To Liz
With all my
respect. Thanks for the
memories.
Jackie

Gender, Sexualities and Law

Bringing together an international range of academics, *Gender, Sexualities and Law* provides a comprehensive interrogation of the range of contemporary issues – both topical and controversial – raised by the gendered character of law, legal discourse and institutions. The gendering of law, persons and the legal profession, along with the gender bias of legal outcomes, has been a fractious, but fertile, focus of reflection. It has, moreover, been an important site of political struggle. This collection of essays offers an unrivalled examination of its various contemporary dimensions, focusing on: issues of theory and representation; violence, both national and international; reproduction and parenting; and partnership, sexuality, marriage and the family.

Gender, Sexualities and Law will be invaluable for all those engaged in research and the study of the law (and related fields) as a form of gendered power.

Jackie Jones, **Anna Grear** and **Rachel Anne Fenton** are based at the University of the West of England.

Kim Stevenson teaches at the University of Plymouth.

Gender, Sexualities and Law

Edited by
Jackie Jones, Anna Grear,
Rachel Anne Fenton and Kim Stevenson

Routledge
Taylor & Francis Group

a GlassHouse book

First published 2011
by Routledge
2 Park Square, Milton Park, Abingdon, Oxon, OX14 4RN

Simultaneously published in the USA and Canada
by Routledge
270 Madison Avenue, New York, NY 10016

A GlassHouse book

Routledge is an imprint of the Taylor & Francis Group, an informa business

Typeset in Times New Roman by Taylor & Francis Books
Printed and bound in Great Britain by CPI Antony Rowe, Chippenham,
Wiltshire

British Library Cataloguing in Publication Data
A catalogue record for this book is available from the British Library

Library of Congress Cataloging-in-Publication Data
Gender, sexualities and law / edited by Jackie Jones ... [et al.].
    p. cm.
  Includes bibliographical references.
    ISBN 978-0-415-57439-6 (hbk) -- ISBN 978-0-203-83142-7 (ebk)
1. Women--Legal status, laws, etc. 2. Sex and law. 3. Gender identity--Law
and legislation. I. Jones, Jackie M.
  K644.G459 2011
  346.01'34--dc22

                                                            2010050851

ISBN13: 978-0-415-57439-6 (hbk)
ISBN13: 978-0-203-83142-7 (ebk)

Contents

Contributors

Alice Belcher: Professor of Law at Dundee Law School, Scotland. Alice has written extensively about company law and corporate governance from a feminist perspective. Her many publications have appeared in *Legal Studies*, *Northern Ireland Legal Quarterly* and *Feminist Legal Studies*. She is a non-executive director of NHS Education in Scotland.

Elsje Bonthuys: Professor of Law at the University of Witwatersrand, South Africa. Elsje's main research interests are in sexual orientation, family law and gender law. She has published widely on these areas, including co-editing *Gender, Law and Justice* in 2007.

Susan B. Boyd: Professor of Law and the Chair in Feminist Legal Studies at the University of British Columbia, Canada. Susan teaches and researches in the fields of family law and feminist legal studies. She is also Director of the Centre for Feminist Legal Studies, University of British Columbia, Canada. Her current research involves the shifting conceptions of motherhood within the law and the changing definitions of legal parenthood.

Todd Brower: Professor of Law, Western State University College of Law, Fullerton, California, Judicial Education Consultant, The Williams Institute, UCLA School of Law, California. Todd has published extensively on the subject of sexual orientation law. In 2002–3, he was an Academic Visitor at the Institute for Advanced Legal Studies, University of London. He is the author of two surveys and reports on sexual orientation fairness in the United Kingdom, published by the Department for Constitutional Affairs (2003, 2005).

Mandy Burton: Professor of Law, University of Leicester. Mandy's research lies in the fields of criminal law, criminal justice and family law with particular emphasis in police and prosecution decision-making, criminal courts, victims' rights and domestic violence. She has produced numerous research reports for UK government departments.

Anna Carline: Senior Lecturer in Law, Liverpool John Moores University. Anna's main research interests are in criminal law, feminist jurisprudence and gender theory. She is currently involved in a research project that analyses the law of rape and consent to sexual activity.

Bridget J. Crawford: Professor of Law at Pace University in White Plains, New York, USA. Bridget teaches courses in the fields of taxation, trusts and estates and feminist legal theory. Her publications include "Toward a Third-Wave Feminist Legal Theory: Young Women, Pornography and the Praxis of Pleasure," *Michigan Journal of Gender and Law*; "Taxation, Pregnancy and Privacy," *William and Mary Journal of Women and the Law*; and "Tax Avatars," *Utah Law Review*. She is the co-editor, with Anthony C. Infanti, of *Critical Tax Theory: An Introduction* (2009).

Anne-Marie de Brouwer: Associate Professor, Tilburg University, the Netherlands. Ann-Marie has developed an international reputation for her research in the field of international criminal law and procedure and human-rights abuses, in particular with regard to victims' rights. Her books include *Supranational Criminal Prosecution of Sexual Violence* and *The Men who Killed Me*. She is the Chair of the Board of Mukomeze (Empower Her), a charitable organisation established to improve the lives of girls and women who survived sexual violence in the Rwandan genocide.

Natasha Erlank: Professor at the University of Johannesburg, South Africa. Natasha heads up the Centre for Culture and Languages in Africa research unit in the Faculty of Humanities. Her interests range from gender, feminist theory, the history of colonialism and public history to current development and political debates. Her research interests currently lie in issues of gender, modernity and nationalism in mainstream Christianity. She is also working on a major project around memory, experience and civic engagement in Sophiatown.

Rachel Anne Fenton: Senior Lecturer at Bristol Law School, University of the West of England. Rachel teaches courses in medical law and gender and has published a number of articles on Italian law, rape and sexual assault and assisted reproduction.

Martha A. Fineman: Robert W. Woodruff Professor, Emory University, USA. Martha is a leading authority on family law and feminist jurisprudence and is an internationally recognised law and society scholar. Her most recent work focuses on the theorisation of vulnerability in relation to political theory. She is founder of the Vulnerability Project at Emory.

Kate Gleeson: Australian Research Council Fellow in Politics, Macquarie University, Australia. Kate's research focuses on modern constructions of sex and gender in political and legal contexts, and she is currently writing a history of abortion politics in Australia.

Anna Grear: Senior Lecturer in Law, Bristol Law School, University of the West of England. Anna works on theoretical aspects of human rights, including her recent work problematising the notion of corporate human rights. She is Founder and Co-Editor in Chief of the *Journal of Human Rights and the Environment* and has recently published a monograph: *Re-directing Human Rights: Facing the Challenge of Corporate Legal Humanity* (2010).

Natalia Hanley: Lecturer in Criminology in the School of Social and Political Sciences at the University of Melbourne, Australia. Natalia has recently completed an ESRC CASE-funded Ph.D. at the University of Manchester on the impact of street gangs on the work of the Probation Service. She is now conducting qualitative research exploring the pathways to imprisonment for Vietnamese Women in Victoria, Australia.

Sue Heenan: Senior Lecturer at Bristol Law School, University of the West of England. Sue specialises in family law, IVF treatments and some aspects of criminal justice.

Rosemary Hunter: Professor of Law, University of Kent. Rosemary is a well-known feminist lawyer who has worked on a range of subjects, including domestic violence law reform and access to justice. One of her most recent projects is 'The Feminist Judgments Project', involving a group of feminist legal academics in a new form of applied socio-legal research.

Jackie Jones: Senior Lecturer in Law at Bristol Law School, University of the West of England. Jackie teaches, researches and writes on equality, violence against women and marriage, broadly defined. She is currently Secretary General of the European Women Lawyers' Association and their representative at the EU Agency for Fundamental Rights, Austria.

Iain McDonald: Senior Lecturer in Law at Bristol Law School, University of the West of England. Iain teaches trusts and equity, contract, and has been teaching gender and the law for a number of years.

Jennifer Marchbank: Associate Professor in the Department of Gender, Sexuality and Women's Studies at Simon Fraser University, Canada. Jennifer has written extensively on gender, including *Introduction to Gender: Social Science Perspectives* with Gayle Letherby.

Leslie J. Moran, Professor of Law, Birkbeck College. Les is well known for his research on matters relating to sexuality and the law, criminal justice, violence and safety, with particular reference to hate-crime and law and visual culture. He has a keen interest in social and legal theory, and much of his work is interdisciplinary.

Ngaire Naffine: Professor of Law, University of Adelaide, Australia. Ngaire has published in the areas of criminology, criminal law, jurisprudence, feminist legal theory and medical law. Her most recent research focuses on the influence of philosophy, religion and evolutionary biology upon law and the conceptualisation of the legal person.

D. Jane V. Rees: Jane is a Ph.D. candidate at Bristol Law School, University of the West of England. Her research is in international law, human rights, gender and jurisprudence. Her Ph.D. is based upon a feminist analysis of aspects of reproduction.

Judith Rowbotham: Reader in Historical Legal and Criminal Justice Studies, Nottingham Trent University. Judith is a leading interdisciplinary scholar focusing on the historical development of the criminal-justice system to illuminate present understandings of crime themes, particularly gender, race and age stereotyping, class and justice. She is co-founder of SOLON: Interdisciplinary Studies in Crime and Bad Behaviour and joint editor of its journal *Crimes and Misdemeanours*.

Philip N. S. Rumney: Reader at Bristol Law School, University of the West of England. Phil's research interests are in criminal justice and criminal law, with a particular emphasis upon the study of rape and sexual assault and the coercive interrogation of terrorist suspects and freedom of expression. He is a member of the Editorial Board of *Crime, Punishment and the Law* and served as a member of an expert group for the Department of Health and NIMHE Victims of Violence and Abuse Prevention Programme (2005–7).

Shilan Shah-Davis: Senior Lecturer at Bristol Law School, University of the West of England. Her research interests lie primarily in the fields of children's rights (in the context of international child law), women's rights (in the context of gender and violence) and in the interplay between culture, law and human-rights norms. She is currently working on a book (with Noelle Quenivet) on girl soldiers and armed conflict in Africa.

Kim Stevenson: Associate Professor of Law, University of Plymouth. Kim specialises in the socio-legal aspects of the criminal law, sexual offences, sexuality and violence. With Rowbotham she co-founded the SOLON research project and jointly edits *Crimes and Misdemeanours*.

Jeffrey Weeks: Emeritus Professor of Sociology at London South Bank University. Jeffrey has written over a hundred articles, papers and books mainly on the history and social organisation of sexuality and intimate life, including *Sex, Politics and Society* (1981), *Sexuality and its Discontents* (1985), *Invented Moralities* (1995), *Same Sex Intimacies* (with Brian Heaphy, Catherine Donovan, 2001), *Sexualities and Society* (with Janet Holland and Matthew Waites, 2003), The World We have Won (2007), Sexuality (3rd edition 2009) and The Languages of Sexuality (2011).

Acknowledgements

The idea for this edited collection arose out of conversations between several members of staff at the University of the West of England who teach and/or research in the area of gender, sexualities and the law (broadly defined). We started off by wanting to put together quite a large interdisciplinary collection, with multiple but coherent themes, that could be used by both teachers and researchers in this area. Over time, the project transformed into a much wider conversation with other scholars, and, eventually, it took the shape of this book. For a variety of reasons, some colleagues who originally wanted to be part of the project are not represented. One particular person we would like to mention here is Professor Gayle Letherby, whose partner tragically died during the course of the project, a sad event which prevented her from continuing.

We would like to thank all the contributors for their enthusiasm, time and willingness to engage with the editorial process. The editors are grateful to Leslie J. Moran for the approval to use the image of Michael Kirby, as granted to him by the artist. The law is as dated in the chapters.

Gender, sexualities and law
Critical engagements

Jackie Jones, Anna Grear, Rachel Anne Fenton and Kim Stevenson

The idea for this edited collection came out of our individual and collective experience of teaching aspects of law and gender over a number of years at different higher-education institutions. That experience, and talking to colleagues elsewhere in the sector who teach aspects of gender, made us realise that increasingly, for today's younger generation, feminism is perceived as old news while equality is perceived as a fact of life. It is a done deal. There is apparently nothing left to say because now men and women are equal. Theoretically at least women can enter any profession they like, rise to the top and get treated and paid the same as men. They can apparently wear what they want, behave as they wish, even as 'laddishly' as the average young male. This perception, moreover, is constantly reinforced in the media through popular imagery, magazines, newspapers, chat shows and many types of television programmes, as well as being implicated in anti-feminist agendas.[1]

In the context of our teaching of undergraduate and postgraduate law students, each of us had noted a certain general reluctance to embrace the feminist cause. There seemed a failure to understand its continued salience. The current younger generation seemed not to believe that glass ceilings still exist, that the representation of sexualised (or pornographic) images of women and girls in the media or their supposed freedom to wear as little as they wish has problematic implications. Feminism, if it means anything positive at all to a broadly 'post-feminist' (and post 'girl power') consumer generation, seems simply to mean 'choice'. Having a choice, in fact, seems anecdotally to be the current student generation's predominant mantra. Individualised choice, moreover, appears all-encompassing, leading many to live in a world where, for them, in effect, consumerism functions as tantamount to a religion. While in some law schools of a more critical tradition the experience of the teaching staff may be different, it seemed that in the context of the majority of law degree courses a relatively 'post-feminist' set of assumptions concerning gender equality remain in play and that the gendered politics that impact upon black-letter law go relatively uninterrogated, in the main.

When we speak about the current younger 'post-feminist' generation we mean (more or less) Thatcher's and Reagan's grandchildren: individuals who have been brought up in the post-1980s 'decade of excess', pursuing (state-sponsored) individualistic aspirations in surroundings that value monetary achievements above community spirit. That post-Thatcher generation arguably sees the world through very different eyes from the mainstream viewpoint of preceding generations. There is, it appears, little space in its cultural comprehension for the fact that, with the rise of consumerism, there has been a kind of marketised 'emptying out' of the political. In such a situation, the feminist assertion that the 'personal is political' can appear tired, old, reactionary and irrelevant.

Meanwhile, the reality of the current situation is that consumerism and related trends accompany a marked rise in the commodification of human beings: forced labour, child labour, human trafficking, forced prostitution. Our own students, in the main, seem to grant little acknowledgement of the significant links between sexualisation of the body and the perpetration of violence against the person and to have little meaningful awareness of the fact that there is no region in the world that has not seen an increase in personal violence in recent times such that, despite the civilising process of two millennia, there are more war/conflict zones now than at any other time in human history.

This, of course, is not the fault of our students. They are the products of a generation whose political sensibilities are shaped by market and consumer dominance, the apparent 'success' of feminism and the arrival of 'equality' (of choice) for all. And there seems to be little natural encouragement for large numbers of youngsters in a society defined by consumer excess to focus, for example, on the effect of the increasing poverty experienced by many in the developing world (especially women). Indeed, many might even be surprised to know that there is no single country in the world in which men and women earn the same pay for work of equal value and that the gender income gap is actually widening.

In other words, as contemporary feminists have argued and the genesis of 'backlash' reveals, many of the improvements fought so hard for – and uneasily gained – in the past are now being eroded or undermined, and our 'post-feminist' generation of young people, in the majority at least (there are, of course, exceptions), seems unable to grasp the seriousness of the situation.[2] While a shift in focus to different areas, perhaps more obviously contemporary in feel, may be necessary and healthy (for example, a focus on sexual orientation and on the fathers' rights movement), and while there are interesting and exciting changes in means of communication with immense political potential (with the rise of Facebook, Twitter and the like), we maintain, as those entrusted with the education of future lawyers, that there is a need to convey the message that the lens of feminism through which to examine injustice and inequality remains vitally important – and that this is a message that the current younger generation need to be helped to understand. Somehow, they need to be captivated by the critical energy latent in the slogan 'the personal is political'.

Is such a critical and near-universal assessment of the younger generation's perception of the current state of gender equality and respect fair? The 'truth' probably lies somewhere in between this narrative concerning the younger generation and a more traditional feminist assessment of the current state of affairs. So how do we bridge the gap between them? After all, it is not as if the 'post-feminist' consumer generation have no political awareness at all. But that awareness does not seem to embrace, at its heart, a focus upon gender justice. So, how do we re-engage with the perceptions of a younger generation that regards the new 'philosophical and/or political' fight not to be so much about women's (or indeed anyone's) empowerment but to be about, for example, the dangers of global warming and other environmental concerns? And this, in the main, from a position where the vast majority of us, but especially the fashion-driven young, continue the consumer practices that so frequently appear to drown out political awareness and to numb political will. In the face of all these pressures and contradictions, how do we, in short, talk to and in the interests of a younger generation *as feminists* and help them to hear and see feminisms through fresh eyes?

The chapters in this collection directly address perennial problems faced by feminism(s) from a range of contemporary perspectives in the hope of presenting a stimulating and relevant set of engagements with real issues facing real people in the contemporary world situation. These perspectives include law, politics, and policies in relation to aspects of gender, sex, culture, race, reproduction, and relational ties to name but a few. Yet, as the title to the collection implies, law is at all times a central unifying theme. Law has presented its authority, in the main, as a neutral form of power committed to abstract, formal equality. In that sense, the nature of law's self-presentation makes the 'post-feminist' generation's assumption that 'equality is here' and that the 'job is done', understandable. However, law is deeply political. Feminism, in this context, alongside 'the personal is political', can just as reasonably assert that 'law is political' and that 'law is personal'.

At the heart of this collection lies the exposure, in virtually every chapter, of the ongoing reality and effects of the intimacy between law, the political and the personal. The collection is divided into six parts, each critically reflecting upon, dissecting and interrogating the relationship between gender, sexualities and law. Five major themes are explored: introductory theoretical reflections, representations of, by and in law, violence (international and national aspects), reproduction and relationships.

Part I: theory, law and sex

Part I offers some introductory theoretical reflections on the person, law and sex. Ngaire Naffine explores the complexity and exclusions of the legal contours of persons as they appear in law, revealing the persistent sense in which women, *as women*, even today, struggle to find themselves genuinely represented by any of the categories of recognised 'legal persons' (Chapter 1). The struggle of women for inclusion within a legal domain built upon the template of masculine personhood also forms a central theme in Rosemary Hunter's exploration of the gendered practices of sexing (and strategic de-sexing) employed within the culture of the legal practice (Chapter 2). Naffine and Hunter, in different but related ways, both point to the intimate relationship between law's theoretical constructions of personhood and the oppressiveness of legal culture – the embodiments and attempted disembodiments of life around the law-office water cooler, in the typing pool and in the courtroom. Gendered hierarchy is mediated through what one wears, what one says (or does not say), what one does as a hobby. The personal is political, and the theoretical is worked out in the day-to-day 'trivialities' of legal cultural life. The politics of cultural capital, in other words, is still a major issue not only for women in particular but also for certain categories of men within the domain of the legal.

The immediacy of the relationship between theory and lived reality also forms a central strand of Anna Grear's account of the linkages between quasi-disembodiment, the abstractionism of liberal law and the oppressions enacted by corporate liberal capitalism, oppressions intimately linked to the destructiveness of oppositional binaries and, in particular, the social construction of a sex binary that is imposed by the law upon sexually diverse human bodies (Chapter 3). In the light of the fact that there are more than two kinds of sexed body, Grear attempts to unsettle the sex binary by invoking a spectrum-conception of sex differentiation, suggesting that law should explicitly embrace sexual variation in its conception of persons. A key theme at the heart of reimagining sex and gender is embodiment, its centrality, its complexity, which, in turn, clearly links to the vulnerability, flowing from our embodiment and which is explored by Martha A. Fineman in the final theoretical chapter (Chapter 4). Fineman's work has long been critical of the formally equal autonomous liberal actor – a construction intimately related to a set of oppressions reflecting substantive inequalities, inequalities which the formality of the liberal construction seeks to occlude. Fineman seeks to present vulnerability as a new and vigorous theoretical value capable of providing a more inclusive, substantive concept of social justice. The constructions of individuals and institutions and the interplay between individual and institutional oppression offers another window onto the complex social power relations of our age.

Part II: representations, law and sex

Part II of the collection highlights the power relations implicit in the legal discourses of (dis)embodiment, sex and the construction of identity. It provides a series of reflections on representation, law and sex. The concerns of the previous section with the legal privileging of a masculinist archetypal legal actor are underlined by Alice Belcher's chapter on 'The "Gendered Company" Revisited' (Chapter 5). It links the masculinism of the corporate form to the masculinism of the social culture of corporate environments. Belcher argues that despite the fact that corporate legal theory invokes a gender-neutral formula of the company as a separate legal person, this concept of the person was male at its inception – and remains so, notwithstanding subsequent legal development, even now.

The partial or deliberate removal of bodies and identities that do not conform to the template of legal masculinism also forms a key underlying theme of Leslie J. Moran's study of the public sex of the judiciary (Chapter 6). His account of 'the individual and the institution', examined through the portraiture of the simultaneously visible and invisible sexuality of the judiciary, and the over-whelming but complexly constituted heteronormativity of judicial office, provides the opportunity to trace the argument concerning the exclusory construction of sexed or sexless 'legal insiders' into one of the most symbolic and archetypically legal of domains. Todd Brower, also focusing upon the judicial, explores the operation of identifiable schemas preventing judges from interpreting legal doctrine and precedent without distortion, in particular the distortion arising from schematic, reductive understandings of lesbian and gay people (Chapter 7). The unconscious nature of schema-matching, he argues, has led to the selective torsion of legal doctrine – revealing a problematic traction in sex-discrimination cases of schemas operating upon the perceptions of judges and other case participants alike.

Arguably, law is at its most potentially oppressive in the context of the criminal trial as this is where the judge operates both as adjudicator and as the institu-tional agent of relatively obvious state power. Turning to the depiction of women in the criminal-justice process, Rowbotham explores the implications of women's increased visibility as defendants. While the visibility of women as offenders challenges traditional tropes of female crime, the profound discomfort exhibited by the criminal-justice system concerning violent interpersonal crimes committed by women reveals that our understanding of the criminal-justice system remains as gendered as ever. The criminal dock itself, that most poignant symbol of the state's piercing forensic gaze, as Judith Rowbotham's argument suggests, is thoroughly and problematically gendered, and she offers the view that the criminal-justice system should develop a conscious awareness of this reality in order to effect change (Chapter 8).

Part III: violence, law and sex

Part III focuses on the current role and impact of the criminal law and its operation through the criminal-justice process in terms of effectively acknowl-edging, managing and responding to the issue of gendered crime, particularly gendered violence. In this context, Kim Stevenson highlights the problems implicit in the representation of crime through gendered tropes and stereotypes (Chapter 9). She argues that media and legal constructions of rape and rape victims mislead the public by failing accurately to reflect the actuality of rape crime. Unchecked dissemination of press 'misinformation' combined with the atti-tudes of certain legal professionals unjustifiably reinforce and perpetuate cultural understandings of rape. Philip N. S. Rumney and Natalia Hanley, by contrast, utilise student-centred research based around the examination of such cultural understandings in order to challenge feminist perspectives concerning rape as a gendered crime and countering the argument that rape laws should be gender-specific (Chapter 10). They argue that while there might be a degree of privileging of male rape in social attitudes, the claim that male victims receive preferential treatment in legal responses to rape appears to have little basis in reality. The issue of distinctively gendered crime, however, is one that Iain McDonald picks up on again, this time in the context of homophobic violence (Chapter 11). Like Stevenson, he highlights the problem of misrepresentation and social understandings linked to stereotypical portrayals of the typical 'stranger-danger' scenario. He suggests that the focus on hate crime is too simplistic to account for the true complexities of the phenomenon of homophobic violence. In particular, he identifies tensions inherent to the dichotomous construction of recognition wherein public 'recognition' of homosexual violence contrasts with the private domain of lesbian violence. This more complex picture reveals the gendered fault lines, arguably, of the familiar public–private divide, an issue invoked by Mandy Burton's discussion of domestic violence (Chapter 12). Burton argues that the civil jurisdiction can be successfully utilised in conjunction with the criminal process in order to 'unmask' the private nature of domestic violence. However, in making this case, she notes the lamentable slowness of the criminal law to specifically criminalise domestic violence, something that, by contrast, the Government managed to achieve relatively easily in respect of child sexual abuse and the Sexual Offences Act 2003. To greater and lesser extents all the authors allude to the invisibility imposed by the criminal law and its failure to acknowledge and address the individual interests of abused victims. Equally, all emphasise the need to provide mechanisms and support that can empower victims to overcome the inequalities of the law.

Part IV: international violence, law and sex

The chapters in Part III are united by the theme of violence, predominantly in the context of domestic law. Can international and European human-rights instruments offer any positive ways of addressing some of the issues involved in systemic gender violence? In Part IV, Anna Carline offers a bridge between domestic and international law's engagement with the theme by examining the UK Government's response to the Council of Europe Convention on trafficking for sexual exploitation (Chapter 13). She argues that despite the human-rights orientation of the Convention, the domestic response is far more punitive than required and unnecessarily moralistic. As an exception to the other chapters in this section, she argues that the law has not been slow in its response but that its impact criminalises those women who, without force or exploitation, wish to be involved in sex work, thereby reinforcing cultural norms and denying the individual interests of women.

The violent imposition of cultural norms and the denial of individual autonomy are also clear central themes of Shilan Shah-Davis's contribution (Chapter 14). The theme of second- and third-order violation haunts this chapter, in that the violence of the honour killing of a Pakistani woman is re-enacted by the social and juridical impunity with which the original violence was carried out. The murder took place in cold blood, at the hands of a paid killer, hired by the victim's own family, but the law merely rendered the victim's status invisible. The overwhelming public support from the Pakistani public for the perpetrators only enhances this sense of a systemic violent excision, by the socio-political and juridical order, of this woman, rendering, as Shah-Davis argues, the death 'a natural occurrence in the cultural order' (p. 189). It is in the forceful nature of the imposition of cultural preference (as embodied in a nation's laws) on women's lives that some of the new, yet old, conversations need to take place. Although the chapter focuses on Pakistan, in no way are these intimate violations of women's and girls' bodies limited to one part of the world. There is a sense in which the international spread of such events can be seen as a by-product of the globalisation and migration flows that bring with them cultural preferences from a range of home cultures.

Anne-Marie de Brouwer's chapter addresses another aspect of the internationalisation of sexual violence, focusing on supranational criminal law and the role of the International Criminal Court and International Tribunals for the former Yugoslavia and Rwanda in dealing with the gendered crimes of sexual violence and torture perpetrated as crimes against humanity and war crimes (Chapter 15). Here the content of the substantive law is not the main issue of concern. The true problem concerns prosecution practices and the enforcement of the law and, in particular, the challenge of finding means to empower victims to bring their cases forward and a related need to educate judges and triers of fact about gender and rape stereotypes. As with all the chapters in this part there is a plea for the law to recognise and acknowledge the individual interests of victims. Physical and sexual abuse are undeniably the most severe personal violation that an individual can endure, and abuse has enduring consequences, exacerbating the criminal seriousness of offences involving this dimension. However, despite apparent advances in criminal legislation, it is, on the basis of these chapters, difficult to argue that present realities do reflect a tangible improvement, certainly from the perspective of the victims of such crime. The evidence is that neither the law nor its agencies have recognised the entrenched gender aspects to the judgments that they make in practice, ensuring that the good intentions behind recent legislation have had little substantive impact.

Part V: reproduction, law and sex

Part V of the collection focuses on varying aspects of reproductive choice. One of the most fundamental decisions that an individual will ever make is the decision to parent, but it is women who, for reasons of biology, remain the primary interest-bearers in reproduction. Kate Gleeson opens this section of the book with a contribution on abortion, which is the most stark or primary arena in which women's self-determination is paramount for reproductive rights, and represents the interest of women in not becoming mothers (Chapter 16). Gleeson's chapter demonstrates how abortion law is not informed by women's agency, rights or choice and how the control of abortion is invested in the autonomous (rational, male) doctor who has become the true subject of abortion law. By contrast, rational women's interests are rendered invisible, and women are denied the right to determine their own reproductive capacity. Gleeson explains how this state of affairs is a product of history as she documents the continual reaffirmation of disinterest in women's autonomy and the correlative increase in the powers of the medical profession in every legal reform in the field since 1803.

Bridget J. Crawford explores the advent of third-wave feminism, its literature and its lack of theoretical and methodological commitment, within the domain of motherhood (Chapter 17). She examines third-wave fertility and motherhood narratives, finding that they reinstate and celebrate the idealism of motherhood that earlier feminisms had sought to dismantle: these texts embrace motherhood as the ultimate personal fulfilment. These narratives are, says Crawford, barometers of the contemporary feminist cultural climate in which motherhood choices have taken place, but that, significantly, any political engagement with the construction of motherhood as an institution, constrained by societal norms and laws, is lacking. Crawford argues that third-wave feminism needs to engage with law and warns that reaffirming motherhood as personal fulfilment may have undesirable consequences. The theme of contemporary motherhood choices and feminism is extended by Rachel Anne Fenton, D. Jane V. Rees and Sue Heenan, who seek to examine women's reproductive autonomy in the arena of assisted reproduction in the UK (Chapter 18). They endeavour to position the meaning of 'choice' when deciding to become a mother through reproductive technologies within the feminist discourse on motherhood as an institution and feminist responses to assisted reproduction. Fenton et al. examine the recent Human Embryology and Fertilisation Act 2008 and its regulation of the types of women who may become mothers, noting that the mothering arena has been widened to include categories of women who were traditionally excluded from it, such as lesbian and solo women. While the new parentage regime and reformed welfare clause may indicate a welcome liberal confirmation of the validity of alternative family forms, the authors note that law may also be simply idealising the status of motherhood for all women.

Thus far, these chapters are concerned with autonomy in the decision to become a mother (or not). Susan B. Boyd, however, takes the theme of autonomy and uses it to discuss the limits placed on women's autonomy once there is an existing child, considered in the context of child-custody law and shared-parenting norms (Chapter 19). Boyd examines the restraints placed upon maternal autonomy due to pregnancy, breastfeeding and cultural expectations about care-giving responsibility – a set of restraints that mean that parenting remains gendered. She then explores modern trends in child-custody law that move away from sole custody towards shared parenting and increased father's rights, noting that whilst sharing parental responsibility should, in theory, enhance women's autonomy, it in fact may do the opposite by forcing burdensome ongoing relationships with the father of the child. Moreover, Boyd reveals that research into the outcomes of shared parenting does not support the presumption, reflected in legal norms, that children's best interests are furthered by such parenting arrangements. Boyd concludes by questioning how women's relational autonomy in the parenting context may be enhanced. This is a salient question, for Boyd's analysis reveals, as does that of Fenton et al., the continued primacy and dominance of the heterosexual and patriarchal family as an ideological unit, evident in both the parentage provisions in cases of assisted reproduction and reproduced by shared parenting norms.

Part VI: relationships, law and sex

Part VI offers a variety of views on relational ties. The family is, of course, a particularly dense site for the construction of idealised relationships in the service of social stability and an arena in which the state takes a high degree of regulatory interest. The traditional assumptions underlying the family unit, moreover, tend to produce growing tensions within states' approaches to the challenge of adapting to new relational and familial forms emerging in contemporary societies. In fact, in the final part of the book, Jeffrey Weeks argues that the debate on same-sex relationships, in particular, drives at the very heart of the traditional assumptions underlying the regulation of marriage and, behind it, issues of family law, the concept of kin, patterned cultural practices of child-rearing, as well as the regulation of the transmission of property through marriage and inheritance (Chapter 20). Using a study of the UK as a lens, Weeks argues that the introduction of civil partnerships is especially significant for what it reveals to us about the evolution of our society and the way in which we understand and construct intimate life. We can also, he suggests, see the emergent shape of a post-traditional society 'bursting to be born', something that the issue of same-sex partnership, uniquely, brings to light.

The unique way in which the state regulation of intimacy in the case of same-sex relationships brings both social movement and resistance to the fore is confirmed by Elsje Bonthuys and Natasha Erlank's study of a specific Muslim community in South Africa (Chapter 21). Here the issues are refracted through the lens of socio-religious power structures and values, and what emerges from their study is an analysis of a peculiarly Muslim combination of willingness to overlook moral and sexual 'transgression' (in the service of maintaining the impression that sexual moral edicts are universally observed) and a closely related opposition to same-sex civil unions, which directly challenge the community's self-presentation and understanding. In this particular setting, state regulation aimed at the production of tolerance runs the risk of misfiring.

Arguably, there is a sense in which the cultural variations revealed by Weeks and Bonthuys and Erlank form part of the background context for Jackie Jones's critical analysis of national cultural variation in the regulation of same-sex relationships within the European Union (EU) (Chapter 22). The implication of Jones's argument is that in the context of civil marriage, as opposed to religious marriage, the state has a particular obligation to be truly inclusive and to make the regulation of intimacy responsive to the complexities and fluidities of contemporary social mores and realities. The supranational regulatory response, in the context of this (in the EU at least), should, as a normative matter, provide a framework in which 'sex' is removed from civil marriage – rendering it the result of free choice between persons of any gender or of any orientation. Marriage, in effect, should be reconstituted as an open-textured institution responsive to the fundamental fluidity of choice and should be rescued by the EU from the inconsistencies and vagaries of national state regulation. However, choice, like gender identities, sexualities and the structure of socio-cultural mediations of varying forms of human sexual embodiment, is a complex matter.

The disaggregation of the meaning of choice and agency in relation to gendered hierarchies forms the centre of Jennifer Marchbank's analysis of the Russian 'mail-order bride' phenomenon (Chapter 23). Addressing what she perceives to be a paucity of genuine knowledge concerning mail-order brides, and the mislead-ing nature of assumptions of brides as the passive victims of a commodifying and instrumentalising dynamic, Marchbank explores the less predictable interplays between agency, choice and power in the context of international marriages, primarily in North America. Again, the oversimplification operative in public and policy perception emerges as a particular problematic. What materialises is a genuine sense in which the women are caught in an entanglement of national immigration impulses, emerging simultaneously constructed as victims and 'conniving migrants'. The victimhood of mail-order brides is thus a complex matter – agency is suppressed in the discourse but, in the final analysis, mail-order brides, in so far as they are victimised, may be the victims, most profoundly, of an international political economy in which material inequality is rife and the pressures for migration strong.

Conclusion

And so we end where we began, reflecting on the power of ideas and ideology, theory and concept to shape the structural dynamics of lived worlds. The personal is indeed political, as is the law and its intimate entanglement with an impact upon the materialities and particularities of life which, in return, both reinforce and disrupt unsettled certainties in a paradoxical age. This collection reveals that questions posed in the past are as relevant today, that new ones emerge, and that shifts in emphasis abound, but that familiar central problematics are in play and difficult to transcend. It is clear that the complex constitution of the relationships between gender, law and sexualities remains as challenging as ever, though increasingly exposed (albeit inconsistently) to critical view within contemporary society at large. This collection is but one contribution to the important task of continuing to render visible the nature, dynamics and implications of those relationships and to keep the conversation open and productive between generations with rather different perceptions of the relevance of the ongoing struggle for gender justice.

Notes

1 Some anti-feminist titles openly suggest this notion of linkages between the gender 'chaos' caused by feminist agendas and their alleged destructive contemporary social 'fallout': A. J. Barron, *The Death of Eve: Women, Liberation, Disintegration* (Toronto: Veritas, 1986); M. Magnet, *Modern Sex: Liberation and Its Discontents* (Chicago, Ill.: Ivan R, Dee, 2001); K. O'Beirne, *Women Who Make the World Worse* (New York: Penguin, 2006).
2 Again, titles are suggestive of the problems now facing feminisms: R. Klein, *Feminism Under Fire* (New York: Prometheus Books, 1996); N. Lyndon, *No More Sex War: The Failures of Feminism* (London: Sinclar-Stevenson, 1992); R. Zubaty, *Surviving the Feminization of America: How to Keep Women from Ruining Your Life* (Chicago, Ill.: Panther Press, 1993).

Part I

Theory, law and sex

Chapter 1

Women and the cast of legal persons

Ngaire Naffine

Introduction: a thought experiment

Let me begin with a simple thought experiment.

1 Picture in your mind's eye a person. Please give this individual a face, a body, a set of clothes and perhaps an activity. This person is just a standard person, no one in particular. But fill in as many details as you can in order to personify them – even a name perhaps.
2 Now picture in your mind's eye a woman, giving her a face and a body, a set of clothes. She too is engaged in an activity. She too is no one in particular.
3 Now return to your first person and ask yourself 'Did they have a sex, and if so, what was it?'

In most cases where this experiment is conducted, most people envisage a man: Mr Anybody.[1] The reason is that there is a deep powerful tradition of thinking of standard, paradigmatic persons as men and of seeing women as something else again. This deep automatic thinking about the sex of persons, I suggest, is to be found in law and remains troubling for the moral and legal personhood of women. Though there are two sexes, and though women are slightly more populous than men, it is a man who forms the automatic idea of a person. Sex and personhood tend to be incompatible legal concepts for women, while they tend to be compatible for men. There is an easy unthinking automatic conflation of men and persons, culturally and in law, which we just witnessed (culturally) in the simple thought experiment. This chapter seeks to explain and defend this proposition: that the personhood and the sex of women remain in tension in law.

Before this chapter comes to look too much like old-style feminism, the sort that alleges that men are the social and legal norm while women are always the exceptions, the odd ones, who must fit themselves to the male case, I need to complicate things by explaining the multifaceted nature of modern legal personhood. The matching or mismatching of women as a sex with legal persons is not as simple as my thought experiment might suggest. For there is serious disagreement in legal circles about what constitutes a legal person, and this disagreement must be factored into the experiment of matching women to persons. This disagreement about the nature of legal personhood is not always made explicit. Sometimes it resides in the background premises about the role that law should take in reflecting what is thought to be our human nature – whether law should reflect that nature or remain fully autonomous. Sometimes it resides in the background premises about what that nature is (supposing that there is such a thing at all). For the present exercise, it is therefore important to identify the varieties of legal persons and to appreciate that women are being matched to different legal beings, depending on context, purpose and the scheme of interpretation of the one doing the matching.

These various competing understandings of our purported human natures (which I will explain shortly), and the role that law should take in reflecting them, must be catered for in our basic exercise. We need to acknowledge that law's concept of the person changes according to the guiding scheme of interpretation; that legal persons are therefore multiple rather than singular; that within different parts of law some views of the person hold greater sway than others. These different understandings of the term 'person', depending on their influence, implicitly determine whether women are fitting legal persons, *as women*. This complex approach to legal personhood (and to women's capacity for personhood) is therefore at odds with the view, once held by some feminists (perhaps myself included), that law adopts a monolithic or singular or static view of the person which, in turn, either forces women out or obliges them to conform to it if they are to be regarded as persons too.

Law's persons

In *Law's Meaning of Life* I expounded four influential ways of thinking about persons in law.[2] I called them legalism, rationalism, religionism and naturalism. Here I suggest that each of these ways of thinking about persons bears a particular relation to women: that there are in effect four related sets or conditions of possibility of women being persons in law *as women*. The relative degree of influence of each of these views of the person tends to depend on the particular legal purpose in view, on the nature of the specific legal relation in question and on the relevant area of law and who and what is involved.

My further suggestion, as a feminist, is that the patriarchal nature of the historical development of these different ways of thinking about persons in law tends to give all of them a masculine flavour which makes it difficult to conceive of legal persons as women. This does not mean that women can never be legal persons. On the contrary, for most of the time, for most legal relationships, women clearly are persons. They can now bear personifying rights and responsibilities in much the same manner as men can as legal persons. But it is far less clear that women, *as women*, are persons in law. As soon as there is something about the condition of women which seems to mark them out as women, as specifically not-male, then problems of personification are encountered.

We might say that the material with which we have to constitute a female legal person, rich and varied though it is, still tends to come in a masculine brand. If we consider a little more closely the repertoire of identities to be found in law, we can see this masculinism at work. Necessarily, in a work of this length, this articulation of the most influential views of the person, and their implications for women, can only be schematic and suggestive.

The rationalist's person

Particularly influential among criminal and contract lawyers is what I call the *rationalist* view of the person as a rational actor, the person of rationalist philosophy and liberal and moral philosophy.[3] In this understanding of law's person, there is a good match between law's person and the liberal philosopher's person. The philosophical literature on the nature of persons is extensive, but for my current purpose I will employ the broadly accepted definition supplied by Brian Garrett, that 'a person is a mental being ... [who] possesses a mind'. As Garrett explains, not just any sort of mind will do: 'Persons possess a range of particularly sophisticated mental states, including – most crucially – self-reflective mental states.'[4] The pedigree of this characterisation of the person can be traced directly to John Locke, who provides the most-quoted definition of a person – as 'a thinking, intelligent being, that has reason and reflection, and can consider itself the same thinking thing, in different times and places'.[5]

Rationalists believe that it is the capacity for reason that most defines and dignifies us and which law should reflect and preserve. Their paradigm legal person is the rational actor. Creatures incapable of reason, on this view, should not be a central concern of law because they are incapable of receiving law's communications and responding to them directly. Only practical reasoners, persons who act for reasons, are the type of people to whom law directly communicates its norms – say, in the criminal trial, ideally understood, as a rational communicative enterprise.[6]

The rationalist view of the person developed with certain educated men in mind and with a quite explicit rejection of women as a sex. The inclusion of women as rational legal subjects of the public realm – who could hold public office, vote, attend university – a move which came with the final 'persons' cases, did not make for a rethinking of this tradition. The nature of reason, its value, why it counted, was not re-conceptualised. Significantly, whether women were thought to possess the natural conditions for rational self-government was not a subject of concern or a cause for rethinking the rationalist person. It was simply a matter of adding women.

The rationalist model of the person has not just been exclusive of women. It has been, and really remains, a model of humanity in which a developed capacity for reason is thought to be the most important thing about us (it is most humanising, most dignifying, most central to our persons) and therefore tends to be exclusive of many men. Paradoxically, it is a view of the person which has had the strongest purchase in criminal law theory.[7] This is paradoxical, because the rationalist's idea of the person poorly describes the majority of the defendant population who tend to be characterised by nearly every indicator of social, economic and cultural disadvantage. And typically they do not engage eloquently in rational dialogue with legal officials.[8]

The religionist's person

Also highly influential in certain parts of law is a *religionist* understanding of the person as sacred being and the correlative idea of human sanctity and inviolability. This understanding of the person is influential in human-rights law generally and also in medical jurisprudence. The idea is that the mere presence of human life generates rights because all *human* life is divinely valued and valuable – we are all sacred. We all have the spark of the divine. (Divine) humanity (defined spiritually, not according to the capacity to reason) is the hallmark of law's true subject. In this view, all human beings are fitting legal subjects, whether or not they are competent to make their own legal decisions, because all human life is sacred – of infinite value.

The idea of human sanctity as the basis for legal personhood is not always expressed in explicitly religious terms, but a religious tradition most clearly informs it and makes sense of it. Those jurists who are willing to employ explicitly religious language in defence of the sacred person in law tend to come from the Roman Catholic tradition. John Finnis has been particularly eloquent about the basis and nature of human sanctity and the nature of the soul and the timing of ensoulment – when the moral and legal person comes into being.[9]

The timing of ensoulment is critical here for women because many religionists believe that the soul enters the body well before birth – and so they render incoherent or compromised the personhood of the pregnant woman. Those who invoke the sacred subject of law, the legal idea of human sanctity, tend to sidestep the problem of the pregnant woman – the problem of two souls in one body and therefore of two potentially conflicting rights-holders inhabiting the very same space.

The naturalist's person

Furthermore, there is also to be found in law a more *naturalistic* view of the person, typically rendered as an embodied and bounded self, a sovereign subject.[10] All laws that protect the right of persons to bodily integrity, often regarded as the most fundamental common law right, tend to conjure up a naturalistic understanding of the person.[11] This view of the person as an enclosed, bounded and sovereign being is highly compatible with rationalism, which emphasises the right of the rational person to exercise autonomy over his own person – what

J. S. Mill thought of as our essential right to physical self-government.[12] The idea is that law should preserve our physical sovereignty – what is thought to be our natural human bodily autonomy and integrity.

The poverty of this theory when it comes to conceptualising the sexual and the reproducing woman has been extensively examined by feminists.[13] That part of the naturalist tradition that emphasises the closed and impermeable body of legal persons seems poorly to describe the female sexed and reproductive body. I will return to this point.

The legalist's person

Finally there is the more *legalistic* understanding of the legal person as an abstract device for endowing a capacity to bear rights and duties. Salmond encapsulated this view in his influential jurisprudential text: 'a person is any being whom the law regards as capable of rights and duties'. He adds that '[p]ersons are the substances of which rights and duties are the attributes'.[14] Salmond insisted that '[i]t is only in this respect that persons possess juridical significance, and this is the exclusive point of view from which personality receives legal definition'.[15]

Legalists, such as Salmond, tend to assert that their task is not to interpret the human condition and that it is not the law's business to engage in such metaphysical disputes and determinations. They profess to be agnostic about the metaphysical nature of persons. They wish to separate law from naturalistic or supernaturalistic views of the person. One's legal nature, they say, should not be confused with one's nature beyond the confines of law, however that is conceived.[16] Law's business is the regulation and the practical organisation of human affairs and the resolution of human differences which are highly variable and may only be obliquely related to these basic existential matters.

Although law has a legal subject known as the 'legal person', legalists say that this is essentially a formal device for enabling a being or entity to act in law, to acquire what is known as a 'legal personality': the ability to bear rights and duties. It is not, nor should it be, a means of recognising or realising what is thought to be our true, essential nature – as sacred beings, or as natural beings or as moral beings, depending on one's legal and moral outlook.

My argument, however, is that for any particular exercise in technical personification, in the endowment of rights and duties, there is always an inexorable pull, even for the legalist, towards one or more of the other three modes of legal personification.[17] There is a constant tug towards one of these other identities (even the corporation is tugged towards the naturalistic or rationalist person whenever there is an invocation of a corporate mind or a corporate body). Within the legalistic tradition, there is no natural person, and certainly no sexing, only abstraction, but there is always a pull towards one of these other realist conceptions of the person – the direction of the drag depending on the particular legal relation in question. And each of these realist conceptions, I suggest, are implicated in patriarchy. In the next part of this chapter I want to illustrate more clearly the point that women, even in the very recent history of persons and right up to the present day, are not fully present as (any of these) persons in law as women.

A very brief selected history of women as persons

If we consider the legal lives of women over the course of the last century – a short historical time – we can observe almost seismic shifts in social and legal thinking about women as persons. These in turn reflect changing understandings of the nature, the reach and the application of rationalism, religionism and naturalism. One can identify a series of moves in which women become public persons (the final persons case), sexual self-governing persons (the removal of the husband's immunity from rape prosecution), but not quite autonomous reproductive persons or subjects (we have achieved only grudging and qualified acknowledgement of the rights of women during labour to self-government). Rationalism, religionism and naturalism and their relationship with legal persons and legal women have their histories and dramatic effects on large parts of the population. What follows is necessarily only the briefest schematic survey of these most defining of moments for women.

Up to the late 1920s, in the anglophone common-law world, women were still not thought to count as legal persons for certain public offices which called for basic public reason.[18] In other words, the rationalist understanding of the person was thought not to include women for some very public legal purposes. Blackstone gave voice to this way of thinking in his famous statement on the law of coverture which is now regarded as patronising, infantilising and unacceptable.[19] Even within the lifetime of the author's mother, it was quite normal, not shocking, to have women legally sequestered from public life based on broadly held assumptions about their female temperament and their limited capacity for public reason. The legal concept of the person was specifically deployed to achieve this exclusion of women from the public sphere.[20]

It *remains* the case that women are still thought not to possess all the necessary and sufficient characteristics of a person who can exercise perhaps the most basic right of the rationalist's person, rational personal self-government: the right to control one's own body.[21] Here I refer to the exclusively female condition of pregnancy. In relation to their own persons, women when pregnant – a thoroughly normal state for women – are still not securely persons in the rationalist sense of this term.

The right of pregnant women to refuse medical treatment considered beneficial or necessary for the welfare of the foetus has always been precarious. In some early American decisions it was explicitly denied and thus women were deprived of rational self-government in a manner which has no parallel for men. More recent medical jurisprudence has formally affirmed the rights of pregnant women to make their own medical decisions whether or not the life of the foetus is at stake, yet the courts remain uncertain about whether such women possess unqualified autonomy. Women in late pregnancy and subsequently in labour still seem to constitute a class of persons of suspect reason when they make decisions which may jeopardise the foetus; we might say that they are still the wrong sort of individual for self-sovereignty. Religionist ideas of foetal sanctity also remain important to legal thinking about persons here.[22]

In *Re MB (Medical Treatment)*, for example, the Court of Appeal was faced with a pregnant woman who refused a medically indicated Caesarean section because of her fear of needles.[23] The Court affirmed the general principle that a 'mentally competent patient had an absolute right to refuse to consent to medical treatment for any reason, rational or irrational, or for no reason at all'.[24] However, MB was found to be temporarily incompetent and thus the right was forfeited. The Court approved a judicial declaration to proceed with a Caesarean against her wishes, with the use of force if necessary.

In *St George's Healthcare NHS Trust* v. *S*,[25] the Court of Appeal disapproved a judicial declaration dispensing with the woman's consent to a Caesarean section (the judge who issued the declaration deemed her incompetent despite a highly articulate written and verbal refusal of consent), but only after the Caesarean had been performed. Here the Court strained to make sense of the competing understandings of the person that seemed to be embedded within the jurisprudential problem before them. It supported the unqualified autonomy of the woman as competent rational legal agent: the rationalist understanding of the woman as legal person. But then the Court said that 'It does not follow ... that this entitles her to put at risk the healthy viable foetus which she is carrying', and it referred to 'the sanctity of human life' as another consideration (essentially a religionist approach).[26] The Court then employed a naturalistic biological understanding of the foetus: '[w]hatever else it may be a 36-week foetus is not nothing: if viable it is not lifeless and it is certainly human'.[27] The Court also asserted that 'pregnancy increases the personal responsibilities of a woman' – her autonomy is qualified – and yet somehow the woman's obligations to the foetus do 'not diminish [the woman's] entitlement to decide whether or not to undergo medical treatment'.[28]

It was only late in the twentieth century that the husband's immunity from rape prosecution was lifted.[29] In South Australia, one of the first jurisdictions in the common-law world partially to lift the immunity, there was great resistance to this change to rape law. It was thought to threaten the very fabric of the family and so only aggravated rape was to be recognised. Full abolition was thought to be too dangerous.[30]

The sexual availability of a wife to a husband has been an entrenched judicially endorsed way of thinking about married women and married life even though it represents a thorough undermining of liberal thinking about self-sovereignty. The fact that it entails the non-application of rationalist theories of personhood to women has been simply accepted. It has been utterly normal and commonplace, a natural way of thinking about women as persons within the legal relation of marriage even though it is entirely incompatible with rationalist liberal humanist thinking about the person.[31]

The husband's immunity from rape prosecution is not an antique legal curiosity but part of the very fabric of recent rape law, even though I suspect it is entirely alien to the thinking of the current generation being trained in law. It has been basic to legal thinking about women and their qualified rights to self-government.

Abortion laws still limit women's will in relation to their own persons, their own body, in the most fundamental way, and in a way which has no parallel for men. There is almost no question of fully decriminalising abortion which would secure women this right. If anything, there is a growing threat that women's access to legal abortion may be diminished or removed.[32]

Can women be persons as women?

These represent deep and yet changing ways of thinking about half the population of rational adults who are supposed to be paradigm legal persons: paradigm rational subjects and paradigm sacred subjects and paradigm natural subjects, depending on the position adopted. They are ways of thinking that have shifted over time and yet some element of patriarchy has endured. At different times, common adult female conditions – marriage and pregnancy in particular (though at the start of the century just being a woman) – have significantly compromised the assignment of reason and the rights which are supposed to flow from its presence. It seems that an adult male form may even now still be needed as a guarantee against compromised rights to self-government; one might say that you need the right sort of human form to be able to reason in the right sort of way. There seems to be a deep masculinism within rationalism, religionism and naturalism. We remain caught in a way of thinking that finds the main theories of the person not fully applicable to women. This further suggests that these three conceptions of the person are not always clearly distinguishable and that they are at times mutually reinforcing, especially in their treatment of women.

Yet much depends on legal circumstance and legal purpose. In different parts of law, legalism, rationalism, religionism and naturalism have differential effects. In the medical jurisprudence that concerns the reproductive lives of women, for example, the religionist's person has a strong presence and women's autonomy is precarious. But when a woman exercises her modern rights as a public person – to vote, to hold public office, the very concerns of the persons cases – then a rationalist model is to the fore. But then, of course, women are not doing anything which would set them apart from men. In effect, they are now acting as men of a certain class have always done.

The metaphysical agnosticism that typifies the legalist – the abstention from any particular view of human nature – has been deployed to considerable effect in aid of women. Legalist judges, for example, have often refused to grant the foetus the sort of rights demanded by religionists. Or they have refused naturalistic claims that the late-term foetus is no different from a baby. They have said that this is not the way rights are recognised and determined in law and so, effectively, have protected the autonomy of women when they are most vulnerable.[33]

And yet the sexual and reproductive lives of women still occasion legal consternation and place women at risk of diminished personhood – suggesting a continuing masculinism in prevailing understandings of the person. Women as sexual or reproductive persons still tend to be treated as exceptional.

Conclusion

In the twentieth century, there have been at least two important historical moments which might have caused jurists to reconsider their concept of the person. One was the final accession of women to legal personhood, for the very important purposes of public office, early in the twentieth century. The other was the accession of married women to private (sexual) self-government in the last decade of the twentieth century. Both changes might have represented occasions for rethinking the legal person. Both legal changes necessarily represented an explicit acknowledgement of the maleness of law's person in that area of law up to that point. The exercise of public reason had been the province of men and was now to include women. Private sexual self-government for married women had been denied; it was now to be extended to them.[34] But this potential re-conceptualisation of the legal person did not occur, even though the concept now notionally embraced women.

The continuing legal puzzlement about the personhood of pregnant women, especially when in labour (are they really rational subjects? Do they represent one individual sacred subject (or two)? Are they sovereign embodied subjects?) also fails to generate a conceptual crisis for any of the varieties of law's persons. The jurisprudence is often criticised as being full of tension, even contradictory in tone and determination. But again personhood in law does not go into spasm. More typically, women in pregnancy and labour are treated as exceptional. They are the problematic ones, not the law.

I do not want to suggest that women are most characteristically women when they are engaged in the act of intercourse with a man or bearing a child. I do not want to say that this is where their personhood resides. I *do* want to say that when activities and experiences are only done or had by women, and those experiences and activities tend to diminish or threaten personhood, the problem is thought not to lie with the concept of the person and its capacity to accommodate typical female experiences; rather, the problem is thought to be with the women themselves. It is the women who are treated as oddities for their failure to satisfy some condition of the concept. And the consequent and necessary masculinism of the concept of the person, variously interpreted, is not even cause for comment. This is why it can be said that legal persons as women tend not to feature in legal thinking and why their absence goes unremarked. Mary Midgley has said there is a genuine philosophical problem here, within the Western intellectual imagination, of two sexes and their proper recognition within a tradition that has only recognised the one (male) sex as full persons.[35] Irigaray has referred to the (female) sex which is not one.[36] MacKinnon has said something very similar.[37] The problem is one of a masculinist pluralism of persons. The solution, perhaps, is non-masculinist pluralism. But, at present, it is hard to see what this would look like. The current cast of legal persons all look like different types of men.

Notes

1   These chances are perhaps diminished by the subject matter of this book and its likely readership.
2   N. Naffine, *Law's Meaning of Life: Philosophy, Religion, Darwin and the Legal Person* (Oxford: Hart, 2009).
3   The leading theorists of criminal law invoke as their central character a rational chooser whom it is fair to call to account for his intentional wrongs. Classical contract law relies on a meeting of minds.
4   B. Garrett, *Personal Identity and Self-Consciousness* (London and New York: Routledge, 1998).
5   J. Locke, *Essay Concerning Human Understanding*, ed. by W. Carroll (Bristol: Thoemmes, 1990), pp. xxvii and 9.
6   This view of the trial has been extensively developed by Anthony Duff. See, for example, R. A. Duff, *Trials and Punishments* (Cambridge: Cambridge University Press, 1986).
7   See, for example, the writings of criminal-law theorists John Gardner, especially, 'The Mark of Responsibility', *Oxford Journal of Legal Studies*, 23 (2) (2003): 157–71; p. 157; and Michael Moore, especially, *Placing Blame: A General Theory of the Criminal Law* (Oxford: Clarendon Press, 1997).
8   See R. Ericson and P. Baranek, *The Ordering of Justice: A Study of Accused Persons as Dependants in the Criminal Process* (Toronto: University of Toronto Press, 1982), on defendants in court and their experiences of the criminal-justice process.
9   See, for example, J. Finnis, '"The Thing I Am": Personal Identity in Aquinas and Shakespeare', in E. Frankel Paul, F. D. Miller Jnr. and J. Paul (eds.), *Personal Identity* (Cambridge: Cambridge University Press, 2005): 250–82; p. 250. See also J. Finnis, 'The Priority of Persons', in J. Horder (ed.), *Oxford Essays on Jurisprudence* (Oxford: Oxford University Press, 4th series, 2000), pp. 1–15; p. 1.
10   The most influential analyses of this bounded embodied being are to be found in the scholarship of Jennifer Nedelsky. See, for example, J. Nedelsky, 'Reconceiving Autonomy: Sources, Thoughts and Possibilities', in A. Hutchinson and L. Green (eds.), *Law and the Community: The End of Individualism?* (Toronto: Caswell, 1989), pp. 219–; 'Law Boundaries and the Bounded Self', in R. Post (ed.), *Law and the Order of Culture* (Berkeley, Calif.: University of California Press, 1991), pp. 162–90.
11   See N. Naffine, 'The Body Bag', in N. Naffine and R. J. Owens (eds.), *Sexing the Subject of Law* (North Ryde: LBC and Sweet & Maxwell, 1997), pp. 79–94, for an interpretation of this character within the category of offences against the person.
12   See J. S. Mill, *On Liberty* (London: Longman, Roberts and Green, 1869).
13   Again, Nedelsky's work is notable here.
14   J. W. Salmond, *Jurisprudence*, ed. G. L. Williams, 10th edn (London and Toronto: Sweet & Maxwell, 1947), p. 318.
15   Ibid.
16   Hans Kelsen was particularly adamant about the need to keep law pure. See H. Kelsen, *A Pure Theory of Law* (Berkeley, Calif.: University of California Press, 1967).

17 The personification of the corporation perhaps representing the most striking and successful effort to pull law away from life, variously understood.

18 The final persons case was *Edwards* v. *Attorney General for Canada* (1930) AC 124. Here the Privy Council finally conceded that women were 'persons' for the purpose of the right to be nominated to the Canadian Senate. A legal history of the British and American persons cases is to be found in A. Sachs and J. H. Wilson, *Sexism and the Law: A Study of Male Beliefs and Legal Bias in Britain and the United States* (Oxford: M. Robertson, 1978).

19 See W. Blackstone, *Commentaries on the Laws of England*, 17th edn (London: Sweet & Maxwell, 1830).

20 See M. Thornton, *Public and Private: Feminist Legal Debates* (Oxford: Oxford University Press, 1995).

21 This is often characterised as the most fundamental common-law right.

22 See Finnis, 'The Thing I Am'; and Finnis, 'The Priority of Persons'.

23 *Re MB (Medical Treatment)* (1997) 2 FLR 426.

24 *Re MB (Medical Treatment)*.

25 *St George's Healthcare NHS Trust* v. *S* (1998) 3 WLR 913.

26 *St George's Healthcare NHS Trust* v. *S*, at 951, 952.

27 *St George's Healthcare NHS Trust* v. *S*.

28 *St George's Healthcare NHS Trust* v. *S*, at 957.

29 The presumptive immunity was lifted by the House of Lords in 1991: *R* v. *R* (1991) 3 WLR 767.

30 If we think about the main criticisms levelled at the leading English rape case of *Morgan* in the mid-1970s and thereafter, it was not that Morgan was immune from prosecution as a principal offender because Daphne Morgan was his wife. It was more to do with the prospect of excusing the unreasonable rapist. At the time of Morgan, the spousal immunity was still accepted.

31 In 1976, South Australia became one of the first jurisdictions to permit the prosecution of a husband for the rape of his wife but there was such concern about the threat this represented to marriage that only aggravated marital rape was criminalised. Basic marital rape was not a crime. It was the intrusion of rape law into marriage that was unthinkable. In the 1990s, South Australia came into line with other jurisdictions and fully lifted the spousal immunity from rape prosecution.

32 With the rise of the Christian right, especially in the USA, there are now sustained efforts fully to criminalise abortion.

33 As a legalist Canadian Supreme Court said in *Tremblay* v. *Daigle* (1989) 62 DLR (4th) 634 at 660, 'The task of properly classifying a foetus in law and in science are different pursuits. Ascribing personality to a foetus in law is fundamentally a normative task. It results in the recognition of rights and duties – a matter which falls outside the concerns of scientific classification.' Consequently, the so-called 'father' of a foetus was denied the right to restrain a pregnant woman from having an abortion.

34 There really was no question that married men lacked this capacity, and, indeed, the very idea that a married woman might rape her husband with legal impunity made little legal sense. It simply did not feature as part of the law.

35 M. Midgley, 'Sex and Personal Identity', in M. Midgley, *Utopias, Dolphins and Computers* (London and New York: Routledge, 1996), pp. 73–84; p. 73.

36 L. Irigaray, *The Sex Which is Not One* (Ithaca, NY: Cornell University Press, 1985).

37 C. A. MacKinnon, *Feminism Unmodified* (Cambridge, Mass.: Harvard University Press, 1987).

Chapter 2

(De-)sexing the woman lawyer

Rosemary Hunter

Introduction

A series of studies of women in the legal profession in the late 1990s, in the UK and Anglo-Commonwealth jurisdictions such as Australia and Canada, revealed that, although women had been entering the profession in significant numbers for over fifteen years, they were still regarded very much as professional 'outsiders'.[1] Legal practice remained not only numerically but also culturally male-dominated. Subsequent studies of professional socialisation and the self-images projected by the solicitors' and barristers' branches of the profession in recruitment materials indicate that, ten years on, and despite rapidly declining numerical dominance, the legal field continues to be characterised by the cultural domination of white, middle-class men, and the marginalisation of women and other non-traditional entrants.[2]

One of the consistent observations of these studies, including the most recent ones, is that, in a profession that imagines its authority as deriving from rational disembodiment, women's status as 'outsiders' is inscribed (among other things) by the forcible embodiment and, specifically, sexualisation of women lawyers. This is evident, for example, in law-firm recruitment practices, work allocation and dress codes; in jokes, comments and put-downs addressed to women lawyers; in attitudes to pregnant lawyers; and in practices of sexual harassment in the profession. In response, women lawyers may play along with 'this complaisant sexual role – smiling, flirting', but at the expense of professional credibility: 'you won't be taken seriously in that role, even though you're doing what is wanted of you as a woman'.[3] More typically, women lawyers have tried to 'fit in' to the paradigm of rational disembodiment by attempting to erase their femininity and to present themselves as non-gendered professionals. This endeavour requires strategic performances and disciplined 'practices of the self', which themselves make professional life more burdensome for women and function as a form of subordination.[4] Neither can they ever be wholly successful. Male lawyers are not, in fact, disembodied, but inhabit a particular form of masculine (hetero)sexual subjectivity, which is both closed to women and entails the repeated performance of that closure, through, among other practices, the sexualisation of women.

It must be noted at the outset that women lawyers are not an undifferentiated category. The forms of professional exclusion that women experience, including the ways in which they are sexualised, and the bodily strategies they adopt, are influenced by their class, race, sexuality and age, as well as (or rather, in combination with) their gender. The literature describing the making of intersectional professional subjectivities is limited, however, because, as Sommerlad points out, 'for several decades', professional outsiders 'were overwhelmingly white middle class women', and it is only recently that the composition of the group of non-traditional entrants to the profession has become more heterogeneous.[5] This is an area requiring further research. Nevertheless, as the following discussion suggests, there are strong grounds for believing that gender and the female body per se remain salient categories for analysis of the legal profession, and that it is far too soon to contemplate jettisoning them in favour of a more differentiated approach.

In addition, the masculinity of the legal profession is not uniform or consistent across different sites. Different forms of masculinity are embodied in traditional, small-town general practices, legal-aid firms, high-street practices and large corporate commercial firms.[6] Similarly, Rogers distinguishes between different areas of practice (the criminal bar versus the commercial/chancery bar) and, more generally, between 'the style of consumption that is offered by the Bar', which she suggests is 'closer to Oxbridge-style social behaviour – drinking with your peers and mentors – than to the corporate consumption – drinking expensive drinks in exclusive bars in London – that is sold by elite solicitors' firms'.[7] As with different forms of femininity, however, and varying reactions to them, the different forms of legal (hetero)masculinity are variations on a theme rather than divergent practices.[8] It remains possible to identify a 'broadly hegemonic masculine style' of lawyering, the essential elements of which remain the same, even though it appears in different guises, and even if individual male lawyers (including gay men) do not all fit the mould.[9]

Sexualising women

The association of men, and law, with disembodied reason, while women are associated with nature, the body and irrationality, is a binary deeply embedded in Western belief systems. The disorderliness of women's bodies – for example through menstruation, pregnancy, birth and female eroticism – stands in sharp contrast to the supposed rationality of the public sphere.[10] Thus, women's corporeality, by its very nature, was considered inimical to the development of the appropriate degree of detachment, sense of justice, analytical skills and rationality required to be a successful lawyer.[11] Although these ideas no longer function to keep women out of the profession altogether, they continue to play a role in women's experiences of professional life. This phenomenon is not necessarily confined to the legal profession. For example, in her study of merchant banking, McDowell observed the operation of various ways of drawing attention to women's female embodiment as a means of constructing them as 'out of place' and '"other" to [the] disembodied masculine norm'.[12] Sommerlad and Sanderson, drawing on Bourdieu, characterise such strategies as a form of 'symbolic violence', a means by which individuals are kept in their place through interactions whose meaning is not objectively visible.[13]

One way in which attention is drawn to women lawyers' bodies is through constant comments about their appearance – their hair, make-up, clothes and general looks.[14] For example, when Heather Hallett QC was appointed as the first woman chair of the Bar Council of England and Wales, *The Times* ran an article in which she was described as 'blonde and bubbly'.[15] Sometimes, such comments directed at women lawyers are intended as compliments rather than as put-downs, making it more difficult to object, but having the same effect: 'I see you as a decorative object, not as a lawyer.'[16] Put-downs abound, however. For example, in a study of an independent bar in Australia in which I was involved, one of the women solicitors we interviewed reported conversations in court in which male barristers would consistently pick on the appearance, weight or 'girliness' (meaning incompetence) of their female opponents.[17] In the context of the game-playing and one-upmanship practised between opposing barristers at the bar table or in negotiations, sexualisation of a woman barrister was an additional strategy available to men as a means of undermining her confidence and credibility as an advocate.[18]

Numerous reports, studies and anecdotal accounts have found high levels of sexual harassment in both solicitors' firms and at the bar.[19] Examples range from 'sleazy remarks', unwelcome requests for dates, ogling and suggestive comments, to judges and older male barristers flirting and making inappropriate remarks to young women solicitors in court, to 'alarming levels of harassment by pupil masters' at the bar and offers of pupillage in exchange for sex.[20] Two recent posts from *The Times*'s BabyBarista blog – a fictional account of life as a junior at the English bar – are illustrative.[21] Other male members of BabyBarista's chambers include HeadofChambers, OldSmoothie and TheCreep, while female members are given names that allude to their appearance and sexuality: TheVamp, BusyBody and UpTights. On 11 January 2010, BabyBarista posted

> HeadofChambers was in pensive mood today and in his most judicial tones, he commented on TheVamp's dress in the following way as she came into tea: 'Is it just me or are skirts getting shorter these days?'
>
> 'Yes, and men's looks are getting longer', replied TheVamp.
>
> 'Particularly a rather well known circuit judge I could mention', said BusyBody. 'I'm sure he's getting worse. I mean, whenever I appear in front of him I get the feeling that his eyes undress me.'
>
> 'Must have very big eyes then', said OldSmoothie somewhat ungallantly.

And the post from 4 January 2010, headed 'Taking the ass out of harass', reads

'Does anyone know anything about sexual harassment?' asked TheCreep this morning, in the clerks room.

'OldSmoothie's the expert in that department', said UpTights smartly.

'It's not sexual harASSment', said HeadofChambers, emphasising the last three letters of harass. 'Harass rhymes with embarrass and embarrassment's exactly what you'll be suffering if you start throwing around that sort of Americanism to an English judge. ... '

' ... I think that you'll find that OldSmoothie has always put the stress on the ass when it comes to harassment', added UpTights.

'You know', said TheCreep earnestly interrupting the flow. 'I was recently invited to join a Facebook group which called itself the 'Sexual Harrassment Action Group ... ' His voice tailed off as he noticed the silence and the smirks which followed.

A notable theme of women's accounts has been the enormous difficulty of making formal complaints or doing anything to stop the harassment other than, in the case of solicitors, leaving the firm.[22] Complaining not only violates professional codes and involves significant professional risk, but it also entails further (self-)identification with one's invidious embodiment.[23] A woman who complains is seen as 'sensitive', hysterical and unable to cope; moreover, complaining about sexual harassment has the effect of 'outing' oneself as (merely) a sex object – yet another form of professional suicide.[24]

High reported levels of sexual harassment are hardly surprising in a context in which, in Sommerlad and Sanderson's words, women's sexuality 'can be a management resource'.[25] That is, women may be recruited and deployed by law firms for their looks, to act as bait for clients and make the firm look good.[26] One of Sommerlad's interviewees in a recent study, who was undertaking the legal practice course for aspiring solicitors, observed that the girls who got training contracts with big firms were all young, slim, blonde, attractive and well-spoken.[27] Thornton notes instances of women lawyers being taken to lunches with clients because they were very good-looking – with intelligent conversation seen as a bonus![28] And McGlynn refers to 'sexualised workplace[s], where (single) women are assets at the marketing activities, where sexual harassment is condoned or seen as a "joke"'.[29] Here, then, young women are offered to clients by their employers specifically as sex objects (not lawyers).[30]

Even when women lawyers are not being used to sell sex, it may be assumed or implied that they are doing so. In McGlynn's words, 'The woman solicitor who invites a male client to lunch/drinks or whatever, as a marketing initiative, runs the risk of her offer being misconstrued.'[31] Remarks are made to women suggesting that they can achieve results by means of their sexual attractiveness which cannot be achieved by men equipped only with legal skills.[32] At the bar, rumours and innuendo abound concerning women barristers' relations with male barristers and solicitors. In our research, we were told of assumptions being made if a junior woman went for lunch with an older male barrister, or if she was seen to work 'too closely' with a particular male QC; and stories circulated about sexual favours being given in return for junior briefs. Such reactions made it impossible for women to participate in either social or mentoring activities on the same footing as their male counterparts.[33] Moreover, it is notable that rumours about sexual intimacy between barristers impugn the woman's professionalism, but not the man's.[34] Thornton asserts that 'sexual activity for a man, even if of questionable legality, is rarely seen to detract from his professional competence ... whereas it is always problematic for a woman, regardless of whether she is the innocent recipient of unwanted advances or not'.[35] Thus, whether in the form of sexual harassment, sexualised marketing, or assumptions and rumours about (hetero)sexual relationships, women lawyers are persistently 'reduced' to their bodies and their sexuality, as a reminder and a reinforcement of their tenuous professional status.

Just as the sexual body of the woman lawyer undermines her professionalism, so, too, does the pregnant body. Pregnant women cannot be taken seriously as lawyers.[36] Thus, for example, barristers we interviewed experienced an unwelcome reduction in the amount of work directed to them by their clerks and solicitors when they became pregnant, and they had to put up with jokes from judges about the risk of them going into labour in court.[37] Moreover, the pregnant female body is viewed with repugnance. In the office, and in contact with clients, it is 'not pleasant to look at' and creates a bad impression, and thus must be hidden away.[38] Presumably, also, part of this repugnance is due to the fact that a pregnant woman signals with her body that she is no longer sexually available, and hence she is even more devalued within the heterosexual economy of the law firm.

De-sexing strategies

Given the frequent, usually unwelcome, attention paid to their own and other women's bodies, it is hardly surprising that women lawyers might feel that they need to suppress their femininity and attempt to 'pass' as male in order to achieve professional acceptance and advancement.[39] As Sommerlad and Sanderson note

> The traditional tactic adopted by women entering single sex professions has been that of assimilation. The ideology of liberal legalism in which all solicitors have been inculcated predisposes many women towards this ... course, based on a belief in the legal labour market as a neutral sphere in which workers are autonomous individuals who make it through their own merit.[40]

Or, in Thornton's words, 'The sexualised workplace has the woman lawyer balancing on a tightrope, trying to fit the image of a competent professional, while simultaneously endeavouring to contain the feminine, if not efface it altogether.'[41] Fitting the image of the competent professional and effacing, or at least containing, the feminine, in turn involves a range of 'practices of the self' – involving clothing, hair, make-up, diet, posture – by which women seek to neutralise their bodies and constitute themselves as professional subjects.[42]

In relation to clothing, Thornton observes that '[t]he male body is invisible in a business suit that disguises both primary and secondary sexual characteristics. As this body is normative within the public sphere, it has come to represent neutrality and *dis*embodiment.'[43] Collier describes the business suit as a 'central icon' which 'serves the crucial function of desexualising the male body, not in the sense of rendering men in suits beyond erotic attachment (far from it) but rather in terms of erasing the sexed specificity of the individual male body'.[44] Thus, women attempting to be professionally 'gender neutral' or 'asexual' adopt the same uniform of smart, dark, tailored suit and plain white or pale-coloured shirt, together with a sensible haircut and minimal make-up, in order to get as close as possible to the male norm.[45] Some may go further, such as the woman noted by Thornton who, in response to being sexually harassed, chose 'to wear the most dowdy pants with polo necks and put her hair up' in order to counter her sexualisation.[46] However, women's choices may be limited in this regard, as some law firms impose dress codes that ensure that women are clearly differentiated from men, for example by insisting that women wear skirts rather than trousers.[47] And even in professional uniform women's bodies are not disguised in the same way as men's, as their breasts, hips and (in a skirt) legs remain more or less visible.[48]

Other 'practices of the self' exercised by women lawyers in order to achieve professional assimilation include acquiring particular forms of knowledge, such as following Rugby League and reading car magazines, and engaging in particular activities, such as learning to play golf and to bet, in order to be able to relate to their male clients.[49] But the disciplining/erasure of the woman lawyer's feminine or sexual body is seen most starkly, perhaps, in relation to attempts to 'fit in' with the long-hours culture of the profession, which is premised on the absence of domestic obligations on the part of the lawyer (and the performance of those obligations by someone else).[50] So, for instance, women lawyers may 'choose' to remain unmarried, childless, or both, to a much greater degree than their male counterparts.[51] And remaining childless may involve terminating a pregnancy. For example, McGlynn recounts the story of a woman being advised by her employer to have an abortion on informing them that she was pregnant and of another being asked in interview if she would consider having an abortion to further her career.[52]

Lawyers who become pregnant, as noted above, are expected to remain invisible, and to carry on regardless, or may feel compelled to conceal the pregnancy for fear of the negative responses and judgements to which they are likely to be subjected.[53] For example, one of the former barristers we interviewed spoke about her friends' behaviours arising from their concerns about the effect of pregnancy on their perceived work capacity.

> Females at the Bar who became pregnant played games with smoke and mirrors. They never announced publicly that they were pregnant. They invested in swing coats to conceal their pregnancies until the last moment. I was frequently sworn to secrecy … They would keep it from their clerks because they felt it would have some briefing impact. … It wasn't talked about with men because they wouldn't understand and they would be judgemental. [They] didn't want to be dismissed as 'a mum'.[54]

Moreover, women are also expected or feel compelled to return to work quickly after giving birth.[55] In our study, women told stories of rushing home to breastfeed, then rushing back to chambers; and one clerk mentioned a 'very well organised' barrister who timed her pregnancies so she could give birth during the summer vacation and return to work without any noticeable interruption to her availability.[56] Women solicitors interviewed by Sommerlad and Sanderson felt the need to work even harder during and immediately after pregnancy in order to overcome the adverse assumptions generated by the pregnancy about their commitment and ability to 'cope'.[57]

Such attempts at disciplining the unruly female body are not always successful. As one of our interviewees explained, for example

> I had a nanny, but I was breastfeeding, the nanny was bringing him in for feeds. I was expressing. I just couldn't coordinate it around court times. I would just be bursting … It was just impossible to try and be an advocate when all you can think about is whether you're going to start leaking milk out of your breasts.[58]

More often, though, in the words of another interviewee, 'you are so keen to be one of them that you sublimate your own real needs'.[59]

As noted earlier, being forced to recognise one's inherent difference and inferiority, and having to work at 'passing', is a form of symbolic violence, part of women's experience of subordination in the legal profession.[60] This is reinforced by Justine Rogers' reading of the message contained in bar recruitment events, that 'outsiders' are welcome to apply, but they must realise that they will have to work harder on themselves and be adaptable in order to achieve inclusion.[61] As both Rogers and Sommerlad and Sanderson observe, too, attempting to 'pass' is a personalised solution which takes for granted and does not challenge established traditions and work practices.[62] Women who adopt individual de-sexing strategies eschew a collective consciousness of women's subordination in the legal profession and hence are unlikely to mentor or support other women.[63] On the other hand, resistance 'might be construed as evidence of precisely the emotionality and irrationality which legal discourse deemed natural female properties, and could thereby emphasise the essential ineligibility of women to be lawyers'.[64] As Justice Catherine Branson of the Federal Court of Australia has observed, women barristers have been offered the 'choice' to be 'an honorary man, or alternatively, an outsider'.[65]

The culture of heterosexual masculinity

Yet the 'choice' of honorary man or outsider is not one that rests with the individual woman. Attempting to be an honorary man does not prevent one's male colleagues from treating one as an outsider.[66] The ability to conform to the male model of the lawyer 'is as dependent ... on subjective and sexist valuations by men as it is on the credentials of the individual woman'.[67] Women 'can have the abjections of their embodiment re-imposed on them ... at the whim of the dominant actors in the field'.[68]

This is not simply a matter of animus, discrimination or sexism on the part of individual male colleagues. Rather, it is because, as noted earlier, the subject position of 'lawyer' is not 'a genderless shell' but is emphatically masculine, albeit that masculinity is generally unmarked due to its appearance as a neutral norm.[69] In recruiting for the bar, for example, Rogers notes that the list of qualities, skills, experience, contacts and all-round excellence required of candidates is 'presented as "disembodied" or devoid of gender, race or class', but reading between the lines a significant image of the bar being projected is that of 'a sanctuary, and indeed a sort of last bastion for an elite, public school (and implicitly masculine) way of life'.[70] Similarly, the depictions of 'hard work' in city law firms' recruitment materials 'evoke ... a distinctively *masculine* notion of labour'.[71] Male corporeality, as noted above, is obscured by the business suit, by the dissociation of men from childcare, and by 'the neutral discourse of law'; but it is at the same time an integral part of the professional habitus, as one of Thornton's informants illustrated graphically when she described groups of male lawyers standing around 'with their hands in their pockets and they flex their buttocks and they rock backwards and forwards. They're so big and it's very difficult to muscle your way into the group.'[72] Thus, not only do women not possess the cultural capital to become full members of the male club, but their attempt to assimilate to the masculine norm is 'a physically impossible performance'.[73]

Legal masculinity conforms to many of the features of hegemonic masculinity identified by Connell and others.[74] It is associated with disembodied reason, a traditional sexual division of labour, sports talk, exclusive homosociality and compulsory heterosexuality.[75] Exclusive homosociality is found in a large range of networking, practice development and social activities in which women are only grudgingly or contingently included (to add sexual frisson), if at all. These include jokes and pranks, lunching and drinking rituals, going on circuit, formal and informal events held at men-only clubs, playing golf and other men's sporting activities.[76] Rogers, for example, describes how potential recruits to the bar were introduced to advocacy weekend – compulsory for training pupils – by '[b]oisterous male practitioners [who] told stories about drinking "copious amounts of Pinot Grigio" and showed photographs of male judges and pupils playing Jenga'.[77]

These homosocial activities are not, of course, done just for fun. They are part of the core business of lawyering. As Sommerlad and Sanderson explain, much of solicitors' business is founded on personalised, patron–client relations, so that 'arguably masculinity per se remains *the* core cultural capital of the profession, largely because this in turn allows the professional to build up the relational capital that is vital to a firm's survival'.[78] Similarly, barristers need to network with solicitors and with senior colleagues in order to generate briefs. So, for example, sporting contacts can be a means of finding employment and of networking and bringing in potential clients, as can membership of the Freemasons and men's clubs.[79] Consequently, it is the ability to forge fraternal bonds, rather than technical expertise, that brings advancement in the profession: 'what may be required for "partnership material" is someone who is "clubbable", or "ladsy"'.[80] Within this masculine economy, two possible roles are open to women: as providers of domestic support or, as discussed earlier, as decoration, entertainment or sexual bait.[81] The de-sexing strategy and attempts to 'pass' can gain only limited traction in this context.

Within hegemonic masculinity, compulsory heterosexuality is the flip-side of exclusive homosociality, as it ensures that the bonds between men remain fraternal rather than erotic. Compulsory heterosexuality constitutes men as desiring subjects and women as objects of desire. Hence, in order to perform their masculine subjectivity, men must inevitably sexualise the women they encounter.[82] The sexualisation of workplace culture, therefore, acts simultaneously to exclude and devalue women and to forge solidarity between men.[83] And client entertainment that involves attending lap-dancing clubs, or drinking and picking up women, operates in the same way.[84]

As Collier observes, 'normative (hetero)masculinity is constituted on a foundational disavowal, a denial of the feminine and femininity which secures the dualism of sexual difference'.[85] This 'otherising' of the feminine must be performed repeatedly in order to sustain the masculine norm, and, as discussed above, this performance takes a wide variety of forms, from sexist comments at Friday night drinks through to the most serious sexual harassment.[86] Indeed, Sommerlad and Sanderson argue that women's increased presence in the legal profession has been met by 'the apparent accentuation of masculinist culture' and increased sexualisation of the legal workplace.[87] The irony is that in order to attempt to assimilate to the masculine norm, women lawyers have also been induced to deny, disavow or 'otherise' the feminine in the disciplining of their own bodily practices. Yet, ultimately, in doing so, they manage not to participate in masculine solidarity but collude in perpetuating the denial of their own professional subjectivity.

Concluding remarks

Before closing, an additional complicating factor must be added to the analysis of legal professional embodiment. As made clear in the discussion of client relations above, lawyers may be characterised as 'interactive service workers' whose personal attributes are part of the product that is being marketed.[88] This requires the surveillance and disciplining of the bodies of all workers – men as well as women.[89] As Collier notes, 'becoming' a (particular kind of) lawyer is a process of subjectivisation involving techniques of care, consumption and self-policing.[90] And he goes on to observe that, for example, the benefits offered by corporate law firms such as private medical insurance, annual health screening, gym or sports club membership, subsidised food bar, in-house medical and dental services and dry-cleaning collection and delivery constitute a '"total package" of body care', which 'facilitate[s] and *make[s] possible* the kinds of physical and psychological investments and practices demanded by the corporate legal employer within a global economy'.[91] So, male as well as female lawyers must engage in 'practices of the self' to conform their bodies to the professional norm. Most notably, this includes absorbing the damaging impact of the long-hours culture on their health and on relationships with their partners and children.[92]

However, as Collier acknowledges, men have a far easier job than women in this regard. They 'appear able and willing to discipline themselves in terms of appropriately masculine dress, voice and authoritative demeanour. The male legal recruit faces few of the disciplinary twists and turns faced by the women [sic] legal initiate', because, of course, he already constitutes the norm, and so is working with, not against, the normative body.[93] The workplace is therefore a more comfortable environment for men than for women, and their physical presence in the workplace goes unremarked.[94] Moreover, the work of disciplining the self has an unambiguous payoff for men in the form of social power.[95] The realisable promise of partnership and high financial rewards makes the personal cost of hegemonic masculine conformity a price worth paying.[96] And, as demonstrated above, the cost of hegemonic masculine conformity is not simply personal but is, to a large extent, externalised onto the abject bodies of women.

Notes

1 In the UK: H. Sommerlad and P. Sanderson, *Gender, Choice and Commitment: Women Solicitors in England and Wales and the Struggle for Equal Status* (Aldershot: Ashgate, 1998); C. McGlynn, *The Woman Lawyer: Making the Difference* (London: Butterworths, 1998); see also, TMS Consultants, *Without Prejudice? Sex Equality at the Bar and in the Judiciary* (London: Bar Council and Lord Chancellor's Department, 1992); in Australia: M. Thornton, *Dissonance and Distrust: Women in the Legal Profession* (Melbourne: Oxford University Press, 1996); R. Hunter and H. McKelvie, *Equality of Opportunity for Women at the Victorian Bar* (Melbourne: Victorian Bar Council, 1998); in Canada: J. Hagan and F. Kay, *Gender in Practice: A Study of Lawyers' Lives* (New York: Oxford University Press, 1995); J. Brockman, *Gender in the Legal Profession: Fitting or Breaking the Mould* (Vancouver: UBC Press, 2001).

2 See R. Collier, '"Be Smart, Be Successful, Be Yourself ... "': Representations of the Training Contract and Trainee Solicitors in Advertising by Large Law Firms', *International Journal of the Legal Profession*, 12 (1) (2005): 51–92; J. Rogers, 'Representing the Bar to Potential Recruits: The Self-Portrait of the Barristers' Profession', paper presented to the Society of Legal Scholars Annual Conference (London: LSE, 2008); H. Sommerlad, 'That Obscure Object of Desire: Sex Equality and the Legal Profession', in R. Hunter (ed.), *Rethinking Equality Projects in Law: Feminist Challenges* (Oxford: Hart Publishing, 2008), pp. 171–94.

3 Sommerlad and Sanderson, *Gender, Choice and Commitment*, pp. 178, 179. See also Thornton, *Dissonance and Distrust*, p. 256.

4 M. Foucault, *The History of Sexuality*, vol. II: *The Uses of Pleasure*, trans. R. Hurley (Harmondsworth: Penguin, 1987), pp. 29–30.

5 Sommerlad, 'That Obscure Object of Desire', p. 171.

6 Sommerlad and Sanderson, *Gender, Choice and Commitment*, pp. 121–2; R. Collier, '(Un)sexy Bodies: the Making of Professional Legal Masculinities', in C. McGlynn (ed.), *Legal Feminisms: Theory and Practice* (Aldershot: Ashgate, 1998), pp. 21–45; p. 28.

7 J. Rogers, email communication with the author, 26 October 2009; Rogers, 'Representing the Bar', p. 13.

8 Sommerlad and Sanderson, *Gender, Choice and Commitment*, p. 122; Collier, '(Un)sexy Bodies', p. 28.

9 Collier, '(Un)sexy Bodies', p. 28.

10 Thornton, *Dissonance and Distrust*, p. 18.

11 Ibid., p. 15.

12 L. McDowell, 'Body Work: Heterosexual Gender Performances in City Workplaces', in D. Bell and G. Valentine (eds.), *Mapping Desire: Geographies of Sexualities* (London and New York: Routledge, 1995), pp. 75–97; p. 81.

13 Sommerlad and Sanderson, *Gender, Choice and Commitment*, p. 85.

14 R. Hunter, 'Women Barristers and Gender Difference in Australia', in U. Schultz and G. Shaw (eds.), *Women in the World's Legal Professions* (Oxford: Hart Publishing, 2003), p. 110.

15 McGlynn, *The Woman Lawyer*, p. 149.

16 Hunter, 'Women Barristers and Gender Difference', p. 110.

17 Hunter and McKelvie, *Equality of Opportunity*, p. 38.

18 Ibid., pp. 130, 136–7.

19 See, for example, Thornton, *Dissonance and Distrust*, p. 255; Sommerlad and Sanderson, *Gender, Choice and Commitment*, p. 131; McGlynn, *The Woman Lawyer*, p. 154; Hunter, 'Women Barristers and Gender Difference', p. 111.

20 Hunter, 'Women Barristers and Gender Difference', p. 110; McGlynn, *The Woman Lawyer*, p. 117; Thornton, *Dissonance and Distrust*, p. 136; Hunter and McKelvie, *Equality of Opportunity*, pp. 130–1; McGlynn, *The Woman Lawyer*, p. 154.

21 Available online at http://timesonline.typepad.com/baby_barista/ (accessed 11 February 2010). Although the blog is fictional, its success depends, of course, on the fact that it reflects reality in an exaggerated form.

22 Thornton, *Dissonance and Distrust*, p. 255; Sommerlad and Sanderson, *Gender, Choice and Commitment*, p. 131; McGlynn, *The Woman Lawyer*, p. 154; Hunter and McKelvie, *Equality of Opportunity*, pp. 130–1.

23 Hunter, 'Women Barristers and Gender Difference', pp. 111, 115.

24 Ibid., p. 115.

25 Sommerlad and Sanderson, *Gender, Choice and Commitment*, p. 3.

26 Ibid., pp. 176–7.

27 Sommerlad, 'That Obscure Object of Desire', p. 190.

28 Thornton, *Dissonance and Distrust*, pp. 136–7.

29 McGlynn, *The Woman Lawyer*, p. 105.
30 Sommerlad and Sanderson, *Gender, Choice and Commitment*, pp. 175–7.
31 McGlynn, *The Woman Lawyer*, p. 105; see also Thornton, *Dissonance and Distrust*, p. 174.
32 Thornton, *Dissonance and Distrust*, pp. 136, 194.
33 Hunter, 'Women Barristers and Gender Difference', p. 111; see also Thornton, *Dissonance and Distrust*, p. 174.
34 Hunter and McKelvie, *Equality of Opportunity*, p. 45.
35 Thornton, *Dissonance and Distrust*, p. 254.
36 See, for example, Ibid., pp. 235, 237; Hunter, 'Women Barristers and Gender Difference', pp. 106–7.
37 Hunter and McKelvie, *Equality of Opportunity*, p. 110.
38 Sommerlad and Sanderson, *Gender, Choice and Commitment*, p. 228.
39 R. Hunter, 'Talking Up Equality: Woman Barristers and the Denial of Discrimination', *Feminist Legal Studies*, 10 (2) (2002): 113–30; p. 120; Sommerlad, 'That Obscure Object of Desire', p. 177; see also Thornton, *Dissonance and Distrust*, p. 229.
40 Sommerlad and Sanderson, *Gender, Choice and Commitment*, p. 19; see also Thornton, *Dissonance and Distrust*, p. 222.
41 Thornton, *Dissonance and Distrust*, pp. 137–8; see also Sommerlad and Sanderson, *Gender, Choice and Commitment*, p. 183.
42 Hunter, 'Talking up Equality', p. 127; Thornton, *Dissonance and Distrust*, p. 228.
43 Thornton, *Dissonance and Distrust*, p. 216.
44 Collier, '(Un)sexy Bodies', p. 29.
45 Sommerlad and Sanderson, *Gender, Choice and Commitment*, pp. 185–6; see also McDowell, 'Body Work', p. 88.
46 Thornton, *Dissonance and Distrust*, p. 136.
47 See, for example, Thornton, *Dissonance and Distrust*, pp. 224, 226; Collier, '(Un)sexy Bodies', p. 29.
48 Thornton, *Dissonance and Distrust*, p. 223.
49 McGlynn, *The Woman Lawyer*, p. 104.
50 The recent introduction by some firms of the possibility of part-time work for partners represents only the slightest concession to lawyers' family responsibilities. First, it is necessary to become a partner in order to make use of this facility, which usually requires conformity to the long-hours culture up to that point (women solicitors who work part-time from the start are less likely to become partners). Second, only a small proportion of partners actually do work part-time (for example, at Freshfields Bruckhaus Deringer, an estimated 1.5 per cent of partners work part-time). See Luke McLeod-Roberts, 'BLM Is Most Female Friendly Firm in UK Top 50', available online at http://www.thelawyer.com/blm-is-most-female-friendly-firm-in-uk-top-50/1003262.article (accessed 11 February 2010). Third, such facilities are usually considered a means of retaining *women* in the firm (see McLeod-Roberts, 'BLM Is Most Female Friendly Firm', and http://www.telegraph.co.uk/finance/newsbysector/supportservices/7047466/Allen-and-Overy-to-let-partners-work-part-time-penalty-free.html (accessed 11 February 2010), thus continuing to mark out women as different from their male counterparts, who are not encouraged to work part time.
51 Thornton, *Dissonance and Distrust*, p. 235; Sommerlad and Sanderson, *Gender, Choice and Commitment*, p. 187; Hunter, 'Women Barristers and Gender Difference', p. 106.
52 McGlynn, *The Woman Lawyer*, p. 100.
53 Ibid., p. 150. Thornton, *Dissonance and Distrust*, p. 234.
54 Hunter and McKelvie, *Equality of Opportunity*, p. 110.
55 Ibid., p. 108; Thornton, *Dissonance and Distrust*, pp. 233, 235; McGlynn, *The Woman Lawyer*, p. 151.

56 Hunter and McKelvie, *Equality of Opportunity*, p. 108.
57 Sommerlad and Sanderson, *Gender, Choice and Commitment*, pp. 228–9.
58 Hunter and McKelvie, *Equality of Opportunity*, p. 108.
59 Ibid., p. 111.
60 Sommerlad, 'That Obscure Object of Desire', p. 193.
61 Rogers, 'Representing the Bar', p. 20.
62 Ibid.; Sommerlad and Sanderson, *Gender, Choice and Commitment*, p. 260.
63 Sommerlad and Sanderson, *Gender, Choice and Commitment*, p. 191.
64 Ibid., p. 260.
65 Quoted in Hunter, 'Women Barristers and Gender Difference', p. 120.
66 Hunter, 'Women Barristers and Gender Difference', p. 120.
67 Sommerlad and Sanderson, *Gender, Choice and Commitment*, p. 272.
68 Sommerlad, 'That Obscure Object of Desire', p. 176.
69 Thornton, *Dissonance and Distrust*, pp. 222, 6; Hunter, 'Talking up Equality', p. 127.
70 Rogers, 'Representing the Bar', pp. 16, 13.
71 Collier, 'Be Smart, Be Successful, Be Yourself', p. 74.
72 Collier, '(Un)sexy Bodies', p. 26; Thornton, *Dissonance and Distrust*, p. 139.
73 McGlynn, *The Woman Lawyer*, p. 105; McDowell, 'Body Work', p. 75.
74 See, for example, R. W. Connell, *Masculinities* (Sydney: Allen & Unwin, 1995);
   R. Collier, *Masculinity, Law and the Family* (London and New York: Routledge, 1995);
   D. Buchbinder, *Performance Anxieties: Re-producing Masculinity* (Sydney: Allen & Unwin,
   1998).
75 Connell, *Masculinities*, pp. 36–7; Collier, *Masculinity, Law and the Family*, pp. 29, 38, 43;
   see also Hunter, 'Women Barristers and Gender Difference', pp. 106–10.
76 Sommerlad and Sanderson, *Gender, Choice and Commitment*, p. 134; Thornton, *Dissonance
   and Distrust*, p. 172; Hunter, 'Women Barristers and Gender Difference', pp. 108–9;
   Thornton, *Dissonance and Distrust*, pp. 168–9.
77 Rogers, 'Representing the Bar', p. 13.
78 Sommerlad and Sanderson, *Gender, Choice and Commitment*, pp. 17, 19 (footnotes omitted).
79 Sommerlad and Sanderson, *Gender, Choice and Commitment*, pp. 138, 140, 170–1;
   McGlynn, *The Woman Lawyer*, p. 104; Thornton, *Dissonance and Distrust*, p. 167.
80 Sommerlad and Sanderson, *Gender, Choice and Commitment*, p. 17; see also Thornton,
   Dissonance and Distrust, p. 166.
81 Sommerlad and Sanderson, *Gender, Choice and Commitment*, p. 175.
82 Hunter, 'Women Barristers and Gender Difference', p. 110.
83 Sommerlad and Sanderson, *Gender, Choice and Commitment*, p. 181.
84 Ibid., p. 141; Thornton, *Dissonance and Distrust*, p. 135.
85 Collier, '(Un)sexy Bodies', p. 34.
86 Thornton, *Dissonance and Distrust*, p. 26. Hunter, 'Women Barristers and Gender
   Difference', p. 112.
87 Sommerlad and Sanderson, *Gender, Choice and Commitment*, p. 149.
88 McDowell, 'Body Work', pp. 76–7.
89 Ibid., pp. 77, 83–4.
90 Collier, 'Be Smart, Be Successful, Be Yourself', p. 65.
91 Ibid., p. 62.
92 R. Collier, 'Work-Life Balance: Ladies Only?', *The Lawyer*, 23 May 2005, p. 33.
93 Collier, '(Un)sexy Bodies', p. 30.
94 McDowell, 'Body Work', p. 85.
95 Collier, '(Un)sexy Bodies', p. 31.
96 Collier, 'Work-Life Balance', p. 33.

Chapter 3

'Sexing the matrix'

Embodiment, disembodiment and the law – towards the re-gendering of legal rationality

Anna Grear

Introduction: the urgency of contemporary justice-contexts

In the early twenty-first century the question of gender justice is more salient than ever. We live in a time of wholesale commodification of the social spheres, in a densely globalising world economic system haunted by a disturbing and growing global gap between rich and poor. We face the related reality of globally spiralling gender violence, burgeoning social complexity and deepening risk – all set against the backdrop of the looming threat of environmental breakdown.[1] At the same time, important challenges are emerging concerning law's need to be more inclusive by extending the protection of legal subjectivity not only to non-human animals and the environment but also to a range of other entities and putative rights claimants, including artificial intelligences, robots and nanotech entities – signalling a vital debate which looks set to inform ethical deliberation on the best way to deliver legal justice in our futures, human and post-human alike.[2] In short, there is an undeniably urgent need for us to reimagine and reconstitute our relationships with each other and with the non-human world of which we are a part. Legal rationality/subjectivity forms an indispensable and muscular thread in the Gordian knot of challenges ahead. Critical reflection on law's gendered rationality, in this context, is arguably especially significant.

The thoroughly gendered nature of law's historical exclusion of persons constructed as 'non-insiders' to legal discourse is radically continuous with identifiable exclusions operative in the burgeoning global capitalist techno-economy. Scholars and activists alike argue that a range of 'outsider' subjectivities disproportionately bear the costs of economic globalisation and the risks it produces. Such accounts draw decisive links between the exclusion of the poor, women, children and other non-dominant humans – such as racial minorities and the disabled, non-human animals, sensitive ecosystem habitats and the environment itself.[3] Importantly, there is a fundamental sense in which all these 'outsider' or 'other' subjectivities can be seen as quintessentially *feminised*.[4] The gender of legal rationality, in the light of law's role as a dominant and legitimating carrier of inclusions and exclusions is, accordingly, a matter in need of continuing critical interrogation.

Of gender and law: some preliminary caveats concerning complexity

In speaking about the gender of law (and legal rationality), we necessarily invoke elusive intellectual terrain. Both law/legal rationality and sex/gender are highly dynamic, open-textured concepts available to a host of competing interpretations and conceptions.

Sex/gender

Traditionally, since Simone de Beauvoir at least, a distinction has been drawn between 'sex' and 'gender'.[5] 'Sex', it has been assumed, refers to an underlying 'natural' 'reality' of a body sexed as either female or male, with vagina or penis, and a general morphology matching the genital identity of an individual. 'Gender', on the other hand, has often been taken to refer to the socio-cultural move from maleness to 'masculinity' or from femaleness to 'femininity'. However, sex and gender turn out to be more complex than this. For a start, as will be discussed below, the biology of sex indicates that sex is not a stable category. Nor does it contain a pair of homogenous binaries, despite the persisting Western socio-cultural (and legal) insistence on a rigid binary sex divide. In fact, the science of sex identification bears out Butler's argument that the 'construct "sex" is as constructed as gender'.[6] Gender, accordingly (following Ahmed), will be understood here to mean the way in which society (and law) names and forms bodies as 'sexed'.

> Gender ... names the discursive regime (including law) which produces bodies, where subjects become bodies, and where bodies become sexually differentiated. As a process (and therefore as temporal and historical) the engendering and embodiment of subjects is not exhaustible or already mapped out, but is the very site where contradictions and meanings are perpetually renegotiated.[7]

Fausto-Sterling has argued that

> labelling someone as a man or a woman is a social decision. We may use scientific knowledge to help us make the decision but only our beliefs about gender – not science – can define our sex. Furthermore, our beliefs about gender affect what kinds of knowledge scientists produce about sex in the first place.[8]

While the precise relationship between sex and gender as constructs involves complexities beyond the remit of this chapter, we can minimally observe that the gendering of legal rationality is related to an 'underlying' *construct* of a 'natural' sexual division imbued with normative implications and that the constructed 'naturalness' of the sex binary is arguably the key justificatory foundation for the 'gendered meanings that seek to establish "sex" for us as ... prior to the cultural meanings that it acquires'.[9]

Law

Law is a complex phenomenon. The very fact that law admits of so many variant jurisprudential accounts bears witness to myriad elements competing for theoretical attention: law simply cannot be adequately accounted for by monolithic conceptions of its nature. However, the very complexity of law, the diversity of its multiple interpenetrations, its multiplicity of perspectives, scenes and contexts, serves, if anything, to underline the power and reach of the central feminist observation that law is 'always and everywhere male',[10] because notwithstanding the kaleidoscopic proliferation of law's systemic and inter-systemic complexities the fundamental feminist critique remains obdurately intact.

Legal rationality and disembodiment

Feminist scholars have identified a key problematic in the gendering of legal rationality as being a tendency towards disembodiment. This is such an important idea in relation to the present chapter that it will be traced out here more fully.

Law presents itself as a 'rational' discourse – a discourse of reason. Western reason has long been dominated by an understanding of reason itself as *disembodied* – meaning that the 'very structure of rationality is regarded as transcending the structures of bodily experience'.[11] But, as feminists have pointed out, the disembodiment of Western rationalism is far from neutral despite the objectivity it implies. The impulse towards body transcendence is, in fact, irreducibly gendered. A wide range of theorists have noted the impact of two sets of binaries conditioning the structure of Western thought and life worlds, binaries that oppositionally and categorically define one another. So pervasive is their influence in Western philosophy that Bottomley argues, identifying them, that 'from Plato to Descartes, the scene was set in which *body/women/emotion/ nature* coalesced into that which was rightfully governed by *mind/men/reason/culture* as the basis for the development of civilised society'.[12]

The fundamental Cartesian insistence on the supremacy of reason over nature entails that the rational self has an inner and outer aspect: mind and body. The body is precisely that which rationality *transcends* and *defines* – externalised, construed as a part of 'nature', an 'object to be controlled and mechanised'.[13] Similarly, the Kantian moral subject – so influential in legal rationality – is defined by quintessentially abstract and 'universal' characteristics transcending embodiment. None of this body excision is remotely neutral in gender terms. There is a fundamental sense in which women are constituted as 'outsiders' to rationality precisely by being identified with embodiment (and its related emotionality). The implications of this are far-reaching. In the co-imbrication of woman/body/emotion/nature, 'nature' is also constructed as thoroughly gendered – it is *feminised*, while rationality is *masculinised*. Keller encapsulates the implications of this as follows

> Having divided the world into two parts – the knower (mind) and the knowable (nature) – [Western] scientific ideology goes on to prescribe a very specific relation between the two ... Not only are mind and nature assigned gender, but in characterising scientific and objective thought as masculine, the very activity by which the knower can acquire knowledge is also genderised. It is that between a subject and an object radically divided ... masculine ... connotes, as it so often does, autonomy, separation and distance.[14]

Keller's statement here suggestively points to the way in which 'nature' itself, the realm of embodied life and its environmental ecosystem habitats, is feminised (because *not-male*). That which is *not-male*, and thus *not-objective-knower*, is *objectified*. That which is 'object' is then left thoroughly available to the action of the (male) subject and to the scopophilic gaze of rationalist 'knowing'. The (male) subject, meanwhile, is characterised precisely by the rational transcendence by his mind of the body, emotion and nature. He is, and rationality is, most emphatically *not-female*. Western *legal* rationality is constituted, in precisely this way, as a gendered but disembodied rationality.

Quasi-disembodiment

Although rationality is constructed as disembodied (as transcending the structures of bodily experience) and *male* (the female is immersed in embodiment), in order to be recognised as *male* a person is typically identified by the possession of a particular *morphology*. In other words, *there is a body in disembodiment*. As Ahmed has argued, 'the disembodiment of the masculine perspective is itself an inscription of a body, a body which is so comfortable we needn't know it is there, a body which is simply a home for the mind, and doesn't interrupt it, confuse it, deceive it with irrationalism, or bleeding, or pregnancy'.[15]

This paradox is fully reflected in law's archetypal subject. The central case liberal legal subject is *disembodied and simultaneously male*: the *paradigmatic* rational agent. The paradoxical impossibility of complete disembodiment is perhaps best reflected by the term 'quasi-disembodiment', which reflects, in the moment of its invocation, the incomplete emptiness of the formally 'empty' legal subject, suggestively alluding to the conceptual sleight of hand that obscures from view the nakedly gendered dimensions of legal disembodiment. Liberal legal justice is in formal terms relatively 'blind' to concrete particularities. It is quintessentially general and 'universal'. This universalism persists, whether we conceptualise the legal subject as a 'citizen', a 'subject' or a 'person'. There is a sense in which liberal rights theory excises the body of its legal subject precisely in order to achieve a formal equality mediated by abstract universalism. Liberal legalism addresses legal subjects as *abstract* wills or personalities 'made possible by the separation of the will from any particular form of embodiment'.[16] But a body remains, nonetheless, and, of course, bodies can never completely disappear in law. When the law does have a body in mind in relation to law's paradigmatic legal actor – the active rational legal subject – that body is almost inevitably the 'bounded heterosexual male body', 'immutable', a construct operative as a 'means of denying bodily integrity to women (and to men who refuse to behave like "true" men who are deemed to lack clear boundary definition)'.[17] The 'male' body of the legal subject is thus constructed through mechanisms of exclusion. The most thoroughly excluded bodies are those presenting the most direct challenge to the masculinist closures of legal individualism, and, most problematically of all, those bodies capable of dividing to become two bodies in one.

Quasi-disembodiment, exclusion and liberal capitalism

The quasi-disembodied legal subject also has a decisive and intimate relationship with the traditional liberal construction of property and with the ideological closures of liberal law's co-imbrication with capitalism. Naffine's survey of the neglected theoretical terrain of legal personhood demonstrates that despite the complex intermingling in law of three identifiable conceptions of law's person, one particular construct takes pre-eminence: an undeniably masculinist construct, 'self-possessed and self-reliant, will-driven, clinically rational and individualistic'[18], which fits perfectly the quasi-disembodied rationalism of property and contract. In fact, this construct has been identified almost univocally by a wide range of critical legal theorists. This is the classical rational (property-owning) agent of contract law, the fully rational juridical individual who can be held fully rationally accountable for his actions.

This quasi-disembodied legal subject is, moreover, thoroughly implicated by important critiques of liberal legal rationality as a form of *rationalising enterprise*[19] committed to the excision of social context in order to privilege the interests of propertied elites. Critical socio-historical accounts, for example, link the contours of the classical rational legal subject with the protection and promotion of the interests of the propertied class in the emergent context of early capitalism, suggesting direct ideological links between the Enlightenment construction of liberal legal individualism and the protection of identifiable propertied interests in the late eighteenth and early nineteenth centuries. The impulses shaping the liberal legal subject thus appear to call upon the binary presuppositions of Western rationalism but, additionally, to reflect the imperatives of liberal capitalism and the related strategic excision of social context. As Norrie puts it:

> In the place of real individuals belonging to particular social classes, possessing the infinite differences that constitute genuine individuality ...

'economic man' or 'juridical man' were abstractions from real people emphasising one side of human life – the ability to reason and calculate – at the expense of every social circumstance that actually brings individuals to reason and calculate in particular ways.[20]

The liberal legal subject was forged in an 'actual historical context' at the time of the 'intellectual birth of liberal Western modernity'.[21] De Sousa Santos has made the related point that the rise of legal positivism and the rise of positivism in the epistemology of modern science go hand in hand, functioning as constructs aimed precisely at the promotion of capitalistic development.[22] Thus, beneath the formal equality of liberal legal rationality we find a paradigmatic liberal legal subject: a socially de-contextualised, hyper-rational, wilful individual systematically stripped of embodied particularities in order to appear neutral, and, of course, theoretically genderless, serving the mediation of power linked to property and capital accumulation. And, although this paradigmatic liberal legal subject is generally thought of as a 'natural (human) person', there is a profound sense, of course, in which this mutilated, de-contextualised, 'emptied out' subject is not really human at all.

In fact, another highly significant implication of the intimate linkages between quasi-disembodiment, liberal abstractionism and capitalism resides in the idea that it is probably more accurate to say that the *corporation, not* the human being, represents the quintessential liberal legal subject. The corporation is a disembodied jural entity, suffering from no gap between itself and the disembodiment of the legal perspective. It is also, as Neocleous has argued, the very personification of capital:[23] the masculinist liberal legal actor writ large. Discussing the construction of the corporate person in the USA in 1886, Federman writes in terms that underscore this:

> the corporation of 1886 represents the production of the normal understanding of the new American man, the bodily expression of male power, the individual self liberated from the constraints of the past and 'the molestations of society or state.' It is now the construct of a well-placed, self-interested enterprising group of persons willing to stake their lives and livelihood for economic success. As such, the corporation meets the requirements of the 'balanced character', that psychological trait necessary (and applied only to elite males) for the emerging commercial economy of the late nineteenth century.[24]

In short, the corporation perfectly fits the thoroughly gendered ideological tilt of liberal law, taking priority in a wide range of contexts and even capturing strategic discursive and legal ground within the field of fundamental human rights.[25] Capitalism itself can meaningfully be understood as a profoundly gendered value system within which the gendered corporate form and its interests are accorded inevitable priority.

Quasi-disembodied capitalistic legal rationality can be linked to the historical and contemporaneous suffering of women, non-human animals and the destruction of the living environment – in short, to all those *feminised 'others'* constituted as *non-male* by their binary exclusion from *male/mind/reason/culture*. These 'others' inhabit/constitute what we can conceive of as the (feminised) 'body-realm' – archetypically 'object' rather than (quasi-disembodied) (male) 'active subject'. Nibert's sociological study of the 'entanglements of oppression' compellingly demonstrates the dense interconnectedness of the abuse of particular groups of human beings ('women, humans of colour, children, humans with disabilities, humans who are older or poor, and those with different sexual orientations'), non-human animals and the degradation of the environment and links these entanglements of oppression unambiguously to the dispersal of *economic power* – particularly to the advent of *corporate capitalism*.[26] There is an almost precise match between Nibert's account and the contours of the exclusions set up by the operative quasi-disembodiment of liberal legal rationality. Behind the 'neutral' mask of formal legal rationality lies a set of profoundly gendered and interlinked injustices, the continuing implications of which could scarcely be more far reaching.

Foregrounding the 'ontic': a strategy for resistance?

We have been considering a critical reading of the relationship between quasi-disembodiment, liberal legal rationality, capitalism and oppression. Fundamental to quasi-disembodiment, as we saw, is the existence of a set of binary constructions of reality – and, in particular, a central and pervasive male/female dualism. It seems useful to ask, in the light of the centrality of this male/female binary, whether rescripting sex/gender as *non-binary* might open an aperture through which to imagine the possibility of a more inclusive legal rationality. One way of doing this is to address quasi-disembodiment directly by focusing on embodiment – and in particular, on the ontic ambiguity of sexed embodiment.

Human beings live lives that are inescapably embodied and materially con-textualised. Our lives are spatially and temporally bound, profoundly socially mediated, but possessing an irreducibly 'ontic' materiality shared with non-human animals and the living environment itself. Life in the 'body realm' is characterised by flesh-and-blood interrelationships with a world of hard and soft objects, gases, water, pollutants, viruses, the impacts of privation, the elements, temperature, weather conditions and so forth. The legal subject, by contrast, is a cipher – an abstraction forced to materialise, and which, when it does, tends to do so as the quasi-disembodied liberal legal construct of 'natural man', and his amplified juridical extension: the corporation. There is thus a complex and ethically significant gap between real 'thick' human beings and the legal subject – the 'thinnest of the thin conceptions of the person'.[27] And while all human beings possess a fundamental embodied vulnerability (or ontic affectability), humans with the power to manage vulnerability – through financial, political, legal and other forms of power – can sometimes become (as history reveals) the very producers of the networked oppressions implicated by critiques of capitalism, liberal law and its 'others'.

While there are many critical advantages to be gained by foregrounding the ontic to counter legal quasi-disembodiment and its production of exclusions and suffering, the key advantage for present purposes is the potential destabilisation of the 'natural' construct of the sex binary so fundamental to law's masculinist closures.

The ontic ambiguity of sex

As noted earlier, feminists have attacked the abstract disembodied universal legal subject for its exclusions. Some have offered strategies for reformulating the legal universal along more gender-inclusive lines. Irigaray, for example, famously attacked the Kantian (disembodied) foundations of the 'neutral' universal legal subject by arguing that it is precisely 'the gender blindness of this male neutrality that perpetuates the forgetting of nature and the social exclusion of women'.[28] She attempted to reconstruct the universal by arguing that

> the most appropriate content for the universal is sexual difference. Indeed, this content is both real and universal. Sexual difference is an immediate natural given and it is a real and irreducible component of the universal. The whole of human kind is composed of women and men and of nothing else.[29]

While this formulation introduces sexed embodiment to the universal, as Otto points out, the strategy fails to transcend the binary.[30] It seems vital to take issue with the idea that humankind is entirely composed of 'men and women *and nothing else*' if the binary is to be destabilised: Irigaray's strategic binary essentialism cannot, by definition, achieve this.

Otto, by contrast, has offered a non-binary reformulation of the universal in direct response to the closures of the abstract (masculine) universal in the field of international human-rights law. Her strategy, unlike Irigaray's, is to attack the *binary* itself. She argues that sex and gender need to be *non-dichotomously* rescripted as *shifting* and *multiplicitous*. For Otto, this rescripting should be achieved by *detaching* sex and gender *entirely* from bodily parts in order to reconstitute sex and gender as a 'hybridity' – a complex of choices and desires not tied to body types (which are, in any case, 'social constructions').[31] But this championing of 'hybridity' confronts her with a crucial theoretical dilemma: the risk of the *erasure* of gender-specific rights and the categories currently vital for political resistance to subjugation. This dilemma, furthermore, is accompanied by the genuine danger that 'hybridity' leaves open the possibility that the masculine will simply reassert itself 'in the universal image of the hybrid'.[32] It is also arguable that by completely detaching sex from bodies, the very mechanism of disembodiment, with its inherent masculinism, will, in fact, *subvert* the rescripting of sex/gender.

Foregrounding *embodiment*, by contrast, means taking *embodied particularity* seriously as a *feature of universality*. When embodiment is rendered central to the human universal we are necessarily drawn close to the contextual, material, lived, flesh-and-blood realities of human lives and invited to imagine a 'concrete universal': a universal filled with bodies in all their variety, capacities, incapacities and context-responsiveness and affectability. Embodiment, in fact, is the very matrix in which our *universality* and *irreducible uniqueness* come into potent symbolic fusion – a fusion with enormous critical energy.

Irigaray's analysis suggests embodied particularity as a way of destabilising the masculinism of the 'neutral' universal but does not follow the implications of embodied particularity through to the destabilisation of the sex binary itself. Otto is right to suggest that the idea of sexual *variation and mutability*, placed at the heart of the universal is more potent in its implications than Irigaray's notion of binary sexual *difference*, but Otto's insistence on the detachment of sex and gender from bodies arguably misses the radical critical potency of *embodiment itself* to suggest a far more ambiguous set of particularities – a *dynamic set of embodied ambiguities* that undermine the sustainability of the sex binary as a 'natural' (normative) imposition on bodies. Sex and gender as constructs are both arguably based on an underlying assumption that 'normal' bodies 'naturally' come as male or female as a matter of 'biology' ('nature's truth'). But the biology of the body's sex, far from being straightforwardly dichotomous, is actually a highly complex matter, and there are bodies, many bodies,[33] 'that present themselves as neither entirely male nor entirely female'.[34]

The sexed body as we currently conceptualise it is simply *not the immutable binary 'given' that law presupposes and then insists upon from birth* while (inconsistently) excising/submerging the body. As we have seen, although the body is transcended in complex ways by (male) legal disembodiment, *the body itself* (cast as female), in a central sense, provides the very presuppositional foundation for the set of feminised exclusions related to legal (quasi)disembodiment – exclusions logically dependent upon differential forms of embodiment (ultimately constructed as 'binary'). While the gendering of legal rationality could continue to insist upon binary gender categories *notwithstanding* the fact that the underlying biology of sex is revealed as *non-binary*, binary legal gendering can only be achieved by *detaching* legal gender from its *own logical foundation*.

Otto insists that bodies themselves are 'social constructions', but, notwithstanding the importance of social constructionist insights, it seems necessary to allow the ontic materiality of the body itself a role in the destabilisation of the binary. We need, arguably, in relation to this, to reconceptualise the biology/social relationship. In fact, sustained attempts to do this are currently underway, questioning the purely social-constructionist approach and allowing the biological a cautious new role, a carefully qualified 'welcome back in'[35] to the task of reconceptualising the body and its social formation. One such approach, for example, emphasises the fact that '[h]uman beings must have a particular physical constitution for social influences to consistently "do their work"'[36], a view allowing materiality to pre-exist, albeit in a qualified and attenuated sense, and in strictly limited ways, the social meanings attributed to it. For present purposes, Grosz provides a most useful figuration in the form of the Mobius strip – a flat ribbon twisted once but joined end to end to form an endless circular twisted surface – to symbolise the way in which the body ('the corporeal exterior') and mind ('the psychical interior') are intimately continuous with each other; demonstrating the 'the passage, vector or uncontrollable drift of the inside into the outside and the outside into the inside'[37], and symbolising the impossibility of disembodied rationality, the inescapability of the ontic. In Grosz's words, the body is

> the threshold or borderline concept that hovers perilously and undecidedly at the pivotal point of binary pairs. ... In the face of social constructionism, the body's tangibility, its matter, its (quasi) nature may be invoked; but, in opposition to essentialism, biologism, and naturalism, it is the body as cultural product that must be stressed.[38]

Nowhere is the interaction between the material body and the social construction of sex differentiation more revealing, yet more covert, than in the case of human intersexual bodies. Intersexualities (for we should not essentialise intersexuality) highlight the sheer empirical unsustainability of the traditional oppositional dichotomy between male and female. In an intersexual body, the genitals, the most visible exterior material markers of sex, confront the sex binary with an ambiguity that directly undermines the claim of binary 'naturalness'. Yet so ideologically fierce is our mainstream cultural commitment to binary sex and gender in the West that the ambiguity or variability of the genitals of intersexual babies are manipulated by surgeons to *construct a sex* that fits a fundamentally *social* (and in some cases, merely aesthetic)[39] insistence on a binary male/female divide.

> Surgeons remove parts and use plastic to create 'appropriate' genitalia for people born with body parts that are not easily identifiable as male or female. Physicians believe that their expertise enables them to 'hear' nature telling them the truth about what sex such patients ought to be. Alas, their truths come from the social arena and are reinforced, in part, by the medical tradition of rendering intersexual births invisible.[40]

And, just as the sex-binary foundational to legal quasi-disembodiment can be inescapably linked to the multiple forms and entanglements of oppression identified by Nibert and others, so too the imposition of the sex binary causes immense suffering to those with sexually ambiguous bodies. In fact, the medical 'cure' for intersexuality often does great harm

> Infant genital surgery is cosmetic surgery performed to achieve a social result – reshaping a sexually ambiguous body so that it conforms with our

two-sex system. This social imperative is so strong that doctors have come to accept it as a medical imperative, despite strong evidence that early genital surgery doesn't work: it causes extensive scarring, requires multiple surgeries, and often obliterates the possibility of orgasm.[41]

Our entire social and legal organisation is predicated, in this light, on *a false binary*. Yet this is a binary, that, as Fausto-Sterling argues, we impose at earlier and earlier stages of development, a move that has the effect of making the binary appear all the more inborn and 'natural'. The presence of intersexual bodies, 'heretical bodies', in an ever-shifting politics of the body, alerts us to the false and violent closures invoked by our binary insistence on the male/female dichotomy, rendering our legal and cultural insistence on 'only two sexes' empirically – and ethically – unsustainable.

Towards the re-gendering of legal rationality?

In the light of the biological instability of sex and the widespread suffering caused by the ideological deployment of binary (and oppositional) sex 'norma-tivity'[42] (including to intersexuals), it seems more just to characterise the uni-versal subject of law not as sexually differentiated in a *dichotomous* sense but as sexually *variegated and mutable*. One way of doing this is to see sex (and potentially gender) not as binary but as existing on an embodied multi-sexed/omnigendered *spectrum* (or continuum)[43] that moves between *notional spectrum-extremes* of 'male' and 'female' but, crucially, without *essentialising* them. This spectrum, thoroughly *embodied*, could embrace a related proliferation of sexual and gender identities and also explicitly allow space for self-ascribed and transgender (and transsexual) identifications – a position, in fact, far more consonant with liberalism's fundamental commitment to individual self-expression than the imposition of the binary sex construct and its gendered 'normativities'. This approach would also be consistent with embracing the complexity of the mutual constitution of the material and social while retaining an important critical role for the ontic materiality of the body itself. And, because this theoretical construct would embrace an explicitly *embodied spectrum*, rather than a *disembodied hybridity*, it retains our important ability to speak of 'maleness/masculinity/masculinisation' and 'femaleness/femininity/feminisation', thus *retaining*, rather than *erasing*, the political languages currently vital to critique of the masculinism of legal rationality and its gendered abstrac-tionism. It may be possible, in this way, to see sex and gender as 'shifting' and 'multiplicitous' as Otto advocates but without embracing yet another form of disembodiment.

There is deconstructive power in the ambiguity of the 'ontic materiality' of human embodment and great potential for its role as an ethical guide in the face of the exclusions implicated by legal quasi-disembodiment. Opening an embodiment-centred imaginative aperture for the re-gendering of legal rationality and its related human universal could just prove to be one of the most critical imaginative leaps we can make in the opening decades of the twenty-first century. Certainly, the important task of reflecting on the extension of legal subjectivity to embrace new entities and to reflect deepening ethical concerns in the face of technological developments and the associated ravages enacted upon the living environment underlines the need to address the foundational dualism underlying the violent historical and contemporary exclusion of all those 'non-insiders' so invidiously feminised by liberal legal rationality.

It is worth recalling, in the closing words of this chapter, that the modern oppositional sex binary was imposed in precisely the same temporal and political matrix that saw the emergence of radical notions of human equality and the birth of rights discourse.[44] The science of physical difference emerged as an ideological tool with which to invalidate equality claims and to protect elite male privilege and 'more than ever, politics necessitated two and only two sexes'.[45] Challenging the foundational sex binary underlying exclusionary legal masculinism and then fully exploring the implications for the gender of legal rationality may be one of the most strategic critical tasks facing us in the context of the inequalities, ravages and intimately interlinked oppressions produced by twenty-first-century neo-liberal globalised corporate hegemony and its related historical exclusions.

Acknowledgements

I would like to thank Patricia Elliot, Lois Bibbings, Alex Rotas and Rosemary Hunter for their comments on drafts of this chapter; Diane Otto for comments on a paper forming the basis of the chapter; and the Centre for the Study of Gender, Sexuality and Law for the generous provision of a Research Fellowship at the University of Keele in 2008.

Notes

1 P. Kirby, *Vulnerability and Violence: The Impact of Globalization* (London: Pluto Press, 2005).
2 See, for a discussion of the implications of post-human insights for human rights, U. Baxi, *Human Rights in a Post-Human World: Critical Essays* (Oxford: Oxford University Press, 2007); see also G. Teubner, 'Rights of Non-Humans? Electronic Agents and Animals as New Actors in Politics and Law', *Journal of Law and Society*, 33 (4) (2006): 497–521.
3 See, for example, D. Nibert, *Animal Rights, Human Rights: Entanglements of Oppression and Liberation* (Oxford: Rowman & Littlefield, 2002).
4 The feminisation of these subjects can be linked to the insights of eco-feminism. See, for example: A. Collard and J. Contrucci, *The Rape of the Wild: Man's Violence against Animals and the Earth* (Bloomington, Ind.: Indiana University Press, 1988). This can also be linked to the impact of 'new wars' and evidence of escalating global violence against women. See the brief but suggestive discussion in B. Turner, *Vulnerability and Human Rights* (Pennsylvania, Pa.: Pennsylvania State University Press, 2006), pp. 13–20.
5 S. de Beauvoir, *The Second Sex* (London: Vintage Classics, 1997).

6 J. Butler, *Gender Trouble: Feminism and the Subversion of Identity* (London and New York: Routledge, 1990), p. 7.
7 S. Ahmed, 'Deconstruction and Law's Other: Towards a Feminist Theory of Embodied Legal Rights', *Social and Legal Studies*, 4 (1) (1995): 55–73.
8 A. Fausto-Sterling, *Sexing the Body: Gender Politics and the Construction of Sexuality* (New York: Basic Books, 2000), p. 3.
9 Butler, *Gender Trouble*, p. 109.
10 J. Richardson and R. Sandland, 'Feminism, Law and Theory', in J. Richardson and R. Sandland (eds.), *Feminist Perspectives on Law and Theory* (London: Cavendish, 2000), pp. 1–22; p. 1.
11 M. Johnson, *The Body in the Mind: The Bodily Basis of Meaning, Imagination and Reason* (Chicago, Ill.: Chicago University Press, 1987), p. x.
12 A. Bottomley, 'The Many Appearances of the Body in Feminist Scholarship', in A. Bainham, S. D. Sclater and M. Richards (eds.), *Body Lore and Laws* (Oxford: Hart Publishing, 2002), pp. 127–48; pp. 134–5. Emphasis added.
13 V. Seidler, 'Embodied Knowledge and Virtual Space', in J. Wood (ed.), *The Virtual Embodied* (London and New York: Routledge, 1998), pp. 15–29; p. 17, cited by B. Ajana, 'Disembodiment and Cyberspace: a Phenomenological Approach', *Electronic Journal of Sociology*, 2005, available online at http://www.sociology.org/content/2005/tier1/ajana.html (accessed 11 December 2009).
14 E. F. Keller, *Reflections on Gender and Science* (New Haven, Conn.: Yale University Press, 1985), p. 79, cited by K. Green, 'Being Here: What a Woman Can Say about Land Law', in A. Bottomley (ed.), *Feminist Perspectives on the Foundational Subjects of Law* (London: Cavendish, 1996), pp. 87–107.
15 Ahmed, 'Deconstruction and Law's Other', p. 56.
16 P. Halewood, 'Law's Bodies: Disembodiment and the Structure of Liberal Property Rights', *Iowa Law Review*, 81 (1996): 1331–93; at p. 1337. See also C. Douzinas and A. Gearey, *Critical Jurisprudence* (Oxford: Hart Publishing, 2005), pp. 127–8.
17 N. Naffine, 'The Body Bag', in N. Naffine and R. Owens (eds.), *Sexing the Subject of Law* (Sydney: Sweet & Maxwell, 1997), pp. 79–93; at p. 84.
18 N. Naffine, 'Who are Law's Persons: From Cheshire Cats to Responsible Subjects', *Modern Law Review*, 66 (3) (2003): 346–67; p. 365.
19 See M. Horwitz, 'Comment: The Historical Contingency of the Role of History', *Yale Law Journal*, 90 (1981): 1057–9.
20 A. Norrie, *Crime, Reason and History: A Critical Introduction to Criminal Law* (London: Wiedenfeld & Nicolson, 1993), p. 23.
21 Ibid., p. 31.
22 B. De Sousa Santos, *Towards a New Legal Common Sense: Law, Science and Politics in Paradigmatic Transition* (London and New York: Routledge, 1995), p. 40.
23 See M. Neocleous, 'Staging Power: Marx, Hobbes and the Personification of Capital', *Law and Critique*, 14 (2) (2003): 147–65.
24 C. Federman, 'Constructing Kinds of Persons in 1886: Corporate and Criminal', *Law and Critique*, 14 (2003): 167–89; at pp. 181–2.
25 See, U. Baxi, *The Future of Human Rights* (Oxford: Oxford University Press, 2006); M. Emberland, *The Human Rights of Companies: Exploring the Structure of ECHR Protection* (Oxford: Oxford University Press, 2006); C. J. Mayer, 'Personalising the Impersonal: Corporations and the Bill of Rights, *Hastings Law Journal*, 41 (1990): 577–663; J. Flynn, 'The Jurisprudence of Corporate Personhood: The Misuse of a Legal Concept', in W. Samuels and A. Miller (eds.), *Corporations and Society: Power and Responsibility* (New York: Greenwood Press, 1987); M. Horwitz, 'Santa Clara Revisited: The Development of Corporate Theory', *West Virginia Law Review*, 88 (1985): 173–224;

G. A Marks, 'The Personification of the Business Corporation in American Law', *University of Chicago Law Review*, 54 (1987): 1441–83.

26 Nibert, *Animal Rights, Human Rights*, pp. 4, xiii.

27 C. Douzinas, *The End of Human Rights* (Oxford: Hart Publishing, 2000), p. 236.

28 E. Porter, 'Equality in the Law and Irigaray's Different Universals', in J. Richardson and R. Sandland (eds.), *Feminist Perspectives on Law and Theory* (London: Cavendish, 2000), pp. 135–52; at p. 145.

29 L. Irigaray, *Sexes and Genealogies* (New York: Columbia University Press, 1993), cited by Porter, 'Equality in the Law', at Note 15.

30 D. Otto, 'Lost in Translation: Re-Scripting the Sexed Subjects of International Human Rights Law', in A. Orford (ed.), *International Law and its Others* (Cambridge: Cambridge University Press, 2006), pp. 318–56; at p. 320.

31 Ibid., p. 355.

32 Ibid.

33 Fausto-Stirling underlines the frequency of such births, citing research she undertook with undergraduate students into the medical literature on intersex. The figure she ended up with, 1.7 per cent of all births, is not, she emphasises, a precise count but would mean, for example, that in a city of 300,000 there would be 5,100 people with varying degrees of intersexual development: Fausto-Sterling, *Sexing the Body*, p. 51.

34 Choi, examining the masculinity of sport, puts the figure somewhat higher in terms of chromosomal sex – at around 10 per cent of the population who are neither XX-female or XY-male: P. Y. L Choi, *Femininity and the Physically Active Woman* (London and New York: Routledge, 2000), pp. 20, 3.

35 A. Fausto-Sterling, S. J. Williams and G. Bendelow, *The Lived Body: Sociological Themes, Embodied Issues* (London and New York: Routledge, 1998), p. 18.

36 Ibid.

37 E. Grosz, *Volatile Bodies: Toward a Corporeal Feminism* (Bloomington, Ind.: Indiana University Press, 1994), p. xii, cited by Fausto-Sterling et al., *The Lived Body*, p. 129.

38 Grosz, *Volatile Bodies*, pp. 23–4, cited by Fausto-Sterling et al., *The Lived Body*, pp. 128–9.

39 See S. J. Kessler, *Lessons from the Intersexed* (New Brunswick, NJ: Rutgers University Press, 1998), pp. 8, 24–8. See also the politically revealing teaching tool, the 'phallo-o-meter', used by the Intersexual Rights Movement: Fausto-Sterling, *Sexing the Body*, p. 59, fig. 3.4.

40 Fausto-Sterling, *Sexing the Body*, p. 28.

41 Ibid., p. 80. For more, see, for example, her chapters 'Of Gender and Genitals: The Use and Abuse of the Modern Intersexual', *Sexing the Body*, pp. 45–77, and 'Should There Be Only Two Sexes?' *Sexing the Body*, pp. 78–114. See also C. Chase, 'Hermaphrodites with Attitude: Mapping the Emergence of Intersex Political Activism', *GLQ: A Journal of Lesbian and Gay Studies*, 4 (2) (1998): 189–211, and C. Chase, 'Surgical Progress Is Not The Answer to Intersexuality', *Journal of Clinical Ethics*, 9 (4) (1998): 385–92 – both cited by Fausto-Sterling. See also, Kessler, *Lessons from the Intersexed*, and A. Domurat Dreger, *Hermaphrodites and the Medical Invention of Sex* (Cambridge, Mass.: Harvard University Press, 1998).

42 To the harms associated with the binary sex divide we can add the harmful effects of the related policing of human sexuality: see L. S. Bibbings, 'Heterosexuality as Harm: Fitting In', in D. Gordon, P. Hillyard, C. Pantazis and S. Tombs (eds.), *Beyond Criminology: Taking Harm Seriously* (London: Pluto Press, 2004), pp. 217–35.

43 Fausto-Sterling, *Sexing the Body*, pp. 20–9.

44 Ibid., pp. 36–44.

45 Ibid., p. 40.

Chapter 4

Vulnerability, equality and the human condition

Martha A. Fineman

Introduction: vulnerability

The concept of 'vulnerability' provides a powerful base for arguments that the state must be more responsive to the needs of those within its purview. I posit vulnerability as a universal and ever-present aspect of the human condition. Human beings – as embodied creatures – are all, always vulnerable. A key aspect of this state of vulnerability is related to the ever-present possibility of finding ourselves physically or otherwise dependent on others for care and support.[1]

I have moved to this vulnerability concept in response to what I see as the failures of American equal-protection law. These failures are a result of law's paradigm of formal equality and its limited ability to respond to the gross and growing economic and material injustice that mars the USA at the beginning of the twenty-first century. The vulnerability thesis focuses attention on the relationship between law and the state, which is understood as a set of social and economic institutions. Vulnerability also calls into question assumptions inherent in the political and ethical systems in which law provides a significant cultural context for shaping expectations and aspirations for both the individual and the state.[2]

The role of the state and its laws in our current American constitutional and statutory regime is to mandate equality through the lens of discrimination, independent of and seemingly oblivious to existing inequalities of distribution: unless there is some distortion introduced by impermissible bias, then the state should not interfere. The list of identity categories found in American equal-protection doctrine is well known: race, gender, religion, national origin and so on. These classifications define individual legal identities and are the basis for the formation of interest groups. Ultimately, the classifications direct the concern and the content of the law itself. The classifications organise equal-protection doctrine, which is framed in terms of disallowing discrimination against someone who occupies one of the categories. Distinctions are made between categories also. Discrimination based on race receives 'strict scrutiny', while gender prompts a less rigorous review.

In my opinion, the major problem with this state of equality jurisprudence is that these categories have become the way in which we understand and explain material, social and political inequalities, as well as the way in which we describe those who may be subject to historic prejudices and stereotyping. Thus, in law, the elimination of discrimination against certain identities becomes the quest, not the elimination of the inequalities for which those identities often serve as proxies: poverty, denial of dignity, subordination and a lack of access to basic social goods.

The difficulty with reliance on these identity categories is that they are both over- and underinclusive in their relation to inequalities. Not all women are paid 75¢ on the male dollar. Some are paid $1.50, or even more. Additionally, not all men are paid $1.00 on the male dollar, and some are even unemployed. To make this point is not to deny that gender and other forms of discrimination exist or that personal characteristics might compound the experience of vulnerability for an individual. The claim is merely that discrimination models based on identity classifications will not produce circumstances of greater equality in many cases and may in fact lead to less equality in real terms.

The first point of this critique is to understand that our existing sense of equality is weak; its promise largely illusory, because it fails to take into account existing inequality of circumstance. The second point is to show how this failure allows responsibility for this inequality of circumstances to be placed solely upon the individual. The institutions of the state are not implicated or involved unless discrimination is found. In this scenario, the equality mandate for the state is fulfilled by the assurance of formal access to those institutions. It is as though these other material, cultural and social inequalities were the product of natural forces beyond the ability of the state or law to rectify, rather than the outcomes of society, produced and reproduced in its institutions.

Note how the individual and the state are positioned in this paradigm. It is the individual who must rise to the occasion. He or she must show initiative and resolve. Society is viewed as a meritocracy in which the individual must be self-sufficient, exercise personal responsibility and be independent on the level playing field that the state ensures. Failure, within this paradigm, is to be understood as individual as well.

Dependency

While dependency has no respected place in the equality regime as it has been defined in American law, I earlier developed a theory of dependency which was also an argument for societal responsibility.[3] The theory began with the recognition that in contemporary understanding dependency is viewed as an extremely negative status. On a political and legal level in the USA there have been repeated attempts to eradicate dependency by removing what are labelled as 'incentives' to dependency, such as social-welfare benefits for poor single mothers. The rhetoric surrounding dependency treats it as something that can be eliminated and as being within individual control. As a result, those who are deemed dependent can be seen as deservingly punished and stigmatised by society.

Interestingly, dependency as a concept has a history, and its meaning has not been fixed over time. Early in American political history the label of dependency was much more broadly applied and was used as the basis for the exclusion of some from political rights (voting) as well as providing justification for second-class citizenship. Dependency was used to describe the position of women and children, certainly, but it also was the term applied to men who were mere wage earners and had no property or capital accumulation. Dependency was conceptualised as the status of having to rely on others for your livelihood – working for wages. Of course, today we consider the wage earner, who has also morphed into the taxpayer, to be the exemplar of the independent citizen. Important in the context of the vulnerability thesis, however, is the realisation that the meaning of such a potent political term in contemporary society can change, and has done so over time. This means that such terms may need to be periodically reconsidered and the assumptions underlying them re-explored.

In contrast to most discussions, my reconsideration of dependency began with an argument about its universality: dependency is inevitable, and it is universal. In this theorisation, dependency is conceptualised as a biological and developmental category, something inherent in the human condition. Another way of recalling the universality of dependency is to remind ourselves that we were all dependent as infants and children. Many – perhaps most – of us also may become dependent once again, in an organic way, as we age, become ill or disabled.

Other types of dependency often accompany this most basic biological form, and we can speak of dependencies as arising in economic, psychological or emotional forms, for example. These types of dependency have not, however, been the focus of my concern; their primary usefulness to the argument being that they help to demonstrate how varied are the relationships crammed into the category of dependency are. Using only one simple word does not begin to capture the range of complex relationships that we could call dependent.

There is another form of dependency that has been central to my work, however. 'Derivative dependency' is what I have called the social or institutional component of dependency. The term 'derivative dependency' signifies a simple concept, and an often overlooked reality: that those who care for others – for the children, the elderly, the ill and others who are the inevitable dependants I referred to earlier – are themselves in need of resources and societal support in order to undertake that care successfully.

Importantly, unlike inevitable dependency, derivative dependency is not a universal experience. Quite the contrary: care work is structured through law and societal institutions, channelled so as to be the responsibility or obligation of only some members of society. In the USA, the ideology of family responsibility does this channelling work.[4] Invoking an ideology of the family is the way in which we privatise dependency, and the family, like the individual, is supposed to be independent and self-sufficient in managing dependency and meeting family members' needs. Families that have to resort to the state for support are deemed to be failures.

Casting the family as separate, private and subject to non-intervention principles in this way allows politicians, philosophers and policy analysts to justify ignoring dependency and its relationship to poverty and inequality. They feel free to assume a competent, functioning private family as they spin out their theories of justice, equality, efficiency and autonomy. Privatisation thus operates in a manner that is highly unjust and should not be ignored by those interested in gender justice. Privatising dependency in the way we do also furthers gender inequality within the family. This is because within the family dependency work is delegated to only some members, and it is still the case that this work and the costs associated with caretaking continue to be borne mostly by women who are socialised into their roles as mother, wife, daughter and so on. In fact, I argue that with this set of social arrangements, in which dependency is primarily the responsibility of the private family, gender equality will be next to impossible for women to achieve, at least when they became mothers.[5] As caretakers, women have historically been uniquely burdened. Undertaking caretaking means diverting time and energy away from activities that are economically rewarded, likely to lead to economic independence and perhaps to societal recognition, power and prestige. As it is now, caretakers are actually punished by the disadvantages attached to family responsibilities in the structure and operation of the so-called free market and the lack of regulatory supervision by the state.

This disadvantage points to a further injustice. Turning a critical gaze to society, it seems that privatising dependency actually fosters freeloading by other societal institutions. Care work built on the back of the family provides an unrecognised subsidy to the state and the market. Looking at the benefits conferred by family labour, it seems clear that the family produces value for the whole of society and its institutions. Care work produces the employee, as well as the CEO, the taxpayer, the soldier, the consumer, the teacher, the student and so on. It seems only fair, in the light of this important reality, to assert that society should share the burdens associated with performing this vital, indispensable labour. At a minimum, society should not tolerate the structuring of its institutions in ways that disadvantage, and discriminate against, caretakers.

Far from sharing the burdens, however, the state and the market appropriate the benefits of the care work that goes on in families, while, at the same time, both the value and the disadvantages associated with that care work are ignored. Therein lies the real injustice, and this injustice provided the basis for my earliest claim against the state on behalf of caretakers and those dependent upon them.[6] The argument was that there is an immediate need for state recognition and structuring of subsidy and accommodation through state institutions in order to reach a more just allocation of responsibility for dependency across societal institutions. This argument about dependency focused on the plight of the caretaker – the exploitation and appropriation of her (or his – it is the activity, not the sex that is relevant) socially productive and necessary labour without corresponding social and economic support and institutional accommodation.[7]

This argument, while persuasive to some, was either ignored or met with the dismissive response that dependency was of little theoretical interest, being only 'episodic' or 'sporadic' in nature and therefore could comfortably be left to the private family and private arrangements. This characterisation is true, arguably, in regard to dependency in its inevitable form, particularly as it may be confined only to early life for some individuals. Further, many individuals escape or effectively manage derivative dependency so that its presence is often attributed to 'choice' rather than to imposition. It was this critique that led me to the concept of vulnerability.

Vulnerability

Vulnerability is what underlies dependency. Like dependency, vulnerability is universal – all human beings are vulnerable. However, vulnerability is not episodic, sporadic or largely developmental in nature. Further, vulnerability is constant throughout life, reflecting not only the realised or inevitable version of dependency (which we experience as children or with some illnesses or disabilities) but also the threat that we might become dependent in the future. Vulnerability underlies, then, the present potential for each of us to be in need of aid and assistance. Further, vulnerability extends beyond the confines of inevitable or developmental dependency to encompass disparate forms of potential human reliance on others, including those based on emotional, psychological, economic, spiritual and institutional needs.

Sometimes our vulnerability is exposed by the need or dependency that arises in the wake of catastrophe or 'natural' disasters, such as errant weather systems that produce flood, drought, famine and fire, as Hurricane Katrina demonstrated to Americans only a few years ago. Our vulnerability might also be exposed as a result of human activities, such as criminal activity or terrorist attacks such as that of 9/11. Further, there are institutions that might fail us, exposing, even increasing and compounding, our vulnerability. In this last category, the worldwide 'great recession of 2008–20?' and unwise, greedy or corrupt practices by corporations and the financial industry should be placed. These categories contain events that we, and society, can attempt to avoid, or, if unable to, to ameliorate, mitigate, or compensate for, but ultimately the inevitability of some such events is beyond human control.

Like dependency, a theory about human vulnerability has both an individual and an institutional component. Both our personal and our social lives are marked by vulnerability. On the individual level, vulnerability encapsulates the universal and constant fragility of the human condition. And while from the perspective of the individual vulnerability may be experienced differently, in particularised ways influenced by the quality and quantity of resources that any individual possesses, it cannot be avoided. What largely defines this experiential differentiation on the individual level is society, which may respond to vulnerability through its institutions. Society cannot eradicate vulnerability, but it is, arguably, created on the foundation of the need to manage and respond to vulnerability through its institutions. In fact, I would argue that to a large degree society and its institutions have been, and continue to be, structured to be responsive to human vulnerability.

The societal and institutional aspects of vulnerability theory focus our attention on the systems that provide resources or 'assets' to individuals. These resources and assets give individuals 'resilience', or the ability to carry on, in the face of our vulnerability, as Kirby has argued.[8] Assets are of varying types: some types of resilience come from assets that may be physical or material in nature: such assets are based on systems of entitlement and ownership that recognise individual rights to income, wealth or property, for example.

In addition, assets may come in the form of human capital or capabilities – provided by systems of education and employment – giving us 'capabilities', in the language of Sen.[9] But assets are also social in nature, provided by systems of family or kin connections and other cultural or group associations and affiliations. Over the past several decades, ideological and political associations organised around characteristics such as ethnicity, race, gender and sexuality have been important assets in this category. Such social systems produce individual and group identities that give individuals a sense of belonging and collective authority.

A vulnerability analysis looks at these asset-conferring systems and considers the obligation of the state to implement and maintain a vital equality regime in regard to the institutions that comprise these systems, assuring that access to them is truly open to all. Thus, a vulnerability approach ultimately is as (or more) concerned with issues of privilege and disadvantage in relation to access and application, as (or than) with equality of outcome. This focus is also the foundation of a discrimination approach, but vulnerability allows for a more nuanced and complex assessment – one that does not accept the existing inequality of circumstances as a given. Instead, a vulnerability analysis asks how and why privilege and disadvantage have occurred and whether this presents an impermissible advantage to an individual or group in regard to building assets or resources.

In such an analysis, the old identity categories are not totally removed from legal consideration. A rigorous anti-discrimination policy should still prevail. However, some of the concerns that have been conceptualised in identity terms and thereby occluded, such as poverty and inequality in education and capital accumulation, would be reframed when we move beyond inherited identity categories towards a larger vulnerability perspective that reveals things otherwise overlooked. The shared, universal nature of vulnerability means that the situation of the whole of society is under scrutiny, not just that of defined minorities. It also means that the focus is not only – even mostly – individual but rather institutional and structural, in recognition of the fact that privilege and disadvantage migrate across identity categories.

Systems

Recalling the basic premise that vulnerability is inherent in the human condition and that, in response, society has developed interlocking systems to attempt to lessen, ameliorate or compensate for that vulnerability, it is crucial to understand the nature and operation of these systems. Some systems are visibly and explicitly controlled by the state, such as those that regulate the formation and dissolution of the family, the required terms and content for basic education and the protection of the young, the establishment of standards for water, food and drug supplies and the delivery and quality of health care. Other systems are perceived, incorrectly, as operating outside state influence or control, such as the free market, globalisation or the so-called private sector, which includes capitalistic and religious institutions, as well as those of civil society.

Within all of these systems, some individuals have been advantaged or privileged, while others are not. Partly based on historic arrangements and allocations of power and privilege, this unequal allocation of advantage and disadvantage has become systemic and represents a distortion for anyone interested in a genuine equal-opportunity society.[10] This distortion has been structured in ways that make it invisible, or at least seem to have rendered it beyond question, for most politicians. What *is* visible, however, is the position of those who are disadvantaged by the systems, and their disadvantage has tended to be viewed as a consequence of their own failure to take personal responsibility for themselves, rather than as the result of their having to compete on an unequal and severely burdened playing field.

When looking at these existing systems of advantage and disadvantage it is important to remember that although we tend to view them in isolation in policy discussions, the privileges and burdens meted out through these systems are both cumulative and interactive. It is not just education alone, for example, but also neighbourhood safety, access to health care and good nutrition and so on that affect an individual's later success in life. The educational system is enmeshed with others, such as banking and zoning, as well as with health care and family-support systems. It is also true that sometimes privilege within one system can mediate, or even cancel out, a disadvantage in another. We have historically relied on education to do this, for example. In contemporary America, where the idea of public education has been reduced to complaints from taxpayers and a rush to private schools for those with resources, this potentially ameliorative asset has been eroded in its ability to counteract other disadvantages. In fact, education in its public, inter-city form often accompanies, and operates in addition to, other disadvantages associated with poverty.

This education example illustrates another reality, which is that disadvantages or privileges accumulated across systems can combine to bring effects more devastating (or advantages more beneficial – if we are considering privilege) than the weight of each separate part being compounded in combination. This argument brings in the phenomena of compounding disadvantage across categories. However, unlike a traditional intersectionality approach, the individual is not at the intersection of identity categories, such as race, class, or gender, but at the intersection of systems of advantage and disadvantage.[11] Thus, the real focus is not on a specific individual but on institutions, producing an understanding of intersectionality that is more realistic and compelling in regard to governmental responsibility. The focus is on the generation and maintenance of the intersecting systems of power and privilege within which individuals act, not on the identity characteristics those individuals claim. It is the systems' interaction that produces advantage and disadvantage by providing an intertwined set of opportunities for the accumulation of resources. It then is clear that existing institutional arrangements, even if seemingly minor or even trivial, can combine or intersect with other systems and effectively bar some members of society from meaningful access to resources that might allow them to mitigate or cushion their vulnerability.

State and structure

What is important in a vulnerability approach is that the emphasis is on the structures of society – the systems in place within society reinforced by politics and legal authority – not individual characteristics or individual actions. Further, the questions asked are not about discrimination but rather about who is privileged and who is disadvantaged. As with current equality jurisprudence, the formal mandate remains for society to establish a regime of equality but the focus and the desired result is very different, with the state's responsibility hugely magnified in a vulnerability analysis. The state must give equal regard to the shared vulnerability of all its citizens, attempting to undo and/or avoid unwarranted privilege in the process and thus transcending the old identity categories and the limits of a sameness of treatment anti-discrimination model.

Vulnerability analysis suggests that we need a more vigilant and more responsive state:

> one that balances out conflicting claims in a more just manner, one which takes into account individual vulnerability and recognizes that there is a societal responsibility to pursue equality by addressing privilege and disadvantage, not just discrimination. This would result in a more inclusive, ambitious and realistic set of aspirations for our social contract than we currently have, at least if we are interested in establishing a more robust equality.[12]

A focus on privilege would also change the nature of the equality inquiry, moving law and politics away from assessing individual members of designated groups within society in order to see if they are the subjects of animus. The focus would not be on membership of a protected identity group, as has been developed over the past few decades under a discrimination paradigm. Nor would the task be to explore the intentional and purposeful nature of actions by individual employees, educators, landlords and so on. Individual intention is not the issue, nor is overt discrimination. You do not need ill will or intentional favouritism if everyone is operating with the same set of assumptions and beliefs in a shared culture that ignores the many ways in which it is systemically organised to privilege some and not others.

Societal structures and the laws that support them, accordingly, must become the focus. Such inquiry should be into the ways in which societal resources are channelled, privileging and protecting some while tolerating the disadvantage and dependency of others. The state has an obligation not to privilege any group of citizens over others unless there are compelling, well-thought-through and fully articulated reasons for doing so. There should be an affirmative obligation on the state to structure the conditions for equality, not just to prevent discrimination.

Conclusion

Equality theory informed by a vulnerability analysis must aspire to ensure the guarantee of true access to resources and asset-conferring institutions, recognising that autonomy is a product of social policy and structuring and not a naturally occurring characteristic of the human condition. State responsibility must be responsive to the inherent and universal vulnerability, and the constant possibility of dependency, which shapes all human lives. Equality must escape the boundaries that have been imposed upon it by a jurisprudence of identity and discrimination and the politics that has grown up around it. The promise of equality cannot be conditioned upon belonging to any identity category, nor can it be confined to only certain spaces and institutions, be they in the public or the private sphere.

Notes

1 We may experience this possibility as particularly frightening if we realise that the societal institutions upon which we will have to rely are themselves vulnerable – potentially unstable and susceptible to challenges, corruption and deterioration caused by both internal and external forces.

2 M. A. Fineman, 'The Vulnerable Subject: Anchoring Equality in the Human Condition', *Yale Journal of Law and Feminism*, 20 (1) (2008–9): 1–24; p. 1.

3 M. A. Fineman, *The Autonomy Myth: A Theory of Dependency* (New York: New Press, 2004).

4 Fineman, 'The Vulnerable Subject', p. 11; Fineman, *The Autonomy Myth*, p. 67.

5 Fineman, *The Autonomy Myth*, pp. 169–75.

6 Ibid.

7 Ibid., p. 172.

8 P. Kirby, *Vulnerability and Violence: The Impact of Globalization* (London and Ann Arbor, Mich.: Pluto Books, 2006).

9 A. Sen, *Commodities and Capabilities* (Oxford: Oxford University Press, 1985).

10 J. W. Lee, 'Class Warfare 1988–2005 Over Top Individual Income Tax Rates: Teeter-Totter from Soak-the-Rich to Robin Hood-in-Reverse', *Hastings Business Law Journal*, 2 (1) (2006): 47–164; p. 47.

11 J. Scales-Trent, 'Black Women and the Constitution: Finding our Place, Asserting our Rights', *Harvard Civil Rights-Civil Liberties Law Review*, 24 (1) (1989): 9–44; p. 9.

12 Fineman, 'The Vulnerable Subject', pp. 19–22.

Part II

Representations, law and sex

Chapter 5

The 'gendered company' revisited

Alice Belcher

Introduction

Over ten years ago I wrote 'Gendered Company: Enterprise and Governance at the Institute of Directors'.[1] That early (1997) article was an attempt to consider how companies and company law intersect with feminist ideas. I argued then that

> a cursory glance at the history of English company law reveals the maleness of the company. In 1604 the advantages of the concept of joint stock were described as follows: 'A whole company, by this means, is become as one *man*'. Lord Halsbury's speech in *Salomon* v. *A Salomon & Co Ltd.* included the following: "Once a company is legally incorporated it must be treated like any other independent person ... " ... Although corporate legal theory has always used the seemingly gender neutral formula of the company as a separate legal person, at the birth of this concept the person was male.[2]

My research during the intervening period has at times returned to aspects of the relationships between women, feminism and companies. I have worked on theoretical concepts at the heart of corporate governance such as risk and uncertainty, trust and corporate culture.[3] I have also investigated how women work in companies, whether they are mothers or not, and highlighted the very small number of women on the boards of the UK's largest companies.[4] My revisiting of 'Gendered Company' is not only informed by developments in UK company law but also reflects the cumulative impact of more than a decade of company-related research on my thoughts and my preferred form of feminism. I here offer reflections tracing the interaction between these research strands and upon 'the gendered company' as an ongoing subject of feminist concern.

Gender and the real presence of the company

The impetus for 'Gendered Company' was a presentation of a more feminine model of the company, by a female academic (not myself), as a serious policy proposition to a predominantly male audience at the Institute of Directors in London in 1995. The model, which was vociferously rejected at the conference, was one that concentrated on relational aspects of the company. At its heart was an argument for the extension of directors' duties and of the categories of persons recognised as having standing to bring actions for breach of those duties. This more feminine model can be placed as a stakeholder model and, accordingly, positioned within the much wider debate on stakeholder and shareholder models of the company. The debate continues and in the UK was recently explicitly addressed in the process of the latest company law reform that led to the Companies Act 2006.

The reform process included a host of commissioned research reports, consultation documents and draft provisions. A major innovation was the codification of directors' duties. In order to produce a statutory version of the existing common-law duties, those common-law duties had necessarily to be considered, and in the context of law *reform*, debates about their exact current meaning were extended into preferred or desired meanings that would change the existing law. Thus, there was, during the reform process, room for the more feminine model proposed at the 1995 conference (or something similar) to be adopted as the preferred model of the company through the reformulation of directors' duties and of the categories of persons recognised as having standing to bring actions for breach of those duties. At the end of the law-reform process, however, the model of directors' duties that has been adopted, termed 'enlightened shareholder value', presents an approach that excludes the direct accountability of company directors to a wide range of stakeholders. Indeed, the main duty connecting stakeholders, other than shareholders, with corporate decision-making is found in Section 172 of the Companies Act 2006 which states 'Duty to promote the success of the company ... (1) A director of a company must act in the way *he* considers, in good faith, would be most likely to promote the success of the company for the benefit of its members as a whole' (emphasis added). This is a duty owed by the directors to the company, and, as such, its exercise can only be challenged by the company or by its shareholders in a derivative action, leaving no room for any other stakeholder to bring an action, despite the fact that Section 172 requires directors to 'have regard' to a list of matters including the interests of employees, relationships with customers and suppliers and impact on the community.

The 'male' company: necessary clarifications

In 1995, I argued that the company was male, as it exhibited masculine traits. It will be suggested below that the company law review has neither diminished nor challenged those masculine traits. It is important to begin, however, by acknowledging a particular challenge: in locating critique of the gendered company in relation to the dichotomous construction of 'othering', the feminist strategy behind 'Gendered Company' is contentious.

The (ideal, masculine) company can be described as rational, logical, strong/dominant, precise, assertive/aggressive, competitive, individually autonomous and as transmitting (rather than receiving) communications. The relevant opposing feminine traits are associated with the irrational, illogical, weak/dominated, vague, yielding, cooperative, exogenously determined 'other' that tends to receive rather than transmit communications. The 'othering' of the feminine implicit in this analysis (the idea that man is treated as human and woman as 'other') is central, not only to a deconstruction of the gendered company but also to many strands of feminist writing.[5] It has been argued, for example, that the view of woman as 'other' has allowed historically, and continues to allow, the mistreatment of women – in the most extreme variants of this view, as witches, as madwomen and as mentally ill.[6] However, notwithstanding their power, a problem attends all such critiques, one that I addressed when I employed the feminist strategy behind 'Gendered Company' a second time, in the context of writing about contract law.

I need to emphasise at this point that the feminist strategy I am employing is that of asking whether there are dichotomies present that relate to the cultural stereotypes of women and men. This is not feminist essentialism although it clearly draws on the work of Chodorow (1978) and Gilligan (1982).[7] Gilligan claimed that, in her research on moral development, the 'care' ethic was found to be more typical among women and the 'justice' ethic more typical among men. This has been badly interpreted as saying that (all) women think differently from (all) men. In fact, Gilligan presented her results as empirically observed tendencies with overlapping statistical distributions. I have referred to masculine and feminine traits, but I want to make clear that I view these as cultural stereotypes and not biologically determined predispositions. In rejecting biological essentialism and referring to masculine and feminine traits as cultural stereotypes, I do not want to be seen as downplaying their power in relation to the lives of women.[8]

While I believe that 'Gendered Company' was a worthwhile endeavour, I acknowledge that the dichotomous deconstructive strategy I employed can result in feminism seeming to chase its own tail or, worse, can be used to reinforce the very problem that feminists seek to highlight and overcome. As Moi has argued

> For more than twenty years now feminist theorists have characterized women as relational, caring, and nurturing; as mumbling and incoherent; or as always seething with feminist rage, just to mention a few well-known leitmotifs. Since nothing distinguishes them from traditional gender stereotypes, such 'gender theories' are all too easy to appropriate for sexist purposes.[9]

With this note of caution sounded, it is submitted that notwithstanding potential pitfalls it remains both meaningful and theoretically useful to assert that the company is male, and remains male, despite the massive opportunity for change offered by a major law-reform exercise.

Remaining male?

In the 2006 Act, the company remains constructed as having a single overriding objective: success 'for the benefit of its members as a whole'. While this is to be informed by relationships with stakeholders, those relationships are important solely because they impact on the company's success. At its most symbolic, the model of the company, as settled during the latest reform process, is a model where the company pursues a masculine, single, objective via a masculine decision-making framework – a claim based in part on the idea of the company as a typical contracting party.[10]

However, another development, in criminal rather than corporate law, may prove to be a more feminising influence on the corporate form. The Corporate Manslaughter and Corporate Homicide Act 2007 introduced the two eponymous offences for England and Wales and for Scotland respectively. The basic elements of the two offences are the same:

- The organisation must owe a duty of care to the victim that is connected with certain things done by the organisation.
- The organisation must be in breach of that duty of care as a result of the way in which certain activities of the organisation were managed or organised by its senior managers. *This introduces an element of 'senior management failure' into the offence.*
- This management failure must have caused the victim's death. The usual principles of causation in the criminal law will apply to determine this question.
- The breach of duty must have been gross.[11]

The notes on the Bill went on to say that senior management failure 'looks at how in practice managers organised the performance of a particular activity, rather than focusing on questions of individual culpability, and *enables management conduct to be considered collectively* as well as individually'.[12] The most important change is that this formulation will enable management conduct to be considered collectively as well as individually. So long as the emphasis remains on 'management' failure as a failure to manage properly and does not become 'senior management' failure, which could drift into meaning the failure of a single senior manager, the collective aspect of the offences should be preserved.[13] The evidential aspect of these offences will mean that collective decision-making by boards of directors will take a more central place than they have hitherto.[14] This is in line with some writings on the real presence of an organisation: Schwartzman states that 'meetings are significant because they are the organisation or community writ small'.[15] Weick argues that

> meetings define, represent, and reproduce social entities. ... Because action that occurs in the meetings is organizational action, this must mean that there really is an organization. Momentarily, at least during the meeting,

there appears to be an organization, and this appearance is reconstituted whenever meetings are constituted ... meetings embody the organization and give it some substance.[16]

While there are many ways in which meetings can be conducted, there is a chance that this focus on collective decisions of the board, rather than on individual decisions of single directors, will help to construct the real presence of the company as collective and relational (feminine) rather than as individuated and single-minded (masculine).

Gender culture and women in the corporate environment

This section will link the development of my feminist analysis of the gender of the company with Probert's ideas on gender culture, in order to provide the context for the following section, which addresses some of the more practical problems facing women within companies as gendered environments.[17] Probert uses a version of the concept of gender culture based on the work of Pfau-Effinger.[18] This version has three elements. First, a set of ideas that define social spheres through which men and women should be integrated into society: 'Is it expected that both men and women will have economically productive roles or is it expected of men only? ... Is the productive sphere seen as equal to or more important than the caring sphere?'[19] Second, the way relationships between men and women are constructed and legitimated, for instance: 'Are women expected to be dependent on men, are men and women increasingly dependent on each other to maintain viable households?'[20] Third, cultural models of motherhood. Probert states that this last element could be crucial as it includes the issue of the stay-at-home mother as contrasted with other child-caring scenarios. This element is also related to the issue of women increasingly choosing to remain childless, at least in Western developed countries.[21]

The very title of Probert's article suggests that gender culture, at least in Australia, limits women either to the feminine role of a perfect mother or to the fate of competing in a masculinised way so as to become 'self-made women' in a world of 'self-made men'. While this section is not offering a summary of where feminism(s) has (have) travelled over the period in view, it seems, nonetheless, that no matter how far today's feminists believe that they are imagining in new ways, many of the issues demanding attention, even in the sphere of the gendered corporation, are reworkings of central problems with long histories. The intractable issues of what it means to be a woman, theoretically and in practice; what it means to attempt feminism and motherhood or chosen childlessness or feminism and being a scientist, writer, company board member or other sort of wage-earner, remain as difficult now as they were, say, for de Beauvoir.[22] These issues are played out across the world in an array of changing cultures, moreover, that remain irreducibly gendered.

One of the central problematics concerning the role of women in corporate workplaces, even today, focuses on the mother/not-mother puzzle.[23] Schwartz expresses this puzzle with a question: 'how can we affirm the significance of motherhood while still trying to free women from the obligation to mother?' The puzzle of how to fit chosen motherhood or chosen childlessness into ordinary life and work is one of the major practical issues facing many if not most (Western) women and is long a theoretical puzzle and cause of debate for feminists. Early feminists linked women's oppression to their reproductive biology and emphasised the need to escape from childbearing, while later feminists reclaim positive maternal images, seeing woman as 'all the more woman as she is mother'.[24] How then, can we provide a theoretical focus for feminism that can easily be applied to motherhood, producing thereby the feminist aim of a society where women can choose motherhood or childlessness in a truly non-defiant way and partake of the advantages of inclusion in culture at large, corporate or otherwise?

Feminism as liberation

My answer to the 'feminist and' dilemma is encapsulated by the term 'liberation'. It is 'liberation' that captures both the spirit of earlier feminist projects and a more current approach to the central feminist debate. My emphasis on the centrality of liberation is inspired by my reading of Toril Moi's 1999 book *What Is Woman?* At first, Moi's line of argument does not appear to approach the 'feminist and' issue, but early in the work she writes

> I want to stress that freedom – not identity, difference, or equality – is the fundamental concept in Beauvoir's feminism. [Then] I am left with the question of exactly what it will take for a woman in a sexist society to be able to speak – or to remain silent – in a genuinely non-defiant way. Non-defiance is still important because defiance is still a reactive stance induced by sexist aggression. ... The problem with the stance [defiance] ... is that it may block us from finding our own voice.[25]

Non-defiance, therefore, is a signal of genuine liberation. Moi is writing for a reader in 1999 about de Beauvoir, and it is clear that, for Moi, feminism remains unfinished business, but it must be recognised that 'post-feminist' ideas have emerged, perhaps especially in France. There are two variations of the French post-feminist theme. According to the first, feminism has achieved its aims and is now no longer necessary. According to the second, feminists have realised the errors of their ways and are now happy to forget it all and re-embrace the French way of being a woman.[26]

However, there is an undercurrent of defiance in both these variations. Women are not truly free in the sense of free to speak in a genuinely non-defiant way. Women, even French post-feminist women, still have to grapple with de

Beauvoir's sexism, expressed by Moi as 'giving a woman the 'choice'' between having to believe that she is a woman through and through at all times and in all circumstances and having to deny that she is one ("I am a writer, not a woman writer").[27] Moi expresses the idea that femininity is a patriarchal constraint and that we should aim for a society where we have ceased to categorise logic, conceptualisation and rationality as masculine, rather than one from which these virtues have been expelled altogether as 'unfeminine'.[28] On the argument put forward against 'male' science by Evelyn Fox Keller, Moi says

> Her critique of dominant forms of Cartesian rationalism is inspiring; her denunciation of the logic and objectification at work in the ideology of science timely. I particularly warm to her idea of undoing the split between reason and emotion ... my only doubt concerns her decision to label the new mode of knowledge 'female'. ... If ... the new mode of thought is superior to traditional ways, why should we not claim it as universal – simply as *the* way to do science?[29]

This criticism clearly applies with equal force to my chosen feminist strategy; if there is a better, more feminine, model of the company it should be claimed as *the* model. In Moi's ideal (theoretical) world, gendered traits would not have any sexist potency. But, for the moment, the world falls short of the ideal. Here, for example, is one very accepting view of the current possible ways in which gender norms operate.

> In contexts where gender roles are well entrenched the corresponding norms function *prescriptively*: not only do they serve as the basis for judgements about how to be (act, and so on), but also we decide how to act, what to strive for, what to resist, in light of such norms. ... However, we should also note that the properties constituting the norms can also function *descriptively*: some individuals have the properties in question and others do not. In a society where gender norms are generally agreed upon and well-entrenched, and where individuals are fairly successful in living up to them, corresponding generalizations about males and females may be descriptively adequate.[30]

It is useful to remember that many indirect sex discrimination actions have only succeeded because courts have accepted descriptive gender norms, for instance, that women are less likely to be able to move their place of work (families move for the man's career not the woman's); or that women tend to have their children in their late twenties, so that limiting applications to a promoted post to those under twenty-eight amounts to indirect sex discrimination.[31]

The gendered traits employed in 'Gendered Company' are, however, less concrete than the social norms used in sex-discrimination jurisprudence. Rather than being either descriptive or prescriptive, they are symbolic. In relation to this it should be noted that the 'feminist and ... ' dilemma has been identified as particularly problematic for women whose work has a symbolically masculine focus. So, for example, for women philosophers a key challenge might concern feminist rejection of the very idea of feminists doing logic. Anthony and Witt state that 'although we consider ourselves committed feminists, the import of the radical critique seemed to be that we must be mistaken – a person cannot, at this stage of the game, be a feminist and still do *that* kind of philosophy'.[32]

According to Lloyd, reason has traditionally been conceptualised as male, and, even if this is regarded as symbolic or metaphorical (rather than part of biological or cultural essentialism), it has the effect of leaving the 'other' to be conceptualised as female.

> The problem for real women is that although they may be symbolised as outside, they are not in fact outside society and its symbolic structures. Symbolic structures cannot be altered by fiat. The symbolism cannot be simply reversed. Nor is it enough to insist that women are in fact rational, because that is not the point. The point is rather the relation of women to the symbolic structures that exclude them.[33]

In the light of these insights, my current form of feminism is an aspiration to the freedom that means the ability to speak, or not, in a non-defiant way – and be heard. But, I recognise that because neither reality nor symbolism can be changed by fiat: women continue to live within structures that have embedded sexist realities and symbolisms, and women continue to have to engage with the 'mother/not-mother' and the 'feminist and ... ' dilemmas. If it is futile to demand change by fiat, then the question becomes whether it is better to attempt incremental change from inside society's sexist structures or to bring change by attempting to be outside them. On this I tend to agree with Rapaport and would suggest that although the following was written in 1993 it remains applicable 'The liberating work of feminist criticism is purely destructive; the positive work of social transformation would begin when there is a critical mass ... Women's speech ... requires that women acquire more power than we have now.'[34]

This emphasis on insider-led change informs my work on women in companies and inspires my calls for more women directors. My feminism has probably not changed since 'Gendered Company', it has simply become more informed. I seem to be a liberal feminist in the short term and a radical feminist in the long term. I am not alone in this stance. For instance, Midgley and Hughes set out a typical liberal feminist agenda with a radical aspiration.

> The immediate aim for women will be to make it possible for them to pass in and out of the child-bearing phase of life without either penalising children or grotesquely interrupting and distorting women's useful careers. This ought to make it possible for the child-bearing years to be an ordinary, rewarding piece of strenuous living, not a bewildering, desolating endurance

test and a sentence of exile from interesting life. … It should make us find it just as natural to hear that 'the Director is on maternity leave this year' as it is now to hear that 'the Director is in America till January'. Of course this is not all that needs to be done, and radicals, as usual, will do well to keep reminding us of other aims. But it will do to be going on with.[35]

Even though this was written a quarter of a century ago, it still remains something to be aimed at rather than something that has been achieved. Despite many policy changes, especially a spate of 'family friendly' moves, the UK's gender culture has not addressed fully the aims of liberal feminists, let alone the aspirations of the radicals.

Women in companies

In the light of the developments in gender culture just discussed, it is now time to address the small number of women on the boards of large UK companies in the context of UK anti-discrimination laws and to introduce some alternative approaches to improving the situation adopted in Norway and Spain. The whole of this section, therefore, adopts a liberal feminist mode but without forgetting the aim of speaking or not speaking in a genuinely non-defiant way as a radical feminist end point.

It was reported in 2007 that women held 13.2 per cent of US Fortune 500 directorships and that only 6 per cent of those female-held board seats were executive directorships, the comparable figure in the UK being that 10.7 per cent of female-held board seats on FTSE 100 boards are executive directorships.[36] In 2008, the *Female FTSE Report* stated that thirty-nine FTSE 100 companies had two or more women on their board that year, compared to thirteen a decade earlier. Also, in 2007, there was just one FTSE 100 company with 30 per cent female representation on the board (the turning point at which female representation has a significant impact across a set of corporate performance indicators), but in 2008 this had risen to five companies.[37] However, there still remain twenty-two companies in the FTSE 100 with no female representation at all at boardroom level.[38] Clearly, there is much yet to do.

Various strategies exist for increasing the numbers of women board members. Current corporate governance best practice includes a main principle stating that: 'There should be a formal, rigorous and transparent procedure for the appointment of new directors to the board' and a provision that if 'external advice or open advertising' is not used, this should be explained.[39] The Higgs Report on the role of non-executive directors stated that nomination committees should insist that their consultants look beyond the 'usual suspects' and was followed by the Tyson Report, which looked at ways of engaging with 'broader pools of talent', including more women, when appointing directors.[40] The approach of encouraging companies to seek a wider pool of candidates coupled with the formalisation of the search and recruitment process may have taken companies away from the former practice of using the old-boy network, a system that perpetuated the norm of men choosing men to join boards. The additions to the voluntary Code of Best Practice and its guidance may explain some of the improvement in the statistics since the publication of the two reports in 2003. In that year, thirty-two of the FTSE 100 companies had no women on their board. By 2008 this had fallen to twenty-two out of the 100. A second strategy could be to jolt companies into action either by a shareholder resolution at an AGM or by a test case in sex-discrimination law.[41] A third strategy would be to have targets or to permit positive discrimination on appointments. Norway and Spain have both put in place legislation with these aims.[42] The Equality Act 2010 includes a permitted form of positive action.[43] There are, therefore, potential improvements on the horizon.

How then, does the presence of women on a board of directors change it – and how are women themselves affected by such an appointment? The effects of women on a board can be observed in board systems or processes, in company behaviour cultures and possibly in the performance of the company as a whole. A review of the literature on 'women directors on corporate boards' that covered 180 published articles, working papers and book chapters was published in 2009.[44] On systems and processes, it has been reported that FTSE 100 firms with women directors adopted and reported the new governance practices recommended by the Higgs Review earlier than firms with all-male boards. Such practices included having director induction and training; conducting a regular review of board performance; reviewing the balance of board skills, knowledge and experience; greater consideration of director succession planning structures; and using external search consultants in the appointment of directors.[45]

The effect on a company of having women on the board could result in improved corporate performance (measured quantitatively) or in changed boardroom behaviour (observed in personal interactions). In terms of performance, various studies have established a correlation between corporate performance measures and women on the board.[46] However, in terms of changed behaviour, it has been reported that

> men are inclined to have very political behavior that is tempered when women are present, partly because women want to get on with the task in hand rather than 'play games'. ... Male directors say that in the presence of women directors, men change their language, become more civilised, and moderate their masculinity. In their view, this led to more effective performance and better governance.[47]

Women also tend to be better prepared for meetings than men, on the board papers generally. But men who want to get a particular item through the board/ or to oppose an item tend to play 'power games' and set things up with allies in advance of the meeting proper. It has also been found that women on corporate boards do not tend to have a feminist change agenda. They have been described as employing the 'tempered radical', small-wins approach. However, it seems many women on corporate boards would not be recognisable as even 'tempered' radicals by radical feminists operating outside the corporate world.[48]

A question remains in relation to whether women are changed by being on a corporate board or by achieving the appointment to a corporate board. In her book *The Third Sex: The New Professional Woman*, McBroom, an anthropologist, studied professional women working in the finance sector in New York and San Francisco. She states that 'women face in the workplace a culture created out of the masculine ethos with its own priorities, values and unique history. That world bears the mark of a gender culture that is ignorant of and intolerant of most human needs other than achievement.'[49] Later in her book she says: 'Over time, corporate culture takes its toll on the personality. Gradually, the professional identity – manipulative, image conscious, functional, independent, rational, emotionally inauthentic and totally focused upon achieving an effect – erodes personal spontaneity.'[50]

Sheppard has identified one of the strategies adopted by women managers and professionals as 'blending' which involves

> very careful management of being 'feminine enough' (i.e. in terms of appearance, self-presentation, etc.) so that conventional rules and expectations of gender behaviour can be maintained by the men in the situation, while simultaneously being 'businesslike enough' (i.e. rational, competent, instrumental, impersonal – in other words stereotypically masculine) so that the issue of gender and sexuality are apparently minimised.[51]

From the literature on women corporate directors it can be concluded that Probert's work on gender culture (as explained in the previous section) is useful both for feminist theorising and as a way of particularising the context for further work on the practical problems encountered by real women working in corporate settings.

Conclusions

In the light of all the considerations discussed above, I conclude, upon revisiting 'Gendered Company', that, despite a major and lengthy company-law review process, the UK company remains symbolically and metaphorically male and that while numbers of women board members in the FTSE 100 are increasing, there remains much to be done by feminism(s) and by feminists. This work, as implied by the argument here, requires liberal feminists working within capitalist structures and radical feminists 'reminding us of other aims'.

Notes

1 A. Belcher, 'Gendered Company: Enterprise and Governance at the Institute of Directors', *Feminist Legal Studies*, 5 (1) (1997): 57–76.

2 (1897) AC 22.
3 A. Belcher, '"Something Distinctly Not of This Character": How Knightian Uncertainty Is Relevant to Corporate Governance', *Legal Studies*, 28 (1) (2008): 46–67; A. Belcher, 'Imagining How a Company Thinks: What Is Corporate Culture?', *Deakin Law Review*, 11 (2007) (2): 1–21; A. Belcher, 'Boundaries, Corporate Decision-Making and Responsibility', *Northern Ireland Legal Quarterly*, 58 (2) (2007): 211–27; A. Belcher, 'Trust in the Boardroom', *Griffith Law Review*, 16 (1) (2006): 151–70. The author is grateful to the Arts and Humanities Research Council for funding the research for these four articles under leave award AH/D500370/1; A. Belcher and T. Naruisch, 'The Evolution of Business Knowledge in the Context of Unitary and Two-Tier Board Structures', *Journal of Business Law*, July 2005, pp. 443–72; A. Belcher, 'The Unitary Board: Fact or Fiction?', *Corporate Ownership and Control*, 1 (1) (2003): 139–48; and A. Belcher, 'Inside the Black Box: Corporate Law and Theories', *Social and Legal Studies*, 12 (3) (2003): 359–76.
4 A. Belcher, 'Equal Opportunities, Staff Development and Assertiveness', in Anne Morris and Thérèse O'Donnell (eds.), *Feminist Perspectives on Employment Law* (London: RoutledgeCavendish, 1999), pp. 43–60; A. Belcher, 'The Not-Mother Puzzle', *Social and Legal Studies*, 9 (4) (2000): 539–56; and A. Belcher, 'Board Diversity: Can Sex Discrimination Law Help?', *Northern Ireland Legal Quarterly*, 56 (3) (2005): 356–72.
5 See, for example, S. L. Bem, *The Lenses of Gender: Transforming the Debate on Sexual Inequality* (New Haven, Conn.: Yale University Press, 1993).
6 J. Ussher, *Women's Madness: Mysogeny or Mental Illness?* (New York: Harvester Wheatsheaf, 1991).
7 N. J. Chodorow, *The Reproduction of Mothering: Psychoanalysis and the Sociology of Gender* (Berkeley, Calif.: University of California Press, 1978); C. Gilligan, *In a Different Voice: Psychological Theory and Women's Development* (Cambridge, Mass.: Harvard University Press, 1982).
8 A. Belcher, 'A Feminist Perspective on Contract Theories from Law and Economics', *Feminist Legal Studies*, 8 (2000): 29–46.
9 T. Moi, *What is Woman? And Other Essays* (Oxford: Oxford University Press, 1999), p. 109.
10 See Belcher, 'A Feminist Perspective on Contract Theories', passim.
11 Corporate Manslaughter and Corporate Homicide Bill, Explanatory Notes, 2006, para. 14, emphasis added.
12 Corporate Manslaughter and Corporate Homicide Bill, para. 15, emphasis added.
13 A. Belcher, 'Imagining How a Company Thinks: What Is Corporate Culture?', *Deakin Law Review*, 11 (2) (2007): 1–21.
14 Ibid.
15 H. B. Schwartzman, 'The Significance of Meetings in an American Mental Health Center', *American Ethnologist*, 14 (1987): 271–94, at p. 288.
16 K. E. Weick, *Sensemaking in Organizations* (Thousand Oaks, Calif.: Sage, 1995), pp. 143, 87.
17 B. Probert, 'Grateful Slaves or "Self-Made Women": A Matter of Choice or Policy?', *Australian Feminist Studies*, 17 (37) (2002): 7–17.
18 Birgit Pfau-Effinger, 'The Modernization of Family and Motherhood in Western Europe', in R. Compton (ed.), *Restructuring Gender Relations in Employment* (Oxford: Oxford University Press, 1999), pp. 60–79.
19 Probert, 'Grateful Slaves', p. 9.
20 Ibid.
21 An issue explored in Belcher, 'The Not-Mother Puzzle', pp. 539–56.
22 S. de Beauvoir, *The Second Sex* (Harmondsworth: Penguin, 1972), passim.

23 J. D. Schwartz, *The Mother Puzzle: A New Generation Reckons with Motherhood* (New York: Simon & Schuster, 1993).

24 H. Cixous, *Stigmata: Escaping Texts* (London and New York: Routledge, 1998).

25 Moi, *What Is Woman*, pp. viii, x.

26 G. Allwood, *French Feminisms: Gender and Violence in Contemporary Theory* (London: UCL Press, 1998), p. 39.

27 Moi, *What Is Woman?*, p. xi.

28 Ibid., p. xii.

29 Ibid., pp. 349–50.

30 S. Haslanger, 'On Being Objective and Being Objectified', in L. M. Antony and C Witt (eds.), *A Mind of One's Own: Feminist Essays in Reason and Objectivity* (Oxford: Westview Press, 1993), pp. 85–125, at p. 90.

31 *Meade-Hill* v. *British Council* (1995) IRLR 478; *Price* v. *Civil Service Commission* (1977) IRLR 291.

32 L. M. Antony and C. Witt (eds.), *A Mind of One's Own: Feminist Essays in Reason and Objectivity* (Oxford: Westview Press, 1993), p. xiii.

33 G. Lloyd, 'Maleness, Metaphor and the "Crisis" of Reason', in Ibid., pp. 69–83, at pp. 72–3.

34 E. Rapaport, 'Generalizing Gender: Reason and Essence in the Legal Thought of Catherine Mackinnon', in L. M. Antony and C. Witt (eds.), *A Mind of One's Own: Feminist Essays in Reason and Objectivity* (Oxford: Westview Press, 1993), pp. 127–44, at p. 133.

35 M. Midgley and J. Hughes, *Women's Choices: Philosophical Problems Facing Feminism* (London: Weidenfeld & Nicolson, 1983), pp. 32–3.

36 S. Terjesen, R. Sealy and V. Singh, 'Women Directors on Corporate Boards: A Review and Research Agenda', *Corporate Governance: An International Review*, 17 (3) (2009): 320–37.

37 Ibid.

38 R. Sealy, S. Vinnecombe and V. Singh, *The Female FTSE Report 2008* (Cranfield: Cranfield University Management School, 2008), p. 6.

39 Code main principle A.4; Code provision A.4.6.

40 D. Higgs, *Review of the Role and Effectiveness of Non-executive Directors* (London: The Stationary Office, 2003), para. 10.19, now embodied in *Good Practice Suggestions from the Higgs Report* (London: Financial Reporting Council, 2006); L. Tyson, *The Tyson Report on the Recruitment and Development of Non-Executive Directors* (London: London Business School, 2003).

41 A. Belcher, 'Board Diversity: Can Sex Discrimination Law Help?', *Northern Ireland Legal Quarterly*, 56 (3) (2005): 356–72, includes a description of how this strategy has been used particularly in the USA. The main argument of this article concerns the possibility of a UK test case.

42 See Belcher, 'Board Diversity', for a discussion of progress in Norway and Terjesen et al., 'Women Directors on Corporate Boards', for references to more up-to-date authorities on both Spain and Norway.

43 Covering the jurisdictions of Scotland and England and Wales.

44 Terjesen et al., 'Women Directors on Corporate Boards'.

45 Ibid.

46 Performance measures include significant positive abnormal returns on the announcement of a woman's appointment, higher returns on equity and total returns to shareholders; see studies reviewed by Ibid.

47 V. Singh, *Transforming Boardroom Cultures* (Bradford: UK Resource Centre for Women in Science, Engineering and Technology, 2008).

48 Terjesen et al., 'Women Directors on Corporate Boards'.

49 P. McBroom, *The Third Sex: The New Professional Woman* (New York: Paragon House, 1986), p. 49.
50 Ibid., p. 64.
51 D. L. Sheppard, 'Organizations, Power and Sexuality: The Image and Self-image of Women Managers', in J. Hearn and D. L. Sheppard (eds.), *The Sexuality of Organization* (London: Sage, 1989), pp. 139–57, at p. 146.

Chapter 6

The public sex of the judiciary

The appearance of the irrelevant and the invisible

Leslie J. Moran

Introduction

Early in an empirical research project on sexual diversity in the judiciary in England and Wales and other common-law jurisdictions, I had to address a particular challenge.[1] Sexuality, I was repeatedly told by informants, was unlike the other strands of diversity: it was a personal and a private matter – strictly extrajudicial. So, while sexuality may appear as a formal strand of judicial diversity policies, officially it is (and ought to be) treated differently: neither recorded nor benchmarked nor audited. In contrast to this official reticence and silence a very different state of affairs was portrayed in the pages of *Who's Who*, an annual volume providing short biographical accounts of England's social elite, including the judiciary.[2] Details of the wives, husbands and siblings of the judiciary were (and remain) the norm. This apparently contradictory landscape generated a number of research challenges. How do you research the institutional operation and effects of that which is apparently not spoken about? How do you make sense of a dominant sexual norm the existence of which is denied yet pervasive? And how do you research and make sense of sexuality that key informants insist is and ought to remain absent and irrelevant in an institutional setting? This chapter is based upon one of the research projects I have developed in response to these challenges.

Queer theory was an invaluable theoretical tool that provided a number of insights enabling me to respond to these methodological challenges. I begin this chapter with some of its key insights before describing one of the research projects I developed to examine the formation and operation of sexuality in the judicial institution. It is a project that some legal students and scholars might find bizarre: a study of judicial images, and more specifically, judicial portraits.[3] One part of this project focuses upon the aesthetic and artistic traditions used in these portraits: how are judges portrayed and why? And in that context how, if at all, is sexuality represented? I use a collection of official portraits of the chief justices of the Supreme Court of New South Wales as a lens through which to reveal the complexity and fragility of potential answers to these questions. The portraits can easily be accessed from the court's website.[4]

The choice of New South Wales is not an arbitrary one. It provides an illuminating context for a more detailed study of a portrait of one particular judge,
the Honourable Justice Michael Kirby. He has a long and distinguished legal
and judicial career, was President of the Court of Appeal of New South Wales
Supreme Court from 1984 to 1996 and then Justice of the High Court, Australia's
Supreme Court.[5] Nationally, he is highly respected and well known.[6] He has a
strong international reputation. Well known for his judicial writings and dissenting judgments, he is also a prolific author, scholar and public speaker.[7] He is
also a gay man. He formally announced his long-term relationship (nearly forty
years) with Johan van Vloten in the pages of Australia's *Who's Who* in 1999. In
1998, Ralph Heimans, a well-known Australian portrait painter, completed a
portrait of the Honourable Justice Michael Kirby that now hangs in the
National Portrait Gallery of Australia and is one of the gallery's most popular
exhibits (see Figure 6.1).[8] Heimens depicts his subject wearing the crimson and
fur robes of the Supreme Court of New South Wales. A particular source of
inspiration for the composition was a speech given by Kirby on his resignation
from the post of President of the Court of Appeal of New South Wales to take
up a post as a judge in the High Court. Using data from interviews with the
artist I seek to answer the following question: how, if at all, is Justice Kirby's

Figure 6.1 'Radical Restraint: Justice Michael Kirby' by Ralph Heimans

sexuality not only figured in the portrait but represented as a desirable quality of judicial office: a judicial virtue?

Public sex

Queer theory offers a number of useful insights. The first is that sexuality is a matter of 'culture', a 'sexual regime'.[9] It is 'a field of sexual meanings, discourses and practices that are interlaced with social institutions and movements'.[10] As such, sexuality, Berlant and Warner explain, is always in play. It is always in public. More specifically, a requirement to be silent about sexuality is not the absence or disappearance of sexuality but rather a key dimension of its mode of public appearance and operation. Thus, the perceived and proposed 'absence' of sexuality from the institution of the judiciary in general, and from judicial diversity debates, in particular, needs to be treated with caution.

Silence is a device by which sexuality appears in public and is one of the devices through which heterosexuality as the norm is reproduced in society in general and in the institution of the judiciary in particular.[11] Sexuality, including gay or lesbian sexuality, is not so much a troubling new addition, a threatening invasion, an inappropriate incivility or an irrelevant matter in judicial settings but a pre-existing, persistent and very public dimension of them. The hesitations, refusals and silences I was beginning to record in the interview transcripts and research notes about sexuality in the judiciary were merely evidence of the existing public sexual culture of that institution.

Silence, absence and invisibility all play a key role in the public fabrication of the heterosexual as privileged sexual subject. As the basic idiom of the personal, and the social, heterosexuality is fashioned as the unmarked. Heterosexuality is in some respects, like the air we breathe, a diffuse all-pervasive presence (a sense of rightness), but, at the same time, out of mind, unnoticed, unrecognisable, often unconscious and immanent to practice or to institutions. The attribution of absence to the pervasive presence of heterosexuality plays a central role in linking certain qualities and values to that subject position. One characteristic attributed to heterosexuality as the unmarked is that of 'a state of nature' which gives rise to a multitude of positive connotations. One is the link between heterosexuality and the ideal. Another is the assumption that heterosexuality is the very pinnacle of moral accomplishment (free from bias, the universal, not the partial). Queer theory identifies all these characteristics as part of a heteronormative regime. In that context, heterosexuality is a rather paradoxical phenomenon, always both present and absent.

Thinking sexuality as a regime or culture, rather than as an identity, requires us to recognise the diffusion of heterosexuality; it has no centre. There is no singular moment of operation or final moment of realisation. It is fragmented, diffuse, inconsistent and contradictory. In a contemporary setting it may simultaneously be formally absent and formally present. At best it is never more than a fragile, provisional unity. No matter how fragile, as Berlant and Warner explain, we must still take seriously 'the metacultural work of the very category of heterosexuality, which consolidates as a sexuality widely differing practices, norms and institutions'.[12] The purported totality of heterosexuality, displays of its cohesion and singularity, not only seek to mask but also tend to expose the fragility of the category of heterosexuality. Its temporal and spatial diffusion potentially poses a major challenge: the increased difficulty of recognising its forms of operation.[13]

So how might a study of judicial portraits contribute to an understanding of the formation of sexuality under a heteronormative regime in the institutional setting of the judiciary? And how, if at all, are non-heterosexual subjects being formed in that context?

Judicial portraits

Various scholars have suggested that an understanding of the judicial image is central to an understanding of the institution of the judiciary. There is in that institution a preoccupation with appearance: with judicial image and image management.[14] While legal rules, such as the rules of natural justice and contempt of court, may play a role in shaping and managing judicial appearance, they are not the only, or primary, means by which the judicial image is produced and managed. The image of the judge is produced through a wide variety of cultural forms and practices that include reported judicial writings, the geography of the courts in which judges perform their office, court websites, popular print media, film, television and portraiture.

Formal judicial portraits are a particular sub-genre of portraiture. In part they are portraits of legal professionals and in part they are portraits of state officials. What impact, if any, does this have on the nature of these portraits? Portraiture of members of professions, Jordonova argues, has distinctive qualities. It plays an important dual role: first in the (self-)fashioning of the sitters and second in the self-fashioning of the institution. Through these portraits the individual's image is fabricated according to the abstract ideas, values and virtues associated with the institution and the collective. Through the sitter's image these institutional values and virtues are made visible, public and more accessible. This plays a role not only in the construction and representation of the identity of the individual sitter but also, importantly, in the composition and construction of collective identities and of the identity of the institution.[15] Judicial portraits are also state portraits, which Jenkins defines as a distinctive type of portraiture, being representations of rulers or their deputies. As state portraits, the nature of the dual function of the portrait shifts. The image of the individual sitter is fashioned by, and made to embody and thereby represent, a set of abstract principles, qualities and characteristics of the state.[16] The judiciary are state officials particularly associated with justice under the rule of law.

What do judicial portraits as state portraits look like? What aesthetic traditions do they draw upon? What are the values and virtues that inform these representations of particular individual sitters? How do they affect the sitter's image? How, if at all, is sexuality represented in and through judicial portraits as state portraits?

The judicial portrait: a case study

Portraits of the sixteen chief justices of the Supreme Court of New South Wales, Australia, offer a useful case study through which to explore the key character-istics of judicial portraits. Spanning the period 1824–2009 it is difficult to dif-ferentiate one sitter from another. The image of the Honourable Sir James Martin, Chief Justice from 1875 to 1886, is remarkably similar to that of the Honourable Sir Lawrence Whistler Street, Chief Justice from 1974 to 1988. The repertoire of poses is limited. With one exception, all are full or three-quarter body portraits. The body of the judge, not the face, dominates the image. The sitter's body is little more than a device to hold and display the insignia of judi-cial office: the full-length scarlet robes with white fur trim, collar and thick cuffs, white neckbands, black waistband and sash, white gloves – a tradition of judicial dress originating in sixteenth-century England.

The face of the sitter, that which perhaps most clearly differentiates one sitter from another and has well-established associations with character and indivi-duality, makes up a small part of the image. The full-bottomed wig, worn by most sitters, further obscures key individualising characteristics such as hair, the shape of the face, the ears and so on. Furthermore, facial expressions are stan-dardised: all depict a certain gravity, a sturdy tranquillity, deep introspection. This aesthetics negates the quixotic, the particular or the idiosyncratic. Last, but not least, a majority set the figure of the judge against a dark background with little or no detail visible. Props are rare and strictly limited to books or papers.[17] The overall composition orientates the viewer's gaze to the symbols of office that cover the body of the sitter.

The chief justice portraits more than amply fit the description of official portraits offered by Charlotte Townsend-Gault; 'bland ... and predictable ... '.[18] She goes on to explain that this often leads to official portraits being, 'dis-missed as vacuous statements and indifferent art' and on that basis largely ignored.[19] But official portraits can tell us much about the nature, meaning and formation of institutional and individual identity, recognition, representation and subjectivity.[20]

The aesthetics described above fashions the sitter according to a long-estab-lished tradition developed to represent social, political and institutional elites in a society. In line with that tradition, the surface of the portrait of each sitter shows a preoccupation with the symbols of power, status, authority and legitimacy. The picture formats, poses, backgrounds, props and so on form the subject of the image according to the values and characteristics of the institution: of indepen-dence, integrity, impartiality and majesty. The sitter's public persona is made to appear as a subject selflessly dedicated to the word of the law. Likeness and individuality in the judicial portrait are produced according to the need to fashion the individual office holder as an exemplar, as the embodied ideal of the values and virtues of the institution. In this regime of representation, the differentiation of one sitter from another is not an aesthetic preoccupation. The individual subject is shaped by an aesthetics that produces the sitter's image as the embodiment of the virtues of sameness: repetition, endurance, continuity and consistency.

Sexuality, judicial virtues and judicial portraiture

What, if anything, can be learnt about how the sexuality of the judiciary is made in and through these portraits? There are a number of possible answers. One is that the preoccupation with the judicial symbols of authority puts the sitter's sexuality out of the frame: sexuality is missing from the image, and not a part of the institution. But queer theory draws attention to other ways of making sense of the portraits. If sexuality is always public then sexuality is necessarily figured in these images as the 'unmarked', the absent presence of heterosexuality as the norm. A third response is that sexuality makes a more formal appearance. Under a heteronormative regime the values and virtues associated with the office and institution of the judge coincide with those attached to heterosexuality: the assumption and expectation that heterosexuality is the basic idiom of personal and social virtue, that it is the natural (unbiased) state or condition, that it is the ideal or the apotheosis of moral accomplishment, free from personal perspective or partiality. The identification and recognition of the judicial virtues in the image of the sitter is the recognition and identification of the institutional subject and of that subject as a heterosexual subject.

But there is a need for caution here in order to avoid what has been described as the 'illusion of immanence': that all the meaning is within the frame of the image.[21] In part, maybe in good part, the meaning of the image comes from outside the frame by way of the social, political and cultural context. The viewer brings a wide array of assumptions about the nature of portraiture into play (that the portrait has strong empirical qualities, being both a likeness of the sitter and the truth of the sitter's character and personality) and contemporary and historical social and political knowledge that may work to ascribe a (hetero)sexuality to the sitter. The form and meaning of the image is the effect of complex social processes and social relations. It begins with the exchanges between the one producing the image (for example, the painter), the sitter and, where relevant, the party commissioning the image.[22] The location and display of the images (which also involve questions about the formats and forms of production and reproduction) and the various audiences for portraits in those different locations all contribute to making the various meanings of the image.[23] Finally, I want to counsel against locating the meaning either in the image or outside the frame of the image. The sexuality of the sitter may be both figured in the image yet only brought into the viewer's consciousness by way of the transactions that take place between the portrait, the viewers and the (sexual) culture or regime outside the frame. Meaning-making is not so much fixed in and by the image. Rather, the image works to generate social relations and interactions that produce its possible meanings.[24]

A portrait of Justice Michael Kirby

How, if at all, does a judicial portrait of a gay man differ from those described above? This brings me to the portrait of Justice Michael Kirby by Ralph Heimans. In some ways it is a portrait of a judge reflecting the long tradition of judicial portraiture. The portrait, the artist explained, has 'only one subject' – Justice Michael Kirby – despite the fact of other figures in the picture.[25] He is portrayed in the full ceremonial robes and wig of judicial office. Again, in line with tradition, the background is devoid of detail. It is also a portrait that devotes considerable attention to the role of a judge. How did this come about? The context of the portrait has particular significance here. This was not a commissioned portrait so there was no particular reason to dwell on the sitter's institutional role. As the artist explained, this opened up many possibilities: 'Do you represent them in their home environment, or do you represent them as no one else might have seen them, as they really might be? So I asked him, "What are your interests? What do you do with your spare time?" And he said, "I work."'[26] At that point, the project became much more closely aligned with judicial portraiture. As Heimans explained, a key theme of the portrait is 'Justice Kirby's judicial approach'.[27]

But in other respects this picture of a judge is far from being a traditional judicial portrait. As the artist explained, 'I quite consciously chose to break with that tradition.'[28] The portrait departs from the tradition of judicial portraiture in three interconnected ways. First, the picture includes other judges. Group portraits of judges are very rare. The first impression is not of a portrait of a single judge whose body is swathed in scarlet but of many bodies; 'It looks like a procession of Santa Clauses.'[29] The 'Santa Clauses' in question are eight judges dressed in their formal judicial robes. Second, the majority of the other judges are literally faceless, being depicted with their backs to the viewer so that in fact the portrait has a single subject. Third, the portrait's shape (a rectangular landscape format where the horizontal axis is longer then the vertical axis) and composition draws upon the traditions of history painting and nineteenth-century genre painting in which the image is composed to evoke a narrative. The artist explained, 'My approach to portraiture is really to try to tell a story through the portrait about the subject, and doing that through context, situation, action, rather than having images of people sitting in armchairs. I like to have a more dynamic portrait.'[30] The composition, pose, props and background all take on a more dynamic storytelling role than is to be found in more traditional judicial portraiture.

It is useful to spend time examining some of these features of the painting in more detail. Let me begin with the painting's use of a group composition. As art historians have noted, in a group portrait the character of the portrait's subject(s) is generated by the interactions among the individuals in the group, their gestures and gazes.[31] In the Michael Kirby portrait this works in a very particular way. The composition suppresses the character of seven of the eight judges. Five have their backs to the viewer. These faceless judicial figures are not subjects but more objects, mere props, used to tell a story about the main character. Their facelessness compositionally singles out the subject of the portrait, Michael Kirby. The two remaining judges further reinforce this state of affairs. The faces of Justice Wallace and Sir Bernard Sugarman (in glasses) are partly covered by the judicial full-bottom wig.[32] Only Kirby's face (and thereby his character) is fully exposed and free from the judicial wig, which he holds. His face stares out of the picture. Positioned at the front of the composition he is 'the only figure looking directly at the viewer and that kind of arrests you', explained the artist.[33] Kirby's face generates 'a real confrontation and exchange' between the subject of the image and the viewer.[34] The viewer has the experience of being observed by Kirby's penetrating gaze.

If the other judges are little more than visual devices used to narrate Kirby's character, what do they depict? The repeated use of the anonymous judicial figure, Heimans explains, 'suggest[s] a judicial lineage, which is important to Kirby'.[35] Further, 'I tried to express something about Justice Kirby's judicial approach through the way I represented him. He is in line with the judges. So there's a degree of him following them. He is also somehow set apart from them, which is something that reflects his more radical approach.'[36]

The contrast between the facelessness of the judicial props and Kirby's fully exposed face and head creates the painting's narrative about Kirby's devotion to qualities associated with the judicial virtues of lineage and tradition (selflessness, impartiality) and also represents his difference, his distinctive contribution to the judiciary as a virtue of office, his willingness to speak out via his dissenting judgments, his role as judge (as public figure) and his active engagement with wider audiences.

The judges as 'props' are also used to represent other individual and institutional characteristics, which the artist described as 'atmosphere'. The spatial arrangement of the figures and their gestures are key. For example, the artist explained that he organised the figures to suggest movement to the left. This is against the dominant compositional tradition that tends to show figures heading right. This compositional format, Heimans explained, is intended to create an experience of disturbance; to generate a, 'greater sense of "unnaturalness"'.[37] Further, 'the fact that they are disappearing into a void heightens the mystery'.[38] Mystery is also evoked by way of gesture. One of the judges, Sugarman, is depicted with his hand on the arm of his neighbour, which the artist explained is to suggest that the judiciary are something of a 'secret brethren'.[39] Mystery is also a theme expressed by the missing and shrouded faces of the other judicial figures. Another individual characteristic and judicial quality depicted in the portraits is that of austerity.[40] Devoid of any particular signs or symbols, the geography of the image is unspecified, which Heimans suggests makes the location 'austere'. The colour and composition that for Heimans produces the Santa Claus effect evokes a different quality, humour. 'Atmosphere' depicts Kirby's qualities and characteristics, 'very regal and very gracious ... and slow ... still ... upright [with] a bit of a smile ... He's got a great sense of humour.'[41]

The faceless judges also carry the traces of another story: a refusal by other judges to be represented in this image with Justice Kirby. In making the painting, Heimans approached several judges to get their approval to depict them in the picture. All refused. One judge was particularly adamant, demanding that the artist sign a document guaranteeing that he would not be depicted in the painting.[42] So, in part, the faceless figures are a trace of this refusal. Is this a trace of a general judicial refusal to be represented? The very existence of so many judicial portraits would suggest that this is unlikely. Or is the refusal more specific: a refusal to be painted by this particular artist, in this particular manner or in relation to this particular judge? And of the two figures that have a face? Heimans explained, 'Sugarman and Wallace are in fact "ghosts".'[43] The image was made after their deaths. Their families happily consented to images of Sugarman and Wallace being used and provided photos; their painted faces are reconstructed from these.

How, if at all, is this sitter's sexuality and more specifically his sexual difference depicted in this image? Following on from the earlier analysis of the tradition of judicial portraiture there are again various answers to this question. One is that there is no reference to Kirby as a sexual subject in this image. Heimans offers us a portrait of Justice Michael Kirby that is fashioned according to symbols and settings commonly associated with depictions of judicial authority, devotion to tradition, independence, austerity and selfless dedication to law.

At the same time, there are aspects of the picture that appear to disrupt this state of affairs. While Justice Kirby wears the symbols of judicial office in common with his fellow judges, the composition takes pains to separate him out. He is the embodiment of its key traditional values but there is also something more. The narrative generated by the image suggests that Kirby embodies some different virtues: the (judicial) virtue of public presence, greater exposure and a distinctive individuality. The exposure of, and composition of, his face adds to this effect. His over-the-shoulder look is a pose that allows for a classic three-quarter-face composition. The contrast between light and shade allows the portraitist to produce a more complex multidimensional representation of the sitter's character. Using these aesthetic forms, flouting some of the conventions of formal judicial portraiture, developing the narrative potential of the picture, figures the 'difference' of Kirby's official persona, his distinctive (dissenting) voice on the Bench of the High Court, his high, and for some, controversial media profile. Does it also depict his different sexuality?

I also want to suggest that his sexuality may be connoted in this portrait image through various characteristics that Heimans refers to as 'atmosphere': the evocation of 'mystery', of 'unnaturalness' and the idea of the subject as a member of a 'secret brethren'. When I asked the artist about Kirby's sexuality and its significance or otherwise in the composition, he explained that at the time the painting was being produced Kirby had not yet announced his long-term same-sex partnership in *Australia's Who's Who*. But his sexuality was 'an open secret', at least in the legal world. It was something the artist knew about. Does the composition's concerns with the representation of mystery and secrecy and with their public display, give visual form to the then status quo, of Kirby's sexuality as an 'open secret'?

And what of the work of factors outside the frame in making the sexual meaning of the image? The title of the portrait; *Radical Restraint: Justice Michael Kirby* is one formal external device that frames the reading of the image. It offers an orientation for the viewer to bring to bear contemporary social, political and cultural contexts upon the meanings to be made by way of the image. Does the 'radical' of the title invite a reading of this image as a depiction of a hugely successful gay man who holds high judicial office and embodies legitimate judicial authority? Does 'restraint' generate similar but rather different connotations – this time connoting the long-standing nature of his sexuality as an 'open secret'?

The prompts that accompany the picture need not necessarily bring sexuality or Kirby's different sexuality into play in making the meaning of the subject of the portrait. For example, the extended text that accompanies the portrait on the wall (and the website) of the National Portrait Gallery of Australia in Canberra, provides a narrative that guides the way the portrait is to be read. It focuses on many of his formal professional achievements and qualities but makes no reference to his sexuality. One interpretation of this is that the accompanying narrative seeks to edit out his sexuality. Another interpretation is that his sexuality is not so much edited out but written according to the heteronormative conventions of sexuality as a formal absence (as heterosexual) or maybe, in the alternative, as the 'open secret' as a love that dares not to speak its name.

I want to consider the impact of the external social and political context upon the (sexual) meaning of the picture made in the interaction between the artist, sitter, image and viewer through one particular example. The version of the portrait displayed in the National Portrait Gallery of Australia is the second version of the painting. In the first version, the doorway to the extreme left of the portrait was filled with a blinding light and 'a rather mysterious figure'. Heimans explained that some viewers suggested the figure 'was a particular judge [Justice Yeldham], who had just been the subject of some scandalous allegations'.[44] Justice Yeldham, a judge of the New South Wales Supreme Court, had committed suicide after allegations were made that he had sex with young men. This particular example of the audience's interpretation (a meaning unintended and unexpected by the artist) draws attention to the way the viewer's reading may be informed by contemporary social and political events. In response, the artist intervened. The shadowy figure was painted out and the doorway repainted as a dark void. Heimans explained that he did this as he wanted to remove any suggestion of sexual 'scandal' from the portrait of Justice Kirby.

Last but not least is the influence of location on meaning.[45] For example, finding the portrait in the National Portrait Gallery of Australia rather than in a courtroom may give licence to read the image differently. When placed in a courtroom with other judicial images in which individuality is formally erased and sexuality appears as heterosexuality as a pervasive absence, similarities between the portrait of Justice Kirby and the other portraits may lead viewers to read them all as representations of heterosexuality.

But, I would agree with Law and Urry that one of the objectives of research into social phenomena must be to resist the temptation to either assume that meanings are single or fixed. Nor should we strive to fix the meaning of a thing or a set of social interactions made in and through an object. The meaning, they suggest, is produced, 'in dense and extended sets of relations. It is produced with considerable effort, and it is much easier to produce some realities than others.'[46] By way of the assumptions associated with the genre of portraiture and the viewer's historical, social and political knowledge, Justice Kirby's sexuality may be figured in the image as both known and unknown, as both a judicial virtue and a judicial irrelevance.

Conclusion

Portraiture, and judicial portraiture in particular, offers a very useful vehicle for examining sexuality in the institutional setting of the judiciary. It is the nature of portraiture to make visible and public the values and virtues of the institution. These are images dedicated to forming and showing the identity of the sitter as the embodiment of institutional values and virtues. In relation to my research on sexuality in the judiciary, portraits provide a means to examine the fabrication of sexuality as an institutional identity that is said to have no place in that institution. The analysis of the aesthetics of the judicial portraits of the Chief Justices of New South Wales has provided an opportunity to examine how sexuality is fashioned as an absent institutional presence. The portrait of Justice Michael Kirby has, by contrast, provided an opportunity to consider how, if at all, sexuality might be represented as a desired aspect of the judicial institution: as a judicial virtue. The portrait of Justice Kirby is particularly interesting as it appears to be produced in contradistinction to an aesthetic of 'ostensible' sexuality. Does this mean that Justice Kirby's sexual difference is unrepresented and unrepresentable in and through that image? My analysis suggests that there is no single answer to that question. It also suggests that it is important not to reduce the answer to an either/or. By way of challenging the illusion of immanence, my argument seeks to highlight the importance of the role of context, setting and social relations in the generation of multiple possible meanings in the institutional image. It seeks, in line with some of the insights offered by queer theory, to highlight the contingency of sexuality in the institution, its fragility as a regime of meaning. This provides an opportunity to reread the traditional aesthetic of judicial portraiture and thereby what counts as values and virtues of the institution of the judiciary and legitimate judicial authority. That aesthetic can no longer be read as one that necessarily fashions the institutional subject of judicial office as heterosexual. But it is an aesthetics that also fashions different sexualities as a desired attribute of an elite institution. That raises some other challenges, such as social class.

Notes

1 L. J. Moran, 'Judicial Diversity and the Challenge of Sexuality: Some Preliminary Findings', *Sydney Law Review*, 28 (4) (2006): 565–98.
2 *Who's Who* was first published 1849. Judges are automatically invited to submit an entry. Available online at http://www.oup.com/whoswho (accessed 17 November 2009).
3 For a study of the interface between the judiciary and sexuality in a popular cultural context, a television documentary, see, L. J. Moran, 'Projecting the Judge: A Case Study in the Cultural Lives of the Judiciary', in *Law and Film: Essays on the State of the Field, Studies in Law, Politics and Society*, 46 (2008): 93–115.
4 Note that these are edited pictures of the portraits, focusing more attention on the upper part of the portraits and the faces of the judiciary. Available online at http://www.lawlink.nsw.gov.au/lawlink/supreme_court/ll_sc.nsf/pages/SCO_chiefjudges (accessed 18 November 2009). For an extended study of these images, see L. J. Moran, 'Judging Pictures: A Case Study of Portraits of the Chief Justices Supreme Court New South Wales', *International Journal of Law*, 5 (3) (2009): 61–80.
5 He retired from the High Court on 2 February 2009 after thirteen years' service. A video of the retirement ceremony is available online at http://www.michaelkirby.com.au/ (accessed 25 March 2009).
6 In the legal community he is well known for his dissenting judgments. For Justice Kirby's response to his reputation, see M. Kirby, *Judicial Activism: Authority, Principle and Policy in the Judicial Method* (London: Sweet & Maxwell 2004).
7 A large collection of his writings and other materials is available online at http://www.michaelkirby.com.au (accessed 18 November 2009).
8 On the gallery's other judicial portraits see L. J. Moran, 'Judicial Portraits', *Portrait*, 24 (winter 2007): 22–5.
9 L. Berlant and M. Warner, 'Sex in Public', *Critical Inquiry*, 24 (2) (1998): 547–66; p. 548, footnote 2.
10 S. Seideman, 'Queer-ing Sociology, Sociologizing Queer Theory: An Introduction', *Sociological Theory*, 12 (2) (1994): 166–77, at p. 169.
11 For an extended analysis of the work that silence does in making sexualities in law, see L. J. Moran, *The Homosexual(ity) of Law* (London: Routledge 1996).
12 Berlant and Warner, 'Sex in Public', p. 553.
13 Ibid., p. 556.
14 W. Haltom, *Reporting on the Courts: How the Mass Media Cover Judicial Actions* (Chicago, Ill.: Nelson Hall, 1998); C. G. Geyh, 'Preserving Public Confidence in the Courts in the Age of Individual Rights and Public Skepticism', in K. Bybee (ed.), *Bench Press: The Collision of Courts, Politics and the Media* (Palo Alto, Calif.: Stanford University Press, 2007), pp. 21–51.
15 L. Jordanova, *Defining Features: Scientific and Medical Portraits 1660–2000* (London: Reaktion Books, 2000), pp. 14–15.
16 M. Jenkins, *The State Portrait: Its Origins and Evolution* (New York: College of Fine Arts Association of America, 1947), p. 1.
17 P. Goodrich, 'The Iconography of Nothing: Blank Spaces and the Representation of Law in Edward VI and the Pope', in C. Douzinas and L. Nead (eds.), *Law and the*

Image: The Authority of Art and the Aesthetics of Law (Chicago, Ill.: The University of Chicago Press, 1999), pp. 89–116.

18 C. Townsend-Gault, 'Symbolic Façades: Official Portraits in British Institutions since 1920', *Art History*, 11 (4) (1988): 511–26, at pp. 511–12.

19 Ibid., p. 511.

20 R. Brilliant, *Portraiture* (London: Reaktion, 1981); C. Soussloff, *The Subject in Art: Portraiture and the Birth of the Modern* (Durham, NC: Duke University Press, 2006); S. West, *Portraiture* (Oxford: Oxford University Press, 2004); J. Woodall (ed.), *Portraiture: Facing the Subject* (Manchester: Manchester University Press, 1997).

21 Soussloff, *The Subject in Art*, p. 5.

22 Brilliant, *Portraiture*.

23 M. Pointon, *Hanging the Head: Portraiture and Social Formation in Eighteenth-Century England* (New Haven, Conn.: Yale University Press, 1993). See also Jordanova, *Defining Features*; and Moran, 'Judging Pictures'.

24 J. Law and J. Urry, 'Enacting the Social', *Economy and Society*, 33 (3) (2004): 390–414.

25 R. Heimans, *Transcript of a Conversation between Ralph Heimans and Andrew Sayers, Simon Elliot, Pamela Clelland Gray, Leoine Hellmers, Suzie Campbell, Kate Eccles-Smith and Sarah Engledow* (Canberra: National Portrait Gallery, 2001). Copy on file with the author.

26 Interview with Ralph Heimans, 4 August 2008. Copy on file with the author.

27 Heimans, *Transcript of a Conversation*.

28 Ibid.

29 Ibid.

30 Ibid.

31 The author's surname is Riegel. His initial is 'A' R. Aloïl, 'Excerpts from "The Dutch Group Portrait"', trans. B. Binstock, *October*, 74 (fall 1995): 3–35; Soussloff, *The Subject in Art*, pp. 33–5. Heimans has suggested that the composition is particularly influenced by Dutch group portraits and Rembrant's *The Syndics* in particular. See R. Heimans, The Doug Moran Portrait Prize 1998, available online at http://www.moran.com.au/art/1998/rh.htm (accessed 11 November 2008).

32 These two figures were respectively the first and second presidents of the Court of Appeal.

33 Interview with Ralph Heimans.

34 Ibid.

35 Heimans, *Transcript of a Conversation*.

36 Interview with Ralph Heimans.

37 Heimans, *Transcript of a Conversation*. The phrase 'secret brethren' has a rich ambiguity suggesting both the strong and enduring patriarchial aspects of the judiciary in the common-law tradition as well as a heteronormative association between homosexuality and conspiracy. For an analysis of the homosocial/homophobic interface in the judiciary, see L. J. Moran, '"May it Please the Court … ": Forming Sexualities as Judicial Virtues in Judicial Swearing-in Ceremonies', in U. Shultz and G. Shaw (eds.), *Gender and Judging* (Oxford: Hart Publishing, forthcoming).

38 Heimans, *Transcript of a Conversation*.

39 Ibid.

40 In part this was because Heimans was uninspired by the courtroom settings he visited.

41 Interview with Ralph Heimans.

42 Heimans, *Transcript of a Conversation*.

43 Ibid.

44 Interview with Ralph Heimans.

45 Pointon, *Hanging the Head*.

46 Law and Urry, 'Enacting the Social', pp. 395–6.

Chapter 7

Sexuality, gender and social cognition

Lesbian and gay identity in judicial decision-making

Todd Brower

Introduction

Our perceptions of the world are shaped by schemas, a set of beliefs about people or situations that guide our interaction with these things.[1] Having a schema about a person or thing enables us to know (or believe we know) a great deal about that individual or object quickly. Thus, we treat that person or object in what we perceive to be an appropriate manner – in accordance with our schema. For example, we may schematically divide furniture into chairs and tables. When we categorise a new object into a schema, we know whether to sit in the thing or to place our drink on it.

Schemas are crucial to our ability to function. If we had to analyse each piece of information or situation anew, we would either be swamped by minutiae or paralysed into inactivity. Schemas, therefore, are how we process the incessant stream of demands and inputs. Schemas permit us to understand new people or situations rapidly and to interact successfully with them. We liberally edit information to fit our schemas: we extract and retain information because it is useful and consonant with them, and reject information when it is inconsistent, or no longer useful.[2] Thus, schemas are idiosyncratic; they are neither necessarily accurate nor consistent with others' models.

We also interact with people according to our social schemas. We develop models that ascribe a range of characteristics to others corresponding to their race, sex and other physical attributes, and these models include schemas for lesbians and gay men, and for homosexuality.[3] One major characteristic of the popular schema about gay people is that they exhibit 'cross-gender' or gender atypical behaviour, behaviour traditionally associated with the opposite sex.[4]

This facet of the lesbian and gay schema has prevented some judges from appropriately interpreting legal doctrine and precedent and has led to anomalous results. Moreover, the relatively non-rigorous and unconscious nature of schema-matching – a feature of both legal and non-legal reasoning – has exacerbated this inaccuracy and distorted legal doctrine involving gay people. This chapter employs some US same-sex sexual harassment cases arising under the sex-discrimination prohibitions of Title VII of the Civil Rights Act of 1964 to illustrate how the insights of cognitive schema models and social-cognition theories inform and misinform decisions of judges and case participants.[5]

Evidence of schema theory at work

One of the thorniest areas in sexual-harassment doctrine centres on the proper application of the Supreme Court's *Price Waterhouse* v. *Hopkins* decision on tradi-tional gender-role enforcement in the workplace.[6] Courts often misanalyse the gender-role claim when lesbian or gay plaintiffs are involved because of the schema's insistence that gay people exhibit gender-atypical characteristics.[7] Accordingly, we can examine these sexual-harassment and gender-role claims to explore how the lesbian and gay schemas interact with sexual-harassment prototypes.

A plurality of the Supreme Court justices in *Price Waterhouse* recognised that an employer who requires traditional gender roles for female employees perpetuates gender stereotypes in violation of Title VII. Despite her recognised professional and business-development abilities, Price Waterhouse denied Ann Hopkins a promotion to an accounting partnership due to her lack of interpersonal office skills, expressed as consequences of Hopkins' gender-atypical (masculine) char-acteristics. She was described as having perhaps 'overcompensated for being a woman' and as needing to enrol in a 'course at charm school' and was advised to 'walk more femininely, talk more femininely, dress more femininely, wear make-up, have her hair styled, and wear jewelry'.[8] The Court found that Price Waterhouse denied Hopkins a partnership in part because her behaviour and characteristics were inappropriate for her gender.[9] The core of the sex discrimination at issue was the employer's insistence on traditional gender conformity.

In contrast, *Hamner* v. *St Vincent Hospital and Health Care Center* exemplifies the distinction between gender and sexual-orientation discrimination. Hamner was a gay male nurse who had a poor relationship with his supervisor, Dr Edwards. Edwards disliked Hamner because he was gay and would harass him by telling gay jokes, parody him by effeminate hand gestures and lisping and scream at Hamner or refuse to communicate with him.[10] Despite Edwards' use of effeminate gestures and speech, indicating that he believed Hamner, as a gay man, was not sufficiently masculine, the record indicated that Edwards' behaviour was due to Hamner's sexual orientation. However, if Edwards had disapproved of men in nursing, or even if he manifested his disapproval by perceiving all male nurses to be gay because of that gender-atypical career choice, the latter two scenarios would evidence sex discrimination and not sexual-orientation bias.[11]

With *Price Waterhouse* and *Hamner* serving as paradigmatic cases, schema-matching should allow judges to categorise new situations appropriately; they do not. Furthermore, even these paradigmatic cases provide evidence of schematic rea-soning. For example, we can draw inferences about plaintiffs' sexuality from the courts' descriptions of plaintiffs, thus demonstrating the effects of schemas. For example, the court described Dixie Adair, another successful female victim of sex stereotyping denied a promotion for being abrasive, patronising, and demanding, as 'present[ing] a most matronly appearance' and 'possess[ing] the very essence of womanhood'.[12] Note the gender-coded terminology. She is the essence of womanhood and also matronly, thus fulfilling one of the central female gender roles: mother.

In contrast, as the court noted in *Hamner*, 'Gary Hamner is a male nurse and a homosexual'.[13] Note the phrase, 'male nurse'. Gary Hamner is a man, thus he is obviously a *male* nurse and not a female one. The gender adjective qualifying 'nurse' is superfluous to identify his sex but demonstrates the schema of nursing as a female occupation. Male nurses are unusual, noteworthy and stigmatised as gender-atypical.[14] Additionally, both the plaintiff's occupation and sexual orientation were noted in *Hamner*. However, atypical gender behaviour alone often triggers the label 'homosexual' because we incorporate confirming information into our schema and edit out disconfirming material.[15] Thus, the schema also attaches to those whom others only perceive to be gay, and it shapes our perceptions irrespective of whether that assessment is accurate or even relevant.

Social cognition research confirms this pattern. Individuals perceive gender cues such as hip sway, gait and body shape in order to assess masculinity and femininity, and also homosexuality and heterosexuality. In one study, research subjects were shown ungendered animated figures walking and asked to judge sex and sexual orientation. Those with a swaggering gait were seen as men; those with a swaying walk as women. Similarly, silhouettes with an hourglass figure were perceived as female and those with a tubular figure as male. When an hourglass figure swaggered – i.e., engaged in perceived gender-atypical behaviour – respondents judged the figure as a lesbian, and when a tubular figure swayed, they called the figure a gay man. Thus, respondents used gender-stereotypical movement cues to make assumptions about sex and sexual orientation and to reveal the interactions between those categories.[16] Indeed, gender atypicality and homosexuality are so schematically linked that some media reports reversed the findings of that research. Those reports erroneously noted that researchers found that lesbians and gay men had distinctive, cross-gendered gaits and body morphology.[17]

Jurisprudentially, this aspect of the lesbian and gay schema encourages a conflation of sex, gender and sexual orientation.[18] Like the morphology study respondents, judges may assume that a male plaintiff who exhibits gender-atypical behaviour is gay, even when he is not. Consequently, judges may transform his Title VII claim from one based on gender to one based on sexual orientation. The conflation often leaves male plaintiffs who exhibit gender-atypical behaviour without a legal remedy and female plaintiffs with limited or uneven results, despite Supreme Court precedent.

In *Smith* v. *Liberty Mutual Ins. Co.*, Smith, a male, applied to be a mail clerk for Liberty Mutual Insurance Company. He was rejected because his interviewer thought Smith was 'effeminate', insufficiently 'male' and therefore unsuited for the job. The government's investigative report confirmed and reinforced gender atypicality and the homosexual schema, stating that Smith's 'offensive' behaviours were 'quite pronounced' and that he had 'interests ... not normally associated with males (sewing)'.[19] Besides illustrating the cross-gender trigger for the gay schema, the investigator's report evidences the tendency to magnify facts that confirm schemas and to downplay or ignore contradictory information.[20] Smith's actual employment application listed four hobbies: playing musical instruments, singing, dancing and sewing.[21] The investigator's report only mentioned sewing, the hobby most gender-identified with women.

Smith tried to prevent gender-atypicality from activating the gay male schema in order to underscore the gendered nature of his discrimination claim. Significantly, he argued that he was a happily married, heterosexual male and was not 'demanding that an employer accept [an] unconventional life style or mores'.[22] Smith's sex-discrimination claim alleged that, since the person eventually hired was a woman, the employer would have expected her to behave 'effeminately' and have interests such as sewing. Those attributes were gender-appropriate for women but not for men. Smith insisted that the employer's 'refusal to hire him was not based on a determination that the plaintiff was in fact homosexual, but rather the subjective determination that he possessed personal traits that Liberty Mutual associated by stereotype with the female gender'.[23] Therefore, the failure to hire him was because of his sex.

Nevertheless, Liberty Mutual neutralised the gender-atypicality evidence that Smith would have needed in order to win his gender-stereotyping case by eliciting the gay schema in the courts. Once the courts schematically read that behaviour as evidencing sexuality and not gender, they transformed Smith's claim from gender-role discrimination to homosexuality.[24] This misreading of the plaintiff's claim as sexual-orientation discrimination rather than as gender discrimination errs analytically and enshrines the gender-atypical-behaviour aspect of the lesbian and gay schema into Title VII doctrine.

In contrast, *Price Waterhouse* focused on the individual nature of Hopkins' claim. Forced conformity to gender norms for behaviour – even commonly accepted ones – still negatively affect individuals. Smith was just as surely precluded from employment as Hopkins was, and for the same reason: their employers' insistence that they conform their gender behaviour to biological sex. The lesbian and gay schema does not always affect women and men equally. Differences in male and female gender roles arguably require asymmetrical treatment of male and female plaintiffs' cases. Women's gender-atypical behaviour may sometimes be acceptable, expected or within gender appropriate boundaries.[25] In those situations, employers and judges do not equate atypical gender behaviour with lesbian identity so they formulate appropriate legal analogies and doctrine.

As *Price Waterhouse* illustrated, some workplaces and careers are predominantly and traditionally male, and women may be under pressure to utilise more masculine attributes in those contexts. In order that women will be hired or taken seriously in business, some advise them not to dress or act in an overtly feminine manner: not to wear too much jewellery, too short skirts, too high heels, etc.[26] At least for some jobs, therefore, a woman with traditionally masculine attributes may be preferred.

Similarly, women's choice of traditionally male careers may be perceived as rational and not reflective of their sexuality, particularly concerning high-status jobs such as accountant, lawyer or business executive.[27] However, cross-gender job choice by males, or by women entering other, more blue-collar fields, implicates the lesbian and gay schema.[28] Contrast, for example, the common perception of a woman who seeks to be a corporate attorney with one who wants to be a bulldozer driver – or a man who desires to be a nurse or receptionist.[29]

One social-psychology study asked men entering traditional female professions about their 'masculinity' (namely, sexual orientation); women were not asked. By using 'masculinity' to refer to homosexuality, the study authors equated gender-atypicality with the gay schema.[30] Thus, the study illustrates the schema's persistence even among gender-role researchers. The difference in treatment between gender-atypical men and women may be partially attributed to the perceived status gains or losses associated with taking traditionally male or female jobs. A man working in a female position, such as a secretary, loses social status; a woman gains status when she chooses a male career. We may perceive the man's choice as peculiar, the woman's as natural.[31] The availability of an alternative explanation for women's choices (that they are seeking increased status) may explain why courts have more readily held that discrimination against women because of gender-atypicality has violated Title VII yet have had difficulty drawing a parallel conclusion in relation to men.

Cognitive psychologists have found that people seize upon even tenuous theories in order to rationalise inexplicable events or behaviour, and schemas often fill this need for order and rationality.[32] Consequently, employers and judges may call upon the lesbian and gay schema when increased status or other acceptable reasons cannot explain gender-atypical behaviour. When masculine women who work in male dominated, high-status careers appear as plaintiffs, they may not elicit the lesbian schema because of the alternative explanation of their desire for increased status. Courts cannot, however, conclude similarly in relation to effeminate male plaintiffs in low-status jobs. Accordingly, the contrast between the outcomes in *Price Waterhouse* and *Smith* appears less confusing, although no more appropriate.

Furthermore, the stronger the inference that the victim of sexual harassment is homosexual, the more difficulty judges have. In same-sex sexual-harassment cases where heterosexual men are perpetrators, they always place their male victims in the receptive role in intercourse or the active role in oral sex.[33] This is not coincidental. Historically, and in some modern cultures, men having sex with other men are viewed in different ways depending on which role they have assumed in sex, the insertive/male role or the receptive/female one.[34] Because concentrating on women's sexuality in the workplace often signals that they are not equals with men, men treating another man as occupying a female sexual role also demonstrates the imposition of second-class status.[35] Both these examples reveal expressions of dominance and inequality towards others seen as insufficiently male to belong to the group. Sexually harassed men are separated from and excoriated by co-workers because of maleness, or perceived lack thereof.[36] Accordingly, the employee's homosexuality is not the ultimate source of the discrimination; rather, the discrimination results from the rigorous enforcement of traditional male gendered behaviour in the workplace.

Similarly, courts more easily accept claims of same-sex sexual harassment through sex stereotyping when they believe that plaintiffs could not be gay, as in the case of the harassment of heterosexual women or schoolchildren.[37] In *Doe* v. *Belleville*, two sixteen-year-old brothers were employed as municipal groundskeepers. Because H. Doe wore an earring, his co-workers called him 'fag', 'queer' and 'bitch', told him to 'go back to San Francisco with the rest of the queers', and threatened to take him into the woods and sodomise him. One worker grabbed H.'s testicles 'to find out if [he was] a girl or a guy'. The court noted

> If the harassment were triggered by that woman's decision to wear overalls and a flannel shirt to work, for example – something her harassers might perceive to be masculine just as they apparently perceived H's decision to wear an earring as feminine – the court would have all the confirmation that it needed that the harassment indeed amounted to discrimination on the basis of sex.[38]

Nevertheless, when an adult gay man was similarly harassed, a different appellate panel of the same court held that the similar epithets, 'fag', 'bitch' and 'drag queen' referred to sexual orientation and not gender stereotyping.[39]

The mechanics of schema theory

Schema mechanisms may explain how this transformation from gender atypicality to sexual orientation occurs. In *Dawson* v. *Bumble & Bumble*, a hair salon in Manhattan employed an openly lesbian woman, Dawn Dawson, as a trainee. Dawson's co-workers included several lesbians and gay men, a bisexual and two transsexuals. Dawson generally wore leather pants and a denim jacket at work, sported a Mohawk haircut and wore no feminine jewellery, perfume or make-up.

After Bumble terminated her employment, Dawson claimed discrimination because of sex, sex stereotyping and/or sexual orientation. Dawson described herself as a 'lesbian female, who does not conform to gender norms in that she does not meet stereotyped expectations of femininity and may be perceived as more masculine than a stereotypical woman'.[40] She was harassed about her sexuality and appearance and told 'that she should act in a manner less like a man and more like a woman'.[41] Her co-workers called her 'Donald' instead of 'Dawn' in front of colleagues and customers.

The courts had significant difficulty in separating gender atypicality from sexual orientation and found that her claim was not based on sex or gender stereotyping but on sexual orientation and, accordingly, was not covered by Title VII.[42] The courts did not understand Dawson's claims; she had difficulty articulating those claims; and the co-workers who engaged in this behaviour may not have separated the two bases for liability. This confusion should not surprise us. Schemas are cognitive images that enable us to classify significant information in compact paradigms by using prototypical features. They tend to be unarticulated and informal. Further, this process occurs semi-automatically, with a relative lack of awareness.[43] We sort and classify information through schemas with little recognition of the fact that this triage is taking place.

Naturally, schemas serve as shortcuts both for people with limited familiarity with a particular situation and those who have significant experience. More experience may lead to more sophisticated and nuanced models, but it might merely solidify an inappropriate paradigm. Therefore, we would expect Dawson to have a schema about lesbian identity and non-traditional gender behaviours that she applies to herself and others. Further, Dawson's and the judges' schemas may either partially overlap or be entirely incongruent. That dissonance explains the following passage:

> Moreover, insofar as Dawson relies on a basis of discrimination that seems to be founded on her status as member of a subset, 'a lesbian who does not conform to gender norms', the theory she essays is not readily definable. ... Under Dawson's hypothesis, Bumble would practice disparate treatment by kinds of homosexuality, discriminating against an admitted lesbian who looks and behaves more like a man than like a woman, and presumably not against another lesbian known to be openly gay but who does not display her sexual preference by any visible expression or appearance.[44]

The court had difficulty understanding Dawson's claim because the court's schema of lesbians insisted on a uniform gender identity. Thus, the court ignored a classic trope of lesbian identity, the butch/femme dichotomy.[45] At one end of the gender spectrum is the butch, a lesbian who rejects traditional feminine roles, trappings and behaviours, opting instead for more traditionally masculine characteristics.[46] At the other end is the femme, a feminine identity that stresses prototypically womanly dress and behaviour.[47] The salon in *Dawson* had a high concentration of sexual minorities. We would expect that the employees in that non-traditional workplace to be aware of, and to incorporate, more sophisticated gender gradations within the schema of sexual minorities than would some federal judges' models of sexual orientation. Consequently, the district judge may not have understood how Bumble may practice disparate treatment by kinds of homosexuality, discriminating against an admitted lesbian who looks and behaves more like a man than like a woman, and presumably not against an admitted lesbian known to be openly gay but who does not display her sexual preference by any visible expression or appearance.[48]

Gender-based divisions among lesbians may not have registered within the judge's more basic schema of homosexuality and gender. Nevertheless, although the judge's model does not encompass a gendered distinction within sexual orientation, this does not mean that it was absent from the workplace or that it did not form part of Dawson's or her former co-workers' schema of lesbians and gay men.

Significantly, if Bumble distinguished between butch and femme lesbians and discriminated against the former but not the latter, that difference is based on gender, as in *Price Waterhouse*, and not on sexual orientation. When our schemas are flawed, we enlist inappropriate or inaccurate analytical models to interpret events or legal precedent erroneously, and thus draw false analogies or distinctions.[49] The mismatch between the judge's schema of gay identity and Dawson's, or that of her colleagues, may have led the courts to misanalyse the appropriate factual and legal context of her claim. The *Dawson* court cautioned:

> When utilized by an avowedly homosexual plaintiff, however, gender stereotyping claims can easily present problems for an adjudicator. This is for the simple reason that 'stereotypical notions about how men and women should behave will often necessarily blur into ideas about heterosexuality and homosexuality'. Like other courts, we have therefore recognised that a gender-stereotyping claim should not be used to 'bootstrap protection for sexual orientation into Title VII'.[50]

The court noted that problems arise because perceptions of sexual orientation and gender-role conformity blend. That insight captures a significant part of the schema for lesbians and gay men: that they engage in cross-gender behaviour. Indeed, without explicit workplace disclosure of an employee's sexual orientation, co-workers may decode a colleague's sexuality solely through gender atypicality.[51] The visibility of openly gay people allows others to notice their sexuality and to mistreat them on that basis, a basis that Title VII ignores. However, that mistreatment can also occur with closeted homosexuals, especially those who exhibit cross-gender behaviour, which is perceived by others to indicate sexual orientation.

The difference between visible and hidden sexual minorities triggers the opposite attribution: sexuality invokes gender atypicality. Openly gay people can have cross-gender behaviours misattributed to them, even if they are conventionally gendered. In contrast, a gender-conforming, closeted gay person does not suffer that misattribution. Accordingly, Title VII doctrine effectively closets sexual minorities. Being out at work means that courts may not remedy any resulting harassment, either because it is non-actionable sexual orientation discrimination or because it is misconstrued as gender discrimination.[52]

Tversky and Kahneman's 'availability heuristic' partially explains this difference. Distinctive information increases in salience and is more readily available for use, while common or unexceptional information recedes.[53] Because heterosexuality is the norm, it retreats from consciousness. Consequently, heterosexuality does not implicate gender. Since courts harbour no cross-gender beliefs about heterosexual women like Hopkins, they can 'objectively' assess appearance or behaviour. But because the gay schema conflates sexual orientation and gender non-conformity, those forms of harassment are often expressed simultaneously, as in *Doe* v. *Belleville*. Doe's co-workers equated effeminacy with homosexuality. His earring and slight build triggered harassment with an anti-gay cast.[54] Nevertheless, because the court believed Doe was heterosexual, his sexual orientation disappeared; the court held that his case concerned gender and not sexual-orientation discrimination.

Openly gay people, however, may activate the schema of cross-gender behaviour for co-workers or judges. Minority sexuality is salient; it intrudes even where irrelevant.[55] This causes a classic double-bind. Open, gender-conforming sexual minorities cannot prevail, even if others harass them through gender stereotypes. A court will view conventional gender-role enforcement claims as a sexual-orientation bootstrap. Alternatively, gender non-conforming gay people like Dawn Dawson also lose because the courts inextricably link their atypical-gender presentation with their sexual orientation. Gender non-conformity claims are reformulated into sexual orientation causes of action. Although courts have stated that Hopkins's gender-stereotyping case would not change if she were a lesbian, *Dawson* illustrates the hollowness of that assertion.[56] Additionally, by using the term 'bootstrapping', *Dawson* employs a schema that implies that open sexual minorities seek to play the system, to surreptitiously transform an impermissible claim (sexual orientation) into a permissible one (gender stereotyping). Since the court began its determinations with a jaundiced eye, it is unsurprising that Dawson lost.

Schema mechanisms also predict that outcome. In addition to cataloguing people or legal problems quickly and efficiently, schemas can incline us to attribute various beliefs to someone. We then attach subsequent interpretations consistent with those impressions. Thus, our 'good student' schema tells us that that person succeeds in school. We may also attach negative characteristics to an otherwise positive schema.[57] 'Good student' might also signify sycophantism. And if our good-student schema includes sycophantism, we may overly attend to hints of currying favour by that student. We might mistrust a new individual simply because something about them resonates with schema components.[58] Accordingly, once the court connects bootstrapping or cheating to openly gay or lesbian plaintiffs' gender-stereotyping claims, those plaintiffs lose, while non-gay plaintiffs win.[59]

Conclusion

As one court perceptively noted,

> We recognize that distinguishing between failure to adhere to sex stereo-
> types (a sexual stereotyping claim permissible under Title VII) and
> discrimination based on sexual orientation (a claim not covered by Title VII)
> may be difficult. This is especially true in cases in which a perception
> of homosexuality itself may result from an impression of non-conformance
> with sexual stereotypes. A homophobic epithet like 'fag' for example,
> may be as much of a disparagement of a man's perceived effeminate quali-
> ties as it is of his perceived sexual orientation. ... It is not always possible to
> rigidly compartmentalize the types of bias that these types of epithets
> represent.[60]

The rigid compartmentalisation required by anti-discrimination doctrine lies at
the root of these issues and contributes to the way in which schematic analysis
distorts legal reasoning. The law requires strict separation between sexual
orientation and gender; litigants and judges are forced to classify in ways that
social scientists often do not and that empirical research shows people generally
may not.[61] Rather than being generally distinct categories, sexual-orientation
prejudice and discrimination often link, for example, to gender and racial bias;
such categories are mutually reinforcing and not rigidly separate.[62] Accordingly,
Title VII's legal constructs requiring sharp classifications between race, ethnicity,
sex, sexual orientation, etc., necessitate distinctions that are often counter-factual
to how people behave. They do not capture the conflations and differentiations
that some individuals make.[63] According to cognitive models, the courts' search
for motivations that completely exclude alternatives is problematic. Correlations
among a range of explanations are more likely.[64] Moreover, if sexual minorities'
schemas interact differently with sexual orientation and gender than do those of
the harassers, or the judges who must decide these cases, then harmonising these
disparate views will be virtually impossible – leaving each participant puzzled or
unsatisfied by others' decisions. Judges will have difficulty accepting plaintiffs'
testimony; plaintiffs will be unclear why they were harassed; and harassers will
mistakenly blend sexual orientation with gender. Consequently, cases will be
inconsistent and under-theorised.

Additionally, regulations protecting against both sex and sexual orientation
discrimination do not, without more, solve the underlying problem that schemas
reveal, although such regulations may alter outcomes. Even when sexual orientation forms a protected class, we still need to legally distinguish between sexual
orientation and sex or gender discrimination – a task fraught with the same
pitfalls and problems demonstrated by this analysis of current US law. Nevertheless, the consequences of improper analysis, i.e. analysis skewed by our schemas of lesbians or gay men, are minimised, to some extent at least, in situations

where both sexual-orientation discrimination and sex discrimination are included within the law's explicit protections.

Judges who understand social cognition can see why court participants may appear inconsistent or to think in ways that the judges find unusual or incomprehensible. Judges may appreciate that their perceptions of events are also shaped by unconscious and idiosyncratic schemas and do not simply chronicle what has occurred. That knowledge can make them mindful of alternative explanations or answers. Of equal importance, jurists and legal scholars may recognise that the sharp classifications that non-discrimination law demands, and the jurisprudential consistency we prefer, must be tempered by a pragmatic acceptance of the limits of doctrine in capturing reality.

Notes

1 For example, A. Brower and P. Nurius, *Social Cognition and Individual Change: Current Theory and Counseling Guidelines* (Newbury Park, Calif.: Sage Publications, 1993), pp. 14–15. See also C. E. Cohen, 'Goals and Schemata in Person Perception: Making Sense from the Stream of Behavior', in N. Cantor and J. F. Kilstrom (eds.), *Personality, Cognition, and Social Interaction* (Hillsdale, NJ: Lawrence Erlbaum, 1981).

2 Brower and Nurius, *Social Cognition and Individual Change*, p. 14.

3 See, for example, K. Clark and M. Clark, 'Racial Identification and Preference in Negro Children', in T. Newcomb and E. Harley (eds.), *Readings in Social Psychology* (New York: Henry Holt, 1947). See, for example, W. Williams, 'The Equality Crisis: Some Reflections on Culture, Courts, and Feminism', *Women's Rights Law Reporter*, 7 (3) (1982): 175–250; at p. 175; D. Stipp and A. H. Moore, 'Mirror, Mirror On the Wall, Who's the Fairest of Them All?', *Fortune*, 9 September 1996, pp. 86–7.

4 See, for example, J. Halley, 'The Politics of the Closet: Towards Equal Protection for Gay, Lesbian and Bisexual Identity', *UCLA Law Review*, 36 (5) (1989): 915–76; 915, 948; A. Taylor, 'Conceptions of Masculinity and Femininity as a Basis for Stereotypes of Male and Female Homosexuals', in M. W. Ross (ed.), *Homosexuality, Masculinity and Femininity* (New York: Herrington Park Press, 1985), pp. 37–53; p. 51.

5 42 USC § 2000 (e) et seq. (2000).

6 *Price Waterhouse* v. *Hopkins*, 490 US 228 (1989).

7 See, for example, *Hamm* v. *Weyauwega Milk Prods.*, 332 F.3d 1058, 1066–8 (7th Cir. 2003).

8 *Price Waterhouse*, 618 F. Supp. 1109, 1117 (DDC 1985).

9 *Price Waterhouse*, 618 F. Supp. 1109, 1112–13, 1117–20 (DDC 1985); *Price Waterhouse*, 825 F.2d 458, 463 (DCC 1987).

10 *Hamner* v. *St. Vincent Hosp. & Health Care Center*, 224 F.3d 701, 705–6 (7th Cir. 2000).

11 See *Bibby* v. *Philadelphia Coca Cola Bottling Co.*, 260 F.3d 257, 262 (3rd Cir. 2001); *Doe* v. *Bellville*, 119 F.3d 561, 598 (7th Cir. 1997); *Hamner*, 224 F.3d at 707 n.5.

12 *Adair* v. *Beech Aircraft Corp*, 782 F. Supp. 558, 562–3 (D. Kan. 1992).

13 *Hamner*, 224 F.3d at 703.

14 See, for example, *Mississippi University for Women* v. *Hogan*, 458 US 718, 729–30 (1982); 'Breaking Barriers', *Jersey Journal*, 8 May 2008, p. 17.

15 For example, *Strailey* v. *Happy Times Nursery*, 608 F.2d 327 (9th Cir. 1979); *Jantz* v. *Muci*, 759 F. Supp. 1543, 1545 (D. Kan.1991). See L. H. Krieger, 'The Content of Our Categories: A Cognitive Bias Approach to Discrimination and Equal Employment Opportunity', *Stanford Law Review*, 47 (5) (1995): 1161–1248; p. 1168.

16 K. L. Johnson, S. Gill, V. Reichman and L. G. Tassinary, 'Swagger, Sway and Sexuality: Judging Sexual Orientation from Body Motion and Morphology', *Journal of Personality and Social Psychology*, 93 (3) (2007): 321–334; p. 321.

17 For example, M. Dahl, 'Gay or Straight? Watch His Walk, New Study Suggests Body Movement Gives Clues to Sexual Orientation', *MSNBC*, 13 September 2007. Available online at http://www.msnbc.msn.com/id/20762841 (accessed 18 April 2009); R. Schneider Jnr., 'BTW, Science Prances On', *The Gay and Lesbian Review Worldwide*, 15 (1) (2008): 11–12; p. 11.

18 See, for example, F. Valdes, 'Queers, Sissies, Dykes and Tomboys: Deconstructing the Conflation of "Sex," "Gender" and "Sexual Orientation" in Euro-American Law and Society', *California Law Review*, 83 (1) (1995): 1–377; p. 1; M. A. Case, 'Disaggregating Gender from Sex and Sexual Orientation: The Effeminate Man in the Law and Feminist Jurisprudence', *Yale Law Journal*, 105 (1) (1995): 1–105; p. 1.

19 Valdes, 'Queers, Sissies, Dykes and Tomboys', pp. 139, nn. 396–7, 400, 144; *Smith* v. *Liberty Mut. Ins. Co.*, 395 F. Supp. 1098, 1101 (NDGa 1973).

20 See, for example, Brower and Nurius, *Social Cognition and Individual Change*, p. 54; M. R. Gottfried and C. Robins, 'Self Schemata, Cognitive Bias and the Processing of Therapeutic Experiences', in P. C. Kendall (ed.), *Advances in Cognitive-Behavioral Research and Therapy* (New York: Academic Press, 1983), pp. 33–9; J. Kilstrom and N. Cantor, 'Mental Representations of the Self', in L. Berkowitz (ed.), *Advances in Experimental Social Psychology* (New York: Academic Press, 1984), vol. XVII, pp. 1–47.

21 Valdes, 'Queers, Sissies, Dykes and Tomboys', p. 139.

22 Ibid., pp. 146–7.

23 Ibid., p. 146.

24 *Smith*, 395 F. Supp. at 1099; *Smith*, 569 F.2d at 327.

25 See *Fudge* v. *Penthouse Int'l*, 840 F.2d 1012, 1016 (1st Cir. 1988).

26 See S. Forsythe, 'Effect of Applicant's Clothing on Interviewers' Decision to Hire', *Journal of Applied Social Psychology*, 20 (19) (1990): 1579–95; p. 1579.

27 See Rosemary Hunter, Chapter 2.

28 R. Levenson, 'Sex Discrimination in Employment Practices: An Experiment with Unconventional Job Inquiries', in R. Kahn-Hut (ed.), *Women and Work: Problems and Perspectives* (New York: Oxford University Press, 1982), pp. 54–64; p. 61.

29 Compare the courts' sympaties to the female plaintiffs in *Price Waterhouse* (accountant) with *Valdes* v. *Lumbermen's Mutual Casualty Co.*, 507 F. Supp. 10 (SDFla. 1980) (lower level warehouse employee).

30 Levenson, 'Sex Discrimination in Employment Practices', p. 61.

31 L. Serbin and C. H. Sprafkin, 'A Developmental Approach: Sexuality from Infancy through Adolescence', in J. H. Geer and W. T. O'Donohue (eds.), *Theories of Homosexuality* (New York: Plenum, 1987), pp. 163–95; p. 177; Levenson, 'Sex Discrimination in Employment Practices', p. 61.

32 R. H. Lauer and W. H. Handel, *Social Psychology: The Theory and Application of Symbolic Interaction*, 2nd edn (Englewood Cliffs, NJ: Prentice-Hall, 1983); Brower and Nurius, *Social Cognition and Individual Change*, pp. 13–14.

33 See *Oncale* v. *Sundowner Offshore Servs., Inc.*, 523 US 75, 77 (1998); *Vickers* v. *Fairfield Med. Center*, 453 F.3d 757, 763, 763 n2 (6th Cir. 2006); *Simonton* v. *Runyon*, 232 F.3d 33, 35 (2nd Cir. 2000); *Rene* v. *MGM Grand Hotel*, 243 F.3d 1206, 1211 (9th Cir. 2001).

34 See, for example, G. Chauncy Jnr., 'Christian Brotherhood or Sexual Perversion? Homosexual Identities and the Construction of Sexual Boundaries in the World War I Era', in M. Duberman, M. Vicinus and G. Chauncy Jnr. (eds.), *Hidden from History: Reclaiming the Gay and Lesbian Past* (New York: Meridian Books, 1989), pp. 294–317; p. 297; T. Almaguer, 'Chicano Men: A Cartography of Homosexual Identity and

Behavior', in H. Abelove, M. A. Barale and D. H. Halperin (eds.), *The Lesbian and Gay Studies Reader* (London and New York: Routledge, 1993), pp. 256–8.

35 C. MacKinnon, *Sexual Harassment of Working Women: A Case of Sex Discrimination* (New Haven, Conn.: Yale University Press, 1979), p. 237.

36 *Bibby v. Philadelphia Coca Cola Bottling Co.*, 260 F.3d 257, 259–60 (3rd Cir. 2001); *Nichols v. Azteca Restaurant Enterprises, Inc.*, 256 F.3d 864 (9th Cir 2001).

37 For example, *Price Waterhouse*, 490 US 228; *Adair*, 782 F. Supp. 558; *Mongomery v. Indep. Sch. Dist.*, No. 703, 109 F. Supp. 2d 1081 (D. Minn 2000).

38 *Doe*, 119 F.3d 563, pp. 566–8.

39 *Spearman v. Ford Motor Co.*, 231 F.3d 1080, 1086 (7th Cir. 2000).

40 *Dawson*, 398 F.3d at p. 213.

41 *Dawson*, 398 F.3d at p. 215.

42 *Dawson v. Bumble & Bumble*, 398 F.3d 211, 213–15, 221–23 (2nd Cir. 2005); *Dawson*, 246 F. Supp. 2d 301, 314–18 (SDNY 2003).

43 D. E. Rumelhart, 'Schemata and the Cognitive System', in R. S. Wyer Jnr. and T. K. Srull (eds.), *Handbook of Social Cognition* (Hillsdale, NJ: Lawrence Erlbaum, 1984), vol. I, pp. 161–88; p. 166.

44 *Dawson*, 246 F. Supp. 2d at 311 (internal citations omitted).

45 See Valdes, 'Queers, Sissies, Dykes and Tomboys', pp. 104–6; E. Q. Shults, 'Sharply Drawn Lines: An Examination Of Title IX, Intersex, and Transgender', *Cardozo Journal of Law and Gender*, 12 (1) (2005): 337–51; pp. 337, 341.

46 E. L. Kennedy and M. Davis, '"They Was No One to Mess With": The Construction of the Butch Role in the Lesbian Community of the 1940s and 1950s', in J. Nestle (ed.), *The Persistent Desire: A Femme-Butch Reader* (New York: Alyson Press, 1992), p. 62.

47 See, for example, B. Denizet-Lewis, 'Putting on a Good Face: Lipstick Lesbians May Favor Makeup and Dress-Up over Political Activism, but Their Very Existence Rejects the Stereotype That Femininity Is Reserved for Straight Women', *The Boston Globe*, 2 March 2003, p. 11.

48 *Dawson*, 246 F. Supp. 2d, at 311.

49 Brower and Nurius, *Social Cognition and Individual Change*, p. 28.

50 *Dawson*, 398 F.3d at p. 218.

51 For how sexual-orientation visibility affects lesbians and gay men, see T. Brower, 'Of Courts and Closets: A Doctrinal and Empirical Analysis of Lesbian and Gay Identity in the Courts', *San Diego Law Review*, 38 (2) (2001): 565–628; p. 565.

52 Cf. K. M. Bovalino, 'How the Effeminate Male Can Maximize His Odds of Winning Title VII Litigation', *Syracuse Law Review*, 53 (3) (2003): 1117–38; p. 1134.

53 A. Tversky and D. Kahneman, 'Availability: A Heuristic for Judging Frequency Probability', *Cognitive Psychology*, 5 (2) (1973): 207–32; p. 207. See Leslie J. Moran, Chapter 6.

54 *Doe*, 119 F 3d at pp. 566–7.

55 T. Brower, 'Multistable Figures: Sexual Orientation, Visibility and Its Effect on the Experiences of Sexual Minorities in the Courts', *Pace Law Review*, 27 (2) (2007): 141–98; pp. 165–71.

56 See, for example, *Bibby*, 260 F.3d at 261; *Heller*, 195 F. Supp. 2d at 1224.

57 Brower and Nurius, *Social Cognition and Individual Change*, p. 14.

58 *Jantz*, 759 F. Supp. at 1545.

59 Compare *Price Waterhouse* and *Back v. Hastings on Hudson Union Free Sch. Dist.*, 365 F.3d 107 (2nd Cir 2004) discussed in *Dawson*. Neither case accused those female plaintiffs of bootstrapping.

60 *Hamm*, 332 F.3d at 1065 n.5.

61 Cf. C. Freshman, 'Whatever Happened to Anti-Semitism? How Social Science Theories Identify Discrimination and Promote Coalitions Between "Different" Minorities', *Cornell Law Review*, 85 (1) (2000): 313–442; pp. 313–14.

62 See, for example, M. M. Bierly, 'Prejudice toward Contemporary Outgroups as a Generalized Attitude', *Journal of Applied Social Psychology*, 15 (3) (1995): 189–99; p. 189; N. M. Henley and F. Pincus, 'Interrelationship of Sexist, Racist, and Antihomosexual Attitudes', *Psychological Reports*, 42 (1) (1978): 83–90; p. 83.

63 See K. Crenshaw, 'Race, Gender and Sexual Harassment', *Southern California Law Review*, 65 (3) (1992): 1467–76; p. 1467; L. McCall, 'The Complexity of Intersectionality', in E. Grabham, D. Cooper, J. Krishnadas and D. Herman (eds.), *Intersectionality and Beyond: Law, Power and the Politics of Location* (London: Routledge-Cavendish, 2008), pp. 49–76; p. 49.

64 E. DeSouza and J. Solberg, 'Women's and Men's Reactions to Man-to-Man Sexual Harassment: Does the Sexual Orientation of the Victim Matter?', *Sex Roles*, 50 (9–10) (2003): 623–39; 632–4.

Chapter 8

The gendered dock

Reflections on the impact of gender stereotyping in the criminal-justice system

Judith Rowbotham

Introduction

Recently, the depiction of women in the criminal-justice process has been contextualised by growing concerns about women's visibility as defendants. The gendered expectations which are an inextricable part of the modern trial process have been challenged by their enhanced visibility, but how far and in what (positive) ways has this challenge affected such expectations? Since the 1990s, commentary has reflected on the extent to which females have increasingly perpetrated offences which are not those traditionally associated with women (property crimes and regulatory offences). They now commonly include interpersonal violence, for instance, thereby investing their offending with a more 'masculine' profile. British Crime Surveys indicate that in 2007–8, 13 per cent of violent crimes were committed by women, with a significant female involvement in a further 11 per cent, entailing a rise of 24 per cent on the 2001–2 levels in the Survey. Police forces also admitted to disquiet about violence committed by all-girl gangs.[1] This unease about female offending reveals how profoundly gendered our gaze on the criminal-justice system remains. As this chapter will demonstrate by drawing on historical illustrations, a gendered perspective has long been an inextricable element in the legal process. This has had a profound impact not just on women's encounters with the courts but also on the male experience of the criminal-justice system.

Equality and the law

Equality before the law has, in theory at least, always been an advertised aim of the English legal process. There was a concerted legislative effort throughout the twentieth century to ensure the equal status of men and women in society and before the law (Sex Discrimination Act 1919, Matrimonial Causes Act 1923, Equal Pay Act 1970, Sex Discrimination Act 1975). One constant problem is that, strictly, equality presumes a quality of being the same, in quantity or value. Therein lies (and always has!) the rub for promoting gender equality via legislation. It is difficult to legislate for the essentially emotional, rather than cerebral, process of establishing a balance in societal esteem.

A functional criminal-justice system must always reflect such societal values in order to sustain its necessary support from the community, ensuring that there is, in practice, an emotional dimension to legal decisions, both in the broad nature of a type of crime and in individual examples. This dimension has consistently been enhanced by the tone of media reportage of cases involving exercise of a gendered judgement. The dilemma is that what is perceived to be a 'just' balance must be at the heart of any genuine equality, whether in the community or the criminal-justice system. Given that a crime is presumed to be an act that damages the welfare of the whole community, not just the aggrieved individual, it inevitably becomes an issue of moral as much as of legal judgement. As Hart has commented, law is rooted in social rules, inflected by moral opinion, reflecting also that, practically, aspects of legal rules will be deduced and so be acknowledged as existing without their being previously formally inscribed.[2]

The usual mantra in today's Britain is that equality is moderated by consideration for diversity.[3] The objective is not to treat every individual in the same way but rather to ensure equity in the sense of 'fairness': acknowledging difference but managing it positively to achieve 'equity'.[4] In practice, such vagueness means that there are always unvoiced assumptions surrounding the strict letter of the law. One way that these become visible is in the contextualising comments of legal professionals when commending conformity to usual practice or when justifying 'deviation' from it on extraordinary grounds. The law of equity originally developed as a means of modifying a perceived harshness of the common law by utilising a set of culturally derived legal principles, relating to accepted concepts of 'natural justice' that sanctioned use of a due modifying discretion by the courts.[5]

Relating this to gender, historically, the law, especially the criminal law, has been masculine in its conception and orientation. Women have, as during the medieval and early modern periods, regularly used the courts as prosecutors or appeared as witnesses in cases.[6] But despite (or because of) this, feminine encounters with the criminal-justice process have always been problematic, and not just in direct juxtaposition to masculine experiences in the courts. The constant contextualisation of women's criminality in terms of their wider socio-economic roles in society promoted associated assumptions about female competence and the desirability of feminine dependence.[7] Such assumptions equally shaped expectations of how men would perform, both in society and the courts, given that gendered identity is 'instituted through a *stylized repetition of acts*'.[8]

Gender and rates of offending

During the eighteenth century there was a visible decline in use of the ecclesiastical courts and, in consequence, an increasing reliance on statute law.[9] Criminality became secularised as more activities (including aspects of personal misbehaviour) previously dealt with by the ecclesiastical courts became matters of temporal concern. It became removed thereby from direct moral judgements equating crime with 'sin'.[10] The moral dimension has never entirely disappeared. However, with crime becoming something formally identified via statute law as a 'normal', if undesirable, secular activity, it assumed the character of an essentially masculine expression of 'bad' behaviour. Women benefited less from this secularising process, especially in the popular gaze which has insisted on maintaining the moral dimension to women's offending, as any survey of comment on modern press stories underlines.[11]

This has conferred on the woman offender a double layer of offending. For example, given that male criminality was 'normal', it was also intrinsically less threatening; leaving female criminality to be characterised as, *ab initio*, *ab*normal, a judgement reflecting on both the deed and the individual. One early criminologist reflected that 'female criminals are infinitely worse than the worst of male criminals'.[12] This negative perspective was enhanced by the reactions of women themselves. Women valued their status as moral arbiters in society, believing it conferred on them both status and power in daily interactions with men. Consequently, even early feminists failed to challenge interpretations emphasising the peculiar moral deviance of woman criminals. This facilitated assumptions that women offenders were a threat to the welfare of society on a scale which men could not match.[13] Deviant masculinities (usually associated with homosexual behaviour in the modern period) have never been identified as equally threatening.[14]

Legal issues shaping the criminalisation of acts or individuals are always complex. Recognition that a crime is culturally as well as legally injurious to the welfare of a community is moderated by ever-changing conceptualisations of that welfare. Consequently, what constitutes criminality in a society will always remain fluid. One feature of modernity has been an increased will manifested by the state, with apparent societal consent, to promote order by expanding the criminalisation process to include ever more actions held to be actually or potentially deleterious to community welfare, whether occurring in a private or a public sphere.[15] Hence the rise to current prominence of regulatory offences in the current over-criminalisation afflicting the UK. It therefore becomes important to identify how that criminalisation process reflects the cultural expectations of any society viewing the conduct of individuals when spotlighted in the courts, using various reportage formats from newspapers to law reports.

At a certain level, a universal system such as the law must rely on stereotypes to establish those boundaries that enable distinctions to be made between offensive and actually offending behaviour. How far do such stereotype-based distinctions rely still on historically engrained assumptions, making them significantly inflected by gendered expectations of individual conduct and understanding?

Female visibility in the criminal-justice system and the gendered implications

It can be easier to comment on the masculine dimension by looking first at the more extensively, if indignantly, documented feminine experience of the criminal-justice system. This is because the interdependent nature of gender relationships enables useful inferences to be made about expectations and stereotypes associated with the silent element to the equation, reversing the process pursued in *Hidden from History*.[16] Legal commentary and media reportage of women within the criminal-justice process in the past two centuries reveals that by the end of the eighteenth century the 'normal' expectation related to women participating in that process as victims of crime, directly or indirectly. Good women's moral sensibilities were, for instance, presumed to be so afflicted by being the victim of or witnessing a crime that they would be unable to describe events in a rational way.[17]

This explains the emphasis placed by practitioners like Fitzjames Stephen on the need for women to be specially protected within and by the law, ensuring a perpetuation of associated assumptions that any *good* woman's 'normal' experience of the criminal-justice process would relate to male perpetrators of crime. Practically speaking, good women were endowed with a status that actively conceptualised them as either present but passive actors within the male-managed legal process or as absent arbiters of the moral damage done to the welfare of the community.[18] For preference, male witnesses could report female reactions to crime women witnessed in ways intended to guide the courts in assessing the relative seriousness of an individual offence. Good women were thus implicitly expected to be practically invisible in the legal process and particularly in the masculine courtroom space.

This effective invisibility of good women was complemented by the condemnations hurled at bad women: those who either perpetrated or promoted criminal acts. Analysis of prosecution rates at the Assizes and Quarter Sessions has encouraged a view that, historically, the woman criminal was a declining category.[19] King, however, has pointed out that a universal case for such a decline ignores the extent to which women's crimes were increasingly relocated to the lower courts.[20] As the modern criminal-justice process evolved, this meant that until the late twentieth century it has seemed increasingly masculine despite women's continuing low-level involvement. Masculine comprehensions of the boundaries to and reasons for criminality, along with associated management strategies, were the governing logic. Thus, any dissenting feminine input became labelled as illogical because of accompanying assumptions about women's 'naturally' emotional natures.[21]

The Victorian period is crucial, as the era when the modern criminal-justice process took on its recognisably modern shape. As a result of the Jervis Acts (Justices Protection Act 1848, Summary Jurisdiction Act 1848, Indictable Offences Act 1848), the modern average of 93 per cent of criminal prosecutions being for summary offences became established.[22] The guinea fee for a summons ensured that Victorian men and women could fairly readily take advantage of the increased opportunity to bring a prosecution to a successful conclusion in the summary courts. It was also the era when a modern mass media in the shape of newspaper reportage developed. That reportage placed a heavy concentration on daily news from the courts, because of the appetite of readers for such news. Reportage from the courts in this period was generally written by legal personnel.[23] This attests to the legal accuracy of the reportage, but examination also reveals its profoundly gendered nature. Women's use of the courts to bring, for example, domestic-violence prosecutions also placed a sharper focus on the masculine aspects of crime. But, using satire as a tool to diminish this development, Victorian newspapers also regularly depicted women as invading the masculine courtroom space by insisting on their right to act as key witnesses in establishing the parameters of criminal events, for instance, and producing thereby a disorder that challenged masculine authority.

Many nineteenth-century legal professionals were uneasy at best with the challenge presented by women. The record of Serjeant Ballantyne clearly attests to his distrust of women's ability to distinguish 'truth' from fiction, referring to what he described as the 'ingenuities of the female mind', amongst other disparaging comments on feminine capacity to act competently within the criminal-justice system.[24] Such men generally considered women to be, *ab initio*, incompetent witnesses.[25] Some legal theorists, notably Fitzjames Stephen, argued that the ability of the law to deliver 'justice' would be best served by excluding women from the courts, leaving it to men to act on their behalf. He argued that the regular presence of female plaintiffs has 'seriously' affected 'public interests', because 'there is a peculiar tortuousness and intricacy about female cases, arising either from a hopeless confusion of facts, or from an absence of facts altogether'. For him, 'The darlings have nothing whatsoever to do with justice.' Justice was a masculine concept, best achieved by making the courts 'a sort of male harem'.[26] If few would have gone quite so far as Stephen, the British emphasis on masculine dominance of the criminal-justice system as the only way to safeguard justice helps to explain the sustained resistance to women as legal professionals in England and Wales.[27] However, this insistence on female legal *in*competence placed an equal insistence on a conceptualisation of a 'normal' male competence to deal logically and effectively with the law.

Gender and the performance/presentation of crimes involving sex and violence

Masculine competence within the courtroom ensured that there, men inevitably intruded on what was, in daily community life, considered the feminine arena of making moral judg(e)ments. The competing moral perspectives on criminality, in and outside the courts, has consequently been considered particularly unfair by feminist commentators because of the unmediated emphasis on the immoral female, as opposed to male, dimension to offending. Even at the start of the twenty-first century, moral pronouncements from the courts have had their most obvious impacts on women, providing testimony to the ongoing relevance and impact of the gendered Victorian constructions of criminality.

Back in 1870, a *Daily Telegraph* editorial insisted that 'No call for public sympathy', was presented by the case of Alice Grantham. A young woman in 'delicate health' and unable to work, Grantham had lived with William Davies, convicted of stealing silk from his employer to maintain his household. Davies received seven years penal servitude, but the court agreed that 'Although Alice Grantham herself did not steal the silk dresses, she lured on Davies to ruin' by committing herself to an immoral relationship. Consequently she was 'hardly less guilty therefore than the man', and was awarded five years penal servitude.[28] Like others, including Edith Thompson, executed in 1923, Grantham was a morally transgressive female and, from a modern perspective, inequitably condemned by the criminal-justice system not on legal grounds but on societally endorsed moral ones. Has the gendered moral differential shown up by such outcomes disappeared? A comparison of recent judgments suggests they have not. In 2005, soldier Andrew Wragg, recently returned from overseas service, was convicted only of manslaughter by a jury when he admitted killing his disabled son and given a two-year suspended sentence. By contrast, devoted mother Frances Inglis was convicted of murder in 2009 for killing her disabled son and awarded a life sentence. The judge told her that 'you cannot take the law into your own hands'. No such comment was made in Wragg's case, indicating continuance of the gendered moral differential.[29]

The chronology of the treatment of both sexual crimes and interpersonal violence (which often overlap) within the criminal-justice system, reflecting on both change and continuity in gendered attitudes in the courts and their reportage, also provides revealing insights. Study reveals the enduring influence of Victorian stereotypes on the workings of the modern criminal-justice system. A consideration of the implications of the concepts of incitement and seduction and their legal realities is informative. Seduction, defined as a man persuading a chaste woman into sexual intercourse, had a presence in common law that did not survive the rise of statute law.[30] This was because, as Stephen pointed out, it was essentially a moral offence, or sin, not a strictly legal breach, which made it unsuitable for translation into the more robustly masculine arena of statute law.[31] The Criminal Law Amendment Act 1885 reimagined the terminology of seduction in the context of *female* persuasion or incitement into intercourse. It became a felony to 'seduce' a girl under thirteen and a misdemeanour to 'seduce' one between thirteen and sixteen. However, an enduring mitigation, certainly for incidents involving girls between thirteen and sixteen was 'evidence' that a girl had incited a defendant into his unlawful action. This had the power to transform the man's moral status at least, identifying him culturally as the victim and thereby enabling the court to take legal account of this aspect of a case, as with the example of *R* v. *Tyrrell* 1893. Aged thirteen, Jane Tyrrell was convicted of 'aiding and abetting' and also for 'soliciting and inciting' Thomas Ford to commit a misdemeanour, to whit of having 'carnal knowledge' of herself. The court was told that she had solicited the sexual contact, testimony then considered entirely plausible. While the conviction was overturned on appeal, the justification for this overturning clearly indicated the gendered con-textualisation in which the law was operating.[32] Coleridge, LCJ, concluded that because the relevant provisions of the Criminal Law Amendment Act 1885 had been intended to 'protect' women, it would be a *reductio ad absurdum* if the Act was then used to convict an under-age girl. If Tyrrell had had the capacity to initiate sexual contact, the fragility of female chastity accompanied by the general lack of female rationality in giving consent meant that such girls required protection against *themselves*, not men. His conclusion also enabled the male perpetrator, Thomas Froud to escape the legal and moral consequences of his action, as Tyrrell's 'seduction' was held to have elicited an entirely 'normal' masculine reaction.[33]

The full details of the encounter cannot be extracted from records of the concurrent Tyrrell trials, as its 'particulars' were deemed 'unfit for publication'.[34] This phraseology was commonly used by both newspapers and the courts when placing cases on public record, essentially because of an anticipated feminine constituency in their public audience which needed protection against such information.[35] Today, the correlation between female chastity and respectability, and popular expectations linked to the feminine stereotype, have, in theory, changed significantly, though rape victims might challenge this. But, at the same time, recent cases involving the concept of 'incitement' indicate that the law remains powerfully gendered. This differently disadvantages men and women because of the ways in which gender expectations continue to contextualise legal judgments, as with Nigel Thomson's recent conviction for having sex with a thirteen-year-old girl. Thomson received a suspended sentence from Mrs Justice Moffat because the girl had 'made the running', meaning that Moffat effectively reached the same gendered conclusion as *Tyrrell* in 1893, with the same socially perjorative reflection on the pivotal female. She commented that 'although she was vulnerable, you too in a sense, are vulnerable as you are a simple man. What occurred was stupidity rather than malice' – making it worth reflecting on how her comment and those of Thomson's lawyers will have affected Thomson's masculine status.[36]

Reportage of another recent case further highlights the problems facing the courts in reaching conclusions that reconcile, rather than divide, the wider community. The coverage in question dealt with the release of two 'foolish, ill-advised lads' who had had sex with a twelve-year-old unnamed girl. Originally sentenced to four years for statutory rape, they were released by the Court of Appeal on the grounds that they had been 'punished enough', especially because the court deemed the girl to have been 'promiscuous', as well as having lied about her age. In the reportage, the girl's mother was 'horrified', and feminist campaigners were outraged that a 'vulnerable child' was not protected by the courts. Feminist outrage that the Court of Appeal took account of the victim's lifestyle when commuting the sentences to community service was exacerbated by the gender of the judge, Mrs Justice Rafferty. She accepted that the youths had been 'genuinely' shocked to find the girl was as young as twelve and agreed with the defence that the sentence had been 'manifestly excessive'.[37]

What these two recent examples suggest is that, despite the advent of a female sexual liberation in the past half century, social attitudes expressed through the criminal-justice system have remained profoundly ambiguous about female sexual activity that can in any way be labelled 'promiscuous', in contrast to a continuing popular acceptance of indiscriminate male sexual activity as 'normal'.[38] Historically, chastity was a defining attribute of respectability in females. Chastity was a key element even in women's own estimation of their social value because it established the superior moral status that women prized.[39] While sympathy for a sexually assaulted woman or girl was possible, the need to protect girls (including from themselves) was central to legal and cultural thought. This located the moral responsibility for masculine sexual deviance upon feminine shoulders. Women had to demonstrate that they had offered no enticement which could be misunderstood by a 'normal' male to evade this responsibility.[40] In both the recent cases involving underage sex cited here, the girls were blamed by the courts, albeit less explicitly than in the historical past, for their 'precocious' attitude to sex or 'promiscuous' habits. This thereby relieved or mitigated the impact of the male promiscuity involved, notwith-standing the equitable intentions of the Sexual Offences Act 2003. None of these cases involved violence in association with the sexual dimension to the cases, but former Director of Public Prosecutions, Sir Ken MacDonald, has recently argued (in relation to rape in the context of alcohol abuse) that the 'promiscuity' of modern women has made it increasingly difficult to obtain rape convictions in British courts, another oblique reference to enhanced female responsibility when allocating blame in rape prosecutions.[41] This underlines the extent to which an aggressive sexuality is still conceived of as 'normally' masculine. Male culpability is thereby depicted as dependent on their lack of restraint, not their 'natural' sexual instincts.[42]

The role of alcohol in inflecting attitudes towards violent criminal incidents involving violence is also illuminating. There is a long tradition, apparently backed by general scientific surveys, of accepting the masculine taste for drink as being more 'normal' than any similar feminine inclination, allied to accep-tance of a superior masculine capacity to manage the negative impacts of alcohol upon their social conduct.[43] Ken MacDonald explicitly identified drink as a factor promoting unacceptable female conduct when discussing strategies for improving the statistics of rape convictions.[44] While Vera Baird has referred to the 'huge political will' behind attempts to ensure that courts do not continue the tradition where drunken women were conceived as having wilfully rendered themselves incapable of giving or denying consent to intercourse, the evidence of recent jury decisions is that this political perspective has yet to win public endorsement.[45] There remains, though, a more forgiving attitude to criminal actions associated with male drunkenness, enshrining a destructive aspect of cultural masculinity in the law. Men are still not considered eligible for protection from themselves in most judgments, cultural and legal.[46]

Generally, the purpose of the criminal-justice system in dealing with masculine violence has been regularly to refresh the parameters surrounding 'acceptable' forms of male force. In this, the scientific labelling of testosterone as a 'masculine' hormone has provided hitherto-unassailable grounds justifying cultural and legal attitudes identifying male violence as 'normal' and 'natural'.[47] The law in action has habitually echoed popular sympathies in demonstrating a contextual under-standing of incidents where some acceptable explanation for a male resort to force could be identified. In terms of male-on-male violence, for instance, Justice Brett, in 1875, and 'for the sake of laws and good government', drew a 'marked distinction' between episodes where 'cowardice and unfairness take place', and those where, as a result of human 'infirm nature', a quarrel would arise which 'normal' and 'manly' men would seek to resolve physically, in the shape of a 'fair fight'.[48] A degree of leniency has consistently been shown towards criminal vio-lence taking place in civilian contexts but involving soldiers recently involved in conflict (as in the Wragg case) something popularly presumed to increase immediately after wars. Ironically, a direct association between an increase in violent crime and post-conflict situations in the UK is not sustained by the sta-tistics. The reality behind those statistics has probably helped in maintaining such popular empathy with defendants presumed to be affected by the 'brutalising' effects of war when seeking to return to a civilian normality.[49]

Female violence is culturally less acceptable than male violence because of the reluctance of society to accept violence as a 'natural' expression of femininity. There is a much greater reliance on external factors (including alcohol or abu-sive upbringings) in any attempt to explain and so justify female violence coming to the attention of the courts. Female-on-female violence has stereotypically been seen as quintessentially lacking in real force or brutality, involving 'unscientific' and by implication less painful or (in the long term) damaging strategies such as hair-pulling or scratching with long nails.[50] Women are not supposed to be 'good' at fighting. Contextualising cultural attitudes include the opposition to female boxing, seen as peculiarly damaging to the welfare of the community as well as to the individual women involved.[51] There is also the continuing emphasis in the reportage on the gender of those killed in conflict, testifying to an enduring popular disquiet over the location of women in active service (unless engaged in a caring role, such as nursing). By contrast, while there may be unhappiness over British involvement in particular conflicts, notably the war in Iraq from 2003, there is a popular acceptance that for men military conflict is not just acceptable – it is admirable. Formalised expressions of violence in this public arena remain quintessentially masculine, and this has undoubtedly had an impact on the operative expectations of the criminal-justice system.[52]

The perspective of the criminal-justice system on crime within the private sphere equally remains gendered. Female abusers acting within domestic or quasi-domestic situations (notably child-minding) have become a more visible fea-ture of the recent criminal-justice landscape. Research shows that historically they were simply less recognised, rather than absent.[53] Female abusers are consistently identified as peculiarly unnatural and 'deviant', as in the case of Karen Matthews as well as Vanessa George, because their very femininity enhances the outrage at their crimes. Men such as Ian Huntley or Peter Tobin are described as evil or twisted in their child abuse, but their masculine instincts are held to 'explain', if not justify, their impulsion to offend.[54] The surprised horror expressed by the courts and media reportage over the actions of teenage girls who terrorise and brutally assault elderly women provides another reinforcing dimension to the gendered expectations associated with criminal violence. Femininity remains associated primarily with physical and emotional gentleness, leaving aggression within the normal masculine sphere.[55]

Conclusion

Taking as a starting point the truism that the law 'is not simply a corpus of practical rules' but a part of the ongoing 'discourse about good and bad states of society', this chapter has explored the enduring issues relating to equity and gender in the criminal-justice process.[56] The 'associations between gender and crime are profound, persistent and paradoxical'; because for as long as people have recorded crime, 'it has been noted that men and women differ in their offence rates and patterns'.[57] There are current 'safeguards' in the law relating to women, but not to men, which are seen by many as inequitable, most notably the anonymity granted to adult women claiming rape but not to adult male defendants. The gender-based primacy given to women as mothers, deriving primarily from the sad Victorian case of Lady Caroline Norton, is now hardly justifiable as a theoretical base for custody judgments demonstrating an equal value for men and women in their parental roles. Courts are beginning to acknowledge this, but fathers still see themselves as unfairly disadvantaged so long as the criminal-justice system remains apparently reluctant to criminalise mothers. It has to be admitted that this gender bias still has a considerable degree of popular support. When, in one recent child-custody case, a child was given into his father's care because of the 'deficient' mothering skills displayed by his mother, the actions of Mr Justice Bond and Lord Justice Wall were uneasily received in the reportage.[58] This enduringly gendered social tension undoubtedly makes it difficult for the courts to achieve a better or more equitable gender balance. However, the persistence of gendered attitudes cannot be condemned as automatically perverse and inequitable. The need is not to avoid gender stereotyping, which is practically and theoretically impossible. It is instead important for the criminal-justice system to develop a conscious awareness of this reality as a continuing issue which is, of itself, neither automatically negative nor positive in its workings. Only then can the courts develop an ability to take gender into equitable consideration, questioning whether practices and conclusions are being adversely affected by gendered assumptions, in order to reach decisions which can be readily explained so that they can be recognised as equitable by both the law and the wider community.

Notes

1 C. Kershaw, S. Nicholas and A. Walker, *Crime in England and Wales 2007/8*, vol. I, Home Office Statistical Bulletin. Available online at http://www.homeoffice.gov.uk/rds/crimeew0708.html (accessed 4 January 2010).

2 H. Hart, 'Positivism and the Separation of Law and Morals', *Harvard Law Review*, 7 (1958): 593–629, at p. 607. Also H. Hart, *Law, Liberty and Morality* (Oxford: Oxford University Press, 1963), pp. 47, 50–1.

3 D. Ben-Galim, Mary Campbell and Jane Lewis, 'Equality and Diversity: A New Approach to Gender Equality Policy in the UK', *International Journal of Law in Context*, 3 (2007): 19–33.

4 Equality Act 2006. See also B. Hepple, Mary Coussey and T. Choudhury, *Equality: A New Framework* (Oxford: Hart Publishing, 2000).

5 J. H. Baker, *An Introduction to English Legal History* (Oxford: Oxford University Press, 2005), pp. 202–4. See also Aristotle, *Nichomachean Ethics*, ed. J. Ackrill, W. D. Ross, D. Ross and J. Urmson (Oxford: Oxford University Press, 1998).

6 See T. Stretton, *Women Waging Law in Elizabethan England* (Cambridge: Cambridge University Press, 1998).

7 J. Kermode and G. Walker, 'Introduction', in J. Kermode and G. Walker (eds.), *Women, Crime and the Courts in Early Modern England* (London and New York: Routledge, 1994), pp. 1–24.

8 J. Butler, 'Performative Acts and Gender Constitution: An Essay in Phenomenology and Feminist Theory', *Theatre Journal*, 40 (4) (1988): 519–31.

9 R. Outhwaite, *The Rise and Fall of the English Ecclesiastical Courts, 1500–1860* (Cambridge: Cambridge University Press, 2007).

10 J. Sharpe, 'The People and the Law', in B. Reay (ed.), *Popular Culture in Seventeenth-Century England* (London and New York: Routledge, 1988), pp. 244–70; pp. 263–4.

11 For instance, reaction to Vanessa George, expressed in comments for the *Mail Online*. Available online at http://www.dailymail.co.uk/news/article-1217415/Nursery-worker-Vanessa-George-internet-accomplices-plead-guilty-sexually-assaulting-young-children.html (accessed 13 January 2010).

12 H. Adam, *Police Work from Within, with Some Reflections upon Women, the Law and Lawyers* (London: Holden and Hardingham, 1908), p. 36.

13 M. Fawcett, *Mr. Fitzjames Stephen on the Position of Women* (London: Macmillan & Co., 1873).

14 *R v. Boulton and Others (Park)* 1871 12 Cox CC 87; *The Times*, 7 May 1870, 14 May 1870; See also L. Bibbings, *Binding Men: Nineteenth Century Criminal Cases and the Policing of Masculinity* (London: Routledge-Cavendish, 2009).

15 E. Avdela, S. D'Cruze and J. Rowbotham, 'Introduction: De-centring Violence History', in E. Avdela, S. D'Cruze and J. Rowbotham (eds.), *Crime, Violence and the Modern State* (Lampeter: Mellen Press, 2010), pp. 1–42.

16 S. Rowbotham, *Hidden from History* (London: Pluto Press, 1975).

17 See, for example, Mrs Henry Wood, *Within the Maze* (London: Bentley, 1872).

18 J. Rowbotham, *Good Girls Make Good Wives* (Oxford: Blackwell, 1989).

19 M. Feeley and D. Little, 'The Vanishing Female: The Decline of Women in the Criminal Process, 1687–1912', *Law and Society*, 25 (1991): 719–57.

20 P. King, *Crime and the Law in England, 1750–1840: Remaking Justice from the Margins* (Cambridge: Cambridge University Press, 2006), pp. 165–225.

21 A point made cogently in much feminist legal and criminological work; see N. Lacey, *Unspeakable Subjects: Feminist Essays in Legal and Social Theory* (Oxford: Hart Publishing, 1998).

22 J. F. Archbold, *Jervis's Acts, 11 & 12 Victoria, cc. 42, 43, & 44* (London: Shaw and Sons, 1848).

23 J. Rowbotham and K. Stevenson, 'Introduction', in J. Rowbotham and K. Stevenson (eds.), *Criminal Conversations* (Bloomington, Ind.: Ohio State University Press, 2005), pp. xxi–xxxii.

24 K. Stevenson, 'Ingenuities of the Female Mind: Legal and Public Perceptions of Sexual Violence in Victorian England, 1850–90', in S. D'Cruz (ed.), *Unguarded Passions: Gender, Class and Everyday Violence in Britain, c. 1850–c. 1950* (Harlow: Longmans, 2000), pp. 89–103.

25 See E. T. Atkinson, *A Manual of Criminal Procedure for British India, for the Magistrate, the Justice of the Peace and the Police Officer* (Calcutta: Barham Hill & Co., 1870).

26 'Ladies at Law', *Pall Mall Gazette*, 7 February 1865.

27 Using the Sexual Discrimination (Removal) Act 1919, in 1922 Helena Normanton accepted the call to the bar, and four women qualified as solicitors. In the USA, women had been able to become lawyers in the last half of the nineteenth century. See Rosemary Hunter, Chapter 2.

28 Leader, *Daily Telegraph*, 4 February 1870.

29 See, for instance, the *Daily Mail*, 12 December 2005, 21 December 2009. The recent acquittal of Kay Gilderdale on a charge of attempted murder raises different issues relating to assisted suicide. Gilderdale's adult daughter was fully mentally competent and sufficiently physically competent to start the suicide process herself, whereas Wragg and Inglis were the sole decision-makers because their sons were incompetent and unable to express their wishes; *The Times*, 26 January 2009.

30 The damage, in the eyes of the law, was to the family: it was a father or brother who brought a prosecution, providing a clear echo with the equally gendered tort of criminal conversation.

31 J. F. Stephen, *A History of the Criminal Law of England* (London: Routledge/Thoemmes Press, 1996), p. 75. First published 1883.

32 *R* v. *Tyrrell* (1894) 1 QBD 710 (Cr Cas Res 1893); *The Times*, 18 December 1893.

33 *R* v. *Tyrrell* (1894) 1 QBD 710 (Cr Cas Res 1893); *The Times*, 18 December 1893. See also C. Sumner, 'Introduction: The Violence of Censure and the Censure of Violence', in C. Sumner (ed.), *Violence, Culture and Censure* (London and New York: Routledge, 1996), pp. 4–5.

34 Proceedings of the Central Criminal Court, 11 September 1893, p. 59. Available online at http://www.oldbaileyonline.org (accessed 13 January 2010).

35 K. Stevenson, 'Unequivocal Victims: The Historical Mystification of the Female Complainant in Rape Cases', *Feminist Legal Studies*, 8 (2000) (3): 346–66.

36 *Daily Telegraph*, 8 January 2010. See also *Daily Telegraph*, 1 December 2009. However, demonstration of intelligence is not presently an automatic dimension to positive masculine identities, in contrast to nineteenth-century expectations. See D. Epstein, J. Elwood, V. Hey and J. Maw (eds.), *Failing Boys? Issues in Gender and Achievement* (London: Taylor & Francis, 1998).

37 *Daily Mail*, 1 December 2009.

38 T. Edwards, 'Sex, Booze and Fags: Masculinity, Style and Men's Magazines', in B. Benwell (ed.), *Masculinity and Men's Lifestyle Magazines* (Oxford: Wiley Blackwell, 2003).

39 Rowbotham, *Good Girls Make Good Wives*. Also, J. Walkowitz, *Prostitution and Victorian Society: Women, Class and the State* (Cambridge: Cambridge University Press, 1986).

40 Adam, *Police Work from Within*, pp. 19–20.

41 *Daily Telegraph*, 15 January 2010.

42 See Kim Stevenson, Chapter 9.

43 J. Rowbotham, '"Only When Drunk": The Stereotyping of Violence in Britain, 1850–1900', in S. D'Cruze (ed.), *Everyday Violence in Britain, c. 1850–1950: Gender and Class* (London: Longman, 2000), pp. 155–69; S. Winslow, *Bad Fellas: Crime, Tradition and New Masculinities* (Oxford: Berg, 2001).

44 *Daily Telegraph*, 15 January 2010.
45 Ibid.
46 Rowbotham, 'Only When Drunk'.
47 For instance, J. M. Dabbs, R. L. Frady, T. S. Carr and N. F. Besch, 'Saliva Testosterone and Criminal Violence in Young Adult Prison Inmates', *Psychosomatic Medicine*, 49 (2) (1987): 174–82. Testosterone research dates back to the mid-nineteenth century.
48 *Daily Telegraph*, 9 April 1875.
49 Compare *Daily Telegraph*, 10 March 1875; *Daily Mail*, 14 April 2004; C. Emsley, *The English and Violence since 1750* (London: Hambledon, 2005), pp. 21–2.
50 L. M. Brown and M. Tappan, 'Fighting Like a Girl Fighting Like a Guy: Gender Identity, Ideology, and Girls at Early Adolescence', *New Directions for Child and Adolescent Development*, 120 (2008), pp. 47–59.
51 See, for instance, *The Times*, 12 August 2009.
52 Robert Verkaik, 'Iraq Veterans Need More Psychiatric Help Says Judge', *The Independent*, 17 August 2006.
53 An acceptance of the existence of female sexual abusers remains problematic for many. See C. Philby, 'Female Sexual Abuse: The Untold Story of Society's Last Taboo', *The Independent*, 8 August 2009; see also L. Jackson, *Child Sexual Abuse in Victorian England* (London and New York: Routledge, 2000).
54 For example, *Daily Mail*, 18 December 2009.
55 Paul Bracchi, 'The Terrifying Rise of Violent Girl Gangs', *Daily Mail*, 16 May 2008.
56 F. Heidensohn and L. Gelsthorpe, 'Gender and Crime', in M. Maguire, R. Morgan and R. Reiner (eds.), *Oxford Handbook of Criminology* (Oxford: Oxford University Press, 2007), pp. 381–430; p. 381.
57 Ibid.
58 *Daily Mail*, 20 November 2009; *Daily Telegraph*, 21 November 2009.

Part III

Violence, law and sex

Chapter 9

'She never screamed out and complained'

Recognising gender in legal and media representations of rape

Kim Stevenson

Introduction

Media representation of crime influences popular understandings of the 'reality' of criminal behaviour. In the context of sex crimes, and rape in particular, there is an additional dimension; namely, that newspaper reportage can significantly influence public attitudes regarding gender stereotypes and rape myths. The terminology and language used in reports of rape and other sexual offences has the potential to exert both direct and subliminal impacts upon its readership. More worryingly, recent findings of a study commissioned by the Lilith Project in 2008, which analysed rape articles from the national tabloid and quality press as well as the BBC website for the year 2006, identified that current media constructions of rape, perpetrators and victims do not accurately reflect published research and crime statistics. This indicates that there are images and attitudes that exist in both the public mind and in the law that underlie the authoritative or established position of the incidence of rape and which are out of step with the realities and actualities of the crime. This miasma undermines official communications and information about rape which in turns impacts negatively upon reporting and conviction rates.

The contemporary stereotypical media construction 'depicts rape as an outdoor crime at the hands of a monstrous or bestial, deviant stranger, who may be "foreign", and uses extreme violence to overpower a victim'.[1] To be acknowledged as a 'proper victim' it is the complainant who must be 'proven innocent' by the press who will test her conformity with gendered expectations relating to conduct, resistance and emotional trauma. Such outdated stereotypifications have more in common with ingrained nineteenth-century expectations of feminine behaviour embedded in legal and media representations of rape (as typified in an episode of the recent BBC television series *Garrow's Law* inspired by the life of late-eighteenth-century defence barrister William Garrow) than the experience of rape in modern times. Yet, despite considerable pressure and criticism, the modern criminal-justice system still seems to have an inherent difficulty in expunging such mythology from its operation, something not made any easier by the external influences of the press. While the twentieth-century development of the scientific study of victimology was a breakthrough in acknowledging the experience of victimisation and victimhood, rape victims still tend to be judged, by the media in particular, according to far more rigid stereotypes.[2] The relationship between rape victim and offender differs from other crimes, not only because of its intimately personal and sexual nature but also because the dynamics of private power play and control make for a very different type of victim.

Surprisingly, it is not just the tabloid press that is responsible for misleading the public in relation to stereotyping and blame-assignment. In July 2009, the *Telegraph* was forced to issue an apology as a result of 'an editing error', after deliberately misrepresenting academic research released in a British Psychological Society press release under the headline 'Scientists Say Women Who Drink Alcohol, Wear Short Skirts and Are More Outgoing Are More Likely to Be Raped'.[3] The reportage completely undermined the results of the study which concluded the opposite: that 'men who engage in highly diverse sexual activities are more likely than their counterparts to coerce a woman into sexual acts against her will'.[4] If the results of an objective inquiry can be so readily misrepresented and manipulated by even the broadsheet press then it is no wonder that rape myths endure in the popular consciousness.

Public recognition of such deceptive stereotypifications and acceptance of the 'real rape' myth (that stranger rape is more deviant and prevalent than intimate rape), allow us to 'distance' ourselves from the fearful actuality: that in fact we are more at risk from partners and acquaintances.[5] As Greer asserts, press representations of gender norms falsely reassure us that 'ordinary' people do not commit sex offences; we therefore need only fear the unrealistic stereotype of the 'predatory stranger'.[6] Contemporary media coverage in the English press, particularly concerning those found to have abused their position of trust, has effectively destroyed such fragile, albeit illusory, security. Public fears now emanate as much from the threat of female perpetrators such as teachers and nursery nurses entrusted with the care of children (notably the Vanessa George case), as from the male stranger waiting at the school gates.[7]

To what extent are the press and the law complicit in promoting such fears? This chapter suggests that responsible reportage of sexual offences is necessarily reliant on a collaborative synergism between law and the press. Historically, this relationship was an inherently symbiotic one though it is less so now. Drawing on historical and modern examples of press reportage and debate, this chapter demonstrates that an awareness of the dynamics of that relationship can illuminate understandings of how rape myths and gender perspectives operate and perpetuate, even today.

Intimate violations

From a historico-legal perspective, reports of sexual deviance have always fascinated audiences by traversing the spectrum from titillating distraction to incomprehensible disgust. In looking to the past, the use of gender-labelling to reinforce cultural stereotypes is blatant, leading to the conclusion that it was endemic. Abusers convicted of sex crimes were portrayed as 'monsters', whereas the banality of modern language, often used frivolously, in words such as 'deviants' and 'paedos', can hide and distort the reality of that historical continuation. As the Lilith study confirms, such labelling can create misleading images of the statistically rarer stranger-rape rather than suggesting the more prevalent forms of sexual abuse by intimates. Going beyond this, there are other important and damaging continuities. Victims are still expected to present themselves as sexually 'modest' and self-protective but are often implicitly represented as 'deserving' or 'accepting' of rape/sexual violence through perceived 'amoral' behaviour or 'inappropriate' dress.

Modern attitudes towards women and sexual violence hardened during the mid-Victorian period with the rise of 'respectability'. They crystallised into legal imperatives, as evidenced in the courtroom, and into cultural constructs, as evidenced in the press.[8] Wykes's late-twentieth-century analysis of press narratives of violence within the wider legal context confirms that the media is a 'significant contributor' to gender discourses.[9] Greer concludes that the sociological phenomena of news production and the construction of sex crimes through press reportage are dependent on a 'diversity of social, cultural, political, organisational and economic factors'.[10] While he does not expressly include law, as either a cultural concept or organisational institution, there is no question that it is nonetheless a significant contributor and that apart from the well-established work of Soothill, Walby, Lees and Wykes it has been largely overlooked in this context.[11] More recently, the two Lilith Reports, *Just Representation: Press Reporting and the Reality of Rape* (2008) and *Rape Convictions in London* (2005), have demonstrated how the limited selection of stranger-rape cases by the media can skew public perceptions and confidence, generating 'multiple negative impacts upon victims of sexual violence'.[12] These 'negative impacts' relate not only to rape myths but also to public perceptions of low conviction rates and low prison tariffs. This is hardly surprising. When a sample of London rape trials heard between April 2003 and March 2005 was mapped against contemporaneous national media coverage, it was estimated that the press selected less than 3 per cent of those trials where a conviction was secured for publication.[13]

The amount of press coverage of sex crimes has fluctuated significantly over the years, tending to mirror the prevailing gender contexts and social culture which in turn have either influenced, or been influenced by, the law and legal discourse. With the rise of respectability and sexual morality at the beginning of the nineteenth century, official transcripts of rape trials at the Old Bailey and Assize courts became heavily censored. This meant that official statistics became unreliable. Equivalent statistical information for the Victorian era is therefore impossible to correlate and so other sources become more important. For example, Victorian newspapers published details of sexual offences in sections on 'crime reports' and 'court intelligence' on a fairly regular basis.[14] Typically, trainee barristers wrote and filed reports of cases in, amongst others, *The Times,* the *Pall Mall Gazette* and the *Daily Telegraph*, based on their understanding of the law and narratives they heard and witnessed.[15] Thus, press reportage of sex crimes was heavily informed by expert opinion, offering a more intellectual level of legal analysis about the arguments presented than is generally the case today.

'Why won't juries at rape trials believe women?'

This 2005 headline preludes a hard-hitting article based on research by Julie Bindell, founder of the Justice for Women campaign, who watched a number of rape trials at the Old Bailey and concluded that enduring negative cultural norms still actively influence jurors and legal professionals alike.[16] Also in 2005, Liz Kelly's Home Office study, *A Gap or a Chasm?*, concluded that powerful and persistent cultural narratives define the meaning of 'real rape' and 'real victim'.[17] Such assertions are nothing new. Stereotypical (primarily masculine) ideals of what constitutes a 'real rape' and who constitutes a 'real victim' have endured for centuries but became entrenched in the public consciousness through print-media representations in the nineteenth century. Of course, there are significant differences in the rhetoric of Victorian and modern media. The Victorian press relied on a mixture of sensationalist and repressive comment and by-lines informing its readership that the details of sexual offences 'were too disgusting' or 'depraved' to reproduce in print or generic comments indicating that another 'moral outrage' had occurred. Though such 'sensationalist' language was often decried on the grounds that it implied considerable and undesirable exaggeration, it often helped to encourage the public to come forward and assist in the prevention and detection of crime. The word 'rape' was hardly ever used. Instead, the Victorian press and legal discourse adopted a range of anodyne phrases and language in the text of the reports, such as, 'he effected his purpose', 'she suffered a fainting fit', 'her person was bruised', etc., that not only sought to protect public morals but also effectively silenced women's voices on occasion, leaving them without the means to effectively articulate their experiences.[18]

Today's press is apparently less censorious, 'sex and violence saturate contemporary popular culture', permitting tabloid emphasis on anything salacious or 'disgusting'.[19] Despite the problems of interpretation, Victorian reportage provides far more detailed narratives of the trial process, courtroom players and judicial direction than modern equivalents. In practice, this enabled fewer superficial judgements to be made about individuals despite the apparent development of more prejudicial gender stereotypes. Victorian gender stereotypes were unequivocally explicit and discriminative. Deference to male respectability was highly influential. Newspapers tended to stress those aspects of conduct or persona that emphasised male/female respectability/unrespectability and the competing strengths of this imperative. Respectable women would dress appropriately, not talk to strange men, not over-indulge in alcohol, be accompanied or chaperoned and not wander off on their own, fight back with all their might if attacked, report any assault immediately, etc. It is easy, therefore, to see the origins of current rape constructions within these press representations of gendered expectations and stereotypes. Equally, it can also be seen how, so long as women at least outwardly conformed and/or could bring witnesses to testify on their behalf, they could use such stereotypes to their advantage. In comparison, the more confused modern stereotypes offer a less certain path, where attention is focused on the actual individual character and her beliefs offering less *generic* protection. While Victorian working-class women, especially those on the verges of economic and thus cultural responsibility, including servants, could find it difficult to make a case, women from other levels of society did find that the stereotypical expectations of them could also blind courts and juries to any *individual* transgressions. In the twenty-first century there is no such defensive barrier for women of any class.

Victorian press reports explicitly highlight the extent to which the evidence of the prosecutrix matched these norms. Could her testimony be shaken? Is she a reliable witness? Did she act according to stereotypical expectations? Who approached whom? Where? When? Did she scream and fight back? What were her injuries? Victim responses in terms of conformity with stereotypical tropes would either confirm or negate her status as a credible 'respectable young lady' or 'respectable married woman' which could then be judged against the defendant's status and respectability. Establishing individual respectability was often more important than proving the evidence and facts presented. A typical example in terms of the reportage, though not the status of the respective parties, which encapsulates such prerequisites is the 1884 trial of Lord St Leonards (Sir Edward Sugden and a former Lord Chancellor) at the Central Criminal Court. This is an unusual case and atypical of Eden's conclusion concerning modern-day reportage: that the contemporary media focus is on rape cases involving 'sports personalities (or celebrities of any kind), asylum seekers and men from a Black Minority or Refugee background'.[20] Victorian reportage was far more representative of everyday violence.

Lord St Leonards was accused of committing an indecent assault (then often charged as an alternative to rape or attempted rape) and a further count of assault with intent to rape, on Emma Cole, a domestic servant in his employ. It is clear from the extensive report in *The Times* that not only was the text written by someone with legal expertise but that gender conformity was the overriding imperative, not just as regards the outcome but in reminding the readership of the cultural standards of conduct expected of them. Key extracts, in the order they appear, evidence this. The first few paragraphs summarise the case for the prosecution:

- Witnesses confirmed that 'she was in an agitated state and she complained to the first person she saw and to her master when he returned home'.
- 'She submitted herself to a medical examination within 24 hours.'

- 'Dr Bentnall found several bruises about her body ... corroborative of the circumstances, and the jury were asked to consider this in order to test the truth of the imputation.'
- Detman [the gardener] was in the garden but 'she did not scream to him ... She made no [immediate] complaint then, she was much too upset to call a policeman'.
- 'She confessed herself to be unchaste ... .'[21]

Interestingly the prosecution argued that this last fact 'corroborated her story' presumably because she had some knowledge of sexual matters which of course respectable ladies should not possess. Cross-examination by the defence barrister, Edward Clarke QC, and his summing-up clearly illustrate the gendered origins of modern rape myths:

- Emma did not make an immediate complaint to the gardener.
- Dr Bentnall 'found bruises on part of her body, [but] there were none on her arms or shoulders where he should have expected to have found them if a violent struggle had taken place'.
- The jury must 'be true to the rule: what was the character of the person making the accusation ... In the case of a pure minded girl the argument would be she would never go through the ordeal of making such a charge in a public court if her story were not true.'
- 'She never screamed out and complained as any other woman would have done if a victim of such an outrage.'
- She only complained later 'to try and get money out of a man in power'.

The jurors, all respectable gentleman, took over an hour to decide (deliberations were often much quicker) and experienced 'some difficulties' in reaching a decision. Their guilty verdict (of assault only, the second count was dismissed) took Clarke and his client by surprise. This was probably because there was evidence that the aristocrat had been drinking, thereby making him less respectable, and, perversely, this was likely to have been aggravated by the public perception that the aristocracy were less respectable than the idealised moral majority, the gentry.[22] Having already spent two months in prison and suffering public disgrace, St Leonards was discharged.

Unsurprisingly, the overwhelmingly male Victorian courtroom struggled with the issue of femininity. On occasion, women met resistance just because they dared make an allegation or because their feminine traits, emotive and expressive, were regarded as irrational by male officialdom. In 1865, the *Pall Mall Gazette* cautioned that female complainants were becoming such 'a common phenomenon in our law courts' that they could seriously affect the public's interest: 'it will be observed that there is a peculiar tortuousness and intricacy about female cases, arising either from a hopeless confusion of facts, or from an absence of facts'.[23] Women could not be relied upon to present their case plainly and logically as the adversarial system required (the 'emotional and highly strung' stereotype), which is something that still frustrates complainants today. Indeed, evidence-in-chief cannot be delivered as a narrative but must be restricted to the questions posited.[24]

Despite such ambiguities and prejudices, Victorian juries were often more willing to believe women than may appear to be the case today, and conviction rates were much higher. Nor can this be explained, as former Solicitor-General Vera Baird QC suggested, in respect of the continuing dire conviction rate of 5–6 per cent for reported rapes, on the basis that they were all 'stranger rapes' and so easier to secure convictions than in respect of rape by intimates. For example, in England and Wales in 2007, the number of rape convictions was 50 per cent higher (over 13,000) than in 1997, but only 6.5 per cent led to a successful prosecution largely because of the increase in reports concerning rape by partners.[25] In comparison, a fair percentage of Victorian women were attacked by their employers, neighbours and guardians, and in any case rape within marriage was not illegal until 1991 and few women lived with their partners outside the bonds of marriage. Perversely then, it can be argued that it was because the Victorians expressly relied on universal gender stereotypifications to determine the outcome of sexual-assault trials that more were successful. By contrast, the modern approach and its preference for extinguishing stereotypes from the courtroom, or at least inculcating a greater awareness amongst both legal professionals and jurors of their impact and effect, may have contributed to achieving the opposite effect.

'The truth about rape: forget the myths and look at the statistics'[26]

Four years after *The Mirror* headline and recent government recommendations to 'educate' jurors about the influence of rape myths, the issue is still proving somewhat controversial. Not so much because of a lack of consciousness of gender but because the manner in which we view and perceive acts of intimate violence has been set in ways that do not encourage impartial reflection. Even the acknowledgement that gender stereotypes, implicitly or explicitly, actively operate in the courtroom is contested despite Baird's insistence that rape myths infiltrate the courtroom at all levels and should be dismissed by jurors. Munro and Ellison's survey of mock juror perceptions confirms that potential jurors still tend to be suspicious of calm complainants and expect credible witnesses to express emotion and demonstrate evidence of violence used against them or in their self-defence.[27] Conversely, Thomas's research for the Ministry of Justice, based on large-scale analysis of over 68,000 jury verdicts during 2006–8, concluded that 'contrary to popular belief and previous government research juries convict more often than they acquit (55 per cent jury conviction rate)'.[28] She asserts that 'juries are not "primarily responsible" for low conviction rates or bias against female complainants but that the rates vary according to the gender and age of the complainant'.[29] Temkin and Krahe's 2007 survey (using some of the same information) confirms the gendered divide: 65 per cent of male rapes resulted in conviction compared to 46 per cent of rapes against women. But they are less dismissive of stereotypical influences, 'Different strategies are needed to boost jurors' *motivation* to engage in a cognitively demanding scrutiny of the available information rather than falling back on well-rehearsed, less demanding stereotype-based judgments.'[30]

In May 2009, in response to public criticism about the Crown Prosecution Service's prosecution of rape crimes and the Brown government's consultation paper *Convicting Rapists and Protecting Victims: Justice for Victims of Rape*, Baroness Scotland, then the Attorney General, wrote, 'Can we influence how juries see an alleged rape victim? Yes, to a degree, by building the most informed case we can and being well aware of the myths and stereotypes that surround this crime.'[31] However, there was no discussion of what is meant by an 'informed case' or of the extent and nature of the myths and stereotypes surrounding the crime. The statement is largely rhetorical, rather than substantive. It is true that the Attorney General's office then embarked on a number of initiatives to reform the role of juries by apparently tackling such pervasive myths. For instance, in June 2009, Baird announced that judges should direct juries to ignore the kind of stereotypical tropes so prominently evident in the Victorian courtroom and so enduringly omnipresent. This was partly in response to similar judicial concern that jurors, albeit unwittingly, may be contributing to low conviction rates. Press headlines, for example, 'Judge and Jury: Freeing Judges to Disabuse Jurors about the Myths' encapsulated the goal of demolishing such myths and stereotypes.[32] Speeches to practitioner audiences, such as the Rape and Sexual Assault Conference, flagged up concerns and proposals to increase the number of Sexual Assault Referral Centres.[33] The Government Equalities Office (then led by Harriet Harman), in conjunction with the Home Office, commissioned a review of rape complaints, chaired by Baroness Stern, to investigate the victim experience and prosecutorial process.

Unfortunately, this has not all been positive, even on the terms set by the present Ministers. Baird, herself, represented the Crown in the Court of Appeal case *R* v. *D (JA)* 2008[34] where the appellant challenged the trial judge's direction to the jury concerning two rape myths. First the judge had advised that a delay in making a complaint of rape does not necessarily mean that it is a false complaint and, second, he had commented in detail about the effects of partner rape addressing the myth that stranger rape is 'worse' than intimate rape. The Court of Appeal accepted that the judge was correct in advising the jury that the trauma of rape might inhibit a woman from making an immediate complaint, provided they weigh this against any comment the defendant may have made about the delay. The conviction was found to be safe but the Court said that he should have limited his comments to the jury about the effects of forced sex within relationships. The decision not only highlights the difficulty judges face in trying to compose a balanced direction but also the fact that juries are denied guidance on understanding the wider context of rape mythology. This is particularly significant given that they are prevented from hearing expert evidence on the issue. While Baird praised the Court for recognising the myth of recent complaint, 'Jurors who are new to these issues can, and frequently are, brought to what the Court of Appeal calls "an unjustified conclusion".'[35] The relative influence of rape myths therefore remains ambiguous. The tragedy is that it has taken 125 years since the St Leonards case for the judiciary to even start to address the iniquity of such myths.

A matter of debate

However, it is not just the judiciary that needs to be persuaded. It has to be recognised that the proactive feminist attack on rape myths, orchestrated by the first ever female law officers, ruffled some masculine feathers amongst both legal professionals and the public. A recent exchange of views published in *The Times* 2009, precipitated by comments from criminal-law barristers David Wolchover and Anthony Heaton-Armstrong, in their ongoing, and not particularly helpful, 'discussion' with Baroness Scotland, Baird, Munro and Ellison highlights the problem. The debate is illustrative of the continuation of profoundly, if unconsciously, gendered discourse, nuanced by expectations relating to both race and social class.[36]

In *The Times* letters page, Wolchover and Heaton-Armstrong declared that, '[we have] over very many years defended in numerous rape trials in which the complainant was submissive or was late in going to the police or showed notable calm in giving evidence and in which the defendant was ... convicted' and bristled at feminist assertions that stereotypical myths still influence police, prosecutors and jurors.[37] Like many, they are offended at the thought that, as enlightened and liberal professionals, they should still be affected by such cultural infelicities. In 2008, first shots had been fired when they criticised the Consultation Paper and the then Solicitor-General, Baroness Baird, for failing to address the issue of false rape allegations.[38] They concede that rape 'myths *may* infect the case-handling of *some* police investigators and Crown prosecutors' but that 'they are not a big problem in trials' and, in their experience, 'rape juries do not *habitually* apply victim stereotypes to acquit defendants'.[39]

Such statements are implicit testimonies to their own effectiveness in presenting cases which are devoid of such stereotypes. But how do they know that juries are impartial? Jury deliberations are secret, so it is impossible for anyone to ascertain the extent to which jurors are influenced. As Munro and Ellison found, if mock jurors are liable to be influenced then the potential for this to be the case with actual jurors cannot be understated.[40] Furthermore, as the Court of Appeal's response in *R* v. *D* suggests, the issue *is* problematic in trials. The barristers instead engage in a 'query the numbers' game challenging Baird over her statistical analysis and comparison with reported cases, conviction rates, false allegations, etc., as compared to other crimes of violence. At one level herein lies the difference: from a feminist perspective rape is a violation distinct from physical violence and so the likely response would be 'men don't get it'. But there is also a need to acknowledge that some women 'don't get it' either and that feminist perspectives can alienate them as much as men. Research undertaken for the Equal Opportunities Commission in 2003 found that 'the concept of "feminism" was seen virtually unanimously in negative terms as old fashioned and "ball-breaking"'.[41] Equally, women may be less empathetic to rape victims because of their perceived fear that it could easily happen to them, if they were, for example, in the wrong place at the wrong time. In contrast to the all-male Victorian juries, if a mixed-sex jury is now the ideal in rape cases then this needs to be acknowledged. Highlighting such gendered understandings is something that the media could responsibly promote.

A letter from another barrister, Ben Morris, written in response to Ellison and Munro's findings, advocates that low conviction rates should be examined not from the position that truthful complainants are disbelieved and that guilty men walk free but rather from the position 'that people are frequently wrongly accused of rape'.[42] He also suggested that extrapolating mock juror attitudes is pointless as there is nothing at stake.[43] This can be taken to support the contention that reliance on extrapolating trends from individual rape cases is particularly problematic and misleading and that it is more important to concentrate on the individual cases themselves rather than trends and theories. Another barrister, Robert English, also accuses Ellison and Munro of failing to take into account the number of cases of false allegations and quite rightly asserts that not every rape trial must end in a conviction. Again, this misses the point: increasing conviction rates is not the same thing as ensuring that all rape allegations result in a guilty finding.[44] Another option to consider is the Victorian practice of downgrading charges which permitted victims some discretion. Many women complainants and their families were quite prepared to lay down alternative charges of indecent assault or even common assault where the actual offence was either rape or attempted rape, as indicated by the St Leonards case. This meant that not only were convictions easier to secure than for formal charges of rape on indictment but that their honour remained intact as respectable women would never 'allow' themselves to be so violated. To downgrade today would be perceived as a public denial that rape had been committed. It was, however, a highly pragmatic solution.

Other barristers have displayed an even more masculine aggressive stance. Ian Macdonald QC's response, publicised on his Chambers website, uses the analogy of Baird 'riding into battle' to combat the low conviction rates and that the result of *R* v. *W* 'was a score draw'.[45] 'Of course it would be very non PC to suggest that those interested in trying to increase the number of convictions might look for solutions nearer to home and ask themselves whether such things as video interviews are actually part of the problem rather than the solution.'[46]

Macdonald then criticises the police for 'endlessly repeating what the witness has already said' and patronising her, 'you're doing ever so well sweetheart'.[47]

The Crown Prosecution Service are targeted because 'no one in the prosecution team dares to challenge an allegation of sexual assault these days'; thus the quality of evidence is only fully tested at trial and is often 'so poor that it would be a great surprise if the jury did convict'.[48] Finally, he somewhat insensitively asserts that 'the emphasis remains on the physical comfort of the complainant, sitting on a comfy sofa and giving evidence in an atmosphere far removed from the realities of the courtroom', demanding 'is it any wonder that conviction rates remain as low as they are?'[49]

While some of these assertions may warrant justification and debate, the overall tone is nonetheless highly disparaging and the comments condescendingly ignore the point that such measures and reforms were introduced precisely because his barristerial colleagues have treated victims so appallingly in the past, and they continue to do so to the extent that cross-examination is commonly seen as a second 'rape' and metaphoric violation. Nor should victims expect female barristers to be any more sympathetic. The defending female barrister, in a case of three thirteen-year-old boys alleged to have raped two sixteen-year-old girls in a park in Bromley, said that one of the girls, who weighed over 12 stone at the time of the rape 'may well have been glad of the attention'.[50] The barrister commented that at the time of the offence she was 'not quite the swan she had now turned into', having slimmed down considerably, and that while 'no-one suggests this is a lesson in politeness and gallantry. It is all too unrealistic that sexual encounters between boy and girls who have never met before must be *against the girls' will.*'[51] The teenagers were boys not men, but counsel's insinuation to the jury that their acts could be considered exculpatory as implied through the victim's 'consent' is a dangerous view and one that only serves to reinforce gender stereotypes.

Conclusion

Informed debate such as that exemplified in *The Times* is both desirable and necessary in order to ensure the continued effectiveness of the law and legal process in practice. Compared to the deliberate press stereotypifications of rape as identified by the Lilith Project and misrepresentation of academic inquiry in the *Telegraph*, the publication of such ongoing debate is an infinitely more responsible counterbalance. But it also has the potential to be counterproductive. Not only can it serve to entrench the positions of those expert legal professionals and academics involved but it also epitomises and replicates the real-life courtroom confrontation that its readership, as potential jurors, will face. The antagonistic and adversarial 'game' that purports to deliver truth and justice as revealed in Victims' Champion Sarah Payne's Report for the Home Office, is often perceived by victims as offering them less protection and respect than the defendant whose human rights are 'guaranteed'.[52] Inevitably, juries must be representative of society comprising those who read the tabloid and the 'quality' press, but it is evident that both readerships are being sent (different) mixed messages about rape. While the law and the press are not intentionally complicit in this it is difficult to escape the conclusion that, for both victims and defendants, being 'judged' by one's peers probably encompasses being indirectly judged by the press. As Jon Collins at the Fawcett Society asserts, 'A more accurate media portrayal of the realities of rape will lead to a better informed public, which in turn will lead to juries and a criminal-justice system that can better deliver justice for victims of rape.'[53]

Notes

1   N. Marhia, *Just Representation? Press Reporting and the Reality of Rape* (London: The Lilith Project, 2008), p. 4. See also S. Brown, *Treating Sex Offenders* (Cullompton: Willan, 2005), p. 1.

2   J. Kitzinger, 'Rape and the Media', in M. Horvath and J. Brown (eds.), *Rape: Challenging Contemporary Thinking* (Cullompton: Willan, 2009), pp. 74–98, at p. 83.

3   'British Psychological Society: Miss Sophia Shaw', *Telegraph* online, 13 July 2009. Available online at www.telegraph.co.uk/science/5818138/British-Psychological-Society-Miss-Sophia-Shaw.html (accessed 10 December 2009).

4   S. Shaw, E. Nye, J. Jamel and H. Flowe, 'The Print Media and Rape', *The Psychologist*, 22 (10) (2009): 1–6.

5   See J. Temkin and B. Krahe, *Sexual Assault and the Justice Gap: A Question of Attitude* (Oxford: Hart, 2008), Chapter 2.

6   C. Greer, *Sex Crime and the Media* (Cullompton: Willan, 2003), p. 185.

7   Childline reported in November 2009 that it had received a 'huge rise in the number of children calling to report sexual abuse by women'. Available online at news.bbc.co.uk/1/hi/uk/8347589.stm (accessed 10 December 2009).

8   K. Stevenson, 'Unequivocal Victims: The Historical Mystification of the Female Complainant in Rape Cases', *Feminist Legal Studies*, 8 (2000): 346–66.

9   M. Wykes, *News, Crime and Culture* (London: Pluto Press, 2001), Chapter 6.

10   Greer, *Sex Crime and the Media*, p. 183.

11   See K. Soothill and S. Walby, *Sex Crime in the News* (London and New York: Routledge, 1991); K. Soothill, S. Walby and P. Bagguley, 'Judges, the Media and Rape', *Journal of Law and Society*, 17 (2) (1990): 211–33; S. Lees, *Carnal Knowledge: Rape on Trial* (London: Hamish Hamilton, 1996); Wykes, *News, Crime and Culture*.

12   Marhia, *Just Representation?* I. Eden, *Rape Convictions in London* (London: The Lilith Project, 2005), p. 31.

13   Eden, *Rape Convictions in London*, p. 30.

14   K. Stevenson, 'Unearthing the Realities of Rape: Utilising Victorian Newspaper Reportage to Fill In the Contextual Gaps', *Liverpool Law Review*, 28 (3) (2007): 405–23.

15   J. Rowbotham and K. Stevenson, 'Causing a Sensation: Media and Legal Representations of Bad Behaviour', in J. Rowbotham and K. Stevenson (eds.), *Behaving Badly: Social Panics and Moral Outrage, Victorian and Modern Parallels* (Aldershot: Ashgate, 2003), pp. 31–46.

16   *The Mirror*, 6 June 2005.

17   L. Kelly, J. Lovett and L. Regan, *A Gap or a Chasm: Attrition in Reported Rape Cases*, Home Office Research Study 293, February 2005, p. 77.

18   See K. Stevenson, 'Taking Indecent Liberties: The Victorian Encryption of Sexual Violence', in J. Rowbotham and K. Stevenson (eds.), *Criminal Conversations: Victorians Behaving Badly* (Columbus: Ohio State University Press, 2005), pp. 232–46.

19   Wykes, *News, Crime and Culture*, p. 138.

20 Eden, *Rape Convictions in London*, p. 28.
21 *The Times*, 23 May 1884.
22 See F. Thompson, *Rise of Respectable Society* (Harmondsworth: Penguin, 1989).
23 *Pall Mall Gazette*, 7 February 1865.
24 See S. Payne, *Rape: The Victim Experience Review*, Home Office, November, 2009.
25 Government Equalities Office/Home Office Press release, 22 September 2009. Of the 6,597 men arrested for rape in 2008–9, 3,495 were sent to trial and 2,018, less than a third, were convicted. *The Times*, 16 December 2009.
26 D. Wolchover and A. Heaton-Armstrong, 'The Truth About Rape: Forget the Myths and Look at the Statistics', *The Times*, 15 October 2009.
27 V. Munro and L. Ellison, *Complainant Credibility and General Expert Witness Testimony in Rape Trials: Exploring and Influencing Mock Juror Perceptions*, ESRC Res-000-22-2374, June 2009; L. Ellison and V. Munro, 'Reacting to Rape: Exploring Mock Juror's Assessments of Complainant Credibility', *British Journal of Criminology*, 49 (2) (2009): 202–19.
28 C. Thomas, *Are Juries Fair?* (London: Ministry of Justice, 2010), p. 47. Available online at http://www.justice.gov.uk/about/docs/are-juries-fair.pdf (accessed 20 September 2010).
29 Ibid.
30 J. Temkin and B. Krahe, 'Addressing the Attitude Problem in Rape Trials', in M. Horvath and J. Brown (eds.), *Rape: Challenging Contemporary Thinking* (Cullompton: Willan, 2009), p. 310.
31 Office for Criminal Justice Reform, Consultation Paper, *Convicting Rapists and Protecting Victims: Justice for Victims of Rape*, 2006. *The Times*, Letters to the Editor: 'Rape and the CPS', 19 May 2009.
32 *The Times*, 15 June 2009.
33 Attorney General's Office, News Report, 23 September 2009.
34 EWCA Crim 2557 (2008).
35 Attorney General's Office, Press Release, 24 October 2008.
36 See *The Times*, Letters to the Editor: A. Heaton-Armstrong and D. Wolchover, 'Rape Complainants Are Not Always Victims', 21 May 2009; L. Ellison and V. Munro, 'Rape Trial Jurors Need Better Guidance', 17 October 2009; V. Baird, 'Rape and the Danger of Making Assumptions', 20 October 2009; D. Wolchover and A. Heaton-Armstrong, '"Typical" Behaviour of a Rape Victim', 23 October 2009; D. Wolchover and A. Heaton-Armstrong, 'The Truth about Rape: Forget the Myths and Look at the Statistics', *The Times*, 15 October 2009.
37 Wolchover and Heaton-Armstrong, '"Typical" Behaviour of a Rape Victim'.
38 D. Wolchover and A. Heaton-Armstrong, 'How Can the "Justice Gap" Between Reported Rapes and Convictions Be Fixed?', *Counsel*, 1 March 2008, p. 10; D. Wolchover and A. Heaton-Armstrong, 'False Rape Allegations Need Constant Investigatory Vigilance', *Counsel*, 23 May 2008, p. 29.
39 Wolchover and Heaton-Armstrong, 'The Truth about Rape'. Italics added.
40 Munro and Ellison, *Complainant Credibility*.
41 M. Howard and S. Tibballs, *Talking Equality* (London: Equal Opportunities Commission, July 2003), p. 10.
42 *The Times*, Letters to the Editor: 'Rape and the Danger of Making Assumptions', 20 October 2009.
43 Ibid.
44 Ibid.
45 Chambers of Ian Macdonald QC, Criminal Law updates. Available online at www.gcnchambers.co.uk/gcn/areas_of_specialisation/areas/criminal_defence/criminal_law_updates/criminal_law_update_15_12_08 (accessed 10 December 2009).
46 Ibid.

47 Ibid.
48 Ibid.
49 Ibid.
50 *The Mirror*, 18 May 2007. Italics added.
51 Ibid.
52 Ibid.
53 *The Independent*, 24 February 2008. Available online at http://www.independent.co.
    uk/news/media/report-calls-for-changes-to-rape-coverage-786543.html (accessed 10
    December 2009).

Chapter 10

Gendering rape

Social attitudes towards male and female rape

Philip N. S. Rumney and Natalia Hanley

Introduction

This chapter will explore the extent to which rape can be said to be a uniquely gendered crime in the context of one particular issue that has been the subject of repeated claims by feminist scholars: the idea that rape is gendered because male and female rape are treated differently in terms of social attitudes.[1] This claim is used by scholars to reinforce feminist theorising on gender which suggests that the bodily violation of women is taken less seriously than the violation of men.[2] Thus, it is argued, male rape is 'privileged' in the sense that it is treated more seriously than female rape in the legal process and in that male victims are less likely to attract negative social attributions.[3] While there is some evidence of the privileging of male rape in social attitudes, a wider examination of the literature reveals that such privileging as does exist is not to the exclusive benefit of males.[4] Further, claims that male victims receive preferential treatment in legal responses to rape appear, on the basis of current evidence, to have little basis in reality.[5]

In order to critically examine claims that male rape is 'privileged', this chapter examines how male and female rape are perceived and constructed in social discourse.[6] It will do so through the use of four focus-group discussions in which participants examined vignettes involving an allegation of male rape. These focus-group discussions will be analysed in order to consider the implications they have for some feminist theorising on gender and sexual assault.

Rape as a gendered crime

Rape can be seen as a specifically gendered crime in several ways. First, most victims are female and most perpetrators are male. Indeed, rape is commonly perceived amongst feminists as a classic example of a 'gendered harm', in that it 'happen[s] overwhelmingly to women, because they are women'.[7] Rape is therefore regarded by many feminists as a form of social control over women.[8] Second, the fear of rape amongst women has been described as 'ever present', experienced as a 'nagging, gnawing sense that something awful could happen'.[9] Baker argues that such fear is not shared by males in the community: 'Rape's prevalence forces women to live with a fear of violation and attack that is essentially unknown to men [...] male prisoners may experience a comparable, if temporary, fear.'[10] Contrary to such assertions, far from being unknown to men outside of institutional settings, it is evident that when males are asked about fear of rape or sexual assault, some do acknowledge both a sense of vulnerability and exhibit behaviour designed to avoid such risks.[11] Thus, while women suffer the fear of sexual violence more often when compared to men, it is evident that this fear is not a uniquely female one. The third potentially gendered aspect of rape relates to its effects. Some scholars argue that the traumatic impact of male sexual victimisation is so different, or even so much less serious, than female sexual victimisation, that the law of rape should not include male victims.[12] Others, drawing on a growing body of empirical evidence, have argued that non-consensual sexual intercourse for both men and women crosses a high threshold of seriousness in terms of psychological and emotional trauma.[13] This does not mean that all men and women react to rape in identical ways. Rather, the evidence suggests that a distinction cannot be easily made between male and female victims of non-consensual intercourse on the basis of relative seriousness. Indeed, in many jurisdictions that have engaged in rape-law reform there has been a recognition that there are significant similarities in the nature and impact of non-consensual penetrative sex on male and female victims.[14]

This chapter will consider a specific issue that has arisen in the feminist literature on rape. That is the claim that, compared to female rape complainants, male complainants receive preferential treatment from society and the legal process. It has been suggested, for example, that male rape has been treated more seriously than female rape during criminal trials and in the law-reform process. Such claims have become more common in the UK in recent times, though they generally lack evidential support or draw dubious inferences from limited data.[15] In the American context, likewise, Dworkin has argued

> Society's general willingness to do anything necessary to protect boys and men from male sexual aggression is testimony to the value of a male life. Society's general refusal to do anything meaningful to protect women and girls from male sexual aggression is testimony to the worthlessness of a female life.[16]

In a variation on Dworkin's notion of privileging, MacKinnon recently suggested that 'when [men] are sexually violated, especially if they are straight and white and adult, it is not generally disbelieved or simply tolerated or found entertaining or defended'.[17]

Such views, encapsulated here by Dworkin and MacKinnon, suggest that male rape victims are treated preferentially compared to their female counterparts as a matter of general social reality. The use of focus-group research cannot fully address the specifics of all the relevant feminist claims in the UK and USA, but it can give an indication of whether male rape is treated preferentially, in broad terms, at the level of social attitudes. This may have further implications for institutional responses to rape which are in turn influenced by negative social attitudes, including myths and stereotypes.[18] Indeed, as an example, there is evidence to suggest that myths and stereotypes held by students concerning male rape are also exhibited by many serving police officers.[19]

The research and its findings

The primary aim of this research was to explore student attitudes towards adult victims and perpetrators of male rape through the use of vignettes featuring an alleged incident of male rape.[20] Research studies that utilise hypothetical scenarios or vignettes have proved useful in uncovering attitudes towards female victimisation, and there is no reason to think that they cannot be effectively applied to the study of male victimisation.

Student participants in the present study were initially informed about the research through an electronic conferencing system attached to compulsory undergraduate criminology modules, staff announcements and email communications. There are a number of advantages to utilising an opportunity sample derived from a student group.[21] Most notably, for the purposes of this research, it ensures that participation is voluntary and that informed consent is given. Students decided which focus-group session to attend. There was no attempt to seek to control, for example, the male–female mix. The self-selection approach resulted in four focus groups, which included male-only (Groups 1, N = 2; and 4, N = 3), female-only (Group 2, N = 7) and mixed-group discussions (Group 3, N = 6). Given that the study involved a small number of participants (eighteen), a level of caution is clearly appropriate when considering the general application of the findings outlined below.

The focus-group discussions were recorded, but there were no researchers present. This was particularly important as it encouraged honest and open discussion of the vignette and minimised the impact of the student–academic relationship on participant responses. The focus-group discussions, which lasted fifty minutes, were conducted at the university in order to provide a comfortable and familiar setting.[22] Due to the sensitivities of the subject matter, participants were fully informed of the nature, purpose and likely outputs from the research process. Participants completed a consent form and were advised that they could withdraw from the study at any time, without providing a reason. Details of support and advice services were also circulated.

As participants were all undergraduate criminology students, there is, of course, a danger that their views may not be representative of the general public, especially as the narrow age range (between nineteen and twenty-three) might produce generationally and culturally specific understandings of sexual violence. However, research involving mock juries has suggested that participants who are students and those drawn from the general public do not differ significantly in the outcome of their decision-making.[23] Additionally, the content of the discussions suggested little prior participant knowledge of sexual victimisation resulting from their studies that might alter the outcome of the research.

Each focus group was provided with one of three fictional vignettes designed to encourage discussion of one of the following variables in the context of a male rape trial: complainant failing to resist during an alleged rape (Groups 1 and 4), delayed reporting by the complainant to the police (Group 2) and an involuntary physical response (erection) by the complainant during the alleged rape (Group 4). The scenario featuring the first variable was run twice due to the small number of participants (two) in Group 1. In summary, all the vignettes featured David and Ian who met at a party and then went back to David's flat to watch a DVD and talk about football. Ian claims that, when he was getting ready to leave the flat, David restrained him, removed his trousers and raped him. Conversely, David claims that during the evening 'one thing led to another' and they had consensual sex. In line with provisions of the Sexual Offences Act 2003, each group was directed to decide whether the complainant consented to intercourse and whether the defendant reasonably believed that there was consent. The aims of the research were to explore the effect of each variable, to investigate attitudes towards male sexual victimisation and, finally, to analyse how group dynamics and interactions impact upon group discussions.[24] Finch and Munro have argued that the use of short, fictional scenarios may increase the likelihood of participants relying on rape myth stereotypes to 'fill in the gaps' in the vignette.[25] Consequently, these findings should be viewed as exploratory at this stage.[26]

The research was not intended to provide detailed analysis of perceptions of female rape; however, it became clear that the focus-group discussions invoked a significant amount of material on female sexual victimisation. This occurred in two ways. First, female rape was used by participants as a standard by which the scenarios involving a male complainant could be analysed. Second, a series of specific issues arose, relating to such things as complainant behaviour, trauma, communication and false allegations in which comparisons were made between male and female rape.

Female rape as the comparator

Participants across all of the focus groups used their perception of the female experience of rape as a source of comparison and a 'standard' against which the information detailed in the vignettes could be evaluated. This comparison occurred on several levels. For example, participants discussed the likely or expected behaviour of female rape victims in terms of reporting, the reliability and credibility of a rape claim and social expectations around behaviour. In the groups, two themes emerged from these discussions. First, a number of participants acknowledged that their attitudes and opinions about the information presented were gender-specific, in other words, these participants reflected upon their responses and admitted that they might arrive at a different conclusion about the vignette if he complainant was female. While these participants were often initially unable to explain their gendered responses, during the course of the group discussion it emerged that these attitudes were largely a result of social expectations of behaviour, as the following exchange from Group 1 (male-only) demonstrates:

ALAN: It's really weird because in my mind, well I am saying did Ian give consent to the intercourse, well my mind I'm saying well from the evidence that's here the fact that he didn't say or do anything to stop it then yes. Did David reasonably believe that he consented, well that's again I would probably say yes. But I'm just thinking that if Ian was a girl, whether I'd have a different opinion, it's quite weird. To actually think that, but I do.

MATT: It's quite reasonable to think that your concepts have changed probably. In what way would they change?

ALAN: Because they were both at a party, if it was a guy and a woman, just because they go back to someone's house, it doesn't necessarily mean he's going to consent to having sex. Again you'd have to say the woman would be pretty naive to go back to guy's house and not think something's going to happen.

Interestingly, this group discussion illustrated the potential fluidity of opinions expressed by the participants. Later in the discussion, Alan applies his earlier reasoning, which he considers in the context of women, to Ian's behaviour. Indeed, Alan makes a characterisation of this behaviour which could be seen as more negative than his earlier description of a woman as 'naive': 'I just think that for Ian to go back to his flat a stranger's house after they've had a few drinks at a party, unless he was very stupid or very innocent.' This illustrates the fact that views towards male rape are not necessarily held in a consistent manner, and, indeed, negative attributions apply to male, as well as female rape complainants.

Second, many of the research participants examined the vignettes from the point of view of the behaviour of the complainant Ian. There was strong evidence that his behaviour was judged by social norms, expectations and notions of personal responsibility for maintaining a reasonable level of safety from potential victimisation. While there was an implication in some of the contributions that women have a significant responsibility for managing personal safety and the perceived risk presented by men. This standard, in some instances, was also applied to Ian with suggestions, for example, that he showed a 'lot of stupidity' for going back to a stranger's flat alone. The following exchange was taken from Group 2 (female-only).

DIANE: If you see things in a female context … this woman went home with this bloke, they were kissing and she was doing all this stuff, and then suddenly she decided not to, do you feel not even legally, but as part of you, she shouldn't have got in this situation.

ALL: Yeah.

BELLA: I do think she shouldn't have got in that situation. But that still doesn't give him the right to rape her ... there was a lot of stupidity on Ian's part to go back.

ANNA: It might mean that 99 per cent you're going to have sex ...

BELLA: It's not consent.

ANNA: I wouldn't go back, I'm not saying it's consent ... I just think if it was a woman, she must have it in the back of her mind if you meet someone at a party you go back to their flat and watch a DVD and one thing leads to another ...

DIANE: Yes, but being a woman, that's completely different.

ANNA: But why ... ?

DIANE: A woman would not go back to a bloke's house if she met him at a party that first night, without wanting something, in my opinion.

HELEN: If I met someone that I've got on with as long as I tell my friends where I'm going I'm quite happy going back to someone's house that I've just met, as long as I feel personally safe.

IRIS: In my opinion I would feel really vulnerable doing that.

Here Iris expresses a sense of vulnerability in the idea of going back to a stranger's flat alone. In several other focus groups where participants saw this type of behaviour as dangerous in the context of women, this sense of danger was projected onto Ian. As a result, Ian's behaviour came under close scrutiny. Interestingly, Anderson and Doherty claim, on the basis of their focus-group discussions involving male and female rape vignettes, that 'victims constructed as heterosexual are culturally exempt from the responsibility of hazard/risk awareness in relation to sexual violence'.[27] This is a conclusion that is contradicted by the findings of this study in which Ian was seen as engaging in risky behaviour irrespective of his sexuality.

While in this exchange there is a reference to Ian's 'stupidity', which was not challenged by other group members, much of the discussion featured expectations concerning the behaviour of women. Diane, who in other parts of the discussion was highly critical of Ian and his behaviour, suggests that a woman who goes back to a man's flat would always 'want something'. She describes the position of women as 'completely different', thus implying that a man may go back to another man's flat without there being an assumption that he consents to any subsequent sexual activity. This exchange also reflects a wider trend within the groups in which participants sought to understand and explain their views in terms of their own likely behaviour and experiences. In their jury research, Pennington and Hastie suggest that jurors make decisions based on 'world knowledge' and the decision-makers' own subjective experiences.[28] Throughout the four focus groups, participants repeatedly referred to their own experiences in order to justify particular conclusions and to 'position' themselves in the fictional vignette, thereby increasing the use and extent of comparative reasoning.

In addition, there were repeated references to Ian 'leading David on' (most notably for accepting an invitation to a stranger's home). The participants also considered sexuality in addition to comparing male and female experiences and expectations. The assumption that 'you're expecting something' if you accept an invitation to go to a stranger's home at night was generally as relevant for men as it was for women. This was justified in terms of the issue of sexuality as evidenced by the exchange below from Group 4:

ANDY: I just don't see this as rape, I know it's hard to think of it from your own point of view … but if you went to a girl's house and you met them that night, and it's not to do with anything but the fact you're attracted to each other, so whether you have sex or snog and stuff, you're expecting something. So something was going to happen, one of them was expecting something to happen and the other one wasn't. You can't go out on a night and go back to someone's, male or female, whatever you like, and not think something's going to happen.

MARK: Because it's not often that something … you get on with someone in a pub, and say do you wanna go back to mine … you go to a party.

ANDY: And get a number.

MARK: But that's the thing you don't generally talk to other guys, you talk to girls. You wouldn't spend the whole night talking to one bloke would you … that seems a bit, contributing to it … if Ian's not gay then I can't really see a straight person doing that … and then going back to theirs.

Here, Ian's behaviour was seen as raising an 'expectation' that sex will take place. Further, non-sexual behaviour, such as talking to someone at a party, 'contributed' to a belief that Ian might be gay and, as was made subsequently clear in later discussions, was used to undermine Ian's claim of non-consent.

Evidence suggests that significant numbers of male and female rape complainants delay reporting to the police.[29] One of the vignettes informed participants that Ian delayed reporting his allegation of rape to the police for three days because 'he was worried that the police would think he was gay and that he wouldn't be believed'. Participants saw similarities in the prospective reasons as to why male and female rape complainants might delay reporting to the police.

> To be honest enough women wait for a few days especially with men. People have a reaction to men being raped anyway 'cause it's the same thing, how could a man be raped? So he's probably feeling a bit weird about going to the police. Because they might say you must be gay you asked for it.

Another participant noted that in the context of delayed reporting: 'It's the same with women who have been drunk.'

Direct comparisons between men and women were also made when participants considered their relative physical size with assumptions being made about
men's ability to resist rape. As one participant commented: 'based on sheer
physics it's easier for a man to restrain a woman than a man to restrain another
man surely. I'm basing that solely on physical makeup.' This might suggest that
to some people an allegation of male rape is less credible than that involving a
female complainant.

Finally, in Group 3 it was suggested by one of the participants that a jury
would 'be more sympathetic' if a rape complainant was female. But this view
was contested when another member of the group referred to a particular belief
that impacts on female rape: that 'if she was dressed provocatively she was
asking for it'. Of course, dress can be invoked to cast doubt on claims of rape in
several different ways. It might be that 'provocative' dress is an issue that substantially impacts on female complainants, but it should not be assumed that
dress does not negatively impact on the reception of allegations of male rape.
This is a particular variable that has not been tested in the current literature,
although within this study clothing was raised as an issue, though not in the
context of provocation. It was argued by one participant that even if David had
pulled down Ian's trousers he still 'would have had a chance and get away'.[30]

False allegations

The fear of false rape allegations continue to play a significant role in social and
legal responses to rape.[31] While it is known that men and women make false
allegations of rape, we know little of how people decide when an allegation of
male rape is false and on what evidential grounds.[32] The issue of false allegations
was a significant feature of the discussions, with participants identifying a range
of possible motivations:

FIONA: People do make things up …
ANNA: You would need a reason to accuse someone of rape.
EMMA: If you weren't gay.
FIONA: But it could have been like she said, he might have been like it might
have been his first full-on gay experience. Wow, yeah, and then suddenly
David is like it's just a one-night thing, and then Ian …
CHARLOTTE: There are crazy people.
DIANE: But we don't know if he has mental-health issues and just wants to be
horrible to someone, it does happen.
EMMA: If that was a woman would you say women would only report a rape?
She wouldn't make it up? … Loads of people go round, 'I got pissed last
night and he raped me … I really wish I hadn't had sex with him.'

Interestingly, the issue of false allegations is further pursued in the context of a
three-day delay in Ian reporting his alleged rape to the police. Included within

this discussion was the suggestion that Ian might fabricate an injury to support his allegation and that it may be more likely for a woman to make a false rape allegation than a male.

DIANE: And also, two days later, if he wanted it make it up as something else, give yourself a whack. You hear about women doing it or whatever … You've got less chance of actually saying it unless it actually happened, whereas with females …

CHARLOTTE: You could quite easily say, 'Oh he's raped me.'

BELLA: It could also happen in terms of pregnancies and stuff like that if they're embarrassed about something they've done and now they're pregnant they probably cry rape, but with men it's harder, you won't fall pregnant.

Of course, taken literally, the claim regarding pregnancy as a motivation to lie about rape is true, as men cannot become pregnant and so lack that specific motivation to lie about rape.[33] However, any assertion that women are more likely to lie about being raped is not supported by the current literature.[34]

Much of the discussion concerning false allegations involved attempts at understanding why Ian might make such an accusation and, where comparison was made with female complainants, similarities were generally emphasised over differences: 'I don't think Ian is gay, because in essence it was a one-night stand, whatever he said, and if it was you or someone, or a woman, she would probably lie and think it was a mistake.' Further discussions also gave an impression that false complaints are easily made, with a range of possible motives.

ANDY: With any rape if someone is claiming they have been raped either I mean I'm just going back to heterosexual [rape], because there's so many more cases of it, it's either there's been a rape and it's been quite significant or it's a girl ashamed of what she did last night and she's gone, and she's saw someone and …

MARK: It's such a harsh thing to say someone could be lying about it but people do … just to try and get attention and get someone put away.

HARRY: Last night I was talking to someone a girl in my seminar group, and we were talking about a rape thing we had to talk about, and she was saying a guy she knew got accused of rape because he had a threesome with this girl and another bloke, and she was just really ashamed of it and cried rape to the police. So it could be like what you are saying … [Ian is] ashamed about having sex with a man …

ANDY: If he consented then he is going to come out and be gay or bisexual and he might not be, he was just drunk and he's straight, and thought this is something different I'll give it a go. I know people who have done that.

The relative seriousness of male and female rape

In their focus-group research, Anderson and Doherty found that some participants viewed the rape of a heterosexual male as more serious than the rape of a homosexual male or woman.[35] Within the wider literature there is evidence of other hierarchies of seriousness which suggest that female rape is more traumatic than male rape.[36] It has even been suggested that males should not be adversely affected by rape or sexual assault at all.[37] In an attempt to justify gender-specific rape laws, some scholars have argued that the rape of women is unique and particularly grave. For example, Williams has argued that the fear and risk of pregnancy, abortion and disease transmission might be a key distinguishing feature of vaginal rape compared with other forms of bodily penetration. She observes that the 'feminist lobby has been surprisingly silent on the point'.[38] One reason for that silence is that such reasoning has come under scrutiny and been found wanting.[39] Williams provides no evidence to suggest that disease transmission is any greater for vaginal rape than it is for other forms of penile penetration or why such consequences should influence the definition of rape rather than be incorporated into sentencing rules.[40]

In the focus-group discussions, a variety of views were expressed on the relative seriousness of male and female rape. In Group 3, two of the participants suggested that a rape is 'more [of] a stigma for a male' and that 'anyone would be embarrassed about getting raped … especially [a] male'. In this group it was also suggested that a hierarchy of seriousness exists between gay and heterosexual males: 'I think a lot of the time especially for males, I think it could be worse for a straight male [who] has never had sex with a man before.' Another participant began to make a distinction between male and female rape but ultimately observed that they were equally serious:

> When I think rape, and then with male rape, probably I don't know there's a high percentage of more dangerous sexual diseases … I mean women can contract it and things like that … but that's probably not on their minds … like HIV … any form of rape if its heterosexual or homosexual I think it's as bad as each other.

Conclusion

The claims of general preferential treatment for male rape complainants asserted by some feminists are largely unsupported by the findings in this research. Most of the focus-group discussions treated male and female rape in a similar manner. There were some departures, for example, in the context of false allegations, victim trauma and in terms of the interpretation of complainant behaviour. Here, expectations and beliefs had a gendered component. But the privileging of male rape was not demonstrated in any consistent way, and in some limited cases there appears to have been more damning judgements made of Ian's behaviour than of female victims placed in Ian's position by the discussants. Given the length and range of the focus-group discussions, any privileging of either male or female rape was relatively limited. A large majority of the discussions indicated no differentiation between male or female complainants.[41] These findings suggest that scholars should show a degree of caution before making, in some instances, sweeping claims or theory-led assumptions about the relative treatment of male and female rape.

Notes

1 For discussion, see P. Rumney, 'Policing Male Rape and Sexual Assault', *The Journal of Criminal Law*, 71 (2008), p. 67 and infra. ns 2,16,17 below.
2 R. Graham, 'Male Rape and the Careful Construction of the Male Victim', *Social and Legal Studies*, 15 (2006), p. 187.
3 Ibid., p. 197.
4 I. Anderson and K. Doherty, *Accounting for Rape: Psychology, Feminism and Discourse Analysis in the Study of Sexual Violence* (London and New York: Routledge, 2008). For examples of the privileging of female rape and sexual assault, see P. Rumney, 'Gay Victims of Male Rape: Law Enforcement, Social Attitudes and Barriers to Recognition', *International Journal of Human Rights*, Special Double Issue on Sexual Minorities 13 (2009), p. 240.
5 See P. Rumney, 'Policing Male Rape' (discussing *inter alia* claims that male victims receive preferential treatment during rape trials and the law-reform process).
6 This work builds on earlier research. See, for example, P. Rumney and N. Hanley, 'The Mythology of Male Rape: Social Attitudes and Law Enforcement', in C. McGlynn and V. Munro (eds.), *Rethinking Rape Law: National, International and European Perspectives* (London: Routledge-Cavendish, 2010); Anderson and Doherty, *Accounting for Rape Psychology*.
7 R. Graycar and J. Morgan, *The Hidden Gender of Law* (Sydney: Federation Press, 2002), p. 300.
8 S. Brownmiller, *Against Our Will: Men, Women and Rape* (Harmondsworth: Penguin, 1975).
9 M. T. Gordon and S. Riger, *The Female Fear* (London: Free Press, 1989), p. 2.
10 K. Baker, 'Once a Rapist? Motivational Evidence and Relevancy in Rape Law', *Harvard Law Review*, 100 (1997): 564 and 624 n3.
11 N. Abdullah-Khan, *Male Rape: The Emergence of a Social and Legal Issue* (Basingstoke: Palgrave Macmillan, 2008), pp. 163–4; C. Carosella (ed.), *Who's Afraid of the Dark? A Forum of Truth, Support and Assurance for Those Affected by Rape* (New York: HarperPerennial, 1995), pp. 201–4.
12 P. Novotny, 'Rape Victims in the (Gender) Neutral Zone: The Assimilation of Resistance?', *Seattle Journal for Social Justice*, 1 (2003), p. 743. See also Williams infra. n. 38.
13 P. Rumney, 'In Defence of Gender Neutrality Within Rape', *Seattle Journal for Social Justice*, 6 (2007), p. 481. Indeed, recent research that compared the impact of adult male and female sexual assault found that males reported greater trauma than females in eight out of ten measures of trauma. D. M. Elliott, D. S. Mok and J. Briere, 'Adult Sexual Assault: Prevalence, Symptomatology, and Sex Differences in the General Population', *Journal of Traumatic Stress*, 17 (2004), p. 203. This notes that 'men with a history of [adult sexual assault] reported significantly higher levels of distress than female victims of [adult sexual assault] on eight of the 10 TSI scales and equivalent

levels on the remaining two scales (Depression and Intrusive Experiences). This occurred despite general equivalence between the sexes regarding the characteristics of the [adult sexual assault]' (p. 209).

14 For discussion, see Rumney, ibid.

15 See for example, H. Codd, 'The Treatment of Complainants', *New Law Journal* (1996), p. 447; Graham, 'Male Rape', p. 187. For responses to these claims, see P. Rumney and M. Morgan-Taylor, 'Male Rape', *New Law Journal*, 14 June 1996, p. 872; Rumney, 'Policing Male Rape and Sexual Assault', p. 1; P. Rumney and J. Jamel, 'The Not So Careful Construction of the Male Victim: A Response to Ruth Graham', unpublished, available online at http://papers.ssrn.com/sol3/papers.cfm?abstract_id=1339585 (accessed 27 January 2010).

16 A. Dworkin, *Pornography: Men Possessing Women* (New York: J. P. Dutton, 1989), p. 56.

17 C. MacKinnon, *Are Women Human? And Other International Dialogues* (Cambridge, Mass.: Harvard University Press, 2006), p. 74. Mackinnon's suggestion that male rape is not found entertaining or amusing is a surprise given that prison rape jokes and other forms of humour associated with male sexual victimisation by women or other men appear common. For a recent example in New Zealand, see http://abs-cbnnews.com/lifestyle/01/18/10/airlines-sexy-cougar-ad-blasted-male-rape-victims (accessed 27 January 2010). See also A. Clark, 'Why Does Popular Culture Treat Prison Rape as a Joke?', *Alternet*, 17 August 2009, available online at http://www.alternet.org/reproductivejustice/141594/why_does_popular_culture_treat_prison_rape_as_a_joke/?page=entire (accessed 27 January 2010).

18 J. Temkin and B. Krahé, *Sexual Assault and the Justice Gap: A Question of Attitude* (Oxford: Hart, 2008).

19 Abdullah-Kahn, *Male Rape*.

20 For earlier research that has examined attitudes to male rape, see, for example, M. Davies and P. Rogers, 'Perceptions of Male Victims in Depicted Sexual Assaults: A Review of the Literature', *Aggression and Violent Behaviour*, 11 (2006), p. 367; M. Davies, P. Pollard and J. Archer, 'Effects of Perpetrator Gender and Victim Sexuality on Blame toward Male Victims of Sexual Assault', *The Journal of Social Psychology*, 3 (2006): 275–91.

21 V. Jupp, *Methods of Criminological Research* (London: Unwin Hyman, 1989); A. Bryman, *Social Research Methods,* 3rd edn (Oxford: Oxford University Press, 2008).

22 S. L. Hamby and M. P. Koss, 'Shades of Gray: A Qualitative Study of Terms Used in the Measurement of Sexual Victimization', *Psychology of Women Quarterly*, 27 (2003): 243–55.

23 Temkin and Krahé, *Sexual Assault and the Justice Gap*, pp. 53–4.

24 J. Kitzinger, 'The Methodology of Focus Groups: The Importance of Interaction between Research Participants', *Sociology of Health and Illness*, 16 (1994), p. 103; H. Frith, 'Focusing on Sex: Using Focus Groups in Sex Research', *Sexualities*, 3 (2000), p. 275; J. A. Hollander, 'The Social Contexts of Focus Groups', *Journal of Contemporary Ethnography*, 33 (2004), p. 602.

25 E. Finch and V. E. Munro, 'Lifting the Veil: The Use of Focus Groups and Trial Simulations in Legal Research', *Journal of Law and Society*, 35 (2008), p. 35.

26 See Todd Brower, Chapter 7, for the use of schemas in sexual-orientation and sex-discrimination cases.

27 Anderson and Doherty, *Accounting for Rape*, p. 81.

28 N. Pennington and R. Hastie, 'Evidence Evaluation in Complex Decision Making', *Journal of Personality and Social Psychology*, 51 (1986), pp. 242 and 254. See also L. Ellison and V. E. Munro, 'Reacting to Rape: Exploring Mock Jurors' Assessments of Complainant Credibility', *Journal of Criminology*, 49 (2009), p. 202.

29 M. King and E. Woollett, 'Sexually Assaulted Males: 115 Men Consulting a Counselling Service', *Archives of Sexual Behaviour*, 26 (1997), p. 579.

30 Rumney and Hanley, 'The Mythology of Male Rape'.
31 P. Rumney, 'False Allegations of Rape', *The Cambridge Law Journal*, 65 (2006), p. 128.
32 Rumney, 'Policing Male Rape'.
33 E. J. Kanin, 'False Rape Allegations', *Archives of Sexual Behavior*, 23 (1994), pp. 85–6.
34 The evidence of false reporting rates for male and female rape is limited. However, what evidence there is does not suggest women are more likely than men to make false allegations. For discussion, see Deputy Commissioner's Command, Directorate of Strategic Development and Territorial Policing, Project Sapphire, *A Review of Rape Investigations in the MPS [Metropolitan Police Service]* (2005).
35 Anderson and Doherty, *Accounting for Rape*, p. 80.
36 For discussion, see Rumney, 'Policing Male Rape', p. 82.
37 Rumney, 'Gay Victims of Male Rape', pp. 241–2.
38 M. L. Williams, *Secrets and Laws: Collected Essays in Law, Lives and Literature* (London: UCL Press, 2005), p. 73.
39 See, for example, C. Wells, 'Law Reform, Rape and Ideology', *Journal of Law and Society*, 12 (1985), pp. 63 and 66; J. Temkin, *Rape and the Legal Process* (Oxford: Oxford University Press, 2002), pp. 60–2.
40 Pregnancy resulting from rape is regarded as an aggravating factor in sentencing under English law: *Millberry* (2003) 2 Cr App R (S) 31, para. 10.
41 In their focus-group research Anderson and Doherty give examples of where male victims are treated more sympathetically than female victims. However, it is less clear from their findings precisely what proportion of the total discussions were gendered in this manner.

Chapter 11

When hate is not enough

Tackling homophobic violence

Iain McDonald

Introduction

Violence against the lesbian, gay and bisexual (LGB) community has only recently emerged more fully as a social problem.[1] This chapter will discuss the importance of understanding homophobic violence as a complex social problem that impacts on gay men, lesbians and the LGB community generally in distinctive ways. Furthermore, the appropriateness of the legal response to homophobic violence, particularly the use of hate-crime legislation, will be questioned. It will be argued here that changes in the criminal law, while vital, will not be sufficient on their own to tackle the continuing violence directed towards the LGB community.

The general use of the phrase 'homophobic violence' rather than 'homophobic hate crime' in this chapter is deliberate. While the concept of 'hate crime' has proved useful in mobilising collective policy responses to crimes and actions based on prejudice or bigotry, 'hate crime' also effects a conceptual and theoretical closure that restricts the scope of any inquiry into homophobic violence and elides the role of the law itself in sustaining a hostile environment for the LGB community.[2]

Revealing the stranger of homophobic violence

The nail-bombing of the London gay pub, the Admiral Duncan, in 1999, the brutal murder of Jody Dobrowski in 2005 and the shocking shootings at the Bar-Noar gay youth club in Tel Aviv in 2009 are all examples of homophobic violence sensational enough to penetrate the news agenda of the day. However, the coverage of such crimes fosters a public understanding that homophobic violence is characterised by acts of extreme, physical violence perpetrated by strangers.[3] Although any coverage of homophobic violence is valuable in raising awareness, research suggests that this value is undermined by the cultivation of a 'stranger danger' discourse and its potentially negative effects.

A focus on 'stranger danger' can disguise the true extent and nature of the behaviour it seeks to address. By focusing on extreme and isolated acts of physical homophobic violence, 'the logic of the stranger obscures our ability to understand the ordinariness of hate crime'.[4] Members of the LGB community undoubtedly face physical violence of the basis of their sexuality.[5] A 2008 survey of 1,721 lesbians, gays and bisexuals found that one in six respondents had experienced a homophobic physical assault in the past three years.[6] It has also been argued that homophobic violence can be among the most vicious of all hate crimes.[7] However, in contrast to the 'stranger danger' associations of isolated physical attacks, homophobic violence comprises a much broader spectrum of actions, including intimidation, verbal abuse and harassment. Stonewall's 2009 report, for example, found that nearly one in six respondents had experienced a threat of violence and that 88 per cent of all the homophobic incidents recorded involved insults or harassment.[8]

This discourse accomplishes two things. Stevenson has argued in the context of discussing myths which impact upon the treatment of rape victims that the identification of 'rapists as strangers and deviants thereby diminish[es] the seriousness with which the public regards rape by men known to their victim'.[9] Similarly, the focus on extreme acts of homophobic violence minimises the general appreciation of the extent to which homophobic violence is part of the 'everyday' experience of many members of the LGB community.[10]

The idea that homophobic violence occurs beyond the boundaries of the ordinary community is a particularly pernicious consequence of 'stranger' discourse. Mason's analysis of racist and homophobic harassment cases is particularly illuminating in this respect. While accepting that homophobic violence is frequently committed by persons unknown to the victim, Mason questions the accuracy of describing such violence as being perpetrated by strangers, noting that in 82.5 per cent of cases analysed victims were able to identify the perpetrator as a 'neighbour' or 'local to home' and, in another 7.5 per cent, as 'local to work'.[11] Victims and perpetrators, therefore, are often connected and familiar through their shared, routine occupation of public, communal spaces – a coexistence which, for the LGB community, cannot and should not have to be avoided.

Therefore, in contrast to the shadowy outsider connotations of the 'stranger' discourse around homophobic violence, 'many incidents are committed by "ordinary" people in the context of their "everyday lives" in patterns consistent with routine activity of crime'.[12] Writing in the context of racial harassment, Sibbett engages the idea of 'perpetrator communities', noting that communities, by their implicit approval or explicit tolerance of violence against certain groups, can shape and confirm the prejudices of perpetrators. Moreover, the predominant focus on the violent stranger of homophobic attacks can also 'serve as markers by which other perpetrators are able to judge their own abusive and intimidatory actions as relatively harmless', insulating the wider community from any need to question their own values and actions.[13]

Understanding the effects and purposes of homophobic violence

In challenging the idea that homophobic violence can be explained purely on an individualistic basis, it is equally important to consider the effects of such violence. Research suggests that the victims of homophobic violence may take longer to recover from the psychological impact of such incidents compared to gay and lesbian victims of crime generally.[14] McDevitt et al. have also suggested that homophobic victimisation may be linked to a greater chance of losing one's employment, more general health problems and greater anxiety in being open about one's sexuality following such an incident.[15]

Moreover, homophobic violence can also be described as a 'message crime' in that the specific identity of the victim is of less significance than their identification as part of a group that is to be denigrated and ostracised.[16] This impersonal aspect of homophobic violence has been likened to a form of 'terrorism' against the LGB community.[17] The pervasiveness and unpredictability of homophobic violence fosters a generalised 'climate of insecurity' that enforces a heterosexist ideology by patrolling the legitimate expressions of sexual orientation in public and enforcing stifling practices of self-policing.[18] Such violence represents 'a form of governance of sexual difference', targeting visible displays of non-heterosexual sexuality for censure and punishment and so constructing them as inferior and unwelcome.[19]

Understanding homophobic violence as a practice of heteronormativity

Understanding the effects of homophobic violence on the LGB community provides a clear imperative to respond. However, if homophobic violence is to be tackled effectively, it is crucial that the purposes of such violence are understood more clearly. While the phrase 'homophobic violence' is used to encompass the broad spectrum of violent acts and conduct directed towards the LGB community on the basis of their sexual orientation, the anti-essentialist insights of queer theory demand that the ways in which sexual orientation may interact with other factors to produce distinctive forms of violence are not overlooked.

Although homophobic violence is most commonly experienced by both gays and lesbians in public contexts, there is evidence to suggest that such an account may predominantly reflect the experiences of gay men.[20] Research into anti-lesbian violence demonstrates that lesbians are more vulnerable to 'privatized forms of harassment or violence'.[21] For example, the recent Stonewall survey recorded that lesbians were more likely than gay men to experience a homophobic incident instigated by work colleagues or family members.[22]

The differential experience of homophobic violence between gay men and lesbians reveals broader, gendered assumptions about the appropriate distribution of power between men and women: anti-lesbian violence reiterates women's violability and a converse acceptance of men's 'right' to control the extent of women's privacy. Furthermore, although research suggests that gay men are more likely to be physically assaulted than lesbians, lesbians remain more likely to experience violence from strangers than heterosexual women.[23] Thus, while paternalistic prohibitions against harming women may constrain the use of violence against lesbians as compared with gay men, the visible display of a non-conformist female sexuality weakens the application of such controls, resulting in the greater use of violence against lesbians than heterosexual women.[24]

Similarly, the major tropes of anti-lesbian violence reveal a common concern with the reinforcement of gendered constructions of the female body and its presumed heterosexuality. Anti-lesbian violence often attempts to (re)feminise the female body through the imposition of forced acts of heterosexuality, thus temporarily restoring the established normative connections between sexed bodies, gendered expectations and heterosexual attraction. The frequent connections made between lesbians and masculinity, confirming the abnormality of masculinised female bodies through their lack of femininity, ensure that traditional notions of heterosexual attraction are sustained.[25] In this way, homophobic violence reinforces the differences (in power and, consequently, in role) between differently sexed bodies.

These important insights expose the very instability of the 'gender order' that such violence strives to preserve. In this sense, homophobic violence must also be understood as a heteronormative discursive practice, perpetually reiterating the centrality and stability of heterosexuality and its associated gender norms.[26] Therefore, while Mason is correct to argue that violence makes a statement about those it objectifies, it is equally important to consider the statements that violence makes about those who use it.[27]

Understanding homophobic violence as a practice of identity

A conception of homophobic violence that exposes its heteronormative foundation challenges the simplistic notion that such acts can be explained solely by perpetrators' individual hatred. It thus locates homophobic violence within the broader social project of maintaining heterosexuality as the dominant expression of gender relations. Moreover, such behaviour has also been demonstrated to have significance in the development of perpetrators' own identity. As Fuss argues, 'heterosexuality secures its self-identity and shores up its ontological boundaries by protecting itself from what it sees as the continual predatory encroachments of its contaminated other, homosexuality'.[28] The key motif here is one of defence. Homophobic violence betrays a vulnerability – an idea that heterosexuality is in need of protection. Thus, homophobic violence does not simply express disapproval; it is also necessary to the production of one's own identity as coherently heterosexual.

This perspective is particularly interesting in light of Connell and Messerschmidt's discussion of hegemonic masculinity. Connell and Messerschmidt argues that 'masculinities are configurations of practice that are accomplished in social action'.[29] '*Hegemonic* masculinity' represents a culturally dominant 'ideal', which is distinguished from forms of subordinate masculinity (including but not limited to male homosexuality) and from femininity in general.[30] While hegemonic masculinity can be expressed in many non-violent practices, for example providing financially for a family or being physically capable, violence remains profoundly compatible with its attainment. Tomsen notes that 'anti-homosexual sentiment is often highly rewarding and enhances the social esteem of those who display it'.[31] Moreover, in their analysis of planned attacks on gay men in a public setting and which resulted in death, Tomsen and Mason note that perpetrators frequently displayed a form of 'protest masculinity', whereby their social and economic marginalisation (which limited their ability to participate in many practices of hegemonic masculinity) was compensated for through exaggerated and aggressive acts of homophobia. In this context, the perpetrators' violence was perceived as a way to establish their own masculinity within their peer group, and its use against gay men helped confirm their own position of dominance in relation to the marginalisation they otherwise shared with their gay victims.[32] Thus, homophobic violence can be conceived not simply as hate but as part of a repertoire of socially validated practices aimed at establishing a 'superior' masculine identity.

The picture of homophobic violence that emerges from this discussion is complex. Far from being merely comprised of acts based on an individual's hatred of the LGB community, homophobic violence is deeply embedded in the everyday 'ordinary' practices of the broader community. Insight into the use of homophobic violence to police homosexual visibility in public has also been supplemented by an awareness of how such practices are necessary in the affirmation of heterosexual (and masculine) ideals. As Moran and Skeggs argue, 'homophobic violence is a violence for the social order, not a violence of social disorder'.[33] It is against this backdrop that the discussion now turns to consider the legal response to homophobic violence.

The legal response to homophobic violence

Although victimisation surveys had been building a picture of the extent of homophobic violence for a number of years, arguably it was only in the aftermath of the Macpherson Report into the murder of Stephen Lawrence in 1999 that sufficient momentum was built to drive a legal response to 'hate crimes' in the UK. However, quite apart from the limitations of the concept of 'hate crime' suggested above, the use of hate-crimes legislation has always been fiercely contested and remains controversial.

A useful starting point from which to discuss the legal response to homophobic violence is provided by Lawrence, who argues that 'it is impossible for the punishment choices made by the society *not* to express societal values'.[34] In other words, a decision not to punish hate crimes expresses an unacceptable rejection of the rights to safety of targeted groups who have been traditionally excluded from society. While Lawrence's basic position is unassailable, it is equally critical, however, to consider the values that are expressed through the decision to punish prejudice in addition to the commission of a criminal offence.

The primary legal response to homophobic violence in England and Wales has been through the criminal law. The two key provisions, contained in Section

146 of the Criminal Justice Act 2003 and Section 74 of the Criminal Justice and Immigration Act 2008, illustrate the broad legal strategies used to tackle 'hate crime', namely, sentence enhancement and the creation of specific 'hate crime' offences.[35]

First, Section 146 of the Criminal Justice Act 2003 imposes a statutory obligation upon the courts, when sentencing, to treat as an aggravating factor the fact that either, in committing any offence, the perpetrator demonstrated hostility towards their victim on the basis of their sexual orientation, or that the offence was motivated (partly or wholly) by hostility towards the victim's sexual orientation.[36] Section 146 can be utilised in conjunction with a conviction for any criminal offence. The provision applies not only to crimes where the victim has been selected on the basis of their (perceived) sexual orientation but to those crimes where such hostility is manifested 'at the time of committing the offence, or immediately before or after doing so'.[37] Moreover, in contrast to the creation of specific 'racially aggravated' offences in Part II of the Crime and Disorder Act 1998, the offender will still be convicted and sentenced for the basic offence, even if the aggravating behaviour cannot be proved. In contrast, Section 74 of the Criminal Justice and Immigration Act 2008 amends Part IIIA of the Public Order Act 1986 to create a more specific range of offences related to the incitement of hatred on the grounds of sexual orientation. The scope of this section is much narrower and is designed to capture the use of words, behaviour or materials which are threatening rather than simply insulting.[38]

A number of justifications have been offered in support of hate-crime legislation. The most prominent of these is that hate-crime legislation is symbolically valuable in expressing the law's disapproval of crimes attributable to prejudice and in reaching out to groups who have been historically excluded from society and the law's protection.[39] Iganski argues that the development of hate-crime legislation in the UK was not primarily aimed at those hardened bigots whose actions are unlikely to be deterred by the presence of criminal sanctions but to effect the 'normative compliance of ordinary people going about their lives'.[40] While it is unquestionable that the state should communicate its commitment to socially inclusive values, the decision to do so through enhanced sentencing provisions remains problematic.

The reasons for this can be explored in considering Moran and Skeggs's argument that efforts to enact hate-crime legislation represent a 'demand for law's violence'.[41] The characterisation of law as violence originated in the work of Cover.[42] While such violence is exemplified in the use of the death penalty, Moran explains, 'Law's violence is manifest not only through the capacity to punish, but in the capacity to draw and enforce distinctions and to impose meanings (the violence of the word).'[43] In this light, the demand for law's violence can be seen as a demand for recognition as a group worthy of the law's protection.

However, to invoke law's violence is to risk being subject to its definitional power and implicated in its closures, so it is important to question the forms it takes. Sentence-enhancement provisions are often justified on the basis that hate crimes are more injurious than ordinary crimes: while all crimes have the capacity to cause lasting effects, crimes that strike at the self-identity of the victim clearly have the capacity to inflict greater and longer-lasting harm.[44] In this sense, an increased sentence reflects the perpetrator's 'just deserts'. Such reasoning takes a potential for greater injury and transforms it into an inevitability. Not only does this risk punishing hate-crime offenders more harshly than 'ordinary' offenders, irrespective of the actual harm inflicted, it also undermines the equality-based argument for hate-crime legislation by feeding into a politics of resentment wherein the general public perceives that certain victim groups are receiving preferential treatment, whether or not that is actually the case.[45]

There is another cost to embracing such an approach. The law's gaze is not neutral; it is violent. In highlighting the dangerous consequences of identity politics, Fraser describes this as a process of 'reification', by generalising the greater harm of hate crimes, the law discursively fixes the identity of lesbians, gays and bisexuals as vulnerable, and as victims.[46] To accept this victimology is to do a great injustice to the resilience of the LGB community, who have been managing their safety and well-being for many years with little protection from the state.[47] As Mason argues, homophobic violence can provide a context in which gay men and women can exercise control: in a society where to be other than heterosexual can still mean being defined, stereotyped and possibly victimised, the power to limit the ability of others to control how one is perceived represents not simply subjugation but also resistance.[48] Thus, it is important to recognise that homophobic violence is not a totalising force and may inadvertently produce positive effects, from the strategic self-management of one's visibility to the development of a stronger LGB community and more determined efforts to campaign for better protection.[49]

Moran expresses further hesitation about turning to the criminal law. When discussing how victim surveys have revealed the extent of homophobic violence, he points out that 'victim surveys [also] record the invisibility of most violence from the institutions of policing and crime control more generally'.[50] Of course, the long-standing inability of criminal-justice agencies to respond to the full extent of criminal activity is not a reason to abandon a criminal-law response. However, the fact that sentence-enhancing provisions may be applied in practice to a relatively limited number of cases gives us pause to question its function.

Drawing on Garland's theories in *The Culture of Control*, Moran argues that the control of crime over the past two decades has been shaped by two distinctive features: the privatisation of personal security through the promotion of individual responsibility for safety and an increasingly punitive approach to criminal justice.[51] Hate-crime legislation (exemplified by the sentence-enhancement approach) provides an example of the latter tendency.[52] These two features are related in that the privatisation of security signals the inability of the state to control crime, while the increasingly punitive use of the criminal law reaffirms the state's centrality as a source of power and legitimate authority. Meanwhile, the bolstering of punitive responses also serves to legitimise the state by deflecting attention from the role of the law and the criminal-justice system in supporting and reinforcing the social conditions in which hate crime can thrive.[53]

The centralisation of the state as a source of law and order is accomplished by promoting the view that 'hate is the problem [and] law the solution'.[54] However, in so far as the goal of hate-crime legislation is not simply to punish offenders but, through those actions, to make a declaratory statement in support of social cohesion, criminal law makes for a somewhat blunt tool. Given its inherent focus on identifying individual responsibility for discrete offences, the criminal law is ill equipped to convey an understanding of hate crimes as an ongoing process of victimisation rooted in a specific historical (and, it is argued) legally permissive context.[55] The focus on single events that meet the legal definition of an offence can exclude the many other legally irrelevant incidents that make up the often systematic experience of abuse. The punishment of individuals also elides the fact that while violence may be experienced at the hands of many, the community is absent within the legal context of hate-crimes legislation. This may also contribute to a sense of frustration for victims of hate crime, in that their experiences are not reflected (or even recognisable) in the legal response.[56]

The limitations of the criminal law in responding to such complex social problems suggest that the enhanced sentencing approach in hate crimes is largely rhetorical and self-serving: it neither understands the problem nor is able to respond to it effectively. Given the proliferation of hate-crimes legislation in the West, it is unlikely that we will witness the demise of a criminal law-focused approach any time soon. Indeed, for many affected communities, it will prove difficult to resist the allure of state recognition and protection, however compromised. Nonetheless, the challenge for the LGB community and others is to campaign for change that brings the criminal law more into line with its professed socially cohesive goals. Hate-crimes legislation does little to challenge, and indeed echoes, the very logic of difference that produces homophobic violence. The enhanced punishment of individual offenders continues to sideline the roots of homophobic violence in the broader community and the institutions of law and order. If the criminal law is to be of use, sentence enhancement should focus on restorative justice measures and tailored community service which might more effectively diffuse the 'tense proximity' of different identities that has exacerbated discord and violence in our society.[57]

From the regulation of homosexuality to the policing of homophobia

Kaplan argues that 'the appeal to the criminal law as a means to equal citizenship invites examination of its role in maintaining historic inequalities'.[58] It is no small irony that in demanding the law's violence it was only a short time before the LGB community was the target of that self-same violence. The law has a long history of punishing, persecuting and discriminating against the LGB community. While the advancements over the past ten years in legal rights for the LGB community have been, in many ways, breathtaking, each step forward has been bitterly contested. Furthermore, as a primary enforcer of law's violence, the police have been a 'pivotal player in the denial of protection', accused of both homophobia and the zealous over-policing of same-sex sexual activity.[59] Such concerns are illustrated in surveys that report a deep mistrust of the law and police, resulting in the under-reporting of homophobic violence to the police through a fear of dismissal or of secondary victimisation.[60]

In essence, the issue becomes a familiar one concerning whether formal changes in the law will be reflected in a corresponding institutional reform. While hate-crime legislation remains dubious in its effectiveness, a more optimistic picture may be emerging in respect of policing attitudes to homosexuality.

There can be little doubt that an effective response to homophobic violence must do more than penalise isolated incidents. It must address and transform the underlying heterosexist structures that produce such violence. In particular, the mutually reinforcing misrepresentations that, first, homophobic violence is exceptional and, second, that the LGB community is a 'troublesome' group to be policed and controlled must be challenged. In respect of the former concern, the Association of Chief Police Officers' (ACPO's) guidance on the monitoring of hate crime obligated under the Crime and Disorder Act 1998 represents an important step forward. The police are now required to record both 'hate incidents' and 'hate crimes'. A 'hate incident' is defined as 'any incident, which may or may not constitute a criminal offence, which is perceived by the victim or any other person, as being motivated by prejudice or hate'. In contrast, a 'hate crime' is 'any hate incident, which constitutes a criminal offence, perceived by the victim or any other person, as being motivated by prejudice or hate'.[61] The advantages of this approach are threefold. Recording 'non-criminal' incidents expands police conceptions of 'criminal activity' and helps communicate both the systematic nature of homophobic violence and the often very ordinary contexts in which it occurs. The obligation to record also reduces the sphere in which officer discretion can operate to restrict the relevance of such activity to police concerns. Finally, the privileging of a victim-defined understanding of 'hate' may empower victims to report to agencies in which they may have little trust.[62]

The difficulty of tackling homophobic attitudes within the police force is rooted in part in the LGB community's (and particularly gay men's) historical position within the law as a target of regulation and punishment. Even following the 'liberalisation' of homosexual acts effected by the Sexual Offences Act 1967, 'homosexuals' retained a 'quasi-criminal' identity that was premised on tolerance and a requirement that expressions of homosexuality remained private.[63]

Arguably, however, there are signs of improvement. While Dick's survey of homophobic hate crime found that 34 per cent of respondents did not report a hate incident because they 'did not think the police could or would do anything', only 10 per cent identified 'concern about homophobia' as the reason for not reporting.[64] The distinction made between 'homophobic' and 'transphobic' violence in ACPO guidance demonstrates an increased sensitivity to issues of identity.[65] Stanko points to the increased use of specific community-liaison officers as helping to generate greater trust and stronger lines of communication. The statutory obligation to include and consult representatives of LGB groups within crime and disorder reduction partnerships also provides greater opportunity for a more constructive dialogue to develop between the police and the LGB community.[66] Moreover, the second *Hate Crime Report* from the Crown Prosecution Service notes an increase in both the charging of and successful prosecution of homophobic hate crime.[67]

But there remain some underlying concerns. Despite the obligation to record hate incidents, Dick's recent survey still found that a quarter of the hate incidents reported by respondents were not recorded as such by the police.[68] This may reflect the continuing strength of police occupational culture and its resistance to change which, it has been argued, continues to valorise key practices of 'hegemonic masculinity'.[69] In addition to promoting negative attitudes towards the LGB community, the emphasis on and prioritisation of aggressive physical action and the thrill of reactive policing may also continue to impact upon police priorities.[70]

Despite the repeal in the Sexual Offences Act 2003 of the offences of gross indecency and buggery, traditionally used to target and criminalise same-sex activity, concern remains that police relations with the LGB community continue to be constructed around notions of the 'good' and 'bad homosexual'.[71] While the police have developed the provision of safety advice to the LGB community, by continuing to focus on traditional constructions of 'stranger danger' over the more commonplace realities of homophobic violence, a strategy of 'responsibilisation' emerges, perpetuating the unhelpful notion that members of the community can 'choose' whether or not to become victims.[72] The element of choice is problematic in two respects. First, it ignores the pervasiveness of homophobic violence that renders choice illusory for the LGB community – the reported greater vulnerability of lesbians to privatised forms of violence illustrates the limitations of 'choice' particularly well.[73] Second, by linking police protection to personal responsibility, those who engage in 'risky' behaviour, such as 'cottaging', are constructed as irresponsible, deflecting attention from the perpetrators' actions and encouraging victim blame.[74] Given the reluctance that such men may feel in reporting homophobic violence, there is still much to be done. However, even here, CPS guidance on prosecuting homophobic hate crime stresses the need for sensitivity in dealing with those who may themselves have been involved in more minor offences.[75] The difficulty of engaging positively with this group is exacerbated by the inclusion of MSMs (men who have sex with men, but who do not identify as gay), for whom reporting homophobic violence may pose particular difficulties and risk an unwanted 'outing' beyond their control.[76]

Conclusion

If we are to tackle homophobic violence effectively, it must be properly understood. Homophobic violence is a complex phenomenon that must be seen as emanating from many different sources: the individual, the community, the law and its agencies. To conceptualise homophobic violence as a problem of hate crime is to invite the law to govern its solution and to ignore the complicity of law and legal enforcement practice in perpetuating the structures that foster such violence. It is vital that we strive to escape the logic of difference that has characterised both the problem and its proposed solutions. Only in this way will we be able to tackle the deeper underlying inequalities that enable society to continue to see the 'homosexual' as 'other'.

Notes

1 This chapter will focus on homophobic violence against lesbians, gays and bisexuals. The issues raised by transphobic violence demand separate consideration, which is beyond the scope of this piece.

2 P. Iganski, 'Criminal Law and the Routine Activity of "Hate Crime"', *Liverpool Law Review*, 29 (1) (2008): 1–17, at p. 3.

3 Ibid., p. 2.

4 E. Stanko, 'Re-conceptualising the Policing of Hatred: Confessions and Worrying Dilemma of a Consultant', *Law and Critique*, 12 (3) (2001): 309–29, at p. 323.

5 G. Mason, *The Spectacle of Violence: Homophobia, Gender and Knowledge* (London and New York: Routledge, 2002), p. 39; N. Chakraborti and J. Garland, *Hate Crime: Impact, Causes and Responses* (London: Sage, 2009), p. 62.

6 S. Dick, *Homophobic Hate Crime: The Gay British Crime Survey 2008* (London: Stonewall, 2009), p. 5.

7 Chakraborti and Garland, *Hate Crime*, pp. 63–4.

8 Dick, *Homophobic Hate Crime*, pp. 5 and 10.

9 K. Stevenson, 'Unequivocal Victims: The Historical Roots of the Mystification of the Female Complainant in Rape Cases', *Feminist Legal Studies*, 8 (3) (2000): 343–66, at p. 349.

10 Iganski, 'Criminal Law'.

11 G. Mason, 'Hate Crime and the Image of the Stranger', *British Journal of Criminology*, 2005, pp. 837–59, at p. 851.

12 Iganski, 'Criminal Law', p. 3.

13 R. Sibbitt, *The Perpetrators of Racial Harassment and Racial Violence* (London: HMSO, 1997), p. 101.

14 G. M. Herek, J. C. Cogan and J. R. Gillis, 'Victim Experiences in Hate Crimes Based on Sexual Orientation', *Journal of Social Issues*, 58 (2) (2002): 319–39, at p. 320.

15 J. McDevitt, J. Balboni, L. Garcia and J. Gu, 'Consequences for Victims: A Comparison of Bias- and Non-Bias-Motivated Assaults', *American Behavioural Scientist*, 45 (4) (2001): 647–713.

16 B. Perry, *In the Name of Hate: Understanding Hate Crimes* (London and New York: Routledge, 2001), p. 10.

17 Herek et al., 'Victim Experiences in Hate Crimes', p. 320.

18 Mason, 'Hate Crime', p. 839; Mason, *The Spectacle of Violence*, p. 68.

19 E. Stanko and P. Curry, 'Homophobic Violence and the Self "At Risk": Interrogating the Boundaries', *Social and Legal Studies*, 6 (4) (1997): 513–32, at p. 514. G. Herek, 'The

Social Context of Hate Crimes: Notes on Cultural Heterosexism', in K. Berrill and G. Herek (eds.), *Hate Crimes* (London: Sage, 1992).

20 S. Tomsen and G. Mason, 'Engendering Homophobia: Violence, Sexuality and Gender Conformity', *Journal of Sociology*, 37 (3) (2001): 257–73, at p. 261.

21 Ibid.

22 Dick, *Homophobic Hate Crime*, pp. 14 and 15, respectively.

23 Tomsen and Mason, 'Engendering Homophobia', p. 261.

24 See Todd Brower, Chapter 7.

25 Tomsen and Mason, 'Engendering Homophobia', pp. 262–4. These issues are explored in greater depth in Mason, *The Spectacle of Violence*, Chapter 2.

26 S. Tomsen, 'Homophobic Violence, Cultural Essentialism and Shifting Sexual Identities', *Social and Legal Studies*, 15 (2006): 389–407.

27 Mason, *The Spectacle of Violence*, p. 43.

28 D. Fuss, 'Introduction', in D. Fuss (ed.), *Inside/Out: Lesbian Theories, Gay Theories* (London and New York: Routledge, 1991), pp. 1–10; p. 2.

29 R. W. Connell and J. W. Messerschmidt, 'Hegemonic Masculinity: Rethinking the Concept', *Gender and Society*, 19 (6) (2005): 829–59, at p. 836.

30 R. W. Connell, *Masculinities* (St Leonards: Allen & Unwin, 1995), p. 37.

31 Tomsen, 'Homophobic Violence', p. 391.

32 Tomsen and Mason, 'Engendering Homophobia', p. 267.

33 L. Moran and B. Skeggs, *Sexuality and the Politics of Violence and Safety* (London and New York: Routledge, 2004), p. 12.

34 F. Lawrence, *Punishing Hate: Bias Crimes under American Law* (Cambridge, Mass.: Harvard University Press, 1999), p. 8.

35 The approach taken by Section 146 has been broadly replicated in Scotland by Section 2 of the Offences (Aggravation by Prejudice) (Scotland) Act 2009.

36 Section 146(2)(a)(i) and Section 146(2)(b)(i). Section 146 also covers offences motivated by or demonstrating hostility towards the victim on the basis of their disability.

37 Section 146(2)(a).

38 Chakraborti and Garland, *Hate Crime*, pp. 60–1.

39 N. Hall, *Hate Crime* (Cullompton: Willan Publishing, 2005), pp. 132–3.

40 P. Iganski, *Hate Crime and the City* (Bristol: The Policy Press, 2008), p. 88.

41 Moran and Skeggs, *Sexuality and the Politics of Violence*, p. 19.

42 R. Cover, 'Violence and the Word', *Yale Law Journal*, 95 (8) (1986): 1601–29.

43 L. Moran, 'Affairs of the Heart: Hate Crime and the Politics of Crime Control', *Law and Critique*, 12 (3) (2001): 331–44, at p. 341.

44 See, for example, Home Office, *Hate Crime: The Cross-Governmental Action Plan* (London: Home Office, 2009). Hall, *Hate Crime*, pp. 66–71.

45 J. Jacobs and K. Potter, *Hate Crimes: Criminal Law and Identity Politics* (Oxford: Oxford University Press, 1998), pp. 130–2; M. B. Kaplan, 'Hate Crime and the Privatization of Political Responsibility', *Liverpool Law Review*, 29 (1) (2008): 37–50, at p. 40.

46 N. Fraser, 'Rethinking Recognition', *New Left Review*, 3 (May/June 2000): 107–20, at p. 112.

47 Moran and Skeggs, *Sexuality and the Politics of Violence*, pp. 17–19.

48 G. Mason, 'Body Maps: Envisaging Homophobia, Violence and Safety', *Social and Legal Studies*, 10 (1) (2001): 23–44, pp. 38–9.

49 V. Jenness and K. Broad, *Hate Crimes: New Social Movements and the Politics of Violence* (New York: Aldine de Gruyter, 1997), Chapter 3.

50 Moran, 'Affairs of the Heart', p. 334.

51 D. Garland, *The Culture of Control* (Oxford: Oxford University Press, 2001).

52 Moran, 'Affairs of the Heart', p. 336.

53 Kaplan, 'Hate Crime', p. 44.

54 Moran and Skeggs, *Sexuality and the Politics of Violence*, p. 29.
55 See B. Bowling, 'Racial Harassment and the Process of Victimization: Conceptual and Methodological Implications for the Local Crime Survey', *British Journal of Criminology*, 33 (2) (1993): 231–50, at p. 238.
56 Ibid., pp. 243–4.
57 J. Dollimore, *Sexual Dissidence: Augustine to Wilde, Freud to Foucault* (Oxford: Oxford University Press, 1991), p. 141. Home Office, *Hate Crime*, p. 10, notes its intention to develop restorative justice approaches in relation to hate crime. However, to reiterate, in order to respond to the inherent difficulties in sentence-enhancement approaches, such an approach would have to supplant and not supplement the existing approach.
58 Kaplan, 'Hate Crime', p. 43.
59 Stanko and Curry, 'Homophobic Violence', p. 515; M. Burke, *Coming Out of the Blue* (London: Cassell, 1993); M. L. Williams and A. L. Robinson, 'Problems and Prospects with Policing the Lesbian, Gay and Bisexual Community in Wales', *Policing and Society*, 14 (3) (2004): 213–32; at pp. 214–15; H. G. Cocks, 'Historiographical Review: Modernity and the Self in the History of Sexuality', *The Historical Review*, 49 (4) (2006): 1212–27, at p. 1224 notes that there were still more prosecutions for homosexual offences in the 1990s than there had been before the Sexual Offences Act 1967 reform.
60 Williams and Robinson, 'Problems and Prospects', p. 215; Herek et al., 'Victim Experiences in Hate Crimes', pp. 332–5; Dick, *Homophobic Hate Crime*, p. 20.
61 ACPO, *Hate Crime: Delivering a Quality Service – Good Practice and Tactical Guidance* (London: Home Office Police Standards Unit, 2005).
62 N. Chakraborti, 'A Glass Half Full? Assessing Progress in the Policing of Hate Crime', *Policing*, 3 (2) (2009): 121–8, at p. 122.
63 D. McGhee, *Intolerant Britain? Hate, Citizenship and Difference* (Maidenhead: Open University Press, 2005), pp. 144–50; K. Glesson, 'Discipline, Punishment and the Homosexual in Law', *Liverpool Law Review*, 28 (3) (2007): 327–47, at p. 344.
64 Dick, *Homophobic Hate Crime*, p. 20. See also Stormbreak, *Homophobic Crime in London* (London: Stormbreak, 2006).
65 ACPO, *Hate Crime*.
66 Stanko and Curry, 'Homophobic Violence', and Stanko, 'Re-conceptualising the Policing of Hatred'; McGhee, *Intolerant Britain?*, pp. 151–3.
67 CPS (2009) *Hate Crime Report 2008–9*. Available online at http://www.cps.gov.uk/publications/docs/CPS_hate_crime_report_2009.pdf (accessed 5 January 2010).
68 Dick, *Homophobic Hate Crime*, p. 25.
69 N. Fielding, 'Cop Canteen Culture', in T. Newburn and E. Stanko (eds.), *Just Boys Doing Business? Men, Masculinities and Crime* (London and New York: Routledge, 1994), pp. 46–63.
70 Chakraborti, 'A Glass Half Full?', p. 124.
71 Stanko and Curry, 'Homophobic Violence'.
72 Ibid., p. 519.
73 Ibid., p. 516.
74 Moran, 'Affairs of the Heart', p. 338.
75 Crown Prosecution Service, *Policy for Prosecuting Cases of Homophobic and Transphobic Hate Crime* (London: Crown Prosecution Service, 2007).
76 Stanko and Curry, 'Homophobic Violence'.

Chapter 12

The legal construction of domestic violence

'Unmasking' a private problem

Mandy Burton

Introduction

In the past thirty years the range of legal remedies for domestic violence in England and Wales has greatly expanded. This is particularly the case in relation to the civil law, where Part IV of the Family Law Act 1996 (FLA) introduced non-molestation and occupation orders for a wider range of applicants, based on more generous criteria than the protection orders that had previously been available under domestic-violence legislation. The criminal law has perhaps been slower to respond. There is no specific criminal offence of domestic violence. The response, therefore, has to be measured in terms of how the courts have adapted generic criminal offences (and defences) to accommodate domestic violence and how the criminal-justice agencies have developed their policies and implemented them in practice. There have arguably been some improvements in the legal response to domestic violence both in terms of substantive law and practice, raising the profile of domestic violence as a 'public' problem. Yet much of the violence that occurs in intimate relationships remains 'private' in the sense that it either does not come to the attention of the legal system or, if it does, the system treats it primarily as a matter to be resolved between the parties out of court. Some commentators would argue that a civil-justice response continues to treat domestic violence as a 'private' matter to be dealt with by the parties. From this perspective, only a rigorous criminal-justice response constructs domestic violence as a 'public' problem. It will be argued here that the 'unmasking' of private violence can be achieved either through the civil or the criminal-justice systems.[1] To do this, legal constructions of domestic violence must challenge rather than reinforce traditional gender roles, empower women and enhance their choices.

There are many hurdles still to be overcome in unmasking the true nature of domestic violence. Legal responses to domestic violence continue to focus on the issue of the conduct of the victim and need to shift their focus from blaming women for being abused to clearly stating the responsibility of men for abusing. A significant step towards further improving legal responses to domestic violence may come from recognition of the gendered nature of the problem. This is because international and European human-rights instruments require an effective response as part of their non-discrimination provisions. Human-rights concepts have the potential to contribute to the project of translating 'private' violence into a 'public' problem either by stimulating policy development or through facilitating challenges to current practices presented by individuals using human-rights law. This chapter begins by examining the gendered nature of domestic violence, then examines current legal practices and concludes by considering some of the possible implications of these practices from a human-rights perspective.

Gendered nature of the problem

There has been considerable controversy in the social-science literature about whether domestic abuse affects men as victims to the same extent as it does women. However, 'family violence' researchers who claim that men are victims as frequently as women have used controversial measurements that exclude some of the significant context and consequences of abuse. In particular, the Conflicts Tactics Scale used by Straus and Gelles failed to distinguish between aggressive and defensive acts, and women are more likely to use violence in a defensive rather than offensive way.[2] Although Gelles has subsequently qualified the results of the original survey, men's groups have continued to use it in order to protest about the focus upon violence against women and to demand similar resources for male victims.[3] It would be wrong to claim that men are never victims of domestic abuse: they are.[4] It would also be wrong to ignore the fact that domestic abuse occurs in same-sex relationships.[5] Gay men and lesbians have had problems in naming same-sex abuse as 'domestic violence', and lesbian women in particular may have suffered from a 'myth' that women are not violent towards each other. Traditional problems with accessing support and protection from domestic violence experienced by heterosexuals may be compounded within same-sex communities by fears about disclosure of their sexual orientation or an unsympathetic response due to their sexuality. It is likely that much violence against men and violence in same-sex relationships remains 'private' in the sense that it is not brought to the attention of anyone outside the relationship. However, the fact that men and same-sex partners may require some specific services in order to access the support and protection they need from abusive partners should not blind us to the fact that, at its most serious, the majority of victims of domestic abuse are female victims of male violence. Domestic violence is a gendered problem; its primary victims are women. These female victims of male violence have significant unmet needs in terms of securing their safety and bringing their abusers to justice.[6] One of the obstacles to meeting these needs is legal constructions of the identities of 'ideal' victims, which continues to deny effective redress to those female victims of domestic violence who deviate from traditional gender roles.

Constructing gendered identities

It has been convincingly argued that the law constructs gendered identities.[7] The way that the law has constructed the identity of the domestic-violence 'victim' shows that historically the law has contributed to the problem of domestic violence. It has done this by defining and reinforcing traditional gender roles that perpetuate the patriarchal attitudes that arguably underlie the most serious manifestations of domestic violence.[8] Numerous examples of the law reinforcing gender stereotypes about appropriate 'wifely/womanly' behaviour can be found in both the civil and criminal law in England and Wales. In the leading case on the interpretation of the pre-FLA provisions for obtaining orders to exclude abusers from the matrimonial home, *Richards* v. *Richards* 1984, the court criticised the allegations made by the wife as 'flimsy and rubbishy'.[9] The conduct of the parties was said to be an important factor, along with other criteria such as the needs of children. In this case, the wife was criticised for having a number of affairs, whereas 'nothing adverse' could be found against the husband. The FLA was supposed to take the focus off the conduct of the parties and place it upon the health, safety and well-being of the applicant and any relevant child. Notwithstanding this, in relation to occupation orders at least, the conduct of the parties remains a relevant factor. Thus, in one case the court concluded that both parties were as bad as each other, despite finding that the husband had struck his wife, whereas she had never been violent towards him except when she intervened in a defensive way to protect their daughter.[10] The courts have always seen orders that exclude the male partner and property owner from the shared home as 'draconian', and this has continued to be the case post-FLA. Their concern to ensure that men are not deprived of their property rights, even temporarily, has led in some cases to the courts refusing to make orders and instead urging the parties to settle their differences 'privately'.[11] In the realm of child contact law, the welfare of the child is legally the paramount consideration, but this has not prevented the courts from criticising women seeking to prevent contact, on the grounds of their allegedly bad behaviour towards the perpetrator of domestic violence. For example, in one case, the mother was criticised for being manipulative and exaggerating incidents of violence, and, despite her having to attend hospital for injuries sustained in one assault, the judge concluded that she had provoked her husband by behaving in an 'autocratic and domineering way'.[12] Non-submissive behaviour is, it seems, a feature viewed as antithetical to ascribing 'victim' status to some judges working in the family-law courts. Examples from the criminal-law arena are no less compelling.

The most obvious 'victim blaming' attitudes of criminal-law judges are evident in the law relating to homicide. This is particularly the case in relation to the operation of the provocation and diminished responsibility defences. When women who kill their violent partners have sought to rely on these defences, they have been more successful in cases where the courts saw nothing in their behaviour to criticise than in cases, like that of Sara Thornton, where they did.[13] When men kill their female partners they have historically been able to rely readily on a defence of provocation where it has been alleged that the victim was 'unfaithful', and attempts by more enlightened members of the senior judiciary to restrict the availability of the defence in such circumstances have failed.[14] The former Labour Government responded with legislation designed to remove the provocation defence from sexually possessive jealous males who kill.[15] Whether this will prevent men who rely on jealousy succeeding with a partial defence to murder is debatable. In recent years, many of these cases have been argued under the defence of diminished responsibility as an alternative to provocation. In one case, Alisdair Sinclair stabbed his wife Sally more than twenty times after she allegedly admitted to having an affair. He was cleared of murder and found guilty of manslaughter on the grounds of diminished responsibility after the jury was told that he was clinically depressed with obsessive-compulsive traits.[16] Despite the fact that the killing was witnessed by children and described by the judge as a 'slaughter', Sinclair was sentenced to only nine years' imprisonment. It is, however, not only prosecutions for fatal violence but all prosecutions for violence which are vulnerable to assertions that the victim 'provoked her own demise'. Edwards used this term more than two decades ago to describe attitudes to domestic violence in the criminal courts.[17] Yet there continues to be evidence that from the top to the bottom of the judicial system decisions are influenced by victim-blaming.[18]

One effect of the persistent negative stereotyping of women who do not conform to judicial expectations of passivity and dutiful service is the denial of justice in the individual case. This in itself is bad enough, but it also has systemic effects: contributing to the problematic legal construction of domestic violence. The message is sent out that domestic violence is only a serious problem worthy of the best response that the legal system can offer when its female victims have conformed to traditional gender roles. This message is surely not lost on the perpetrators of abuse who see 'second-class' justice or no justice for women whose reputations are denigrated in the courts, often on the basis of little evidential foundation.[19] The 'evidence' in the Sinclair case consisted of a Post-it note allegedly attached to a document addressed to a male colleague stating 'I lust after you.' The victim's stepfather insisted that he had asked his daughter, who was seeking a divorce, if she was in another relationship, and she had told him that she did not have the time. Frequently, victims and their families are silenced in the legal system, particularly in homicide cases where the killer's story often goes unchallenged.[20]

Empowering victims

While law has often played a negative role in the reinforcing cultural stereotypes that support domestic violence, there is empirical evidence that some victims do find legal interventions helpful and that these interventions have the potential to change violent men. It would therefore be incorrect to characterise legal responses to domestic violence as failing all victims. In the civil-law context, empirical research has shown that women's experiences of protection orders did improve after the FLA was implemented. In one study, about one-third of women who had used civil-protection orders said that they were helpful and that the abuse stopped. Another 40 per cent said that the orders were of some help.[21] Some of the continuing problems that women had with accessing protection via the civil law included the costs of obtaining an order and difficulties with enforcement if the order was breached. There has been long-standing criticism of the restricted availability of legal aid to fund applications for protection orders. There is a perception, particularly amongst solicitors working in this area, that public funding is not readily available. This is partly due to the funding rules themselves, which seem to favour the pursuit of a criminal complaint as opposed to a civil remedy. Whether these criticisms are justified is a matter of debate and one that has certainly been contested by the Legal Services Commission (the body responsible for administering public funding in England and Wales). Some commentators have suggested that a decline in applications for non-molestation orders in recent years may be attributable to the restricted availability of public funding, especially in a climate of vast budget cuts. But there are a range of other explanations which may account for this.[22] Victims of domestic violence would certainly be better off if there were no means or merits test to be satisfied in order to obtain public funds with which to apply for protection orders under the FLA, but this is unrealistic given that unlimited resources cannot be devoted to legal aid. A trade-off inevitably has to be made with the allocation of resources to other publicly funded services such as health and education. Victims of domestic violence need appropriate support from health services as much as they need it from the law. However, help from specialist solicitors who are knowledgeable about the dynamics of domestic abuse, the FLA and ways to argue for public funding on behalf of victims who have 'good reason' for not pursuing the criminal route, would perhaps go towards empowering victims who are put off by ill-informed solicitors who buy into the victim-blaming attitudes found elsewhere in the legal system.[23]

It is sometimes argued that the criminal law has a key advantage over the civil law in that it places the burden of protecting the victim on the state and therefore relieves the victim of the costs, both financial and non-financial, of pursuing a remedy herself. This argument rests on the assumption that participation in the criminal-justice process does not place any real burdens upon the victim. Empirical evidence tends to suggest that the role of the victim is crucial to police and prosecutorial decision-making. Historically, the practices of the police have been found to be influenced by the type of cultural beliefs described above; if the victim's behaviour was less than 'ideal' then the police might deny assistance; in particular, they might refuse to make an arrest. In more recent years it has been suggested that it is not so much negative stereotyping of victim behaviour that influences police and prosecutorial decision-making but the attitude of the complainant towards the continuation of a prosecution. In the absence of a willing complainant, the police and Crown Prosecution Service (CPS) are reluctant to proceed with cases.[24] In this sense it can be argued that victims retain power over prosecutions: if they withdraw their complaint, then usually the prosecution will be discontinued, although the CPS can proceed, in theory, if they are satisfied that it is in the public interest and they have sufficient evidence to do so. Some commentators have argued that victims are empowered by the control that they have over prosecution decisions: it gives them a tool to negotiate against/with their abuser and may more effectively contribute to their safety than a prosecution.[25] However, the counter of this argument is that the 'control' that the victim retains over the prosecution places her in a more vulnerable position in relation to intimidation and further abuse by the defendant aimed at getting her to withdraw her complaint and thereby bring any prosecution to an end. This is one of the arguments used by those who support mandatory prosecution policies. They point out that the victim's decision to withdraw is often not truly voluntary, and, even if it were, there are interests at stake which go beyond those of the parties in the case. The arguments for and against mandatory prosecution are difficult to balance, but the circumstances of individual domestic-violence cases can vary enormously, and this perhaps lends support to a discretionary, rather than a mandatory, approach. It may be further disempowering for victims to replace the control of the abuser with that of the state through mandatory prosecution policies. The system should do what it can to ensure that victims are protected from intimidation and abuse when they have made a complaint, thereby supporting the victim to continue a prosecution if she believes that it is the best route to her future safety. In this way, the legal system can enhance women's choices rather than diminishing them.

Enhancing choices

How far have recent developments in legal responses to domestic violence enhanced women's choices for seeking protection and justice under the law? The civil-justice system theoretically gives most choice to the victim because the pursuit of a remedy rests with her initiative: in England and Wales it is not possible for third parties to seek protection orders under the FLA on behalf of a victim of domestic violence.[26] Traditionally, the 'choice' of the victim has also been central to the issue of the enforcement of protection orders that are breached. In the past, the main route for enforcing civil orders was via civil proceedings for contempt, usually initiated by the victim with the help of a solicitor (if she could afford it) or legal aid. The advent of the FLA saw a presumption in favour of powers of arrest being attached to orders in specified circumstances, and in recent years the majority of non-molestation orders have had such powers attached. Thus, the police, if they could be persuaded to act, took over some of the responsibility for responding to breaches of civil-protection orders although the victim still has the 'choice' about whether to report a breach to the police. Most recently, the

Domestic Violence Crime and Victims Act 2004 made breach of a non-molestation order a criminal offence punishable with up to five years' imprisonment. There is disagreement about whether this has improved the enforcement of protection orders and about whether it enhances or erodes victim's choices. It can be argued that it has eroded victim's choices in the sense that the police and prosecution authorities act on behalf of the state, rather than the victim, and could decide to continue a prosecution for breach of an order against the victim's wishes if they thought that it was in the public interest. However, we have seen from empirical research how unlikely it is that the CPS will prosecute cases in the absence of a willing complainant and so, although the spectre of a 'victimless' prosecution cannot be discounted, there is probably not a great deal for victims to fear in this respect. Also, ultimately, the decision to report a breach continues to rest with the victim, save in the relatively few cases where domestic violence might be brought to the attention of the criminal-justice agencies by a third party such as a neighbour. However, criminalisation of breach may be off-putting for some victims who wish to see their abusers held to account but do not wish to see them criminalised and who may now find the residual route of contempt proceedings more difficult to pursue. In that sense, victims' choices may have been eroded rather than enhanced. Furthermore victims cannot force the police to take action where victims want it but the authorities are unwilling. The effectiveness of civil-law responses to domestic violence are now entwined with the criminal-justice response to domestic violence, which makes improvements in this area even more important.

The most significant recent developments in the criminal-justice response to domestic violence have come in the form of specialist domestic-violence courts. These courts operate mainly in the summary jurisdiction and usually cluster cases to a single court session with specially trained magistrates and other criminal-justice personnel. The aim of the courts is to improve the safety and satisfaction of victims and to increase the accountability of perpetrators. The courts have had some success on these measures, but, overall, victim withdrawal remains high even within the specialist court setting. There is also continuing concern about the appropriateness of penalties imposed by specially trained magistrates. Low-level fines and conditional discharges continue to feature in a large number of cases despite training which should alert the magistrates to the limited impact of such penalties in comparison to referral to a perpetrator programme or a custodial sentence. From the victim's perspective, specialist domestic-violence courts do have an advantage over traditional processes in that there is at least a victims' advocate who can keep them informed about the progress of the case and relay information to the criminal-justice agencies on their behalf. Whether the criminal-justice agencies use this means of communicating with the victim in the way that victims would like is debatable; some victims continue to report disappointment at the way in which their cases are handled both in terms of the process and the outcome. Nevertheless, the introduction of specialist domestic-violence courts has probably overall enhanced the experience of the criminal-justice process for victims and increased the input that they have into the case. When critiquing the current practice, it is worth remembering how poor the response of the criminal-justice system has historically been. One flaw in the current drive to specialisation might be that it seems to be concentrated on traditional criminal-justice measures of success, such as increasing guilty pleas and convictions. While these can reap benefits for victims, it is also the case that victims may measure the success of a case very differently from the criminal-justice agencies. There is a danger that, under the guise of enhancing victims' rights, victims are being harnessed for the pursuit of crime-control goals which have little to do with genuinely improving victim safety and choice. Thus, advocates of criminal-justice reforms should remain mindful of the potential for victims' 'rights'-based claims to backfire. There is no doubt that victims' rights will become an increasing feature in the legal discourse surrounding domestic violence as international and regional human-rights conventions are interpreted in ways that seem to compel more appropriate state intervention.

Domestic violence as gender discrimination and a human-rights violation

Because domestic violence has historically been seen as a private matter, it has not been taken seriously as a human-rights violation and the responsibility of the state. This, however, is changing. The gendered nature of domestic violence, discussed at the beginning of this chapter, has been recognised by the United Nations (UN). In 1992 the UN Committee on the Elimination of Discrimination Against Women (CEDAW), made a general recommendation requiring all countries to include information in their reports (submitted every four years) to the Committee about the prevalence of violence against women and the measures being taken to protect them. CEDAW regularly expresses concern about the pervasiveness of domestic violence in individual states and the inadequate efforts to tackle it as a gender-discrimination issue.[27] Where the UN has led, the European Court of Human Rights (ECHR) has belatedly followed. In the landmark judgment of *Opuz* v. *Turkey* 2009, the Court finally recognised domestic violence as a form of gender discrimination and an inadequate response by state authorities as a breach of the non-discrimination provisions of Article 14 ECHR.[28] The Court expounded the positive obligations upon states to protect victims of domestic violence from 'torture, inhuman and degrading treatment' under Article 3 and to protect their 'right to life' under Article 2.[29] The European Council is now working on a convention to address violence against women as a form of gender discrimination.

These human-rights developments may provide impetus for governments, including the UK, to address their strategy for dealing with domestic violence from a gender perspective. They may also give individual victims of domestic violence a route of redress where they have received an inadequate response from state authorities to their calls for protection from an abusive partner. How effective human rights are in this respect remains to be seen.[30] The decision in *Opuz* v. *Turkey*, for example, does not require states to put in place mandatory prosecution policies for domestic violence; the court was highly critical of a law that prevented prosecution without the complainant's support but implicitly approved the discretionary prosecution policies that are in place in many states. Nevertheless, the judgment underlines the importance of judicial practices that question traditional patriarchal attitudes about appropriate female behaviour and cultural practices that tolerate abuse. The imposition of a fine rather than a term of imprisonment on Mr Opuz for stabbing his wife seven times because she had not cooked his dinner and because he was fed up with interference from his mother-in-law in his marriage was just one example of the inadequate response of the Turkish criminal-justice system. The most potent failure was the ignoring of complaints about threats to his mother-in-law's life which culminated in her being shot dead as she and her daughter were fleeing the area. For this crime he received a reduced sentence because his mother-in-law had allegedly offended his 'honour' by taking his wife away and leading her into an 'immoral life'.[31] The Turkish authorities were criticised for creating 'a climate that was conducive to domestic violence' through a combination of prosecutorial inaction and judicial passivity.

While human rights have often been seen as men's rights and not especially helpful to improving the situation of women, cases such as *Opuz* show that human rights do have the potential at least to challenge traditional legal responses to domestic violence that have tolerated and reinforced gender stereotypes, providing excuses for men who abuse their female partners. The domestic-violence policy of the CPS in England and Wales is likely to be convention-compliant because it does allow for a range of factors to be weighed in the public interest in prosecuting, even when the victim withdraws. However, the implementation of police and prosecution policies, in practice, might be subject to a successful challenge in Strasbourg, if not necessarily in the domestic courts.[32] Domestic courts still tend to insist that the police are given considerable discretion in deciding what action to take when receiving complaints, even when their inaction has fatal consequences.

Conclusion

Law can never be a complete solution to domestic violence, but it can reduce the role it plays in contributing to the problem when it reinforces patriarchal attitudes. Victims of domestic violence have paid a heavy price individually for departing from traditional gender roles. And the price paid by victims collectively is even higher as the legal system reinforces rather than challenges the gender roles that contribute to the perpetuation of domestic abuse. Developments in substantive law and practice are slowly improving the legal responses to domestic violence. Some developments, such as reforms to the law of provocation, specifically aim to overcome the 'victim-blaming' approaches which have proved so problematic in the past. Whether they will be successful is difficult to gauge. Changes in law and policy are often met by the resistance of those called upon to put the changes into practice. Despite some reservations about the power of law, I would support the position of the sceptical reformist: although cultural attitudes are hard to change, they are worth trying to change.[33] It is only by doing so that the nature of domestic violence as a societal problem will be 'unmasked', made visible as a gender problem and one worthy of appropriate state intervention. Such state intervention should be the kind that empowers women and supports the choices they make while seeking safety and justice via both the civil and criminal law. If human-rights law can help in this process then it is to be welcomed. Feminist campaigners and law-makers know the value, as well as the limitations, of rights claims.[34] Rights claims can shape public discourse and can help the legal system to acknowledge the gendered nature of domestic violence and the pressing need for more effective responses. State intervention in domestic violence has the potential to challenge patriarchal attitudes, rather than to perpetuate them.

Notes

1 The public/private dichotomy is contentious, and many have rejected it as a useful analytical or practical tool in the domestic-violence context. See, for example, M. Dempsey, *Prosecuting Domestic Violence* (Oxford: Oxford University Press, 2009). However, despite its limitations, it does on some levels offer a useful framework, see M. Burton, 'Domestic Violence, "Nuisance Neighbours" and the Public/Private Dichotomy Revisited', *Child and Family Law Quarterly*, 20 (1) (2008): 95–108. At a descriptive level, making 'private' violence 'public' entails taking something that has previously been unregulated and opening it up to public scrutiny and state intervention.

2 R. Dobash and R. Dobash, 'Women's Violence to Men in Intimate Relationships: Working on a Puzzle', *British Journal of Criminology*, 44 (3) (2004): 324–49.

3 R. Gelles and D. Loseke, *Current Controversies in Family Violence* (Thousand Oaks, Calif.: Sage, 2003).

4 A. Grady, 'Female on Male Domestic Violence: Uncommon or Ignored?', in C. Hoyle and R. Young (eds.), *New Visions of Crime Victims* (Oxford: Hart, 2002), pp. 71–95.

5 C. Donovan and M. Hester, *Comparing Love and Domestic Violence in Heterosexual and Same Sex Relationships: ESRC End of Award Report* (Swindon: Economic and Social Research Council, 2007).

6 C. Humphreys and R. Thiara, *Routes to Safety* (Bristol: Women's Aid Federation England, 2002); M. Hester and N. Westmarland, *Tackling Domestic Violence: Effective Interventions and Approaches* (London: Home Office, 2005).

7 C. Smart, *Feminism and the Power of Law* (London and New York: Routledge, 1989). In addition, see Ngaire Naffine, Chapter 1.

8 Although researchers disagree on the 'causes' of domestic violence, it has been convincingly argued that domestic violence in its 'strongest' sense presents issues of patriarchy as well as domesticity and violence. See Dempsey, *Prosecuting Domestic Violence*.

9 *Richards* v. *Richards* (1984) AC 174.

10 *Re Y (children) (Occupation Order)* (2000) 2 FCR 470.

11 See *Chalmers* v. *Johns* (1999) 1 FLR 392, in which occupation orders were described as 'draconian' and one judge suggested that the parties attend mediation with a view to resuming their relationship.

12 *Re H (A Child) (Contact: Domestic Violence)* (2006) 1 FCR 102.

13 *R* v. *Thornton (No. 2)* (1996) 2 All ER 1023.

14 See *R* v. *Weller* (2004) 1 Cr App R 1.

15 The relevant provisions of the Coroners and Justice Act 2009 met opposition in the House of Lords but were reinstated by the House of Commons.

16 It is not difficult to envisage the psychiatric profession coming up with medically recognised illnesses, sufficient to satisfy the newly reformulated defence of diminished responsibility, in cases where men kill due to excessive jealously. See M. Burton, 'Intimate Homicide and the Provocation Defence: Endangering Women?', *Feminist Legal Studies*, 9 (3) (2001): 247–58.

17 S. Edwards, '"Provoking Her Own Demise": from Common Assault to Homicide', in J. Hanmer and M. Maynard (eds.), *Women, Violence and Social Control* (London: Macmillan, 1987).

18 See E. Gilchrist and J. Blisset, 'Magistrates Attitudes to Domestic Violence and Sentencing Options', *Howard Journal of Criminal Justice*, 44 (2002): 348–63. They found that magistrates' decisions were influenced by victim-blaming.

19 This is particularly so in rape cases, where attempts to restrict the type of evidence that can be adduced at trial (for example about sexual history) have not prevented counsel and jurors relying on stereotypes about the respectability of the complainant and other features of her behaviour in the aftermath of an assault to guide their advocacy and decision making. See C. McGlynn and V. Munro (eds.), *Rethinking Rape Law* (London: Routledge-Cavendish, 2010) and Kim Stevenson, Chapter 9.

20 J. Radford and D. Russell, *Femicide: The Politics of Woman Killing* (Buckingham: Open University Press, 2002). In recent years, victims' families have been given more 'rights' through victim advocacy schemes, but the systemic impact of these has yet to be seen in any significant way.

21 Humphreys and Thiara, *Routes to Safety*, p. 53.

22 M. Burton, 'Why Are Applications for Non-Molestation Orders Declining', *Journal of Social Welfare and Family Law*, 31 (2) (2009): 109–20.

23 Poor advice given by some solicitors may be one factor putting victims off applying for protection.

24 C. Hoyle, *Negotiating Domestic Violence* (Oxford: Oxford University Press, 1998).

25 D. Ford, 'Prosecution As a Victim Power Resource: a Note on Empowering Women in Violent Conjugal Relationships', *Law and Society Review*, 25 (2) (1991): 313–34.

26 There is an unimplemented provision in Section 60 of the FLA which would allow this, but issues of victim consent and who might be authorised as the third party have proved problematic when implementation of this provision has been considered. See M. Burton, 'Third Party Applications for Protection Orders in England and Wales', *Journal of Social Welfare and Family Law*, 25 (2) (2003): 137–50.

27 R. McQuigg, 'The Responses of States to Comments of the CEDAW Committee on Domestic Violence', *International Journal of Human Rights*, 11 (2007): 461–79.

28 *Opuz* v. *Turkey*, Application no. 33401/02 (June 2009).

29 In the particular case it was held that the inadequate response of the Turkish police, prosecutors and courts breached the right to life of the applicant's mother and the applicant's Article 3 rights.

30 Some commentators are more optimistic than others. For an optimistic perspective, see S. Choudhry and J. Herring, 'Righting Domestic Violence', *International Journal of Family Law and Policy*, 20 (1) (2006): 95–119. For a more pessimistic view, see

M. Burton, 'Failing to Protect: Victims' Rights and Police Liability', *Modern Law Review*, 72 (2) (2009): 283–95.
31 On this subject area, see Shilan Shah-Davis, Chapter 14.
32 Burton, 'Failing to Protect'.
33 M. Burton, *Legal Responses to Domestic Violence* (London: Routledge-Cavendish, 2009).
34 E. Schneider, *Battered Women and Feminist Law Making* (New Haven, Conn.: Yale University Press, 2000).

Part IV

International violence, law and sex

Chapter 13

Criminalisation or protection?

Tensions in the construction of prevention strategies concerning trafficking for the purposes of sexual exploitation

Anna Carline

Introduction

Trafficking of human beings constitutes a major global and international issue and is described by many to be the 'modern form of slavery'.[1] The UK is one of the major destination countries, and the UK's Action Plan Against Trafficking details the steps already taken and those needed to be taken in order to tackle trafficking.[2] As part of the Action Plan, the then Labour Government committed to ratifying the Council of Europe Convention on Action Against Trafficking in Human Beings 2005 (hereafter 'the Convention') and eventually did so in December 2008. Due to the ratification of the Convention it could be argued that the Labour Government constructed trafficking as primarily a human-rights issue. This chapter will, however, show the extent to which trafficking as a criminal-law issue has had, and continues to have, a major impact on domestic law. It will be argued that the Labour Government was more concerned with adopting increasingly punitive approaches to prostitution, approaches which, if uncritically adapted by the Coalition Government, will only increase the vulnerability of all of those engaged in prostitution, as opposed to protecting the human rights of victims of trafficking.

In order to develop this argument, the chapter will critically analyse two aspects of the criminal law: the definition of trafficking as contained in Sections 57–9 of the Sexual Offences Act 2003 (SOA) and the new strict liability offence of purchasing sexual services from a prostitute who is subject to force, etc. The chapter will argue that the criminal law goes much further than is required under the Convention, but not in a positive manner. Indeed, it will be contended that the new strict liability offence potentially contravenes the Convention.

Trafficking: a brief overview

Despite the widespread nature of the problem of trafficking, formulating exact statistics is exceptionally difficult due to its covert and criminal nature. Estimates suggest that, globally, somewhere between 12.7 million and 27 million people are in forced/bonded labour or sexual servitude. Out of those, 80 per cent are female and 50 per cent are children.[3] The difficulty with regards to precise numbers is evinced in the research conducted by Kelly and Regan. They estimate that on a yearly basis anywhere from 142 up to 1,420 women and girls will be trafficked in the UK for the purposes of sexual exploitation.[4]

Policies and conventions on trafficking generally draw a distinction between trafficking and smuggling, although commentators argue that in reality the distinction is by no means clear-cut. Anderson and O'Connell Davidson state that 'the trafficking/smuggling distinction represents a gaping hole in any safety net for those whose human rights are violated in the process of migration'.[5] On a basic level, trafficking occurs when an individual is coerced or deceived into being transported and forced into labour for a third party. In contrast, smuggling occurs when an individual consents to being transported, invariably by illegal means, but is not forced into labour. Trafficking generally involves transportation across national borders but also occurs within a country (internal trafficking) – a type of trafficking often used to snatch children from one region to another for sexual exploitation, especially those in care.[6]

This chapter will focus on trafficking for the purposes of sexual exploitation/prostitution. It has been argued that trafficking in women and children for sexual exploitation 'is the third largest and fastest growing criminal activity in the world'.[7] Nevertheless, it is important to acknowledge that trafficking for other purposes does occur and can be just as exploitative. Although trafficking is undoubtedly gendered, with traffickers being overwhelmingly male and victims overwhelming female, due to the 'feminization of poverty', men also fall victim to trafficking, albeit for forced labour (such as on marijuana farms) rather than for sexual exploitation.[8] Both trafficking and smuggling are exceptionally complex phenomena, and it is important that stereotypes and generalisations are deconstructed in order to expose their presuppositions and exclusions.

International and European conventions on trafficking

The United Nations Protocol to Prevent, Suppress and Punish Trafficking in Persons, especially Women and Children 2000, which supplements the United Nations Convention Against Transnational Organised Crime 2000, contains the international definition of trafficking, which is reproduced on a European level in the Convention. Article 3 of the Protocol states:

> 'Trafficking in persons' shall mean the recruitment, transportation, transfer, harbouring or receipt of persons, by means of the threat or use of force or other forms of coercion, of abduction, of fraud, of deception, of the abuse of power or of a position of vulnerability or of the giving or receiving of payments or benefits to achieve the consent of a person having control over another person, for the purpose of exploitation.

Exploitation includes, at a minimum, 'the exploitation of the prostitution of others or other forms of sexual exploitation, forced labour or services, slavery or practices similar to slavery, servitude or the removal of organs'. The Protocol further states that a victim's consent to being trafficked is 'irrelevant where any of the means set forth in subparagraph (a) have been used' (Article 3b).

This definition of trafficking represents a compromise between two different schools of thought: those who adopt a radical feminist perspective and maintain that all prostitution amounts to violence against women (abolitionists), and those who argue that prostitution can amount to legitimate work and is not always necessarily and fundamentally exploitative (autonomists).[9] These two differing perspectives have led to a debate at the international level as to whether or not the Protocol should explicitly connect trafficking and prostitution or focus more generally on the non-consensual, exploitative aspects of trafficking.[10] The definition manages to represent both perspectives. The capacity to consent to being 'trafficked' is recognised in a negative manner, as Article 3(b) states that a person's consent will be irrelevant if it is obtained by certain means. This concurs with those who draw a distinction between forced and voluntary prostitution. Trafficking for purposes other than prostitution is also recognised; nevertheless, Article 3(b) explicitly refers to sexual exploitation, conforming to the requests of the anti-prostitution camp.

As argued below, while the approach adopted by the Labour Government (and probably retained by the Coalition Government) appears to suggest an allegiance with the radical feminist school of thought, a different agenda can be seen to be in play: that of moralism. The Labour Government's approach, in reality, draws upon a conservative moral perspective under which being paid for or paying for sex is considered to be immoral. The move to increase the criminalisation of prostitution has more to do with promoting a moral perspective concerning appropriate consensual sexual encounters than with protecting those who engage in prostitution.

Dealing with trafficking: prevention, protection and prosecution

Signatories to the International and European Conventions undertake to deal with trafficking in three ways: prevention, protection and prosecution. The aims of the European Convention are set down in Article 1:

(a) to prevent and combat trafficking in human beings, while guaranteeing gender equality;
(b) to protect the human rights of the victims of trafficking, design a comprehensive framework for the protection and assistance of victims and witnesses, while guaranteeing gender equality, as well as to ensure effective investigation and prosecution;
(c) to promote international cooperation on action against trafficking in human beings.

Prosecution of traffickers is therefore only one element in the fight against trafficking. Significantly, Egan has argued that states have tended to be more concerned with developing criminal laws to deal with traffickers than with implementing policies and procedures which protect and support victims of trafficking.[11] More positively, the Convention has been heralded as being victim-centred and adopting a more human-rights-based approach.[12] In particular, Article 13 requires states to allow rescued victims a reflection period of at least thirty days, during which the state will not be allowed to 'enforce any expulsion order' against the victim. This is prescribed in order to give victims sufficient time to 'recover and escape the influence of traffickers and/or to take an informed decision on cooperating with competent authorities'.[13] Furthermore, under Article 14, states are required to issue residence permits to victims of trafficking not only in order to enable them to assist with any investigation or criminal proceedings but also to permit them to remain if it is considered that 'their stay is necessary owing to their personal situation'. Hence, the right to remain is not solely based upon a victim's willingness to provide evidence in criminal proceedings, arguably demonstrating a more victim-focused attitude.

The initial UK Action plan focused more on the issue of prevention and prosecution, as opposed to the human rights of victims and drew over-whelmingly upon discourses of immigration policy and crime control.[14] The Home Office was, to begin with at least, reluctant to promote a more human-rights centred approach due to the fear that measures that protected victims might operate as a 'pull' factor: that individuals would claim to be victims of trafficking in order to take advantage of the protections offered.[15] In 2009, the Home Office introduced reflection periods of at least forty-five days and also the appropriate residence permits.[16] In order for an individual to gain the relevant rights, he or she must first of all be recognised by the state authorities as being a genuine victim of trafficking. Identifying victims of trafficking is an exceptionally difficult process due to various issues, including the reluctance of victims to come forward and the lack of training for frontline staff. To this end, and in accordance with the Convention, the national referral system aims to enable victims to be identified and dealt with accordingly.[17] It has, however, been heavily criticised recently.[18]

Both a victim and not a victim? The SOA 2003 and definitions of trafficking

In order to further substantiate and explore the contention that the Government's approach to trafficking is a moralistically based strategy of criminalisation, legal definitions of trafficking will now be evaluated. This will underline, it is suggested, the claim that the reality of the UK Government approach under Labour accorded with a crime-control, rather than a human-rights protection, model, as the criminal-law definition is significantly wider than the one used to determine whether a victim should be afforded protection as required under the Convention.

Trafficking for the purposes of sexual exploitation is governed by Sections 57–9 of the SOA 2003. The offences cover trafficking into, within and out of the UK; however, in the light of space limitations, Section 57 will be used as an example. Section 57 provides that 'a person commits an offence if he intentionally arranges or facilitates the arrival in the UK of another person' and either he intends to, or believes another person is likely to, 'do something to or in respect of B, after B's arrival but in any part of the world, which if done will involve the commission of a relevant offence'. Significantly, the offence does not require any form of threat, deception or coercion, contrary to the Convention's definition, and neither is B's consent, or lack of it, referred to. The phrase 'relevant offence' refers to a range of sexual offences, including causing a person to engage in sexual activity without consent (Section 4), causing or inciting prostitution for gain (Section 52) and controlling prostitution for gain (Section 53). These latter two offences do not necessarily require any form of exploitation or coercion. Indeed, in *R* v. *Massey* 2007 it was confirmed that the word 'controlling' in Section 53 did not require any force or coercion on behalf of the defendant and would be satisfied if a third party simply directed or instructed a sex worker.[19] The offence of trafficking, therefore, can be committed in the absence of any form of exploitation or coercion, arguably rendering the current UK formulation of the offence conceptually problematic in its relation to the international definition.

The adoption of this wider definition impacts upon the construction of trafficked victims and trafficking offenders. If a woman has consented to being transported from another country in order to work in prostitution, any person who facilitates her travel may potentially contravene the law, despite the lack of any untoward measures or exploitation. Indeed, since 2004, forty-six men and women have been convicted for transporting willing sex workers.[20] Arguably, the criminalisation of such persons is problematic, not least because the women involved are not in fact victims in the human-rights sense. This wider approach problematically encourages the police to use the law against easier targets, those who help and assist willing sex workers, as opposed to those who use coercive and exploitative measures to traffic women into prostitution and to render their escape, if not impossible, then very difficult.

It could be argued that such an approach conforms with a radical feminist perspective, a perspective in which all forms of prostitution amount to violence against women, meaning that the state must step in to arrest those who encourage, enable, facilitate or force such behaviour and which indicates that the women should be considered to be victims in a strict sense, notwithstanding any alleged 'consent'. However, it is relatively clear that this radical feminist approach is not adopted in the definition of who is a victim of trafficking for the purposes of human-rights protection. The UK Action Plan on Trafficking defines trafficking as 'the movement of a person by coercion or deception into a situation of exploitation'.[21] Similarly, in the documentation regarding the ratification of the Convention, the then Government stated that human trafficking 'consists in a combination of three basic components – an action (recruitment); by a means (e.g., threat of force, or fraud); for the purpose of exploitation'.[22] This three-step approach coincides with international perspectives and academic commentary.[23] However, trafficking under the SOA 2003 seems to dispense with the 'means' component of the definition, with the logical implication that a person could be a victim of trafficking for the purposes of the SOA 2003 but simultaneously fall outside the definition as contained within the UK Action Plan. We therefore have, as a result of this legal conceptual disjunction, a possible situation in which an individual is both at once a trafficking victim and not a trafficking victim. Moreover, it is of note that the UK Government problematically adopted a narrower definition when dealing with issues of human rights than it did when developing criminal offences. Accordingly, it can be argued, with justification, that the key underlying concern of the law remains the punishment of traffickers and the implicit promotion of a moralistic approach to prostitution, rather than a concern to protect human rights.

As a lens through which to further examine these themes, we can explore the criminal-law definition of trafficking by reflecting upon its application, by the Court of Appeal, in the case of *R* v. *Delgado-Fernandez and Zammit* 2007.[24] The appellants were convicted for conspiring to:

1   traffic women into the UK for sexual exploitation;
2   control prostitution for gain;
3   facilitate a breach of immigration law.

Miss Delgado-Fernandez was sentenced to five years' imprisonment, which was challenged by the Attorney General on the grounds that the sentence was too lenient, while Mr Zammit appealed against his sentence of seven years on the basis that it was manifestly excessive. The Court of Appeal held in both instances that the sentences were manifestly excessive and accordingly reduced them to four years and five years respectively. What is significant about this case is the knowledge and agency displayed by the presumed 'victims'. The women trafficked had already freely engaged in sex work in Spain and were fully aware, when they were recruited by Miss Delgado-Fernandez, of the nature of their employment in the UK. The women did not fit the stereotype of innocent and naive women duped by deceitful men, an image generally drawn upon by the Government in order to justify increased criminalisation. Rather, it could be argued that the women were economic migrants. Indeed, research suggests that many migrants in the sex industry are not only aware of the work they will engage in but that they have also employed traffickers to help them enter the sex industry in the UK in a bid to improve their living conditions.[25] Furthermore, it is estimated that two out of three rescued 'trafficked victims' return to work within the sex industry.[26] The key concern in this case, in real terms, turned on the issue of the breach of immigration law. As the Attorney General stated, that 'was where the gravamen of the offence lay'.[27]

Significantly, it can be argued that this case supports the contention that the criminal law does not require the existence of any exploitative 'means' in order for a trafficking offence to be committed. The approach of the Court of Appeal hints, furthermore, at a tension between the Judiciary and the Government. The definition of trafficking relied upon by Lord Chief Justice Phillips, who delivered the leading judgment, mirrors that which is contained in the UK Action Plan and also the Convention. His Lordship considered trafficking to be a process involving three stages: recruitment, transportation and management at the destination.[28] *Prima facie*, this does not appear to require exploitative 'means'. However, activities amounting to exploitation and deception were considered to occur at the recruitment stage. Citing the Sentencing Advisory Panel, Lord Phillips states:

> the recruiting process may involve deception of the victims as to the nature of the work they will ultimately be doing ... Others are fully aware that they are to work in prostitution but may be deceived about the conditions of work, the number of 'clients' ... and the amount of money that can be earned.[29]

Although Lord Phillips's approach does not seem to necessarily require exploitation in order for the trafficking offence to take place, it appears that exploitation needs to be 'read in to' the facts of the case in order for the women to be presented as victims.[30] Lord Phillips's phraseology clearly implies the need for genuine and informed agency in respect of all the circumstances relevant to the choice to be made by the woman herself and that any failure in this respect can reasonably be interpreted as deceptive, misleading or potentially exploitative. In this particular case, for example, while the women were already working in prostitution and were aware that they would be required to provide such services in the UK, it was noted that they had been 'encouraged ... to offer a wider range of sexual services than originally appealed to them'.[31] Furthermore, the amount of money taken from them was also considered to amount to exploitation. However, when discussing the length of the sentences, the Court of Appeal contrarily states that there 'was no deception or coercion'.[32]

The approach of the Court of Appeal appears to demonstrate a difference of opinion to that of the then Government. In the opinion of the court, exploitation remains pivotal to the definition of trafficking. However, it can also be argued that the vagueness of the SOA 2003 leads to inconsistencies in this regard. As suggested above, deception and coercion both at once existed and did not exist. The case raises a further related question: if the Convention had been ratified at the time of this case, would the women involved have been labelled as victims by the national referral system? If the trafficking offences were drafted in a tighter manner, one which emphasised the importance of 'means' by which the women were trafficked as opposed to focusing on the existing criminal offences relating to prostitution, the legal responses would be more certain and coherent, avoiding the conceptual bifurcation implicated in the simultaneous 'victim'/'non-victim' disjunction.

Clients of trafficked victims and the criminal law

The UK Government's ideological commitment to moralism, the related conceptual tensions inherent to the law and the related definitional complexities at the interface between UK law and the Convention can be placed alongside the somewhat unpalatable exploitation, by the former Labour Government, of the theme of victimisation, not in order to protect women but to punish those who visit prostitutes. The plight of the trafficked victim was drawn upon by the Labour Government, precisely in order to increase the criminalisation of those who visit prostitutes, a strategy that reflects the moralistic perspective identified here.

Section 14 of the Policing and Crime Act 2009 criminalises those who use the services of people trafficked into prostitution. This is undoubtedly a radical reform. Prior to this section, adult prostitution per se was not criminalised.[33] If an individual did use the services of a trafficked victim they could be guilty of rape. Under Section 1 SOA 2003, rape is committed when A engages in sexual intercourse with B, without B's consent, and A does not reasonably believe that B consents. Section 74 states that a person consents if 'he agrees by choice and has the freedom and capacity to make that choice'. Clearly, if a person has been forced into prostitution by traffickers they do not have the freedom to make a choice, and, if the defendant was aware of this, he would be guilty of rape. Moreover, under Section 75(2)(c), an exclusive presumption comes into play if the complainant was, and the defendant was not, unlawfully detained at the time of the relevant act. Thus, in a trafficking scenario, there would be a presumption that consent was absent, as the woman was unlawfully detained. In such situations, the defendant would have to adduce sufficient evidence to rebut the presumption (Section 75(2)).

The consequences for a rape conviction are rightly severe. The offender can face up to life imprisonment and is also placed on the sex-offenders register.[34] Without any doubt, if a person pays to engage in sexual intercourse with a woman whom they know has been forced into prostitution, a hefty sentence should follow. However, due to concerns that the offence of rape is too difficult to prove in trafficking cases, the Government introduced Section 14, making it a criminal offence to pay for the sexual services of a prostitute who has been exploited by a third party for the purposes of gain. Exploitation is defined as the use of force, threats (whether or not relating to violence), any form of coercion or any form of deception (Section 14(3)(a)(b)).[35] If a person is found guilty they may be fined up to £1,000. Clearly this is markedly lower than the penalty for rape, and this is due to the issue of *mens rea*.[36] The proposed offence is one of strict liability. It matters not whether the defendant knew that the prostitute was exploited.

To say that this reform has caused consternation is an understatement. Liberty, for example, argued that it appeared to lead to the criminalisation of prostitution by the back door; however the Labour Government rejected such claims.[37] The stated aim of the offence was to reduce demand, and it was argued that the creation of a strict liability offence would radically impact and deter those who purchase sexual services, leading to a reduction in demand which would accordingly reduce supply. The belief underlying this appears to be that if supply is affected then trafficking will become less lucrative and that, consequently, fewer women and children will be forced into prostitution.[38]

Other difficulties with the offence include: the distinct lack of supporting empirical evidence; the under-theorisation of the link between demand and supply and the notion of deterrence; an unsubstantiated and unshakable belief that the creation of another criminal offence will make a radical impact; a lack of clarity as to whether the aim is to reduce all forms of prostitution or just the more exploitative end of the market; and the fear that this offence will capture a significantly wider range of prostitutes than those who have been trafficked or coerced, hinting, again, at a more moralistic approach to prostitution.

The imposition of strict liability: contravening the convention?

Those in favour of the offence argue vehemently that a strict liability offence is necessary in order for the offence to be effective, as knowledge of circumstances, even on an objective level, would be too difficult to prove. Indeed, this is the argument made against relying upon the offence of rape. It is asserted that many trafficked victims would simply lie about their circumstances if a client made any enquiries so consequently a conviction would not be forthcoming as the defendant would not possess the relevant mental state.[39]

The fate of trafficked victims and the Government's duties under the Convention are both relied upon in order to support this offence.[40] However, it is unusual to use the principles of strict liability in order to deal with sex offences. The only existing crime which does so is Section 5 of the SOA 2003: sexual intercourse with a child under the age of thirteen. Under this offence it is irrelevant how old the defendant believed the victim to be. Those who oppose Section 14 distinguish Section 5, maintaining that whereas it is possible to objectively verify the age of a person, it is not as possible to objectively verify the circumstances of a sex worker.[41] The problem is that those who purchase sexual services will simply not be able to ascertain whether they are committing a criminal offence. In real terms, it is difficult to avoid the impression that the strict liability offence conveys an underlying conservative moralism in the light of which paying for sex is deemed 'wrong' and 'immoral'. It is notable, for example, that there is no concerted effort to permit the non-exploitative side of the industry. Rather, all clients live under a constant threat of punishment.

The extent to which strict liability is promoted and considered absolutely necessary might be taken to imply that anything less would fail to satisfy the requirements of the Convention. In reality, however, there is no support in the Convention for this approach. Indeed, the Convention explicitly refers to knowledge. Article 19 sets down that the State should consider criminalising 'the use of services which are the object of exploitation ... with the knowledge that the person is a victim of trafficking in human beings'.[42] The explanatory report further states that to be liable for punishment under Article 19, a person using the services of a trafficking victim must do so 'in the knowledge that the person is a victim of trafficking in human beings'. In other words, the user must be aware that the person is a trafficked victim and should not be penalised if unaware.

While the Convention acknowledges the complexities of proving knowledge, this does not justify, or even suggest, the appropriateness of a strict liability offence. On the contrary, Paragraph 235 of the explanatory report surmises that the problem may be overcome 'without injury to the principle of presumption of innocence – by inferring the perpetrator's intention from the factual circumstances'. The use of 'inferences' is not new to the law, and, rather than invoking the blunt instrument of strict liability, it should be left to the jury to infer, on a factual assessment of a case, whether or not a defendant had 'intended' to commit an offence.[43] This approach accords with the main thrust of the relevant international instruments. For example, Article 6(2)(c) of the Convention on Laundering, Search, Seizure and Confiscation of the Proceeds of Crime 1990 states: 'knowledge, intent or purpose required as an element of an offence set forth in that paragraph may be inferred from objective, factual circumstances'. A jury, or a magistrate, looking at all the circumstances in which the transaction took place, is able to infer that the defendant had knowledge. Furthermore, since Article 19 refers to the 'objective' circumstances, it is concerned with what the reasonable person can be taken to have known, as opposed to the subjective knowledge of the defendant. The issue turns on whether, looking at the objective facts of the circumstances of the case, it can be inferred that the defendant had knowledge of the exploitative circumstances. This is very far removed from the draconian imposition of criminality implicit in the strict liability offence.

Throughout the parliamentary debates, there were various challenges to the imposition of a strict liability offence. Proposals were put forward for the amendment of the law to require a belief, or a reasonable belief, that the prostitute was a victim of exploitation, but these proposals were constantly rejected by the Labour Government on the basis that they would be unworkable.[44] A considerable and relevant lacuna in this respect was the failure to discuss the wording of Article 19, a failure that meant that there was no consideration of how enabling a jury or a magistrate to draw an inference would deal with the difficulties of proof that might enhance the efficiency, justice and fairness of the law's application.

The creation of a strict liability offence is worrying and is not supported by various groups, including the Criminal Bar Association and Liberty.[45] The Joint Committee on Human Rights argue that it breaches Article 8 of the European Convention of Human Rights: the right to a private and family life, on the basis that it interferes with a person's sexual conduct.[46] In addition, the English Collective of Prostitutes have expressed concern that further criminalisation will only lead to more violence and exploitation.[47] Significantly, if the new Government were to repeal the strict liability offence this would enable the penalty for Section 14 to be increased substantially. It is impossible to reconcile the Labour Government's contention that trafficked victims suffer a terrible fate that is akin to being raped many times a day with such a disproportionately small penalty amount: a mere maximum £1,000 fine. This discrepancy underlines the main question driving this chapter: about what was the Labour Government really concerned? Not only does the strict liability offence potentially contravene the Convention, it also further strengthens the argument that the true foundation of the relevant UK Government's approach to trafficking reflected a moralistic attitude that paying for sex is wrong rather than a genuine or coherently expressed legal concern for the victims of trafficking.

Conclusion

When we critically analyse the criminal law's definition of trafficked victims and the new offence of purchasing sexual services from a prostitute subject to exploitation, it is clear that the relevant definitions and offences contained within domestic criminal law are significantly more expansive than required under the Convention. Although it might be easy, on the face of it, to assume that the Labour Government was concerned with the human rights of trafficking victims, further scrutiny demonstrates that the main focus is something quite different and infinitely less benign in its impacts on the victims of trafficking: the criminalisation of traffickers and those who purchase sex, without nuanced consideration of the economic agency of the women involved in sex work. Underlying this focus is a conservative moralistic agenda concerning prostitution which means that ultimately criminalisation is pursued at the expense of genuinely responsive human-rights protection. Whether or not the new Coalition Government will move away from this moralistic approach remains to be seen.

Author's note

This chapter was written while the Labour Government was still in power. Although trafficking was mentioned three times in the new Conservative/Liberal Democrat Agreement, no proposals have as yet appeared. It is therefore possible that the arguments put forward here are broadly the same as can be levelled at the new Government.

Notes

1 United Nations Office on Drugs and Crime, *Global Report on Trafficking in Persons* (UNODC, 2009), p. 6. Available online at http://www.unodc.org/documents/Global_Report_on_TIP.pdf (accessed 23 October 2009).

2 Home Office and Scottish Executive, *UK Action Plan Against Trafficking* (London: Home Office and Scottish Executive, 2007); Home Office and the Scottish Government, *Update to the UK Action Plan on Tackling Trafficking* (London: Home Office and the Scottish Government, 2009).

3 US Department of State, *Trafficking in Persons Report* (Washington, DC: US Department of State, 2008), p. 7. Available online at http://www.state.gov/documents/organization/105501.pdf (accessed 20 October 2009).

4 L. Kelly and L. Regan, *Stopping Traffic: Exploring the Extent of, and Responses to, Trafficking in Women for Sexual Exploitation in the UK* (London: Home Office, 2000), p. 22.

5 B. Anderson and J. O'Connell Davidson, *Trafficking: A Demand Led Problem? A Multi-Country Pilot Study* (Stockholm: International Organisation for Migration, 2003), pp. 5–17; p. 13.

6 For an overview of the factors causative of trafficking, see M. Melrose and D. Barrett, 'The Flesh Trade in Europe: Trafficking in Women and Children for the Purpose of Sexual Exploitation', *Police Practice and Research*, 7 (2) (2006): 111–23, at p. 115.

7 Women Aid International Conference, *Code Red: An Integrated Response to Global Trafficking*, London, Publicity Material, cited in Ibid., p. 115.

8 See, for example, V. Munro, 'A Tale of Two Servitudes: Defining and Implementing a Domestic Response to Trafficking on Women for Prostitution in the UK and Australia', *Social and Legal Studies*, 14 (1) (2005): 91–114, at p. 92. UNODC, *Global Report on Trafficking in Persons*, pp. 48–51.

9 See, for example, the website for the Coalition Against Trafficking in Women, www.catwinternational.org. (accessed 2 October 2009) and the Global Alliance Against Traffic in Women, www.gaatw.org. (accessed 2 October 2009). See also V. Munro and M. Della Giusta, 'The Regulation of Prostitution: Contemporary Contexts and Comparative Perspectives', in V. Munro and M. Della Giusta (eds.), *Demanding Sex: Critical Reflections on the Regulations of Prostitution* (Aldershot: Ashgate, 2008), pp. 1–12.

10 For a more detailed debate, see A. Carline and Z. Pearson, 'Complexity and Queer Theory Approaches to International Law and Feminist Politics: Perspectives on Trafficking', *Canadian Journal of Women and the Law*, 19 (1) (2007): 73–118; and S. A. FitzGerald, 'Putting Trafficking on the Map: The Geography of Feminist Complicity', in V. Munro and M. Della Giusta (eds.), *Demanding Sex: Critical Reflections on the Regulations of Prostitution* (Aldershot: Ashgate, 2008), pp. 99–120.

11 S. Egan, 'Protecting the Victims of Trafficking: Problems and Prospects', *European Human Rights Law Review*, 1 (2008): 106–19, at p. 107.

12 Ibid., p. 112.

13 Article 13(1).

14 See Carline and Pearson, 'Complexity and Queer Theory Approaches', pp. 99–107.

15 Home Office and Scottish Executive, *UK Action Plan Against Trafficking*, pp. 17–18.

16 Home Office and The Scottish Government, *Update to the UK Action Plan*, pp. 19 and 50.

17 Home Office and The Scottish Government, *Update to the UK Action Plan*, pp. 19–21. For further details regarding identification and referral mechanisms, see T. Kroger, J. Malkoc and B. H. Uhl, *National Referral Mechanisms: Joining Efforts to Protect the Rights of Trafficked Persons* (Warsaw: OSCE Office for Democratic Institutions and Human Rights, 2004).

18 *The Guardian*, 16 June 2010. Available online at http://www.guardian.co.uk/law/2010/jun/16/trafficking-victims-let-down-rights (accessed 22 June 2010).

19 EWCA Crim 2665 (2007), para 20.

20 N. Davies, 'Prostitution and Trafficking: The Anatomy of a Moral Panic', *The Guardian*, 20 October 2009, p. 7.

21 Home Office and Scottish Executive, *UK Action Plan Against Trafficking*, p. 4.

22 Home Office, *Trafficking Questions and Answers*. Available online at www.crimereduction. homeoffice.gov.uk/humantrafficking005qanda.pdf (accessed 5 October 2009), p. 1.
23 See, for example, Melrose and Barrett, 'The Flesh Trade in Europe', p. 116.
24 EWCA Crim 762 (2007).
25 N. Mai, *Migrants in the UK Sex Industry* (London: Institute for the Study of European Transformations, London Metropolitan University). See also R. Kapur, *Erotic Justice: Law and the New Politics of Postcolonialism* (London: Routledge-Cavendish, 2005).
26 More4 News, 'Two in Three Rescued Women Off the Radar', 16 September 2009. Available online at www.channel4.com/news/articles/uk/two+in+three+rescued+women +off+the+radar/3346517 (accessed 16 October 2009).
27 EWCA Crim 762 (2007) para. 38.
28 EWCA Crim 762 (2007), para. 31.
29 EWCA Crim 762 (2007), paras. 45–6.
30 EWCA Crim 762 (2007), para. 9.
31 EWCA Crim 762 (2007), para. 46.
32 EWCA Crim 762 (2007), para. 46.
33 Section 47 of the SOA 2003.
34 Section 1 of the Sex Offenders Act 1997. Note, however, that a conviction for the trafficking offences contained in Sections 57–9 of the SOA 2003 do not lead to an entry on the sex-offenders register.
35 For a critical discussion of the meaning of 'exploitation', see V. Munro, 'Exploring Exploitation: Trafficking in Sex, Work and Sex Work', in Munro and Della Giusta, *Demanding Sex*, pp. 83–97.
36 See HC Public Bill Committee 3rd Sitting, col. 91, 29 January 2009.
37 HC Public Bill Committee 3rd Sitting, cols. 91–4.
38 See Home Office, *Tackling Demand for Prostitution: A Review* (London: Home Office, 2008); and Jacqui Smith, Labour MP and former Home Secretary, HC Deb, vol. 486, col. 524, 19 January 2009.
39 See, for example, Fiona Mactaggart, Labour MP, HC Deb, vol. 486, col. 546, 19 January 2009.
40 See, for example, Fiona Mactaggart, Labour MP, HC Deb, vol. 492, col. 1431, 19 May 2009; also HC Deb, vol. 486, col. 547, 19 January 2009.
41 See, for example, Lord Pannick, HL Committee 2nd Sitting, col. 261, 1 July 2009.
42 It is important to note that whereas states *must* enact offences to criminalise those who traffick people (Article 18 of the Convention), governments are not so bound in relation to individuals who use the services of trafficked victims. Under Article 19, governments only have to consider adopting such legislation.
43 *R* v. *Woollin* (1999) 1 AC 82. See also *Prosecutor* v. *Akayesu*, case no. ICTR 96–4-T Judgment 688, 2 September 1998. This latter case specifically dealt with drawing inferences in cases involving rape during times of armed conflict.
44 See, for example, the comments made by Labour MPs Alan Campbell and Denis McShane, HC Deb, vol. 492, cols. 1403–4, 19 May 2009.
45 See HC Public Bill Committee, 3rd Sitting, cols. 81–93, 29 January 2009.
46 Joint Committee of Human Rights, *Legislative Scrutiny: Policing and Crime Bill*, Tenth Report of Session 2008–9 (London: House of Lords and House of Commons, 2009), paras. 1.21–1.37.
47 Niki Adams, HC Public Bill Committee, 1st Sitting, col. 33, 27 January 2009.

Chapter 14

A woman's honour and a nation's shame

'Honour killings' in Pakistan

Shilan Shah-Davis

'The right to life of women in Pakistan is conditional on their obeying social norms and traditions'.[1]

Introduction

On 6 April 1999, Samia Sarwar, a twenty-nine-year-old woman, was shot dead by a man hired by her own family in her lawyer's office located in a bustling business district of Lahore, Pakistan. Why was she so callously summarily executed, in public, in broad daylight? Married off to her cousin as a seventeen-year-old, in a match arranged by her family, Samia had been seeking a divorce from her husband after enduring years of abuse and domestic violence by him.[2] Having failed to get the divorce through family deliberations, she had sought help from the law firm AGHS, and taken refuge in the AGHS-run women's shelter, Dastak.[3] While staying at the shelter, Samia, fearing for her life, had refused to meet with male relatives but had reluctantly agreed to a meeting with her mother (who was allegedly going to hand over papers needed for the divorce) at the office of her lawyer, Hina Jilani.[4] Samia's mother had arrived at Jilani's office accompanied by her brother and a driver. The lawyer asked the men to leave the room but Samia's mother objected, averring that she could not walk and needed the driver's assistance.[5] In the next moment, the driver pulled out a gun and shot at both Samia and her lawyer. While Samia died instantly, Hina Jilani narrowly escaped injury.

Samia's family believed that by seeking a divorce Samia had brought shame and dishonour to the family and that such a brazen act of defiance called for punitive action in order to restore the family name and honour.[6] It can be argued that the fact that the killing was carried out so overtly denotes that the 'perpetrators were convinced they were doing the right thing, were not afraid of publicity' and felt no need to hide their identity, as they felt sure that they could count on widespread support and that the state would not hold them to account.[7] In light of the events that followed, it seems that the perpetrators were not wrong in their belief.

If there is anything more shocking than the killing itself, it is the impunity with which the act was carried out. Although Samia was clearly murdered, no one has been convicted for her death. Thus, despite the fact that Samia's parents had hired a man to kill their daughter, and that Samia's mother and uncle had even accompanied the killer, the law in Pakistan allowed them to escape conviction.[8] Moreover, when the case went to court, Samia's parents appeared as her heirs, and, under the Qisas and Diyat Ordinance, forgave the murderer whom they had hired to kill their daughter in the first place.[9]

In contrast, however, there was overwhelming support for the perpetrators from the Pakistani public, a number of politicians and provincial leaders and some segments of the press. Many contended that since the killing was in accordance with tradition, it could not amount to a crime.[10] Others simply emphasised that the parents should have first obtained a local tribal council verdict as this would have given the act 'legitimacy' and avoided any subsequent procedural issues.[11] Thus, the issue was not the premeditated murder of a woman but the procedural oversight by the parents. In light of this immeasurable backing, the meta-message that emerges here is that Samia's death was a natural occurrence in the cultural order.

Indeed, even during the associated parliamentary discussion at the time, much sympathy was evoked for Samia's parents who were regarded as upstanding members of the community, acting to safeguard social traditions and their family's honour.[12] Samia's behaviour, conversely, was deemed to be honour-defying, self-serving and egotistical.[13] In addition, this event triggered bitter religious-tribal agitation against Samia's lawyer, whereby there were calls from members of certain groups not only for her arrest but also for her death because of her (supposed) role in corrupting women by encouraging them to rebel against traditional norms and customs.[14] Negative sentiments against Hina Jilani were voiced in the Pakistani Senate too, where one senator asserted, 'We have fought for human rights and civil liberties all our lives but wonder what sort of human rights are being claimed by these girls in jeans.'[15] Moreover, members of the Government accused human-rights organisations supportive of the lawyer of 'spreading vulgarity and obscenity in the name of human rights' and threatened to penalise such groups.[16]

Nonetheless, this one high-profile incident did place the practice of 'honour killings' (which until then had been occurring in Pakistan with limited public attention) firmly within the country's national discourse, with reverberations across the global media. The case sparked vigorous discussion, debate and open demands for action from individuals and groups, both nationally and internationally. As one Pakistani politician put it, 'Samia in her death has no doubt become a metaphor for all honour killings. She has become a symbol for all brutalities against women.'[17]

Since 1999, besides myriad activities undertaken by various non-governmental organisations (especially women's groups) and other human-rights activists to try and bring to an end the practice of honour killings, there have been a number of legislative changes in Pakistan that purport to effect the prevention of such gender-based violence and other discriminatory practices against women and girls. Irrespective of such notionally promising changes, the country continues to be notoriously prominent as a state where the number of honour killings remains amongst the highest in the world.[18] While reliable data providing a true representation of the extent and magnitude of the problem is virtually impossible to obtain, a recent report estimates that between 2004 and 2007 there were 1,957 incidents of honour killings of women reported in the media.[19] It must be remembered, though, that this figure is just the tip of the iceberg, as significantly more occurrences of honour-related killings actually go unreported.[20]

In its investigation into the phenomenon of honour killings against women in Pakistan, this chapter analyses three aspects of the issue.[21] First, the concept of honour killings is outlined. Second, the rationale behind honour killings is examined, paying particular attention to the notions of honour and its corollary shame, masculine and feminine divides and power and control. Third, the regulation of honour killings is delineated, focusing on both the state law and non-state adjudicatory mechanisms. This chapter concludes that within the Pakistani context the right to life of women is intrinsically linked to their obeying social norms and traditions where the concept of honour is represented by male 'honour'.

The concept of honour killings

Defining the term 'honour killings' is not a straightforward task. This is largely because cultural understandings of the term vary locally depending upon who kills whom and upon what the perceived transgressions of social norms leading to the killings are.[22] At its most basic, the term is commonly used as shorthand, to flag an extreme type of gender-based violence against women 'characterized by (claimed) "motivation"' to preserve familial codes of honour.[23] A more comprehensive definition, and the one used for the purposes of this chapter, is that it comprises of ritualised acts of violence in the form of murders, committed usually by male family members (including extended family members) against female family members who are perceived to have brought dishonour and shame to the family.[24] Furthermore, the 'dishonourable and shameful behaviour' that triggers such killings need not be actual. It can be merely perceived or suspected.[25] In other words, because such behaviour is something imputed by others, material truths concerning what is real and what is not become irrelevant.

At this stage, it is worth pointing out that the very terminology – honour killings – is in itself problematic for two reasons. First, for taking the description articulated by the perpetrators and thereby not only retaining the ideological emphasis on 'male' honour, but also masking the high levels of violence involved.[26] And, second, for concealing, in some instances, the real motivation behind the act, as it is argued that a whole 'honour killing industry' has sprung up wherein the excuse of honour is regularly used 'as a blanket cover for a multitude of [other] sins'.[27] For example, men have been known to manipulate the tradition of honour killings to settle land disputes and old enmities.[28] In such contexts, the underlying motive is clearly not the restoration of honour. Accordingly, in light of this, feminists have argued for the rejection of the term 'honour killings' in search of another more suitable phrase which does not allude to a misconceived ideology of honour that disguises the true nature of the violent manifestations.[29] However, in the absence of a better alternative phrase, this chapter shall continue to use the expression 'honour killings' to describe this gender-based murder of women.

Although a common occurrence in various cultures and communities, the practice of honour killings seems to be most prevalent in more collectivist societies where the sentiment of honour is lived out openly before other people and any dishonourable conduct of an individual is taken to reflect upon the rest of the family and other members of the community.[30] That being said, owing to the extensive media reports in the past few years about the frequency of honour killings in places such as Pakistan, Jordan, Palestine, Turkey and certain other Islamic states, and amongst Muslim diaspora communities (including those in Western Europe), a popular belief exists that this practice is somehow based on the tenets of Islam. Such a view is erroneous and misplaced.[31] Put simply, if certain Muslims have committed honour killings, or if honour killings have been carried out in some Islamic states, it does not automatically follow that the practice is prescribed, condoned or tolerated by Islam. On the contrary, Shari'ah (Islamic) law repeatedly condemns murder.[32] Rather, it prescribes respect for human life and human dignity and discourages interference with other people's lives and speculation about other people's affairs.[33] Additionally, Shari'ah law is highly critical of individuals falsely accusing others of crimes they did not commit. Such behaviour is called *al-kadf*, which literally means to throw something at someone.[34] So, for instance, those who falsely point the finger at chaste women and fail to bring forth witnesses to prove allegations should be lashed eighty times and their testimony should never be accepted again, unless they repent and admit their wrongdoing.[35]

What is more, family killings and other forms of violence committed in the name of honour are by no means tied to a particular religion or group: 'Murder of kin on the justification of restoring family honour is frequent not only in ... Muslim society, but also in other societies ... for example ... Sardinia and Sicily. This does not mean that Roman Catholicism encourages it.'[36] In fact, the notion of honour was certainly a part of the legal history of Western civilisation before its institutionalisation in Muslim countries, and, as a result, honour killings existed even before the advent of Islam.[37] For instance, honour played an important part in the structure of Roman society and in the evolution of Roman law, and, accordingly, justifications for honour killings can be found in the family law of the Roman Empire.[38]

In Pakistan, honour killings occur in all four provinces of the country and in the tribal areas adjoining the border with Afghanistan.[39] Nonetheless, it must be pointed out that the phrase 'honour killing', as understood by many, is of the English language. In the various languages and dialects spoken in Pakistan, this extreme manifestation of violence has historically been mentioned in ways that directly brand the victims of the act as 'black'. For instance, in Sindh it is called *karo kari* and in the Punjab it is referred to as *kala kali*. Both literally mean 'black male' and 'black female', traditional metaphoric terms for adulterer and adulteress. The branding as 'black' implies that the community must be cleansed of the deed that blackens it.[40] Traditionally, honour killings were socially sanctioned to punish women for (often allegedly) engaging in extramarital sexual activity. However, over the years, claimed justifications for the practice 'have widened to include women's expressions of autonomy by, for example, exercising choice in marriage or a decision to seek divorce.'[41]

There is no definitive local consensus regarding the origins of honour killings in Pakistan.[42] For instance, some allege that it originates from the various Baloch tribes of Balochistan and spread to other communities when members of these tribes migrated to different parts of the country.[43] On the other hand, Pathans of the North Western Frontier Province claim that the Muslims adopted this practice from the Hindus since the subcontinent had been home to both Muslims and Hindus.[44] Despite the uncertainty about the origins of the custom, it would be fair to deduce that in Pakistan the killing of women in response to perceived breaches of honour finds endorsement in local (tribal) traditions and culture.[45]

Rationale behind honour killings

Within local traditions, the perception of honour used to rationalise killings 'is founded on the notion that a person's honour depends on the behaviour of others and that behaviour, therefore, must be controlled.'[46] As a result, other people's conduct (as opposed to one's own) becomes a key factor in one's own feelings of self-worth and community regard. Hence, honour acts as a pivotal link between the individual and the community. In this context, it offers a moral framework for behaviour, norms and rules that provide a basis for acceptance in collective life.[47] Indeed, within Pakistan, it is through the holding of honour, in the form of familial respect (*izzat*) and social prestige (*ghairat*), that individuals find a place in their community.[48] Consequently, in this regard, honour is imbued with great power and becomes foundational to the individual's identity.[49] What is more, once an act deemed to be shameful becomes public knowledge (as in Samia's case when she sought the help of the law firm AGHS), this can adversely affect the individual's and family's standing in the community, and, therefore, the transgressor of the dishonour must be punished as almost a matter of social inevitability.[50]

In addition, in collectivistic cultures such as Pakistan, the family is the 'core unit that the individual identifies with and is naturally a powerful institution in the way communities are organized'.[51] Thus, here honour is not something that is simply important and achieved individually; rather, it encapsulates the whole worth of the family and the community. In other words, honour is shared and belongs to the collective.[52] It also transcends time in that the lives of the unborn members of the community depend upon it as well. Therefore, losing honour invites ridicule and disgrace and subjects not only the family but also the entire community to shame. Such a collective attitude of honour, for example, was certainly evident following Samia's death when members of the Pashtun community vigorously defended Samia's parents' actions and alleged that Samia, by her actions, was responsible for her own demise.[53]

Moreover, just as honour can be lost, it can also be regained by avenging the offensive act.[54] Accordingly, actions, including murder, carried out to restore the honour and remove the shame, are not only condoned but often valorised. In many instances, perpetrators of honour killings are viewed as victims by fellow members of the community because, in their view, 'what the perpetrator had to go through was worse than death'.[55] What is more, by carrying out the act of killing, it is considered that the perpetrator displayed courage and lived up to expectations, i.e. became *ghairatmand* (possessing honour and brave).[56] In a nutshell, a Pakistani folk saying says it all: *Daulat khonay pur kuch naheen khota; sihat khonay pur kuch kho jaata hai; ghairat khonay pur sub kuch kho jataa hai* (When wealth is lost nothing is lost; when health is lost something is lost; when honour is lost everything is lost).[57]

It is further argued that collectivist societies can be fiercely patriarchal and hegemonic. In this context, honour becomes the operative perspective of the power-holding group that relies on the behaviour of others.[58] More to the point, such patriarchal structures are modulated by a gender construct whereby women and their activities are taken to represent the behaviour that must be controlled.[59] In other words, women are seen as the repositories of their family's honour and men are considered to be the protectors of this honour.[60] But, rather than possessing honour themselves, women are merely symbolic vessels of male honour, and for that reason all of their actions are seen to reflect upon male family members. Hence, the behavioural qualities that are deemed to be honourable for women and men contrast dramatically, and the qualities required of women are anchored in the assumptions underlying male definitions and expectations of appropriate female behaviour.[61] One scholar maintains that in this patriarchal setting women are bestowed with immense negative power for the reason that any 'misbehaviour on their part can bring shame and dishonour to the male members of a whole community, lineage or family.'[62] There is a powerful sense in which, just as the concept of honour does for men, it is primarily a woman's shame, or potential for shame, that summarises her public reputation and social position.[63] As a result, in order to prevent the dishonouring of the manliness of men, the quality required of women is, in essence, shame. Therefore, while men have honour, women have shame.[64] And, for men, female shame and dishonour must be responded to, violently if necessary, if male reputation and social prestige are to survive.

What is more, in order to protect their shame and men's honour, women are expected to behave modestly. In fact, modesty and chastity are considered essential components to preserve male, and thereby the family's, honour. Besides, female chastity also represents the 'symbolic capital' of male hegemony.[65] Women are regarded as an object of value that is worthy of possession and that must be controlled. Basically, 'women are considered the property of the males in their family ... [and] the owner of the property has the right to decide its fate.'[66] So, by engaging in behaviour that compromises her chastity, a woman undermines the ownership rights of her male family members and loses her inherent value as an object worthy of possession.[67]

It is also averred that in many societies, including Pakistan, the very 'ideal of masculinity is underpinned by a notion of "honour" – of an individual man, or a family or a community – and is fundamentally connected to policing female behaviour and sexuality.'[68] In this context, honour can be understood in terms of dominance and a male-derived social interest. Consequently, because of the vesting of such an interest in the conduct and body of a woman, in order to protect it, men accord themselves complete authority and control over their female family members.[69] Thus, a man who is unable to take authoritative action against a transgressive female family member becomes ungendered, as he has failed to exert his power and, therefore, his masculinity. Indeed, within the Pakistani context, it can be argued that a man who fails to kill the woman of his household who has damaged his honour would be regarded, by other male family members and by members of the community, as 'socially impotent and *beghairat* (without honour).'[70] Furthermore, it can be argued that while femininity is an ascribed status masculinity is something that must be achieved, i.e. a process that can only be realised through the effective control and punishment of female misbehaviour.[71] And such control, like other forms of oppression, is often deeply rooted in violence.

Regulation of honour killings

Within Pakistan, due to the existence of plural adjudicatory systems which comprise of both formal and informal laws, the regulation of honour killings evokes competing spheres of simultaneous legal subjection. In turn, such pluralism gives rise to different, competing normative systems that seek to order human behaviour.[72]

The formal justice system in Pakistan today operates as a hybrid of secular and religious models, and, therefore, like in many Islamic states, there is a secular court system as well as Shari'ah courts.[73] However, 'tribal council arbitration, although not part of the formal justice system, [also] wields incredible control over all manner of disputes.'[74] Such arbitration systems, in the form of *jirgas* and *panchayats* (tribal and community councils) have existed in South Asia for centuries and their decisions have been handed down from one generation to the next, resulting in sets of codes delineating acceptable standards of social conduct.[75] These traditional codes of conduct, as can be seen from Samia Sarwar's case, for instance, continue to have a more commanding hold on the behaviour of the members of contemporary Pakistani society than the state's formal laws.

In addition, the governance of communities through *jirgas* and *panchayats* has allowed the development of a lasting informal, non-state parallel system of regulation in Pakistan. At present, a high proportion of the population in Pakistan live in rural areas as opposed to urban centres.[76] For such members of society, the tribal and community councils (which continue to operate in all the provinces) remain the first and, more often than not, the final source of authoritative adjudication.[77] Such forums are composed solely of men, particularly those who already exert great financial and/or inherited power.[78] Women are not allowed to appear before these gatherings, either as the accused or the complainant, nor can they be witnesses.[79]

Jirgas and *panchayats* deal with a variety of issues that not only consist of resolving disputes between members of the community but also involve passing pronouncements on matters deemed to be of relevance to the honour of the community – including (alleged) acts by women that defy the traditionally formed social order and morality. The pronouncements delivered in cases involving women who have supposedly transgressed the cultural normativity are 'gendered articulations of patriarchal privilege' that resonate structurally inbuilt inequities towards women.[80] In other words, in a quest to preserve communal solidarity and (male) collective honour, tribal and community councils are known to order the killing (frequently on the slimmest suspicion) of female transgressors or to endorse the murder of such women by male family members.[81] Here the goal is not to elicit the truth and punish the culprit but, rather, to restore the balance disturbed by a woman's (often assumed) indiscretion.[82]

The Government seems to have little control over the activities of *jirgas* and *panchayats*. On the contrary, it is reported that many members of parliament have been or are actually part of such councils.[83] Moreover, as demonstrated by the reaction of some members of the Pakistani Senate to Samia Sarwar's murder, there is endorsement for the preservation of traditional social codes and customs even in the country's highest law-enacting body. Consequently, the rule of tradition becomes more powerful than the rule of law. Notwithstanding the fact that this cultural ideology generally remains relatively intransigent in Pakistan, in early 2000, intent on promoting an enlightened and moderate image, the then Government stipulated that it was determined to take strict measures to curb violence against women in the name of culture and tradition and to ensure the safety of women in Pakistani society.[84] As a result, a number of legislative changes have been introduced.

In the context of honour killings, one such change that is of particular relevance is the Criminal Law (Amendment) Act 2004. In fact, this Act is the first piece of legislation that officially acknowledges the problem of honour-related violence in Pakistan.[85] It prohibits offences 'committed in the name or on the pretext of honour' and introduces a number of modifications to the laws relating to murder via amendments to the Pakistan Penal Code.[86] During its enactment, one government minister hailed it as 'a landmark decision as the law protects the rights of women and eliminates ... archaic rituals'.[87]

However, women's-rights advocates have criticised the Act as 'defective and incomplete'.[88] Critically, the Act does not address the crucial problem of 'statutory concession' available to perpetrators through the *Qisas* and *Diyat* laws which posit 'forgiveness' powers in the hands of the victim and his or her legal heirs. The Qisas and Diyat Ordinance was promulgated in 1990, following the Supreme Court Shariat Appellate Bench's decision in the case of *Federation of Pakistan* v. *Gul Hassan* 1989, where the court found certain sections of the Pakistan Penal Code and the Criminal Procedural Code concerning deliberate murder and deliberate hurt to be contrary to Islam.[89] In introducing major changes to penal provisions dealing with such offences, the Ordinance had (and still has) far-reaching consequences for the legal prosecution of honour killings as it shifted the emphasis of murder as a crime against the state to a private offence against the individual.[90] Accordingly, the charge of implementing legal justice for a wrongful death is effectively placed in the hands of the deceased's *wali* (legal heir[s]) rather than the government.

In a nutshell, the heirs may seek *qisas* (retribution), *diyat* (i.e. enter into a compromise with the accused in return for compensation – often referred to as compounding) or total forgiveness of the accused.[91] In addition, even if the case is being heard under *qisas*, any one of the heirs may, at any stage of the prosecution, waive their right of *qisas* and invoke the other options available to them.[92] Furthermore, the court is obliged to accept the decision unless it exercises its discretion under Section 311 of the Pakistan Penal Code which grants the court discretion to prosecute in certain circumstances (irrespective of whether there is a waiver, compromise or pardon). However, in reality, this provision has rarely been applied.[93] In fact, in the context of honour killings, due to the familial structure in which such crimes occur, perpetrators walk away free (as evident in Samia Sarwar's case). Consequently, the message that emerges here is that murders of family members are a family affair and that prosecution and legal redress are not inevitable but are open to negotiation.

Conclusion

As explored in this chapter, the right to life of women in Pakistan is indeed conditional on their obeying social norms and traditions. The structures that perpetuate honour killings are socially constructed, and the related rhetoric of violence is a product of a historical and cultural process that is neither essential nor time-bound in its manifestation. The concept of honour in such a process is represented by the ideological construction of male 'honour', whereby killing transgressive females is deemed essential not only for the restoration of the family's *ghairat* and *izzat* but also to ensure the collective identity. What is more, this masculine hegemony is reinforced by the regulation of honour killings within both the formal legal system and the non-state adjudicatory mechanisms.

Notes

1 Hina Jilani, lawyer and human-rights activist in Pakistan, quoted in Amnesty International, *Pakistan: Violence Against Women in the Name of Honour*, ASA 33/017/99, 1999, p. 2. Available online at http://www.amnesty.org/en/library/asset/ASA33/017/1999/en/5d9201f4-e0f2-11dd-be39-2d4003be4450/asa330171999en.pdf (accessed 30 January 2010).

2 K. Lasson, 'Bloodstains on a "Code of Honor": The Murderous Marginalization of Women in the Islamic World', *Women's Rights Law Reporter*, 30 (3) (2008/9): 407–41; p. 418.

3 In fact, when Samia spoke with her parents about her intentions to seek a divorce, rather than offering support they threatened her life; see S. Palo, 'A Charade of Change: Qias and Diyat Ordinance Allows Honor Killings to Go Unpunished in Pakistan', *UC Davis Journal of International Law and Policy*, 15 (1) (2008/9): 93–101; p. 94. AGHS (Law Firm) Legal Aid Cell is the first law firm established by women in Pakistan.

4 R. A. Ruane, 'Murder in the Name of Honor: Violence Against Women in Jordan and Pakistan', *Emroy International Law Review*, 14 (3) (2000): 1523–80; p. 1524.

5 Amnesty International, *Pakistan: Violence Against Women*, p. 22.

6 T. S. Khan, *Beyond Honour: A Historical Materialist Explanation of Honour Related Violence* (Karachi: Oxford University Press Pakistan, 2006), p. 274.

7 Amnesty International, *Pakistan: Violence Against Women*, p. 22.

8 K. N. Ahmed, 'Concurrent Session B–1, Gender (In)justice, Comments', *SPDI Research and News*, 6th Special Bulletin, 10 (6) (2003): 42–4. Available online at http://www.sdpi.org/help/research_and_news_bulletin/SDPI_%20research_and_news_bulletin_nov_dec_2003/articles/Day%20three%20articles/Gender%20 (In)%20Justice.htm (accessed 30 January 2010).

9 Ibid. It is also argued that the family's financial status and social and political influence allowed them to take the law into their own hands and murder Samia; see Khan, *Beyond Honour*, p. 275.

10 Amnesty International, *Pakistan: Violence Against Women*, pp. 22–3.

11 In Pakistan, alongside the formal legal system, there exists an informal adjudicatory system as well where non-state forums such as tribal and community councils play a highly influential role in regulating and resolving various issues. R. A. Ruane, 'Murder in the Name of Honor: Violence Against Women in Jordan and Pakistan', *Emroy International Law Review*, 14 (3) (2000): 1523–80; p. 1525.

12 A. H. Jafri, *Honour Killing: Dilemma, Ritual, Understanding* (Karachi: Oxford University Press Pakistan, 2008), p. 92.

13 Ibid.

14 Ibid., p. 2.

15 M. Hussain, '"Take My Riches, Give Me Justice": A Contextual Analysis of Pakistan's Honor Crimes Legislation', *Harvard Journal of Law and Gender*, 29 (1) (2006): 223–46; 242–3.

16 Ibid., p. 243.

17 Jafri, *Honour Killing*, p. 3.
18 See, for instance, Khan, *Beyond Honour*, p. 135; A. Knudsen, *License to Kill: Honour Killings in Pakistan* (Bergen: Chr. Michelsen Institute, 2004), p. 2. Available online at http://www.cmi.no/publications/file/1737-license-to-kill-honour-killings-in-pakistan.pdf (accessed 17 January 2010); and Lasson, 'Bloodstains on a "Code of Honor"', p. 418.
19 M. Nasrullah, S. Haqqi and K. J. Cummings, 'The Epidemiological Patterns of Honour Killing of Women in Pakistan', *European Journal of Public Health*, 19 (2) (2009): 193–7, p. 194.
20 Asian Human Rights Commission, *Pakistan: Conditions for Women are More Precarious on International Women's Day 2009*, Statement, 8 March 2009. Available online at http://www.ahrchk.net/statements/mainfile.php/2009statements/1926/ (accessed 26 January 2010).
21 In this chapter, the term 'women' also includes girls.
22 S. A. Warraich, '"Honour Killings" and the Law in Pakistan', in L. Welchman and S. Hossain (eds.), *'Honour': Crimes, Paradigms and Violence Against Women* (London: Zed Books, 2005), pp. 78–110; p. 78.
23 L. Welchman and S. Hossain, '"Honour", Rights and Wrongs', in L. Welchman and S. Hossain (eds.), *'Honour': Crimes, Paradigms and Violence Against Women* (London: Zed Books, 2005), pp. 1–21; p. 4.
24 Sometimes female family members are involved as well, as can be seen, for example, from Samia Sarwar's case where a mother was a major participant in the killing of her own daughter. Although less common, men can also be the victims of honour killings. Knudsen, *License to Kill*, p. 1; and Human Rights Watch, *Integration of the Human Rights of Women and the Gender Perspective: Violence Against Women and 'Honor' Crimes*, Intervention Before the 57 Session of the UN Commission on Human Rights, 6 April 2001. Available online at http://www.hrw.org/press/2001/04un_oral12_0405.htm (accessed 26 January 2010).
25 Welchman and Hossain, '"Honour", Rights and Wrongs', p. 5.
26 Welchman and Hossain, '"Honour", Rights and Wrongs', p. 8; P. Baxi, S. M. Rai and S. S. Ali, 'Legacies of Common Law: "Crimes of Honour" in India and Pakistan', *Third World Quarterly*, 27 (7) (2006): 1239–53; p. 1239.
27 Welchman and Hossain, '"Honour", Rights and Wrongs', p. 8; Amnesty International, *Pakistan: Violence Against Women*, p. 25.
28 Amnesty International, *Pakistan: Violence Against Women*, p. 26. Shirkat Gah, *There is No 'Honour' in Honour Killing: National Seminar Report* (Lahore: Shirkat Gah, 2002), p. 26.
29 See, for instance, U. Chakravarti, 'From Fathers to Husbands: Of Love, Death and Marriage in North India', in L. Welchman and S. Hossain (eds.), *'Honour': Crimes, Paradigms and Violence Against Women* (London: Zed Books, 2005), pp. 308–31; p. 308.
30 Jafri, *Honour Killing*, p. 18; P. Bourdieu, 'The Sentiment of Honour in Kabyle Society', in J. G. Peristiany (ed.), *Honour and Shame: The Values of Mediterranean Society* (Chicago, Ill.: University of Chicago Press, 1970), pp. 192–241; p. 208.
31 N. A. S. Kakakhel, 'Honour Killings: Islamic and Human Rights Perspectives', *Northern Ireland Legal Quarterly*, 55 (1) (2004): 78–89; p. 82; and C. A. Madek, 'Killing Dishonor: Effective Eradication of Honor Killing', *Suffolk Transnational Law Review*, 29 (1) (2005): 53–77; p. 55.
32 Hussain, 'Take My Riches, Give Me Justice', p. 235.
33 See, for example, the Qur'an, verses 5:32, 6:151, 17:33, 49:12.
34 F. K. Nesheiwat, 'Honor Crimes in Jordan: Their Treatment Under Islamic and Jordanian Criminal Laws', *Penn State International Law Review*, 23 (2) (2004): 251–82; p. 264.
35 The Qur'an, verses 24:4–5.
36 S. D. Lang, 'Sharaf Politics: Constructing Male Prestige in Israeli–Palestinian Society', unpublished doctoral thesis, Cambridge, Mass.: Harvard University, 2000, p. 55; and Jafri, *Honour Killing*, pp. 19, 27. Alessandro Bausani, quoted in G. M. Kressel,

'Sorocide/Filiacide: Homicide for Family Honour', *Current Anthropology*, 22 (2) (1981): 141–58; p. 153.

37 Hussain, 'Take My Riches, Give Me Justice', p. 235.

38 Jafri, *Honour Killing*, p. 30; Lasson, 'Bloodstains on a "Code of Honor"', p. 418.

39 Warraich, '"Honour Killings" and the Law', p. 79.

40 Jafri, *Honour Killing*, p. 7.

41 Warraich, '"Honour Killings" and the Law', p. 79

42 Ibid., p. 80.

43 Shirkat Gah, *There is No 'Honour' in Honour Killing*, p. 16.

44 Ibid., p. 17.

45 See, for instance, Jafri, *Honour Killing*; Khan, *Beyond Honour*; and Hussain, 'Take My Riches, Give Me Justice'.

46 N. V. Baker, P. R. Gregware and M. A. Cassidy, 'Family Killing Fields: Honour Rationales in the Murder of Women', *Violence Against Women*, 5 (2) (1999): 164–84; p. 165.

47 P. Sen, '"Crimes of Honour", Value and Meaning', in L. Welchman and S. Hossain (eds.), *'Honour': Crimes, Paradigms and Violence Against Women* (London: Zed Books, 2005), p. 44.

48 Knudsen, *License to Kill*, p. 4.

49 Sen, 'Crimes of Honour', p. 44.

50 Baker et al., 'Family Killing Fields', p. 171.

51 Jafri, *Honour Killing*, p. 22.

52 Ibid., p. 23.

53 Ruane, 'Murder in the Name of Honor', pp. 1524–5.

54 Knudsen, *License to Kill*, p. 4.

55 Jafri, *Honour Killing*, p. 24.

56 Kakakhel, 'Honour Killings', p. 81.

57 Jafri, *Honour Killing*, p. 24.

58 Baker et al., 'Family Killing Fields', p. 165.

59 Hussain, 'Take My Riches, Give Me Justice', p. 227.

60 Ruane, 'Murder in the Name of Honor', p. 1530. Madek, 'Killing Dishonor', p. 55.

61 Baker et al., 'Family Killing Fields', p. 166.

62 D. Kandiyoti, 'Emancipated but Unliberated? Reflections on the Turkish Case', *Feminist Studies*, 13 (2) (1987), 317–38; p. 322.

63 Ibid.

64 See, for example, N. Shah, 'Faislo: The Informal Settlement Office and Crimes Against Women in Sindh', in F. Shaheed, A. S Warriach, A. S. Balchin and A. Gazdar (eds.), *Shaping Women's Lives: Laws, Practices and Strategies in Pakistan* (Lahore: Shirkat Gah, 1998), pp. 227–52.

65 Knudsen, *License to Kill*, p. 4.

66 J. Chahine, 'Laws in Arab World Remain Lenient on Honour Crimes', *The Daily Star* (Lebanon), 9 September 2004. Available online at http://www.dailystar.com.lb/article.asp?edition_id=1&categ_id=1&article_id=819 (accessed 24 January 2010).

67 Ruane, 'Murder in the Name of Honor', p. 1531.

68 R. Coomaraswamy, 'Violence Against Women and "Crimes of Honour"', in L. Welchman and S. Hossain (eds.), *'Honour': Crimes, Paradigms and Violence Against Women* (London: Zed Books, 2005), pp. xi–xiv; p. xi.

69 Hussain, 'Take My Riches, Give Me Justice', p. 227.

70 Ruane, 'Murder in the Name of Honor', p. 1532.

71 Jafri, *Honour Killing*, p. 21.

72 N. Khouri, 'Human Rights and Islam: Lessons from Amina Lawal and Mukhtar Mai', *Georgetown Journal of Gender and the Law*, 8 (1) (2007): 93–110; p. 95.

73 Palo, 'A Charade of Change', p. 95. Furthermore, it must be pointed out that within the folds of the formal legal system there exists another judicial scheme called the Frontier Crimes Regulations (FCR) (introduced during the British colonial rule) which is applicable to the Federally Administered Tribal Areas (FATA) situated in northern Pakistan. Basically, the FATA are under the direct executive authority of the President of Pakistan, and laws passed by Parliament (and applicable to the rest of the country) do not apply in this region unless so ordered by the President.

74 Hussain, 'Take My Riches, Give Me Justice', p. 233.

75 Baxi et al., 'Legacies of Common Law', p. 1243; M. Castetter, 'Taking Law into Their Own Hands: Unofficial and Illegal Sanctions by the Pakistani Tribal Councils', *Indiana International and Comparative Law Review*, 13 (2) (2003): 543–48; p. 558.

76 See statistics provided by the Population Census Organization (Pakistan). Available online at http://www.sbp.org.pk/departments/stats/PakEconomy_HandBook/Chap_10.pdf (accessed 20 February 2010).

77 Khan, *Beyond Honour*, p. 230; Hussain, 'Take My Riches, Give Me Justice', p. 233.

78 Hussain, 'Take My Riches, Give Me Justice', p. 233.

79 Khan, *Beyond Honour*, p. 232.

80 Baxi et al., 'Legacies of Common Law', p. 1243.

81 Asian Human Rights Commission, *The State of Human Rights in Pakistan: 2008*, Hong Kong: Asian Human Rights Commission 2008, pp. 14–15. Available online at http://material.ahrchk.net/hrreport/2008/AHRC-SPR-014–2008-Pakistan_AHRR2008.pdf (accessed 15 February 2010).

82 Ruane, 'Murder in the Name of Honor', p. 1536.

83 See, for example, Asian Human Rights Commission, *Pakistan: Order an Honour Killing – Become a Minister*, Statement, 4 March 2009. Available online at http://www.humanrightsblog.org/2009/03/pakistan_order_an_honour_killi.htm (accessed 26 January 2010).

84 Khan, *Beyond Honour*, p. 263.

85 Hussain, 'Take My Riches, Give Me Justice', p. 239.

86 Criminal Law (Amendment) Act, 2004, para. 2.

87 O. Tohid, 'Pakistan Outlaws "Honour" Killings', *The Christian Science Monitor*, 20 January 2005. Available online at http://www.csmonitor.com/2005/0120/p06s01-wosc.html (accessed 31 January 2010).

88 Hussain, 'Take My Riches, Give Me Justice', p. 239.

89 Subsequently passed by Parliament as the Qisas and Diyat Act in 1997; Warraich, '"Honour Killings" and the Law', p. 84.

90 Knudsen, *License to Kill*, p. 8.

91 Palo, 'A Charade of Change', p. 100.

92 Warraich, '"Honour Killings" and the Law', p. 86.

93 Ibid., p. 87.

Chapter 15

Supranational criminal prosecution of sexual violence

Anne-Marie de Brouwer

Introduction

During practically every conflict in the world, from time immemorial, rape and other forms of sexual violence against women have taken place on a massive scale.[1] Men too fall victim to sexual violence in conflict, although seemingly in smaller numbers than women.[2] The consequences of sexual violence are severe and enduring: many survivors contract sexually transmitted diseases including HIV/AIDS, face unwanted pregnancies and health complications resulting from botched abortions and suffer from sexual mutilations and other injuries. In addition, they often face stigma, isolation and severe trauma. Typically, they are confronted by poverty and by having to take care of orphans as well as their own children.

This chapter addresses the adequacy of the supranational criminal law system (on both a substantive as well as a procedural level) of the International Criminal Tribunal for the former Yugoslavia (ICTY or Tribunal) and Rwanda (ICTR or Tribunal) and the International Criminal Court (ICC or Court) from the perspective of victims/survivors of sexual violence.[3] In particular, the ICC's Rome Statute, Rules of Procedure and Evidence (RPE), Elements of Crimes (EoC) and case law are examined and compared to the ICTY and ICTR Statutes, RPE and case law, in the necessary light of the reality of sexual violence taking place in conflict situations.[4] Recommendations are offered in regard to how sexual violence can and should be prosecuted before the ICC, which is currently examining the situation of Uganda, the Democratic Republic of the Congo (DRC), Darfur/Sudan and the Central African Republic (CAR).

Sexual violence in supranational criminal law

Article 5 of the Rome Statute stipulates that 'the jurisdiction of the Court shall be limited to the most serious crimes of concern to the international community as a whole', namely genocide, crimes against humanity, war crimes and the yet-to-be-defined crime of aggression. What do these first three crimes entail and to what extent can sexual violence be prosecuted as such? In order to address this question, the acts and the common elements pertaining to these crimes need to be examined.

Crimes against humanity and war crimes

Articles 7 and 8 of the Rome Statute explicitly, and for the first time in supranational criminal law, prohibit rape, sexual slavery, enforced prostitution, forced pregnancy, enforced sterilisation and any other form of sexual violence as crimes against humanity and war crimes. With the exception of the crimes of rape and enforced prostitution, these specific sexual violence crimes have previously never been laid down in an international instrument at either the international or supranational criminal law level. In addition, previously no clear definitions of the crimes of rape and enforced prostitution existed on the supranational criminal law level (despite their criminalisation), let alone of any of the other sexual violence crimes. What are, or what should be, the definitions of sexual violence crimes in the context of the supranational criminal law system? When trying to answer this question one should bear in mind that although the ICC's EoC provide a detailed overview of the elements of sexual violence crimes, the EoC are, strictly speaking, not binding; they are merely intended to guide the judges in interpreting and applying the stated 'definitions' of the crimes (Article 9 of the Rome Statute).

With regard to the definition of rape, the EoC do not focus on the issue of non-consent but rather on force, threat of force, coercion or a coercive environment. This definition of rape is a mixture of the definitions provided in the ICTR *Akayesu* and ICTY *Furundžija* cases. In the *Akayesu* judgment, the first definition of rape in supranational criminal law was put forward. The Chamber chose to formulate rape as follows: 'a physical invasion of a sexual nature, committed on a person under circumstances which are coercive'.[5] In the *Furundžija* case, another definition of rape was accepted, which would better take into account the common denominator of the crime of rape to be found in national jurisdictions. The focus of the definition of rape as pronounced in the *Furundžija* case is therefore on sexual penetration and coercion, force or threat of force.[6] By contrast, the ruling in the ICTY *Kunarac, Kovač and Vuković* case, taken by an Appeals Chamber and after the EoC were drafted, focuses on sexual penetration (like *Furundžija*) but also lack of consent as elements of the crime of rape.[7] It was held that lack of consent was part of the definition of rape in the major national legal systems in the world and that the *Furundžija* judgment had mistakenly not incorporated this element in the definition. Yet, lack of consent as an element of the crime of rape (or any other sexual violence crime for that matter) is immaterial within the supranational criminal law context, especially in light of the violent and oppressive contexts in which rapes take place during genocide, crimes against humanity or armed conflict. In other words, when the common elements of these crimes are established (see below), the issue of consent quickly becomes irrelevant. In addition, no matter how questions are phrased by the

Prosecutor ('Did you consent?' or 'Was it done against your will?'), such questions may insult rape victims and may cause further traumatisation, especially if questions like these are asked after the victim has already set out the coercive circumstances in which the sexual violence was inflicted. The reaction of Witness 95 in the *Kunarac, Kovač and Vuković* case to the question posed by the Prosecutor (at the request of one of the judges) whether the sexual contact had been against her will, was met with outrage and is illustrative in this regard: 'Please, madam, if over a period of 40 days you have sex with someone, with several individuals, do you really think that is with your own will?'[8] Witness 95 had just explained to the court that she had been selected for the purpose of rape more than 150 times in a period of forty days.

Once it has been established that a crime was committed, questions concerning consent become irrelevant. In the (presumably) rare cases in which the Defence may want to advance consent as a defence, this is still possible, but the relevance and admissibility of such evidence must first be confirmed in an in-camera procedure (a closed session) in order to spare the victim from painful propositions which have not been tested beforehand (Rule 72 of the RPE). It is suggested that the *Kunarac, Kovač and Vuković* Appeals Chamber judgment on the definition of rape, focusing, as it did, upon the issue of consent, should not, therefore, be followed by the ICC.[9] In fact, in general terms, the Akayesu and ICC definition of rape in the EoC best fits the reality of the crime in relation to genocide, armed conflict and crimes against humanity and should therefore be taken as the leading definition of rape in supranational criminal law.

As far as the crime of sexual slavery is concerned, the crime is defined in the EoC in conformity with the definition of enslavement, to 'exercise any or all of the powers attaching to the right of ownership over one or more persons', with the addition that the perpetrator caused the victim to engage in one or more acts of a sexual nature. Although the definition may at first give the impression that some sort of commercial aspect is involved as 'ownership' may be understood to refer to, for example, purchasing and selling, a footnote attached to the first element of the crime of sexual slavery makes it perfectly clear that sexual slavery includes 'forced labour', 'reducing a person to a servile status' (including forced marriage) and 'trafficking in persons, in particular women and children'. It can therefore be concluded that sexual slavery does not necessarily require any financial benefits to accrue to the enslaver nor the confinement of the victim in a particular place. The crime of enforced prostitution, on the other hand, focuses mainly on pecuniary advantages. In most situations, the act committed may be better charged as sexual slavery rather than enforced prostitution. In times of genocide, crimes against humanity and armed conflict, women are frequently captured for the prime purpose of sex without any financial benefits being involved. The so-called 'comfort women' were for a long time wrongly thought to have been captured by the Japanese for the purpose of enforced prostitution whereas they were in fact held in sexual slavery.[10] Situations falling short of sexual slavery are nevertheless prosecutable as enforced prostitution.

According to the EoC, the crime of forced pregnancy should be understood as one where 'the perpetrator confined one or more women forcibly made pregnant, with the intent of affecting the ethnic composition of any population or carrying out other grave violations of international law' (see also Article 7[2][f] of the Rome Statute). It remains to be seen how this crime will be interpreted by the judges of the ICC, but it must be noted that a narrow interpretation, for example requiring that the confinement of a woman implies that a specific amount of time needs to have elapsed, will certainly not be in conformity with the reality in which forced pregnancy takes place in times of genocide, crimes against humanity or armed conflict. The crime of enforced sterilisation may additionally capture, for example, the situation in which women were raped so viciously that their reproductive system was completely destroyed. The residual category, that of 'any other form of sexual violence of *comparable* gravity' (emphasis added) need not be interpreted strictly, as this might lead to the conclusion that all other sexual violence crimes need some degree of penetration. Such an interpretation is undesirable and would, moreover, not take into account the Tribunal's case law on this matter, in which, for example, forced nudity was found to fall within the ambit of 'other inhumane acts'.[11] All these factors, taken together, force the conclusion that the Rome Statute incorporates an impressive list of specific sexual violence crimes.

Genocide

The definition of the crime of genocide (Article 6 of the Rome Statute) does not include specific references to rape and other forms of sexual violence and follows the definition of genocide contained in the 1948 Genocide Convention verbatim. The EoC, however, do refer to rape and sexual violence in a footnote (which has the same standing as an element), explaining that these crimes fall within the ambit of sub-heading (b) of the crime of genocide, namely 'causing serious bodily or mental harm to members of the group'. This acknowledgement was directly inspired by the 1998 *Akayesu* judgement before the ICTR, in which, for the first time, it was explicitly recognised that rape and sexual violence can constitute genocide in the same way as any other act, provided that the criteria for the crime of genocide are met.[12] The Trial Chamber held that 'sexual violence was an integral part of the process of destruction, specifically targeting Tutsi women and specifically contributing to their destruction and to the destruction of the Tutsi group as a whole'.[13]

Despite this recognition, it needs to be stressed that an explicit inclusion of sexual violence as crimes constituting genocide would render the law on the supranational criminal law level consistent with the crimes against humanity and war-crimes provisions. The specific sexual violence provisions laid down in the latter two crimes as outlined above (rape, sexual slavery, etc.) should therefore be incorporated into the genocide definition. Explicit reference to the specific sexual violence crimes would properly recognise and emphasise that they can be genocidal crimes in and of themselves. In addition, in light of the reality of what genocidal rapes entail, the genocide definition should be amended to include a reference to group destruction on the basis of gender also.

Apart from charging an accused under the specific sexual violence crimes, prosecutions at the ICC can also still take place under non-specific sexual violence crimes if this serves to establish the totality of the accused's conduct and the different and multiple harms experienced by victims. Of particular interest could be the crime of torture as a war crime, which imposes an additional purposive element. Rape, for instance, could be cumulatively prosecuted as both the war crime of rape and the war crime of torture, the latter when the rapes were inflicted in order to humiliate, intimidate, punish and/or to discriminate on the basis of gender. Whereas the Prosecutor at the ICTY and ICTR was, to a certain extent, also bound to prosecute sexual violence under non-specific sexual violence crimes in the absence of any equivalent to the specific sexual violence crimes of the Rome Statute, the ICC Prosecutor can consider both options: prosecuting under non-specific sexual violence crimes and/or under specific sexual violence crimes, of which the latter should form the forefront of the prosecutorial strategy on sexual violence. Prosecuting sexual violence *as* sexual violence undeniably recognises the true nature of the crime.

Common elements to genocide, crimes against humanity and war crimes

For a successful prosecution of sexual violence, the elements common to genocide, crimes against humanity and war crimes all need to be fulfilled in order that rape or any other form of sexual violence should also qualify as an international crime. Specific intent to destroy a certain group, the common elements for genocide, can, for example, be found in speeches of the accused calling for the rape of women of a particular group or in statements made by the rapists themselves during the rapes.[14] As far as crimes against humanity are concerned, it has been established in ICTY and ICTR case law that the act of rape or any other form of sexual violence does not itself need to be committed in a widespread or systematic manner; the act need simply form part of a widespread or systematic attack.[15] The elements common to war crimes include that the conduct took place in the context of, and was associated with, an international or non-international armed conflict, and that the perpetrator was aware of factual circumstances that established the existence of an armed conflict. Yet an unfortunate element has been added to the war-crimes provision: war crimes must, *in particular*, be prosecuted when committed on a systematic or large-scale basis. Although the Court focuses on high-profile individuals and cases first and foremost, this addition could keep isolated cases of serious sexual violence outside its jurisdiction. Naturally and finally, for sexual violence to be attributed to the accused, a link between the crime and the accused needs to be established.

The charging practice at the ICC

By the end of 2009, out of four situation countries, eight cases have emerged, with a total of sixteen persons facing charges, fifteen of whom are still alive. So far, four accused are in The Hague to face trial. The question that comes to mind is to what extent sexual violence has been successfully investigated, charged and prosecuted in the cases before the Court. As concerns the DRC cases, it is clear that former militia leaders Thomas Lubanga Dyilo and Bosco Ntaganda are not facing any charges of sexual violence. In the Ugandan case, three out of five Lord's Resistance Army commanders have not been charged with sexual violence. Of the Sudan cases, three individuals have not been charged with sexual violence. Thus, in the case of eight out of the (originally) sixteen individuals facing charges (50 per cent), no charges of sexual violence were made, despite the suspects' leadership positions and the available evidence of widespread sexual violence in the conflicts concerned, including evidence that links the suspects to the sexual violence committed.[16] Several NGOs, including local NGOs, have heavily criticised the Court for failing to include sexual violence amongst the charges facing Thomas Lubanga Dyilo in particular.[17]

The remaining eight suspects (50 per cent) are charged with certain forms of sexual violence. However, for all of these individuals, the charging of sexual violence could be considered to be rather narrow, especially in the light of the senior positions held by the accused and the documented magnitude and range of the sexual violence crimes committed in the situations concerned. For example, in some cases, just rape is charged whereas, in other cases, a number of sexual violence crimes are charged, but other charges have been left out such as forced marriage in the Lord's Resistance Army case and sexual slavery, forced pregnancy and torture in the Sudan cases.[18] Leaving out charges pertaining to the sexual violence inflicted, or not charging sexual violence at all, does not do justice to the victims and survivors of the conflict and does not reflect the totality of the crimes committed. In the long run, it might even deter victims from coming to the Court to testify and/or to participate.

Sexual violence in supranational criminal procedure

Having examined the main substantive issues, we now focus on sexual violence in supranational criminal procedure in order to examine the way in which both participation and reparation could (and the extent to which it does or does not as yet) assist victims of sexual violence taking part in ICC proceedings.

Participation of victims/survivors of sexual violence

The ways in which victims of sexual violence have 'participated' at the Tribunals and the challenges faced by the Court in attempting to effectuate victim participation in a gender-sensitive manner are important concerns. With respect to the Tribunals, it has sometimes been argued that the Prosecutor, because he or she is held to protect the interests of the international community, also takes care of the interests of victims.[19] On a number of occasions, however, the interests of victims of sexual violence and those of the Prosecutor have failed to coincide, to the detriment of the former.[20] Some mechanisms, such as *amicus curiae* interventions and directly addressing the Office of the Prosecutor by sending letters, have been helpful in addressing victims' concerns and bringing the situation out in the open. However, the effectiveness of these interventions is dependent on a number of issues, in particular judicial and/or prosecutorial discretion, but also on *amici* who care enough to take up the plight of victims. This is compounded by the fact that victims themselves have no right to submit victim impact statements to the court.

This situation changed with the establishment of the ICC. For the first time within supranational criminal procedure, victims have the right to participate in the Court's proceedings, often through a legal representative (see, for example, Article 68[3] of the Rome Statute and Rule 16 of the RPE). In their capacity as participants, victims may present their views and concerns where their personal interests are affected. The modalities of participation leading up to and during the trial, for example, include access to the public record; submission and examination of evidence if this assists in the determination of the truth and if the Court has requested the evidence; access to hearings, status conferences and trials; filing written submissions and making opening and closing statements.[21] The overall control of the proceedings, of course, remains with the judges of the Court. It is of note that the Court must permit the participation of victims of sexual violence in gender-sensitive ways that take into account the well-being, dignity and safety of the victim (Article 68[1] of the Rome Statute and Rule 16[5] RPE). For victims of sexual violence, this means that they may be represented by a legal representative with experience in dealing with cases of sexual violence and/or trauma counselling. A prior condition is that victims of sexual violence should be notified about their participatory rights and the gender-sensitive arrangements available to them. Exactly because of the stigmatisation, shame and fear that disproportionally attaches to these crimes, the Court should give victims of sexual violence extra attention so that they will be able to realise their participatory rights to the fullest extent. For this purpose, the Victims Participation and Reparation Section (VPRS) should, on behalf of the Court, reach out to international and national women's groups working in the countries concerned. Yet, despite an increase in outreach activities since the Court became operational, many victims in the situations concerned are still unaware of the purpose and function of the Court and how they can play a role in its proceedings.

By the end of September 2009, the Court had received a total of 1,814 applications from persons seeking to participate as victims in the ICC proceedings, mostly from males and from persons from the DRC.[22] This seems to be a small number bearing in mind that the crimes over which the Court has jurisdiction affect large groups of people. While accurate statistics are hard to find, it is estimated that in the DRC alone 500,000 women have been raped during the conflict there.[23] Outreach, then, seems to be crucial. Moreover, of the received applications, only 771 applicants (43 per cent) have been authorised by the ICC to actually participate in the proceedings.[24] The Court has decided that in order to participate as a victim in *a case* (rather than the situation at large) there should be a causal link between the harm suffered by the victim applicants and the crimes for which the accused is charged.[25] It is not clear how many of the recognised applicants are victims of sexual violence. In light of the phase that the trials at the ICC have reached, and the relative lack of charges of sexual violence, the number is likely to be very small. The low number of participating victims to date, in light of the gravity of the crimes with which the Court is dealing, is a cause for worry. Furthermore, if no charges of sexual violence are brought in the case, victims of sexual violence cannot easily participate in expressing their views and concerns pertaining to the sexual violence they endured.

The problem of low participation is exacerbated (and partially explained) by the Court's complicated application process. The considerable length of the forms and the amount of (legal) detail needed in order to complete the application forms is troublesome for many victims.[26] Offering victims an opportunity to apply for standing in the proceedings and then disappointing them by failing to meet their expectations is a powerful source, moreover, of potential secondary victimisation. In order to address some of these failures, it would arguably be preferable to develop more regulation rather than to depend so heavily on ever-changing case law.[27]

It is likely that large numbers of victims may ultimately participate before the Court and that it may prove necessary to have one or more common legal representatives (Rule 90 of the RPE). The group representation of victims of sexual violence, however, may be more difficult than it first appears. For example, groups of victims that appear homogenous may in reality not be so: they may, for instance, come from different regions and/or have been sexually violated by perpetrators of different ethnicities. One possible solution might be to organise subgroups within a group of victims. The need to be responsive to the distinct interests of victims also impacts on the qualifications required from common legal representative(s) (Rule 90[4] of the RPE and Article 68[1] of the Rome Statute). In cases of sexual violence, representatives would need to have expertise in dealing with victims of sexual violence and may need to come from the same region as the victims and speak their language. The gender of legal counsel may be important for victims too. Unfortunately, it appears that the list of legal counsel does not yet contain any significant number with expertise in sexual violence, that very few women are on the list (19 per cent or fifty-seven out of 302 persons) and that very few counsel come from the situations under consideration before the Court – 13 per cent or thirty-nine out of 302 persons, of whom only four, three from the DRC and one from the CAR, are women.[28] This current imbalance should be addressed by the Court immediately. It is, furthermore, suggested that the Court should not appoint too many common legal representatives in any given proceeding at the same time, as this would most probably lead to unacceptable delays and to fragmentation of the trial.[29] A balance will therefore need to be found between appointing a limited number of common legal representatives and, at the same time, ensuring that the distinct interests of victims are accounted for.

Reparation and assistance to victims/survivors of sexual violence

Despite provisions on restitution of property or proceeds as well as compensation, the issue of reparation to victims has traditionally hardly been dealt with by the ICTY and ICTR Tribunals.[30] The judges of the Tribunals have instead always held that their primary task lies with retributive justice, that is, with prosecuting perpetrators for serious violations of international humanitarian law.[31] The Rome Statute and the RPE, on the other hand, contain an elaborate reparation regime (Articles 75 and 79 of the Rome Statute and Rules 94–9 of the RPE): for the first time in history, an international criminal court is able to provide reparation awards to victims. In addition, a Trust Fund for Victims and their Families was created and is able to complement the Court's work where reparation is concerned.

The main difficulty with reparation awards provided by the Court is that they are only awarded once the accused has been found guilty, whereas victims of sexual violence may need physical, psychological and medical support much earlier. Indeed, since the ICC became operational in 2003 after the election of senior staff members, not one single trial has been concluded. For this reason, assistance is to be offered by the Trust Fund in an earlier phase, allowing for a broader system of reparation accessible at any stage of proceedings. The Trust Fund has therefore a double mandate: it will not only implement reparation awards from the Court but may also implement programmes that will assist victims of mass crimes in terms of physical and psychological rehabilitation as well as material support (Rule 98 of the RPE; Regulation 50 of the Regulations of the Trust Fund for Victims).[32] Thus, the Trust Fund can assist victims in an early stage of proceedings, even those whose cases may not have been taken up by the Prosecutor, reaching, potentially, many more victims and assisting them by meeting their immediate needs.

The Trust Fund has started to implement several activities in Uganda (eighteen projects approved) and the DRC (sixteen projects approved) already, benefiting an expected total of 226,000 direct and indirect victims.[33] The projects implemented in these countries include specific activities that support survivors of sexual violence in a collective manner. In particular, survivors are assisted through physical and psychological rehabilitation projects and socio-economic activities.[34] Some illustrative activities include: fistula repair, trauma counselling, the provision of sanitary supplies and referrals to HIV and reproductive health services, screening and intake centres, job-training programmes for victims, community awareness of sexual violence to address stigma and discrimination, special initiatives for children born out of rape and the reintegration into communities of men and boys who have raped.[35] In Uganda, three of the eighteen projects in total (16.6 per cent) are specifically focused on survivors of sexual violence; in the DRC, eight of the sixteen projects (50 per cent) are for programmes focused on survivors of sexual violence.[36] In 2009, a scaling-up of these projects and the start of projects in Sudan and the CAR occurred: €650,000 has been allocated for the CAR expecting to reach some 130,000 victims.[37] On 10 September 2008, the Board of Directors announced the launch of a global appeal for €10 million to assist 1.7 million victims of sexual violence in the situations falling within the jurisdiction of the Court.[38] A total of €702,481 was pledged and received from states, and these funds are currently being used for approved activities in Uganda and the DRC.[39] The attention that the Trust Fund is giving to projects benefiting survivors of sexual violence is promising, and it is to be hoped that the Court will similarly provide reparation in a collective manner in order to reach as many survivors of sexual violence as possible. However, the Secretariat and the Board of the Trust Fund should continue to actively fundraise as the monies in the Fund, taking into account the number of victims and situations before the Court, are arguably insufficient, a mere €3,131,248 on 1 July 2009.[40]

Conclusion

Rape and other forms of sexual violence were long considered by-products of war before their recognition as self-standing crimes worthy of criminalisation and prosecution. The ICC Statute and its EoC and RPE can be considered more or less as model legislation as far as the prosecution of sexual violence is concerned. However, current ICC practice shows that the charging, investigation and prosecution of sexual violence is in certain cases completely lacking. Even when present not all sexual violence is comprehensively charged. This does not do justice to the sexual violence actually perpetrated against victims. In order to recognise fully the crimes committed, to prevent these crimes from taking place in the long run and to treat victims of sexual violence with respect, the Court needs to mainstream its gender and sexual violence policies on multiple levels, embracing, for example, its investigation and charging practices, participation and reparation modalities, outreach strategies and staffing (in order to provide staff with relevant expertise and adequate gender and geographical representation). The legislation on sexual violence that the Court is working with is sound in many respects but for future success requires much more potent implementation approaches.

Notes

1 For an overview, see A. de Brouwer, S. Ka Hon Chu and S. Muscati, *The Men Who Killed Me: Rwandan Survivors of Sexual Violence* (Vancouver: Douglas and McIntyre, 2009), pp. 23–6.

2 See E. Carlson, 'The Hidden Prevalence of Male Sexual Assault During War', *British Journal of Criminology*, 46 (1) (2005), pp. 16–25; R. Carpenter, 'Recognizing Gender-Based Violence Against Civilian Men and Boys in Conflict Situations', *Security Dialogue*, 37 (1) (2006), pp. 83–103.

3 For further reading, see A. de Brouwer, *Supranational Criminal Prosecution of Sexual Violence: The ICC and the Practice of the ICTY and the ICTR* (Antwerp: Intersentia, 2005).

4 The Statutes, RPE, EoC and case law of the Tribunals and Court can be found on their websites. See www.icty.org, www.ictr.org and www.icc-cpi.int.

5 *Prosecutor v. Jean-Paul Akayesu*, judgment, Case No. ICTR-96-4-T, 2 September 1998 (hereafter Akayesu judgment), paras. 598, 688.

6 *Prosecutor v. Anto Furundžija*, Judgment, Case No. IT-95–17/1-T, 10 December 1998, paras. 180, 185.

7 *Prosecutor v. Dragoljub Kunarac, Radomir Kovač and Zoran Vuković*, Judgment, Case No. IT-96-23-A and IT-96–23/1-A, 12 June 2002, para. 128.

8 *Prosecutor v. Dragoljub Kunarac, Radomir Kovač and Zoran Vuković*, Transcripts, Case No. IT-96-23-T and IT-96–23/1-T, 25 April 2000, pp. 2235–6.

9 The opportunity of the 2006 *Gacumbitsi* Appeals Judgment, to overrule the *Kunarac, Kovač and Vuković* Appeals Judgment on the definition of rape and to clarify the definition, was unfortunately missed. See further A. de Brouwer, 'Commentary on the *Gacumbitsi* Judgment', in A. Klip and G. Sluiter (eds.), *Annotated Leading Cases of International Criminal Tribunals: The International Criminal Tribunal for Rwanda, 2005–2006* (Antwerp: Intersentia, 2009).

10 See, further, Y. Yoshiaki, *Comfort Women: Sexual Slavery in the Japanese Military During World War II* (New York: Columbia University Press, 2000).

11 See *Akayesu* Judgment, para. 697; and *Prosecutor v. Eliézer Niyitegeka*, Judgment and Sentence, Case No. ICTR-96-14-T, 16 May 2003, paras. 459–67.

12 *Akayesu* judgment, para. 731. ICTY and ICTR practice has, furthermore, shown that prosecution of sexual violence under any of the five subheadings of the definition of genocide is possible.

13 *Akayesu* judgment, para 731.

14 See *Akayesu* judgment, para. 729; *Gacumbitsi* judgment, paras. 200–2, 215, 224, 227 and 259.

15 *Prosecutor v. Dragoljub Kunarac, Radomir Kovač and Zoran Vuković*, Judgment, Case No. IT-96–23 and IT-96-23/1, 22 February 2001, para. 417.

16 See Amnesty International, *Democratic Republic of Congo: Mass Rape – Time for Remedies*, AI Index: AFR 62/018/2004, 26 October 2004; Amnesty International, *Uganda: Doubly Traumatised: The Lack of Access to Justice by Women Victims of Sexual and Gender-based Violence in Northern Uganda*, AI Index: AFR 59/005/2007, 30 November 2007; Human Rights Watch, *Sudan: Five Years On – No Justice for Sexual Violence in Darfur*, April 2008; United Nations (UN News Service), *Thousands Fall Victim to Sexual Violence in Central African Republic*, 22 February 2008.

17 See Women's Initiatives for Gender Justice, *Letter to the Prosecutor*, 2006; and the Beni Declaration, *Womens' Rights and Human Rights NGOs from the Democratic Republic of the Congo on the Prosecutions by the International Criminal Court*, 16 September 2006.

18 See, further, A. de Brouwer, 'What the International Criminal Court Has Achieved and Can Achieve for Victims/Survivors of Sexual Violence', *International Review of Victimology*, 16 (2) (2009): pp. 183–205.

19 See V. Morris and M. P. Scharf, *An Insider's Guide to the International Criminal Tribunal for the former Yugoslavia* (New York: Transnational Publishers, 1995), vol. I, p. 167.

20 For example, when the Prosecutor entered into a plea agreement with the accused by dropping the count on rape in exchange for a guilty plea on the other counts, he did not necessarily take into account the interests of the victims of rape. This happened,

for instance, in *Prosecutor* v. *Omar Serushago*, Sentence, Case No. ICTR-98–39-S, 5 February 1999, para. 4; and *Prosecutor* v. *Predrag Banović*, Sentencing Judgment, Case No. IT-02-65/1-S, 28 October 2003, paras. 9–19.

21 *Prosecutor* v. *Thomas Lubanga Dyilo*, Decision on Victims' Participation, Trial Chamber I, ICC-01/04-01/06, 18 January 2008, paras. 101–22.

22 Women's Initiatives for Gender Justice, *Gender Report Card on the International Criminal Court 2009*, October 2009, p. 95.

23 Christophe Boltanski, 'Congo: Le viol comme arme de guerre', *Le Nouvel Observateur*, December 2008. Available online at http://hebdo.nouvelobs.com/hebdo/parution/p2300/articles/a389902-congo_le_viol_comme_arme_de_guerre.html (accessed 3 March 2010).

24 Women's Initiatives for Gender Justice, *Gender Report Card*.

25 See *Prosecutor* v. *Thomas Lubanga Dyilo*, Decision on Victims' Participation, Trial Chamber I, ICC-01/04-01/06, 18 January 2008; *Prosecutor* v. *Thomas Lubanga Dyilo*, Judgment on the Appeals of the Prosecutor and the Defence Against Trial Chamber I's Decision on Victims' Participation of 18 January 2008, Appeals Chamber, ICC-01/04–01/06 OA 9 OA 10, 11 July 2008; *Prosecutor* v. *Thomas Lubanga Dyilo*, redacted version of 'Decision of "Indirect Victims"', ICC-01/04-01/06-1813, 8 April 2009.

26 See, further, K. Glassborow, *Victim Participation in ICC Cases Jeopardised*, Institute for War and Peace Reporting, AR No. 148, 20 December 2007.

27 A. de Brouwer and M. Groenhuijsen, 'The Role of Victims in International Criminal Proceedings, in S. Vasiliev and G. Sluiter (eds.), *International Criminal Procedure: Towards a Coherent Body of Law* (London: Cameron May, 2009), pp. 149–204; p. 204.

28 List of Counsel, 1 September 2009, available at http://www.icc-cpi.int/Menus/ICC/Structure+of+the+Court/Victims/Legal+Representation (accessed 22 December 2009).

29 See M. Groenhuijsen, 'Victims' Rights and the International Criminal Court: The Model of the Rome Statute and its Operation', in W. van Genugten, M. Scharf and S. Radin (eds.), *Criminal Jurisdiction 100 Years after the 1907 Hague Peace Conference* (The Hague: T. M. C. Asser Press, 2009), pp. 306–7.

30 See Articles 24(3) of the ICTY Statute and 23(3) of the ICTR Statute (on restitution); and common Rule 106 of the ICTY and ICTR RPE (on compensation).

31 *Victims Compensation and Participation*, report prepared by the Rules Committee, 2000, Sections I and III.

32 ICC-ASP/4/Res. 3, 3 December 2005.

33 See *Report of the Court on the Activities and Projects of the Board of Directors of the Trust Fund for Victims for the Period 1 July 2008 to 30 June 2009*, ICC-ASP/8/18, 29 July 2009, p. 2.

34 Trust Fund for Victims Program Overview, undated.

35 ICC Press Release, *Global Appeal for €10 Million to Assist 1.7 Million Victims of Sexual Violence Launched*, 10 September 2008.

36 See Annex II to the Report to the Assembly of States Parties on the Activities and Projects of the Board of Directors of the Trust Fund for Victims for the Period 1 July 2008 to 30 June 2009, ICC-ASP/8/18*, 18 September 2009.

37 See the *Proposed Budget Programme for 2010 of the International Criminal Court*, ICC-ASP/8/10, 30 July 2009, pp. 135–40.

38 ICC Press Release, *Global Appeal*.

39 See Report to the Assembly, p. 4.

40 Ibid., p. 6.

Part V

Reproduction, law and sex

Chapter 16

The strange case of the invisible woman in abortion-law reform

Kate Gleeson

Introduction

Abortion is the most common surgical procedure for women of reproductive age. In the United Kingdom, around one in three women will have at least one abortion during their lifetime, with most being performed for social and psychological reasons.[1] In 2008, only 1 per cent of all abortions were performed for reasons of foetal disability.[2] Globally, the legal status of abortion has profound ramifications for women's health and mortality. Although it is obvious that abortion directly affects and concerns women, the focal subject of British abortion law is, nonetheless, the medical doctor. Since the nineteenth century, abortion law has been reformed periodically to reflect the heightened status of the medical profession and its influence on abortion, culminating in the full medical authorisation of abortion practice in the Abortion Act 1967. While historically abortion was performed routinely by women on themselves, and on each other as part of the practice of midwifery, abortion is now a fully medicalised procedure that, legally, only doctors may perform. This consolidation of medical autonomy and medical control of abortion correlates with a related disinterest in women's autonomy embodied in the law: a pattern that is strikingly apparent within each legal reform enacted since 1803. Abortion law regulates a medical procedure *crucial to* women, and *peculiar to* women, yet the interests of women in the control of their reproduction appear as all but invisible when examining the text of the 1967 statute, and the legislation preceding it.

Feminist critical legal theory has long identified the falsehood of a system and practice of criminal law that purports a 'neutrality and objectivity of liberal legal forms', thereby exposing the 'substantive preconceptions' of these forms and 'the ways in which they in fact favour systematically certain kinds of interests'.[3] For example, Lacey argues that women's lack of representation within and by the supposedly neutral category of the 'legal subject' in the criminal law has meant that 'the views and assumptions built into legal forms, rules and principles as well as the values and goods recognised by legal arrangements express the experiences and viewpoints not of the abstract individual' but of the 'privileged white male'.[4] The basic feminist argument with the criminal law is, according to

Lacey, that the 'paradigm legal subject' has been constructed as an individual 'abstracted from its social context', characterised by masculine-identified capacities for 'rational understanding, reflection and control of their own actions'.[5] An essential method of this construction is the systematic exclusion of 'certain features of experience' that may be 'extra-legally crucial to the shape of women's lives', yet which are deemed irrelevant to the process of the law. This exclusion performs a function, in Lacey's terms, of silencing women by disallowing the context of their experience in law's abstract formation of the rational (male) subject.[6]

Feminist theory and jurisprudence has made inroads in deconstructing, problematising and partially rectifying this bias by influencing the passage of some legislation aimed to 'right past wrongs' and improve the lives of women.[7] But within abortion law in particular the disinterest in the representation of women's interests, as predicated on concerns for their bodily integrity and reproductive autonomy, remains startling; and it appears boldly to transcend ideals of even the (falsely) asserted neutrality and objectivity that is characteristic of the criminal law, for the subject of abortion law is explicitly the autonomous (male) doctor. In a fate more comprehensive than silencing, the autonomous, rational woman is invisible within a law that was driven by the medical establishment and which does not grant her the 'right to determine [her] own reproductive capacity' but simply licenses the medical profession to 'act benevolently' towards her, if it is inclined to do so.[8]

In one unforeseen (and ironic) outcome of the 1967 Act, however, women's autonomous, rational subjectivity has appeared as visible and effective within another legal arena. As a direct result of the 1967 Act, the invisible, silenced female subject of criminal abortion law has made her appearance vocally, albeit belatedly and retrospectively, in cases of remedial tort associated with legal abortion in the case of foetal abnormality. The Abortion Act changed the thrust of abortion law by providing an explicit defence for doctors who provide abortions on the grounds of foetal abnormality. Prior to 1967, abortion law made mention only of women and those who procured their miscarriages: abortion prohibitions were aimed to protect 'His Majesty's subjects' from unlawful abortions, and the law allowed for abortion only when doctors decreed that the risk to the woman of continuing the pregnancy outweighed the Crown's interest in childbirth. These sentiments persisted in debates over the 1967 Act, but, decisively, what emerged at the same time was an explicit focus on the foetus and its characteristics. Although abortion performed on the basis of foetal indications accounts for only a marginal proportion of all procedures, this category has been instrumental in reforming the law in its entirety and, subsequently, in facilitating the rise of the wrongful birth suit.

As a result, it will be argued in this chapter that, despite its successful aim of protecting doctors from criminal allegations, the Abortion Act 1967 has placed doctors (unexpectedly) in a newly vulnerable position, as being subject to lawsuits concerning wrongful birth. And, in an unpredicted yet logical extension of its rationale, the Act has also provided for both the representation and actualisation of women's interests regarding their reproductive autonomy beyond the narrow constraints of the criminal law, retrospectively, in the forum of the tort of wrongful birth. This paradoxical state of affairs means that while within the *criminal* law of abortion a woman's autonomy and interests are discounted, the *civil* law points the way forward to an actualisation of women's agency through tort actions undertaken by women seeking to recoup compensation for their interests having been undermined by unintended pregnancy outcomes. It is in this arena, therefore, that we may witness the operationalisation of legal redress by an autonomous female legal subject, contextualised and defined by its relationship to pregnancy, which challenges the hegemony of the invisible, silenced female subject as instantiated in criminal abortion law. This female subject of the civil law presents a powerful contrast to the orthodox (male) legal subject, typically 'abstracted from its social context, including the context of its own body, and of the dependence of its own identity on its relationship towards and affective ties with others'.[9]

The conundrum underlying this important possibility is that the right to redress for women depends upon a criminal law in which this particular con-textualised female subject does not appear. In order to establish the argument, the chapter traces the history of abortion regulation with a view to illuminating the passage of the conundrum presented by the strange case of the invisible woman in abortion law reform and her unanticipated appearance in actions for civil redress. It does so in order to inform the greater project of critical feminist analysis, to help identify examples of the female legal subject in practice, and the historical factors that have contributed to its varying states of efficacy and recognition in abortion-related law.

The origins of the law and the consolidation of medical authority over abortion

In 1803, Lord Ellenborough's Act criminalised the unlawful procurement of a miscarriage as part of a general consolidation of assault offences. Debate continues today about the aim of the miscarriage provision of the Act, which appears 'almost incidental' to the general prohibition against attempting to poison with intent to murder.[10] Rather than a focus on the foetus, Waller and others argue that the miscarriage provision was aimed primarily at protecting women from dangerous and deadly procedures.[11] Throughout the nineteenth century, ther-apeutic abortion was acceptable to many doctors, but others within the medical establishment and the judiciary condemned the practice.[12] Influenced by the nascent doctors' lobby and its campaigns against 'irregulars' (midwives and homoeopaths), abortion law evolved to become less discretionary and to make it easier to secure convictions. After a series of further consolidating reforms, abor-tion came to be governed by the Offences Against the Person Act 1861, which targeted those who intended to unlawfully procure a woman's miscarriage, as well as women who intended to procure their own miscarriages, regardless of whether the woman was actually pregnant. There remained, however, a general acceptance of *therapeutic* abortion in medical jurisprudence.

In the 1920s, the rate of puerperal sepsis contributing to maternal mortality was scrutinised.[13] In 1936, the Birkett Committee was established in order to inquire into the incidence of abortion and how to reduce maternal mortality. From the 1930s onwards, the British Medical Association (BMA) lobbied for the clarification of 'obscure' abortion law, in order to 'enable the doctor to concentrate upon his proper duty to his patient without distracting visions of judges and juries reviewing his decisions at the assizes', and in 1938 the case of gynaecologist Aleck Bourne provided an opportunity for this clarification.[14] Bourne was a member of the BMA and the Abortion Law Reform Association (ALRA) who regularly performed abortions and was committed to trying to 'establish the legality of his practice'.[15]

In April 1938, a fourteen-year-old girl was gang-raped by guardsmen at the Horse Guard's Barracks at Whitehall, and became pregnant. She was refused an abortion at St Thomas' Hospital, but her case was taken up by the birth-control campaigner Dr Joan Malleson, who wrote to Bourne asking if he would 'risk a *cause celebre* and undertake the operation'. Malleson advised that the abortion should be performed on prophylaxis grounds, because 'no nervous disorder appeared to be present' and that 'many people held the view that the best way of correcting the present abortion laws was to let the medical profession extend the ground for therapeutic abortion in suitable cases until the law had become obsolete as far as practice went'.[16] Bourne agreed to perform the procedure. The police were informed, and, when they arrived at the hospital, Bourne admitted that he had performed an abortion and 'wanted the officers to arrest him'.[17] He was charged under Section 58 of the 1861 Act for unlawfully procuring a miscarriage.

Bourne commanded widespread sympathy for his 'courage in placing his professional career in jeopardy to obtain legal clarification which might help others' in the medical profession.[18] Witnesses for the defence included former physician to the Prince of Wales, Lord Horder, the house surgeon of London hospital and others.[19] In court, the Attorney General did not suggest that therapeutic abortion was unlawful but questioned whether Bourne's case constituted a therapeutic abortion performed to the save the woman's life. The focus of the trial was not on the wishes of the pregnant woman but on her medical diagnosis. Contrary to Malleson's position, Bourne claimed that he had performed the abortion for therapeutic reasons related to the young woman's mental health and that, after eight days' surveillance to test her 'nature', he had agreed to grant her an abortion only after she 'broke down', thus indicating to him that there was 'in her nothing of the cool indifference of the prostitute'.[20] The trial judge, Justice Macnaghten, noted approvingly that Bourne would not have performed the operation 'if he had found that the girl was either feeble-minded or had what he called a "prostitute mind", since in such cases pregnancy and child-birth would not be likely to affect a girl injuriously'.[21]

In directing the jury, Macnaghtan J noted that even at common law there may be justification for an action 'where an unborn child is killed', just as there may be justification in the case of homicide. He stated that the burden rested on the Crown to satisfy beyond reasonable doubt that the defendant 'did not procure the miscarriage of the girl in good faith for the purpose only of preserving her life'.[22] Bourne was acquitted. The judgment confirmed the legality of abortions performed by doctors to save a woman's life, broadly interpreted to include psychological factors. The *Lancet* hailed the decision as a 'sample of public opinion' but also criticised it for making the law 'only a little less obscure than before'.[23] The judgment was also criticised for appearing not to provide for lawful abortion on humanitarian grounds, unrelated to physical or mental health.[24]

Bourne confirmed the medical establishment's authority over abortion – over both women's abortion decisions and the procedure's legitimacy. At this time, the female lay abortionist was frequently demonised as a 'predatory harpy' and, unsurprisingly, the overwhelming majority of those arrested for procuring abortions were women.[25] In *Bourne*, Macnaghten J summed up the case to the jury by explaining the moral difference between Aleck Bourne, who believed he was performing his medical duty, and a selfish woman abortionist, who, after being paid her fee, left 'the victim of her malpractice ... dead on the floor'.[26] Macnaghten J also confirmed that doctors were the only practitioners qualified to perform abortions. Although Bourne had testified that he had not consulted another doctor, because he 'regarded himself as the second opinion', Macnaghten J said that he expected that doctors would not perform an abortion in future without 'consulting some other member of the profession of high standing' in order to demonstrate that the operation was undertaken 'in good faith'.[27]

Perhaps the greatest significance of the *Bourne* judgment, therefore, was its ruling that it was immaterial whether medical opinions on the mental or physical condition of the woman were correct in some objective sense, or even in the opinion of the woman concerned. Although it is 'not self-evident' that doctors are 'well qualified to determine whether or not a pregnancy should be terminated', abortion was deemed 'legitimate if based on medical decisions made in good faith'.[28] Whilst, arguably, the 1803 Act was aimed to protect women from dangerous procedures, in 1938 doctors and their reasoning were confirmed as the subjects of the law, rendering women's interests invisible behind the medical diagnosis.

The Abortion Act 1967

In 1939, the Birkett Committee recommended the codification of the *Bourne* test, but this did not eventuate. Therapeutic abortions began to be performed for psychiatric indications on an increasingly large scale in Britain under the authority of *Bourne*. The BMA advised doctors to consult with 'professional colleagues of recognised status' in order to indicate 'good faith' and to help protect against interpretations of the law less liberal than Macnaghten J's.[29] A dual economy arose of costly 'abortion on demand' in the private medical sector, competing with cheaper and more often dangerous, 'back-street' abortions. The ALRA lobbied to rectify this inequality and for abortion to be protected in legislation for 'good women' in dire circumstances, while the BMA continued to lobby for a law to clarify the existing legal position and to protect doctors who provided abortions in the case of foetal abnormality, especially after the 1941 identification of the congenital effects of rubella embryology. In 1967, the joint lobbying was successful, and the Abortion Act, sponsored by Liberal MP David Steele, was passed after one of the 'hardest fought parliamentary encounters' of the era.[30]

The Act reaffirmed that the medical profession was the subject of abortion law, offering it protection by providing a set of defences for doctors to perform abortions in the instances outlined in *Bourne*: where two doctors agree in good faith that to continue the pregnancy would either risk the woman's life or injure her physical and mental health, or the physical and mental health of her already existing children. In addition to the *Bourne* test, abortion was permitted if two doctors agreed that there was a substantial risk that if the child were born it would suffer from such 'physical or mental abnormalities as to be seriously handicapped'.[31] By law, a doctor was not compelled to perform abortion if holding a conscientious objection, thereby protecting him from allegations of malpractice. The Act ensured the protection of doctors who were in professional agreement (or collusion) about the 'need' for an abortion by requiring the consultation of a doctor of 'high standing', as advised by Macnaghtan J in *Bourne* and promoted by the BMA. However, this requirement is redundant and overly careful in its solicitude for the medical profession, because the Act *spells out* the legal defences to abortion, thus disallowing the possibility of narrow judicial interpretations that might compromise or convict doctors.[32] Jackson characterises the requirement for two doctors' agreement as currently 'the principal statutory barrier to abortion'.[33]

Thalidomide and the campaign for reform

1960s parliamentary support for abortion reform was not secured due to the emergence of a women's movement, as might be thought. As Brookes observes, historically, women have been 'on the periphery' of the medical and legal debate over abortion,[34] and the women's movement emerged later. The 1967 Act was influenced in part by new expectations of the regulation of families encouraged by the launch of the contraceptive pill in 1961, which provided for a more open discussion about fertility control as a 'desirable social goal'.[35] But, more crucially, the ALRA was able to gain parliamentary sympathy once Law Professor Glanville Williams assumed its leadership in the 1950s and he identified eugenic terminations as providing the best case for law reform. The ALRA and the BMA had a shared interest in eugenics (and little else), which allowed them to form an allegiance in the campaign for reform.[36] After six failed attempts in Parliament the lobbies finally secured widespread support as a direct result of the thalidomide catastrophe in the early 1960s.

Thalidomide, the anti-nausea drug marketed to pregnant women as Distaval, and withdrawn from sale in the UK in 1961, is estimated to have caused varying degrees of deformity in around 466 babies across Britain. The drug caused international uproar once it became known that American *Romper Room* host, Sherri Finkbine had to travel to Sweden (via Japan, where she was refused) in order to obtain an abortion after having taken thalidomide; and Belgian, Suzanne Vendeput, was acquitted of murdering her newborn baby who was thalidomide affected. This outcome angered some, while many were also sympathetic to her plight. In the case of thalidomide, abortion was viewed as a *sympathetic* response to innocent women to which many could relate.[37]

Along with consideration of eugenic terminations, such as in the case of thalidomide, the ALRA lobbied for the provision of social indications for legal abortion, aimed to protect the family. Consequently, Steele's original 1966 Bill included a 'social clause' to permit abortion if the woman's capacity as a mother would be 'severely overstrained' by the care of the child and a clause to permit abortion in the case of the woman being 'defective' or having become pregnant before the age of sixteen, or by rape. However, these clauses were abandoned once the BMA advised that they were 'objectionable in specifying indications which are not medical'.[38] In acceding to the medical case for eugenic terminations, the ALRA lost control of the reform campaign. In 1966, following an international rubella pandemic, the BMA formed a Special Committee to direct law reform. The BMA argued that legislation should clarify the existing legal position of doctors in order to satisfactorily protect the 'honest medical man' from persuasion or pressure to perform abortions with which he did not agree, and that the law should be altered so that the risk of 'serious foetal abnormality may be taken into account in deciding whether or not to *recommend* termination of pregnancy'.[39] These recommendations came to form the basis of the 1967 Act.

Women were, accordingly, not recognised as the subjects of twentieth-century abortion law. Their agency, their rights and their choice did not inform the law. In *Bourne*, the woman was considered only in terms of her dire medical diagnosis, rendered dependent upon the medical profession for its benevolence and judged in terms of innocence or prostitution. Similarly, Sheldon notes that the woman of the 1967 Act was constructed as an 'emotionally weak, unstable (even suicidal) victim of her desperate social circumstances' or by the conservative opponents of reform, as 'a selfish, irrational child'.[40] A woman was treated in the Act as someone who could not make decisions for herself. Instead, responsibility was 'handed over to the reassuringly mature and responsible (male) figure', the doctor.[41] Moreover, the normal, rational, autonomous woman with genuine self-interest in abortion appears to have been *invisible*, both to lobbyists and to the government. Despite estimates of abortion in the 1950s ranging from 100,000 to 250,000 per year, women in need of abortion were constructed in the parliamentary debates, and by the BMA, as abnormal (except, perhaps, those who had the misfortune to conceive a disabled foetus through no fault of their own). The BMA, Parliament and even the ALRA were so convinced of the 'peripheral' nature of the abortion demand that provisions were not made in the NHS for the extra influx of abortion patients after 1967, and it was caught unprepared for the subsequent demand.[42]

The Human Fertilisation and Embryology Act 1990

Despite periodic public debates, the Abortion Act 1967 operated unamended until the enactment of the Human Fertilisation and Embryology Act 1990. The debate surrounding the 1990 Act considered abortion in the context of assisted reproduction and embryo research and turned to the discussion of gestation limits for all abortions. The Abortion Act 1967 had set no gestation limit, but it was understood that the Infant Life Preservation Act 1929 prohibited the destruction of a foetus after 28 weeks, except when performed to save the life of the woman. Twenty-eight weeks was considered to be the stage at which a foetus was viable in 1929. By the 1990s, the medical consensus on this point had changed, and the Human Fertilisation and Embryology Act was used to recast abortion law to reflect this development. Section 37 of the 1990 Act amended the 1967 Act by providing a statutory time limit of twenty-four weeks for abortions procured to prevent risk to the physical or mental health of the pregnant woman (or any existing children of her family): the primary indication for abortions in Britain.

The new time limit did not apply to the other indications for abortion: to save the life of the woman, prevent her grave permanent injury or the risk of foetal disability. In fact, the 1990 Act rescinded the ambit of the Infant Life Preservation Act for these indications, which potentially provide a legal basis for abortion until the moment of birth if two doctors are in agreement. In the case of the disability clause, the rationale for this is that amniocentesis might not provide information until late in the pregnancy, and doctors must not fear the law when performing late terminations in response to late diagnoses. The time limit for abortion remains a subject for periodic public debate.

Following the 2008 House of Commons Science and Technology Committee on the Scientific Developments Relating to the Abortion Act 1967, the Government agreed that there was no medical case for lowering it in the case of abortions performed before twenty-four weeks, as the medical case for viability before this stage of development had not improved significantly since the Act was last amended.[43] But after an intensive public lobbying campaign, legislation to reduce the time limit was introduced in Parliament. Following protracted emotional debate, it was rejected.[44]

Repercussions of reform: the wrongful birth suit

The two fundamental changes to modern abortion law, the 1967 and 1990 Acts, were influenced not by considerations of women's interests in abortion, or their autonomy, but by *medical consensus* around questions concerning the foetus: its viability and medical opinion on the 'substantial risk' of its disability (handicap). This was in part the outcome of lobbyists adopting the pragmatic strategy to focus on eugenic terminations, to persuade Parliament of the greater case for reform. Thus, despite the very marginal proportion of late-term abortions, and of abortions in cases of foetal abnormality, these considerations have deflected the thrust of abortion law towards the subject of the foetus, when arguably this was never its historical focus. Historically, abortion law addressed women and those who procured their miscarriages. The thalidomide crisis shifted the focus towards the defence of doctors operating in consideration of foetal characteristics, with the unexpected result that the 1967 Act has altered both the law and practice of abortion. Genetic screening is now common, especially for Down's Syndrome, and while screening was once offered only to women aged over thirty-five, in the 2003 *Genetics White Paper* it was proposed that by 2004/5 *all* pregnant women would be offered screening through the NHS.[45] This suggests that *no pregnancy* within the public health system should progress without the spectre of abortion, for, as Jackson notes, the risk of miscarriage associated with testing creates a presumption in favour of termination in the case of a positive diagnosis.[46] This is an extraordinary development of the situation, as compared with 1967 when the law was debated and designed predominantly for the medical profession, with only the so-called marginal and desperate women in mind as its patients.

The 1967 Act was drafted to provide doctors with legal authority to judge in good faith 'that the defence to what would otherwise be a crime is made out'.[47] This was despite the fact that prior to 1967 doctors were rarely prosecuted for criminal abortions; the true targets of the law were the 'back street' lay women abortionists.[48] In regard to criminal matters, perhaps unsurprisingly, the law has continued to provide the medical profession this protection.[49] The law also grants authority to doctors to assess the risk of 'serious handicap' of the foetus, based on medical prognosis, unguided and uninformed by the 'woman's (or her partner's) perception of the risk'.[50] Scott identifies the shift towards foetal characteristics as the soliciting of, 'if not an objective then at least a more impersonal assessment' than is involved in assessing the other indications for abortion, which concern the woman's health and/or situation.[51] And she describes the recognition of the wrongful birth claim, which corresponds (indirectly) to the terms of the Abortion Act as developing in response to scientific and legal developments to 'enhance the deliberative quality of the abortion decision'.[52] But, ironically, the hegemony of the 'handicapped clause' has placed doctors in a newly vulnerable position.

The ubiquity of genetic testing, and the normalisation of abortion for foetal abnormality, means that the medical profession, and health services, are now liable for not providing pregnant women adequate information about a 'substantial risk' of 'serious' handicap.[53] Since the 1980s the courts have recognised that in light of the 1967 Act, a doctor's (or health service's) duty of care embraces providing genetic information to women lest liability arise for damages and the costs of raising children with disabilities. In other words, medical services have been found to have 'a duty to take reasonable steps to ensure the parents can exercise their choice under the Act', which would appear to imply not only a duty placed upon doctors but also a corresponding right of women to abortion not explicit or apparent from the Abortion Act itself.[54]

Doctors still possess power and authority over abortion in this domain because it is their diagnosis of what constitutes a 'serious handicap' that will dictate if an abortion is permissible. Should a woman disagree with her doctor on this point, it would appear that she does not have the 'right' to abort (she needs another two doctors to agree with her). Nonetheless, it seems that despite and because of the entrenched medicalisation of abortion in the Abortion Act, women have realised rights of recourse. Because the test for causation in a wrongful birth suit is whether or not the woman would have aborted had she been 'correctly advised of the foetus's health or condition', an assessment involves both subjective and objective factors: the supposedly objective medical appraisal of the foetus and the woman's subjective appraisal of her decisions about the pregnancy and abortion.[55] It is within this subjective test of self-appraisal that the autonomous female subject, with a self-regarding interest in abortion, becomes apparent. The female subject contextualised by its relationship to pregnancy, invisible within criminal abortion law, has made its belated appearance in tort law.

Conclusions and implications for feminist theory

Abortion in Britain is generally safe and accessible, a fact that correlates directly with abortion's legal status. But the law remains the subject of criticism and complaint. In 2008 a group of eighty-five medical experts and academics called on the Government to modernise the law, to reflect contemporary ideals of patient autonomy whereby a doctor's role is to 'support' a patient to make medical decisions rather than to make these decisions for her.[56] The capacity for autonomy is 'central to what it means to be a person', just as the social and political recognition of autonomy is at the 'heart of respect for persons'.[57] Yet the criminal law of abortion is not centred on concerns for women's autonomy, despite the fact that this arena is central to the regulation of women's reproductive praxis. Instead, as the product of the history outlined here, the Abortion Act authorises doctors to make decisions about women's reproductive lives, rendering women's self-regarding interests invisible in the abortion decision. The 2008 campaign for modernisation did not succeed in changing the law. But this does not mean it is not possible for the law to represent the autonomous interests of women, or to address the female subject. The example of the wrongful birth suit, an unintended consequence of the Abortion Act, reveals that the female subject, contextualised by its relationship to pregnancy, is compatible with modern law. Although presently women's autonomy would appear to be exercised more readily through tort *as a remedy*, than through abortion law *as a right*, the ideal female subject does possess efficacy. Lacey argues, with regard to feminist critical reform of the law, that 'what we need is not an abandonment of the legal and political project, but rather the development of more sophisticated understanding of legal practices, their strengths, as well as their evident and important limitations'. This would entail a commitment to both 'strategy and ideal' and an 'aliveness' to the different ways in which each must be assessed.[58] In the case of abortion, one strategic move, therefore, would be to look toward the female subject of tort and to point to its inconsistencies with the invisible counterpart (mis)represented in the criminal law.

Notes

1 E. Jackson, *Regulating Reproduction: Law, Technology and Autonomy* (Oxford: Hart Publishing, 2001), p. 72.
2 Department of Health, 'Abortion Statistics, England and Wales: 2008', *Statistical Bulletin 2009/1* (London: Department of Health, 2009). Available online at http://www.dh.gov.uk/en/Publicationsandstatistics/Publications/PublicationsStatistics/DH_099285 (accessed 2 March 2010).
3 N. Lacey, *Unspeakable Subjects: Feminist Essays in Legal and Social Theory* (Oxford: Hart Publishing, 1998), p. 28.
4 Ibid.
5 Ibid., p. 193.
6 Ibid., p. 200. See Ngaire Naffine, Chapter 1.
7 C. Smart, *Law, Crime and Sexuality: Essays in Feminism* (London: Sage, 1995), p. 128.
8 Ibid., p. 129.
9 Lacey, *Unspeakable Subjects*, p. 193.
10 S. Gavigan, 'The Criminal Sanction as it Relates to Human Reproduction: The Genesis of the Statutory Prohibition of Abortion', *Journal of Legal History*, 5 (1) (1984): 20–43; p. 21.
11 L. Waller, 'The Tracy Maund Memorial Lecture: Any Reasonable Creature in Being', *Monash University Law Review*, 13 (1) (1987): 37–55. J. Keown, *Abortion, Doctors, and the Law* (Cambridge: Cambridge University Press, 1988), p. 60, disputes this line of argument about the aim of the 1803 provision.
12 Waller, 'The Tracy Maund Memorial Lecture'; R. Sauer, 'Infanticide and Abortion in Nineteenth-Century Britain', *Population Studies*, 32 (1) (1987): 81–93; p. 84.
13 'Medical Societies', *Lancet*, 15 November 1924, p. 1011.
14 'The Law of Abortion', *Lancet*, 9 May 1936, p. 1074.
15 K. Hindell and M. Simms, *Abortion Law Reformed* (London: Peter Owen, 1971), p. 70.
16 'A Charge of Illegal Abortion: *Rex v Bourne*', *Lancet*, 23 July 1938, p. 220.
17 Ibid., p. 221.
18 *King* v. *Bourne* [1939] 1 K.B. 687 at 688, per Macnaghten J.
19 'Doctor Acquitted', *Canberra Times*, 20 July 1938, p. 4.
20 Hindell and Simms, *Abortion Law Reformed*, p. 70.
21 Ibid.
22 *King* v. *Bourne*, pp. 690–1.
23 '*Rex v Bourne*', *Lancet*, 23 July 1938, p. 201.
24 F. Talbot, 'Abortion and the Law', *Lancet*, 30 July 1938, p. 281.
25 J. Peel, 'Attitudes in Britain', in Family Planning Association, *Abortion in Britain* (London: Pitman Medical Publishing Co. Ltd, 1966), pp. 66–73; p. 67; J. G. Weir, 'Lay Abortionists', in Family Planning Association, *Abortion in Britain* (London: Pitman Medical Publishing Co. Ltd, 1966), pp. 35–41; p. 39.
26 *King* v. *Bourne*, p. 690.
27 'A Charge of Illegal Abortion', p. 222. *King* v. *Bourne*, p. 695.
28 Jackson, *Regulating Reproduction*, p. 80; P. Richards, *Parliament and Conscience* (London: George Allen & Unwin, 1970), p. 88.
29 BMA Special Committee, 'Therapeutic Abortion', *British Medical Journal*, 2 (5504) (1966): 40–5; p. 40.
30 H. L. A. Hart, 'Abortion Law Reform: The English Experience', in Robert L. Perkins (ed.), *Abortion: Pro and Con* (Cambridge: Schenkman, 1971), p. 189.
31 Abortion Act 1967, Section 1(b).
32 Abortion Act 1967, Section 1(a)–(d).
33 Jackson, *Regulating Reproduction*, p. 80.
34 B. Brookes, *Abortion in England 1900–1967*, London: Croom Helm, 1988, p. 79.
35 Ibid., p. 34.

36 K. Gleeson 'Persuading Parliament: Abortion Law Reform in the UK' *Australasian Parliamentary Review*, 22 (2), 2007, pp. 27–32.

37 It was not until 2010 that the Government made an apology to the victims of thalidomide and offered them a compensation package of £20 million. S. Bosely, '50 Years on, an Apology to Thalidomide Scandal Survivors', *Guardian*, 14 January 2010.

38 In Hindell and Simms, *Abortion Law Reformed*, p. 170.

39 BMA Special Committee, 'Therapeutic Abortion', p. 41. My emphasis.

40 S. Sheldon, '"Who Is the Mother to Make the Judgment?" The Constructions of Woman in English Abortion Law', *Feminist Legal Studies*, 1 (1) (1993): 3–22; p. 6.

41 Ibid., p. 17.

42 V. Greenwood and J. Young, 'Ghettos of Freedom, an Examination of Permissiveness', in National Deviancy Conference (ed.), *Permissiveness and Control: The Fate of the Sixties Legislation* (London: Macmillan Press, 1980), pp. 149–74; p. 170; V. Greenwood and J. Young, *Abortion in Demand* (London: Pluto Press, 1976), p. 29.

43 Department of Health, 'Government Response to the Report from the House of Commons Science and Technology Committee on the Scientific Developments Relating to the Abortion Act 1967'. Available online at http://www.dh.gov.uk/en/Publicationsandstatistics/Publications/PublicationsPolicyAndGuidance/DH_080925 (accessed 2 March 2010).

44 The debate was considered in the context of the Human Fertilisation and Embryology Act 2008, which did not address changes to the abortion provisions of the 1990 Act. Late-term abortion is very rare. In 2008, 90 per cent of all abortions were carried out at under thirteen weeks' gestation; 73 per cent at under ten weeks; 1 per cent after twenty weeks: Department of Health, 'Abortion Statistics, England and Wales: 2008'.

45 Department of Health, *Our Inheritance, Our Future: Realising the Potential of Genetics in the NHS* (London: Department of Health, 2003), p. 42. Available online at http://www.dh.gov.uk/prod_consum_dh/groups/dh_digitalassets/@dh/@en/documents/digitalasset/dh_4019239.pdf (accessed 2 March 2010).

46 Jackson, *Regulating Reproduction*, p. 97.

47 R. Scott, 'Interpreting the Disability Ground of the Abortion Act', *Cambridge Law Journal*, 64 (2) (2005), pp. 388–412; p. 400.

48 Weir, 'Lay Abortionists', p. 39.

49 Scott, 'Interpreting the Disability Ground', p. 388. The reported crisis in British abortion provision indicates that doctors are exercising their right to refuse to perform terminations. See J. Laurance, 'Abortion Crisis as Doctors Refuse to Perform Surgery', *The Independent*, 16 April 2007.

50 Scott, 'Interpreting the Disability Ground', p. 392.

51 Ibid.

52 Ibid., p. 400.

53 Abortion Act 1967, Section 1(d).

54 Newman J, in Scott, 'Interpreting the Disability Ground', p. 400. See *Rand* v. *East Dorset Health Authority* (2000) 56 BMLR 39.

55 Scott, 'Interpreting the Disability Ground', p. 405.

56 L. Creedon, 'Call to Modernise Abortion Laws', *Press Association National Newswire*, 17 October 2008.

57 Lacey, *Unspeakable Subjects*, p. 105.

58 Ibid.

Chapter 17

Third-wave feminism, motherhood and the future of feminist legal theory

Bridget J. Crawford

Twenty years ago, young women in the USA boldly proclaimed the onset of feminism's 'third wave'. Third-wave feminists embraced the 'fun', 'sexy' and 'girly', rejecting the (supposedly) strident, humourless feminism of the 1970s and 1980s, while also taking up the feminist mantle. They critiqued pop culture, identity politics and their feminist foremothers, all the while pushing social, sexual and generational boundaries with tongues in cheek. Now there is a substantial body of third-wave feminist literature in the USA.

For many young women, third-wave feminism has an intuitive appeal. Gender-awareness provides an entrée for understanding differentials in social, economic and political power, but it does not inevitably lead to marginalisation. If anything, a third-wave feminist's embrace of all aspects of her personal identity functions as a claim of right to a place in the mainstream. The thirteen-point third-wave feminist 'Manifesta' is now required reading in some university women's and gender-studies classes.[1] That agenda makes several claims about the law, and yet third-wave feminism has had little or no impact on feminist legal theory. This is because third-wave feminist writing fails to grapple with gender equality or *law* writ large. Far from improving on the feminism of the past, third-wave feminists retreat, to women's detriment, from their predecessors' theoretical and methodological commitments. Nowhere is this clearer than in third-wave writings about fertility and motherhood.

Much of third-wave feminist writing has taken the form of the first-person narrative. In the 1990s and the first few years of the twenty-first century, there appeared several anthologies of collected essays by women (and some men), mostly in their twenties, writing about interning for political organisations, working as a nude dancer, consuming pornography or enjoying hip-hop music. Somewhat predictably, as third-wave feminists have aged, their subject matters have changed. For third-wave feminists now in their thirties and forties, the personal account of one's 'journey' toward motherhood seems to have become the new rite of passage. Rebecca Walker's *Baby Love*, Evelyn McDonnell's *Mama Rama* and Peggy Orenstein's *Waiting for Daisy*, are three representative examples of such milestone narratives.[2]

Taken together, these third-wave fertility and motherhood narratives contribute (perhaps unwittingly) to a mythology of motherhood that earlier feminists sought to dismantle. These works pay lip-service to the notion that motherhood should not be the measure of a woman's worth, but they embrace motherhood as the ultimate personal fulfilment. Second-wave feminists critiqued the influence of state systems, especially law, on motherhood as a practice and status. But third-wave feminists keep most critical theory at a distance.

Third-wave feminism, however, needs law, and law needs third-wave feminism. Joining the two forms an opening move in the development of an equality jurisprudence that acknowledges women's reproductive capacities but neutralises the role those capacities play in women's legal subordination. By offering a critique from squarely within the generation of women who have proclaimed a 'third wave' of feminism, this chapter speaks directly to my peer group of Western legal scholars. I am a third-wave feminist by strict demographic definitions, but not necessarily by preference, politics or proclivity.[3] Women like me (and our allies) who grew up and first studied law in a post-co-education era need to develop our own account of the law's limitations and potential. This account should be informed by our own experiences but also needs to take into account preceding feminist concerns and methodologies. In fusing contemporary third-wave feminist writing with extant feminist legal scholarship, one can discern the beginnings of a 'third-wave' feminist legal theory with its sights set on pragmatic gender justice.

The perpetual daughter syndrome

To the extent that third-wave feminist writers initially addressed the subject of motherhood at all, they spoke from the perspective of the perpetual daughter. This was an inevitable consequence of the generational bookends that young feminists in the USA used (and continue to use) to distinguish themselves from feminists who emerged out of the 1970s and 1980s. Their difference from those earlier feminists – their political, intellectual and actual mothers – is the primary trope of third-wave feminism. Its methodology is the first-person narrative. When Walker proclaimed in the pages of *Ms.* Magazine in 1991, 'I am not a postfeminism feminist. I am the Third Wave', she was twenty-two years old.[4] Walker is now in her early forties. Pregnancy and motherhood have replaced activism and fluid gender identity as primary third-wave subjects. On one level, this shift in subject-matter focus is a natural consequence of the methodological reliance on the first-person narrative. On another level, this shift marks a potentially conservative aspect of third-wave feminism.

In Rebecca Walker's case, her complicated relationship with her own mother, the poet and novelist Alice Walker, undergirds her memoir, *Baby Love*. One of Walker *fille*'s first concerns upon finding out she is pregnant is her mother's likely reaction. 'I had a tempestuous relationship with my mother, and feared the inevitable kickback sure to follow such a final and dramatic departure from daughterhood.'[5] Becoming a mother, then, in Rebecca Walker's construction, is the process by which one becomes an adult and *un*becomes a daughter: 'The fact is that until you become a mother, you're a daughter.'[6] Walker sees motherhood as the ultimate destination of a self-described fifteen-year journey taking place roughly between the time of her college graduation and the impending birth of her child.[7] With synecdotal swiftness, Walker then reads her own pregnancy as a watershed moment for feminism writ large. She describes her 'journey' toward motherhood:

> Ultimately it was like trying to steer a boat with a banana. I had no idea what was going on, no clue whatsoever … I didn't know that the longing, fear, and ambivalence were part of the pregnancy, the birth, and everything that came after. I didn't know that the showdown between the ideas of my mother's generation and my own was inescapable, and slated to play out personally in our relationship. I didn't know that those fifteen years constituted my real first trimester, and all that time my baby was coming toward me, and I was moving toward my baby.[8]

Walker reads the shift from daughterhood to motherhood as a personal trans-migration that portends change, if not in the leadership of the women's movement then in its focus and tenor. The 'showdown' that she perceives between her mother and herself becomes generalised into a 'showdown' between younger feminists and older feminists. As third-wave writers shift from their identities as activists, writers and cultural producers towards motherhood, they perceive themselves moving from the margin to the centre of feminist leadership.

Fertility and motherhood operate as a claim of right over menopausal women of the preceding generations. In Walker's story, third-wave feminists' literal and figurative mothers are passé, spent and past their prime.

If Walker were correct that motherhood marks the end of daughterhood (and that they are mutually exclusive identities), then the pages of *Baby Love* would not be replete with accounts of continued emotional skirmishes between mother and daughter. For example, the Walker *mère* threatens to publish an angry response to the Walker *fille*'s claim in a memoir that, 'my parents didn't protect or look out for me, but fed, watered, and encouraged me to grow'.[9] Walker describes her mother as overwhelmed by ambivalence about the maternal role: 'When I was in my twenties, my mother told me that she had to decide to love me, that she could have gone either way and she *chose* to love me.'[10] In contrast, Walker writes after her son's birth, 'There is no choice involved in my love for Tenzin, and if there were some secret place where I wondered, and there isn't, I would never tell him about it.'[11] So for Walker motherhood brings at the very least a duty to act as if one loves unconditionally (which Walker claims she does), even if the feeling does not come naturally. Mothers have special obligations to children.

> Because mothers make us, they map our emotional terrain before we even know we are capable of having an emotional terrain, they know just where to stick the dynamite. With a few small power plays, a skeptical comment, the withholding of approval or praise, a mother can devastate a daughter.[12]

Walker generalises about motherhood and feminism from her experience of being a particular woman's daughter. The solipsism of the narrative distracts from a potentially conservative interpretation of her text: motherhood is the key to women's personal fulfilment.

The inevitable mother syndrome

Unlike Walker's story, Evelyn McDonnell's *Mama Rama* does not, at least initially, make motherhood its central quest. A former freelance writer for the *Village Voice* and other publications, McDonnell is the popular culture critic for the *Miami Herald*. Her memoir is as at least as much about sex and rock 'n' roll (as the subtitle promises) as it is about motherhood. She relates her experiences as a stepmother and mother in the context of her rich professional and personal lives.

After McDonnell marries a man with two daughters, she learns to navigate the tricky role of step-parent: 'Raising a family would undoubtedly be easier if I had started from scratch … step parenting is a delicate balancing act, and I'm a klutz. Harsh words must roll off your back. You must never expect instant, or even deferred, gratification.'[13]

Biological motherhood was never a strong impulse for McDonnell, in her own estimation. She and her husband had unprotected intercourse for 'a couple' of years without conceiving, but they 'didn't get all repro-crazy, didn't see a fertility doctor or have sex when my temperature rose'.[14] Her eventual pregnancy comes as a (seemingly) pleasant surprise: 'I didn't need to be a biological mother to feel complete; I had just hoped for it as a bonus', McDonnell explains.[15] And even though she embraces her identity as the mother of a spirited boy, McDonnell says, 'I continue to believe that women shouldn't have to have kids to feel successful or complete.'[16]

McDonnell's rejection of motherhood as woman's one, true vocation pays homage to her feminist commitments, but it does not sufficiently disguise the tone of inevitability that dominates the last third of her narrative. She revises, or at least revisits, the life story she has just told in the previous two-thirds. 'I assumed I would be a mother, but I barely imagined it', McDonnell claims.[17] Then, reflecting on the memoirist's act of reconstituting the past, the book's last two sentences attempt to construct a retroactive narrative frame: 'Children laughed and cuddled in the future of my dreams. Sometimes I couldn't hear them over the music, but they were there.'[18] For all of the sex and rock 'n' roll of the preceding pages, then, motherhood is what makes McDonnell's dreams come true. A child is the ultimate fulfilment after years of pursuing personal and professional success.

The natural mother syndrome

The subtitle of Rebecca Walker's book (*Choosing Motherhood After a Lifetime of Ambivalence*) would be an appropriate one for Peggy Orenstein's memoir *Waiting for Daisy*, as well. Orenstein's story (in fact subtitled *A Tale of Two Continents, Three Religions, Five Infertility Doctors, an Oscar, an Atomic Bomb, a Romantic Night, and One Woman's Quest to Become a Mother*) is one of delayed parenthood, illness and infertility. In the early years of her marriage, Orenstein views her professional work as a writer as incompatible with starting a family. She feels unable to live up to her own stay-at-home mother's model.

> Although I publicly stood up for working mothers and day care, I knew that, for me, motherhood meant one thing: being there for your children like my mom had been there for me ... The issue wasn't whether I wanted to turn into my mother or even whether I feared I would; it was that I believed I should.[19]

Orenstein avoids addressing her 'chronically, maddeningly conflicted' state until the death of her father-in-law precipitates the decision to have a baby.[20]

Her plans are derailed by a diagnosis of breast cancer at thirty-five years of age. After recovery from cancer, she becomes pregnant, loses the pregnancy and begins fertility drugs. When those and intrauterine insemination are unsuccessful, she turns (unsuccessfully) to IVF and an egg donor. Orenstein describes the way infertility took over her life: 'I'd been so leery of being trapped by motherhood, so wary of its threat to my career and marriage, to my hard-won sense of self. Here I was instead, defined by my longing for a child, by my inability to become a mother.'[21]

When Orenstein becomes pregnant a second time, she says that she felt 'a current, almost like a silvery thread, running between me and my little zygote'.[22] When she miscarries at eight weeks, 'I felt the thread, that silvery strand connecting us, snap. Just like that.'[23] Orenstein is simultaneously punished by, and master of, her own body, subject to the odds of infertility treatments while also being attuned to the most minute biological changes.

As much as she pursues biological motherhood with determination, Orenstein and her husband consider adoption after the loss of her second pregnancy. Through work contacts, they meet a Japanese woman who arranges for private placement adoptions. But when Orenstein sees a picture of the child she and her husband plan to adopt, she feels none of the connection that she felt to her previous pregnancy: 'I looked at that squalling, outraged creature and felt ... nothing. Was I supposed to love him on sight? Was I supposed to know that he was my son? Who was this child, anyway, and what were we signing up for?'[24] The conflict is exacerbated when Orenstein learns that she is pregnant (for a third time) just five days before flying to Japan to visit her intended adoptive son, whom she has named Kai. 'Surprisingly, I didn't have a strong preference for a biological child over Kai; or perhaps more correctly, I was afraid to have one. The [biological] baby within, as I'd come to think of it, was too precarious, impossible to believe in after three losses.'[25]

Her experiences of loss are an obstacle to biological motherhood and an emotional stumbling block to adoptive motherhood.

After spending several days with her intended son, Orenstein overcomes her doubts about her ability to love a non-biological child.

> Sometime over the next few hours as I listened to his freight train breathing, I felt something in my heart release. I didn't know what was right anymore, didn't know what we ought to do, but I knew that I could love this baby; I knew he could be my son.[26]

When immigration and international restrictions prevent the couple from adopting the child, the baby is placed with another family. Orenstein later mourns the loss of her son: 'We had only spent a short time together, he and I, but I missed him. I still do.'[27]

Read against Orenstein's narrative, Rebecca Walker suggests that motherhood is as much (or more) a state of being as a state of mind. Walker is at pains to distinguish her own feelings for the biological child she birthed from those she has for a former partner's child whom Walker quasi-adopted: 'It's not the same ... I don't care how close you are to your adopted son or beloved stepdaughter, the love you have for your non-biological child isn't the same as the love you have for your own flesh and blood.'[28]

Walker posits an innate, inevitable, permanent and even mystical connection between a mother and a biological child. Poetically, she says that she and her biological son are, in her words,

> bound through space and time in the beginningless beginning, that place of infinite mystery. We have met there, on that ground, in a meeting impossible to erase. Even when we are far from each other, we will each possess a fragment of that encounter, buried in the loamy dirt we call our separate selves. I am no longer inexperienced enough to diminish this connection.[29]

In other words, if Walker had feelings of affection or even love for her quasi-adopted child, they were motivated by 'inexperience'. Walker, in her new role as the 'experienced' woman, elevates the importance of biology (i.e., the impending birth of her biological child) above affinity – or at least treats biology as generating affinity.

Evelyn McDonnell's narrative is far less self-centred than Walker's, and yet McDonnell, too, suggests the uniqueness of a biological parent's bond with her child. She explains her mistakes as a step-parent as the product of trying to exert too much control over her husband's children: 'I've learned to let Bud raise his daughters the way he wants, which is not always the way I want. I've gone from being mad that they weren't taking the right college-prep courses to praying that they don't flunk another year.'[30]

McDonnell's sensitivities originate in the fact that her stepdaughters were six and eight when she entered their lives; by that time in a child's development, 'the molds have been set'.[31] It is not, then, the absence of a biological tie that precludes a particular relationship between McDonnell and her stepdaughters but rather the presence of other influences at earlier stages of their lives.

Praise and blinders

Martha Fineman remarked in 1995 on the 'ambivalence' she perceived in the feminist legal scholarship of the preceding five years. She said that feminist scholarship of the early 1990s treated motherhood as 'burdensome, oppressive', at least initially, and then developed a 'sympathetic or empathetic mode' to account for other aspects of motherhood, its 'political, legal, and practical aspects'.[32] It is this sympathetic mode that third-wave feminists partially extend and from which they partially disengage. Third-wave feminists such as Walker celebrate motherhood and recommend it for all women. She says to a college audience that 'being pregnant is the best. I highly recommend it. I really do.'[33] With comments like these, Walker both inverts the notion that the physicality of motherhood is burdensome and endorses a hierarchy of values and commitments in which 'family' (read: motherhood) should come before activism and careers. Walker recounts her speech to a college audience:

> I talked about how since I have been pregnant, I've been more concerned than ever about the need for people in politics and the public eye to have healthy personal lives. So often the momentous cultural work happens at the expense of family and sustained intimacy with loved ones. I saw a lot of heads nodding as I spoke, and several couples came up afterward to talk about their trying to keep their families together in the midst of giving so much of themselves to the work they care so much about.[34]

Walker would likely disavow the view that motherhood is the right choice for every woman, but her remarks are not qualified. Pregnancy is simply 'the best'. Young women can stop debating the relative merits of careers, service or family. Walker has the answer and takes it on the lecture circuit.

Both Evelyn McDonnell and Peggy Orenstein are more self-conscious than Walker, to the point of bordering on apologetic, in their praise of motherhood. McDonnell, for example, says that being a successful woman need not include having children, but that it need not exclude having children, either: 'We shouldn't have to not have kids to feel like successful women.'[35] Orenstein describes the physical confidence that she gained from giving birth and then confesses, 'what's more, as it turns out I adore being a mom, though I am a little uneasy saying so'.[36] The reader senses that McDonnell and Orenstein, at least, are almost apologetic about the importance that they place on motherhood and the enjoyment that they derive from it. At least in part, that may be the legacy of the ambivalence about motherhood that Fineman read in the feminist legal scholarship in the early 1990s. Walker perhaps overreacts in her praise of motherhood, but all three writers embrace motherhood as a part of their personal identities.

Three memoirs cannot represent an entire generation's attitudes toward motherhood, but these three women's personal choices, explained by them in extraordinary detail, are important barometers of the cultural climate in which those choices occurred. The second-wave feminist connection between individual choice and the construction of motherhood as an institution remain uninterrogated by the memoirists, making a (small) possible allowance for one paragraph in McDonnell's book. Motherhood is entirely personal, with a slight nod to the outside world. It is a deeply desired choice for each of Walker, McDonnell and Orenstein, but it is not a political engagement as second-wave feminists would understand it. Fineman, for example, praised the work of feminist legal scholars in the 1990s who 'place[d] motherhood in a primarily political context', by understanding motherhood 'from a pragmatic and material perspective, restrained by law and other societal norms'.[37] Third-wave feminism, the intellectual beneficiary of multiple feminist critiques of motherhood as a cultural practice, retreats from the challenge entirely.

In the third-wave version of feminism, the political is personal, notwithstanding McDonnell's protestations to the contrary. She claims that through motherhood she has discovered that 'once again, the personal is political. As in every stage of my life, I've found great comfort in womankind, other mothers have helped me figure out how to manage my load ... They're my new sorority, and many of them are my old sisters.'[38]

Support and reassurance are necessary conditions for human flourishing. But sharing experiences is not by definition a political act. By infusing meaning into those shared experiences, one develops a basis for institutional engagement – a far different project than sorority.

The institution of motherhood

McDonnell, unlike Walker or Orenstein, briefly positions motherhood as the basis for activism. She imagines a 'motherhood movement' that would be to the twenty-first century 'what civil rights were to the '60s'.[39] McDonnell reasons that women have lost sons in war, women are more responsible than men for their children's education and that women care about parental leave and health care. 'Our numbers are certainly strong; hear us roar', she says.[40] At one level, McDonnell's call reflects a belief that women can unite around political causes. Her solution to 'problems' faced by mothers is political activism. On another level, though, her call to action oversimplifies issues as 'women's' issues and fails to take into account the legal and structural norms that make them into 'women's' issues.

Apart from this brief foray by McDonnell, the memoirists do not apply their significant critical skills to motherhood as a social, cultural or legal practice.

Absent from their personal stories is any hint of an analysis of the implications, practices and behaviours associated with motherhood, i.e., childrearing, childcare, unequal allocation of parenting responsibilities, underemployment and unequal pay for women, limited career opportunities and financial instability upon divorce. None of the narratives gives the reader any hint that motherhood is something more than the pleasurable fulfilment of a personal desire. In third-wave feminist writing, motherhood is reclaimed as the ultimate *personal* destiny for all women.

An institutional analysis of motherhood, which is so significant in earlier feminist writing, is noticeably absent from third-wave writing about motherhood and other topics.[41] In 1976, for example, Adrienne Rich published a book of essays with the title *Of Woman Born: Motherhood as an Experience and Institution.*[42] Rich sees a woman's ability to bear children as the primary vehicle for her marginalisation throughout history.[43] Of motherhood, she says:

> This institution has been a keystone of the most diverse social and political systems. It has withheld over one-half the human species from the decisions affecting their lives; it exonerates men from fatherhood in any authentic sense; it creates the dangerous schism between 'private' and 'public' life; it calcifies human choices and potentialities. In the most fundamental and bewildering of all contradictions, it has alienated women from our bodies by incarcerating us in them. ... Motherhood as an institution has ghettoised and degraded female potentialities.[44]

Walker, McDonnell and Orenstein would disagree that motherhood constrains women's choices, and the writers perhaps even lean towards a cultural feminist view that women's reproductive capacities make them special. Third-wave feminists imply that women's experience of mothering is inevitable, biologically driven and rooted in femaleness itself. In this sense, one might interpret Walker and McDonnell as embracing a more relational feminism, in the style of Robin West. West says that women's reproductive roles mean that, through pregnancy, women experience the literal physical dependence of another person and take on (or are assigned) a 'distinctive nurturing role' in caring for infants.[45] Whether the cause is biological or social, though, is less important to West than the fact that

> more than do men, we live in an interdependent and hierarchical natural web with others of varying degrees of strength. ... If women's 'difference' lies in the fact that our lives are relational rather than autonomous, and if autonomy is a necessary attribute of a human being, then women's difference rather abruptly implies that women are not human beings.[46]

West encourages feminists to 'insist on women's humanity – and thus on our entitlements', while also embracing women's interdependence on and with others.[47]

For Walker, the fact that she will physically give birth to her expected child is the foundation for her indignation at her husband's preference for a semi-private childbirth experience (with healthcare providers at the ready), over a home birth attended by friends reciting poetry and prayers.[48] McDonnell, for one, embraces her role as primary decision-maker in parenting matters. McDonnell says that she has more responsibility than her husband does for raising their son, but that she is not unhappy with that division of labour: 'That's generally fine with me: Cole's [my husband's] third child and my one and only. Bud's in charge of the girls; I want to be in charge of the boy.'[49] In other words, McDonnell embraces her caretaking role, even if she suspects that sexism may be at work.

Orenstein is brutally honest with herself when she asks whether becoming a mother allowed her to maintain her relationship with her husband. Had she not become pregnant, she asks 'would I have ultimately destroyed the most precious, sustaining thing in my life: my marriage? I'd hate to think that the only way I could have righted myself was to have a baby. I'll never know whether that was the case.'[50]

Seeing her husband parent is a source of great pleasure to Orenstein. His involvement in caretaking, something that she does not detail but that she implies is significant, is the reason that Orenstein says that she does not feel 'personally or professionally compromised by motherhood'.[51] Orenstein's account opens the door to the possibility, as Fineman has suggested, that men can be 'mothers'.[52]

Third-wave feminists have insisted that men must be included in any successful transformation of society.[53] In the absence of a structural analysis of the institution of motherhood, it will be difficult to map that transformation. That is where prior feminist legal scholarship might give a boost to third-wave feminism.

The future of feminist legal theory

The power of personal storytelling is demonstrated by second-wave feminist consciousness-raising groups and on third-wave feminist blogs about employment and workplace advancement for women.[54] But storytelling in a vacuum is nothing more than that. For society or culture to be able to respond to women's needs, through the law or otherwise, storytelling must be accompanied by critique. To insist on critique from within the personal memoir may be unrealistic, but it is not an unreasonable expectation of Walker, Orenstein and McDonnell. Walker's own writing, for example, is considered one of the inspirations for third-wave feminism.[55] Before publishing *Waiting for Daisy*, Orenstein was a well-known author of two books that adopted an explicitly feminist perspective: *Flux: Women on Sex, Work, Kids, Love and Life in a Half-Changed World*, and *School Girls: Young Women, Self-Esteem and the Confidence Gap*.[56] And before *Mama Rama* Evelyn McDonnell was an established rock critic known for an edited volume of women's writing, *Rock She Wrote: Women Write About Rock, Pop and Rap*, as well as her work at the *Village Voice* and the *San Francisco Weekly*.[57] Each of these authors had a public feminist profile before writing her memoir. Feminism is a product of what feminists say, do and write, and so the three authors' personal narratives, taken together, do function as a partial bellwether for contemporary feminism.

The law needs to take into account women's personal, subjective truth. The common-law system relies on individuals' narratives. Without the telling of a personal story, there can be no legal claim and no case law. Fostering the telling of women's personal stories is a vehicle for developing a legal vocabulary that can recognise inequality that women experience. Robin West makes a similar claim with her call for an emphasis on women's 'subjective, hedonic lives'.[58] She says that women experience pain in a different way than men do, and that they must give voice to that subjective experience. Acknowledging women's differences from men, West says, will encourage the development of 'a vocabulary in which to articulate and then evaluate them, as well as the power to reject or affirm them'.[59] Third-wave feminist narratives about motherhood are a means of translating women's hedonic lives into literal verbiage that the law requires in order to do justice. That is where third-wave feminism may give a boost to law.

So far, third-wave feminist writings lack an explicit, concrete emphasis on law. The power of third-wave feminist work has been mostly rhetorical; its greatest influence has been to create or exacerbate existing generational fault-lines within feminism. The wave metaphor positions 'incoming' women in conflict with those who came before them. 'Young' women are set up in contrast to 'older' women. The fertile are pitted against the menopausal. If being a mother, or having the same sex as those who have the biological ability to be mothers, defines all women to a certain extent, then feminists would do well to abandon the wave metaphor.

Uniting a feminist legal theoretical perspective on motherhood as an institution with third-wave narratives about the personal joys of motherhood is laden with both promise and pitfalls. In identifying the pleasures, satisfactions and joys associated with motherhood, we might appreciate the real needs of women for protection against discrimination in the workplace and more generous family-leave policies. Perhaps maternal preferences in custody might re-emerge, if courts recognised some special ability of women to provide the nurturing and care that young children need. Yet women who fail to meet the idealised standards of a 'perfect mother', such as women who have extramarital relationships, might invite a shift in US divorce law back towards a fault-based paradigm. That paradigm would penalise both non-conforming women as well as make it more difficult for all women to leave untenable marriages.

A more nuanced vocabulary for describing women's needs carries with it the possibility that women's own words will be used to justify either the status quo or even regressive policies. If motherhood is embraced as the 'true' woman's experience, gender-neutral parenting leave might disappear entirely. Women who do not meet normative expectations for 'motherly' behaviour might be subject to additional scrutiny or punishment. Protections for mothers might translate into protection for those who most resemble some 'idealised' version of a mother. Although describing that mother is difficult, she is unlikely to be someone who is poor, who works too much, who uses drugs, has non-traditional sexual partners, is incarcerated, does not speak English or belongs to a 'wrong' religion.

Close analysis of these third-wave writings about motherhood reveals a tension in their claims. The narratives make both normative claims (as in Rebecca Walker's universal endorsement of motherhood as 'the best') and descriptive ones about the joys of motherhood, tempered by disclaimers about universalising from individual experience (as in McDonnell's statement that women should not have to become mothers to feel successful).[60] Third-wave feminism's emphasis on the joys of motherhood might empower women to advocate for laws – such as parental leave and protections for breastfeeding mothers – that support mothers. But legal theorists should be cautious about normative strains in third-wave feminism that portray motherhood as desirable for all women.

Third-wave feminism suggests that political activism, cultural critique, marriage and motherhood are all feminist experiences and that those experiences are not as disparate as they might seem. McDonnell, for one, links her youthful topless marches in the New York City gay-pride parade to the experience of toplessness (or at least partial toplessness) as a breastfeeding mother.[61] Third-wave writings suggest the complexity of the feminist experience. In third-wave feminist hands, feminism is a framework that permits simultaneous critique and embrace of motherhood. Feminist legal theory, then, can work to both dismantle structural and institutional inequalities in the law, while also demanding that the law secure women's ability to choose motherhood (or not).

Notes

1 J. Baumgardner and A. Richards, *Manifesta: Young Women, Feminism, and the Future* (New York: Farrar, Straus & Giroux, 2000).
2 R. Walker, *Baby Love: Choosing Motherhood After a Lifetime of Ambivalence* (New York: Riverhead, 2007); E. McDonnell, *Mama Rama: A Memoir of Sex, Kids, & Rock 'n' Roll* (Cambridge, Mass.: DaCapo, 2007); P. Orenstein, *Waiting for Daisy: A Tale of Two Continents, Three Religions, Five Infertility Doctors, an Oscar, an Atomic Bomb, a Romantic Night and One Woman's Quest to Become a Mother* (New York: Bloomsbury USA, 2007).
3 Third-wave feminists define themselves as feminists 'whose birthdates fall between 1963 and 1973'. L. Heywood and J. Drake, 'Introduction', in L. Heywood and J. Drake (eds.), *Third Wave Agenda: Being Feminist, Doing Feminism* (Minneapolis, Minn.: University of Minnesota, 1997), pp. 1–20. See also L. Jervis, 'The End of Feminism's Third Wave', *Ms.* (winter 2004/5): 57: 'I was born in 1972, right smack in the demographic that people think about when they think about the third wave'. I was born in 1969.
4 R. Walker, 'Becoming the Third Wave', *Ms.* (January/February 1992): 39–41; reprinted in *Ms.* (spring 2002), at p. 86.
5 Walker, *Baby Love*, p. 5.
6 Ibid., p. 47.
7 Ibid., p. 8.

 8 Ibid.
 9 Ibid., pp. 75–6.
10 Ibid., p. 187.
11 Ibid.
12 Ibid., p. 6.
13 McDonnell, *Mama Rama*, p. 149.
14 Ibid., p. 170.
15 Ibid.
16 Ibid., p. 237.
17 Ibid., p. 169.
18 Ibid., p. 245.
19 Orenstein, *Waiting for Daisy*, pp. 10–11.
20 Ibid., p. 14.
21 Ibid., p. 74.
22 Ibid., p. 100.
23 Ibid.
24 Ibid., p. 203.
25 Ibid., p. 208.
26 Ibid., p. 214.
27 Ibid., p. 220.
28 Walker, *Baby Love*, p. 69.
29 Ibid., p. 72.
30 McDonnell, *Mama Rama*, p. 153.
31 Ibid.
32 M. A. Fineman, 'Preface', in M. A. Fineman and I. Karpin (eds.), *Mothers in Law: Feminist Theory and the Legal Regulation of Motherhood* (New York: Columbia University Press, 1995), pp. ix–xii.
33 Walker, *Baby Love*, p. 137.
34 Ibid., pp. 35–6.
35 McDonnell, *Mama Rama*, p. 237.
36 Orenstein, *Waiting for Daisy*, p. 222.
37 Fineman, 'Preface', p. xiii.
38 McDonnell, *Mama Rama*, p. 240.
39 Ibid., p. 239.
40 Ibid., pp. 239–40.
41 See, for example, B. Crawford, 'Toward a Third-Wave Feminist Legal Theory: Young Women, Pornography and the Praxis of Pleasure', *Michigan Journal of Gender and Law*, 14 (1) (2007): 99–168.
42 A. Rich, *Of Woman Born: Motherhood as Experience and Institution* (New York: W. W. Norton & Company, Inc., 1976).
43 Ibid., p. xv.
44 Ibid.
45 R. West, 'The Difference in Women's Hedonic Lives: A Phenomenological Critique of Feminist Legal Theory', *Wisconsin Women's Law Journal*, 3 (1987): 81–142, at p. 130.
46 Ibid., p. 131.
47 Ibid.
48 Walker, *Baby Love*, p. 50.
49 McDonnell, *Mama Rama*, p. 191.
50 Orenstein, *Waiting for Daisy*, p. 223.
51 Ibid., p. 222.
52 M. Fineman, *The Neutered Mother, the Sexual Family and Other Twentieth Century Tragedies* (London and New York: Routledge, 1995), p. x.

53 M. Chapman with R. Elwood, 'Explaining Feminism and Experimenting with Labels: Where Do Men Fit Within the Movement?', in S. Weir and C. Faulkner (eds.), *Voices of a New Generation: A Feminist Anthology* (New York: Pearson Education, Inc., 2004), pp. 121–7.
54 A. Stein, 'Women Lawyers Blog for Workplace Equality: Blogging as a Third-Wave Feminist Legal Method', *Yale Journal of Law and Feminism*, 3 (2) (2009): 357–408.
55 Walker, 'Becoming the Third Wave', at p. 86.
56 P. Orenstein, *Flux: Women on Sex, Work, Kids, Love and Life in a Half-Changed World* (New York: Doubleday/Anchor, 2000); P. Orenstein, *School Girls: Young Women, Self-Esteem and the Confidence Gap* (New York: Doubleday/Anchor, 1994).
57 E. McDonnell, *Rock She Wrote: Women Write About Rock, Pop and Rap* (New York: Dell, 1995).
58 West, 'The Difference in Women's Hedonic Lives', p. 123.
59 Ibid., p. 132.
60 Walker, *Baby Love*, p. 137; McDonnell, *Mama Rama*, p. 237.
61 McDonnell, *Mama Rama*, p. 182: 'As a kid, I was a shirtless tomboy running through sprinklers. As a young woman, I marched down Fifth Avenue for top-freedom. As a mama, I sat bare-breasted in restaurants, malls, and even one work meeting. Nothing was going to stop me again from suckling my child.'

Chapter 18

'Shall I be mother?'

Reproductive autonomy, feminism and the Human Fertilisation and Embryology Act 2008

Rachel Anne Fenton, D. Jane V. Rees and Sue Heenan

Introduction

Women are the primary interest holders in reproduction. While traditional gender roles have altered and technology has advanced, pregnancy and child-birth remain a woman's burden and are entirely gender-specific.[1] As the decision to become a mother 'is crucial to [a woman's] personal well-being, definitive of her social persona, and predictive of her economic horizons',[2] the centrality of motherhood to women's lives means that reproduction has been an important focus of feminist literature. Situating motherhood within feminism has, however, been hugely problematic: feminist analysis has encountered a 'profound ambivalence' as to whether motherhood is empowering, oppressive or both.[3] As the decision to mother or not is so essential to a woman's sense of self and her life plan and, if it is correct that 'the interconnection between all aspects of women's unequal status – particularly race, class, and age – are nowhere clearer than in the potential consequences of maternity and motherhood',[4] then it is important that 'natural' mothering or assisted mothering decisions are characterised by real choice and autonomy rather than being conditioned by socially constructed notions of idealised motherhood.

In the UK, assisted conception is regulated by the Human Fertilisation and Embryology Act 1990, recently updated by the amending statute of the same name in 2008 (hereafter HFE Act). The UK has a relatively permissive and liberal regime and, as such, occupies a middle ground between some countries whose regulation is prohibitive and other countries, such as the USA, which have no formal regulation and where treatment provision is purely market-based. The HFE Act regulates women's reproductive autonomy in so far as assisted mothering choices are concerned. However, it is recognised that assisted reproductive technology (ART) choices are not made in the abstract. Rather, it is suggested that the ART decision is in a sense a 'micro' decision, which can only be entered into once the 'macro' decision to become a mother has been made. This chapter will explore women's choices to become mothers and, subsequently, to use ARTs, before examining the extent to which women are granted self-determination under (some parts of) the UK's regulation.[5]

To be mother

Feminist arguments about motherhood tend to fall into two categories: those organised around notions of reproductive autonomy as a means of empowering women and those that consider all reproduction as a means, if not a form, of oppression.[6] The concept of reproductive autonomy originates in liberal feminism's desire to empower women and allow them to act on their own agency through self-determination and freedom of choice.[7] Considered by many women as a 'right', birth control and abortion are areas for which women have fought and now expect and demand, self-determination, control of their own bodily integrity and the ability to make lifestyle choices.[8] Reproduction as oppression has its origins in second-wave feminism. Patriarchal dominance and female subordination were so woven into the fabric of society[9] that it was suggested that the most oppressive experiences were those where male dominance had become invisible because it had become the norm.[10] Nowhere was this considered more the case than in the burden of reproduction. Indeed, Rich suggested that, 'under patriarchy, female possibility has been literally massacred on the site of motherhood'.[11]

While society may have moved on from the position whereby those without children were perceived as 'selfish, peculiar or disturbed'[12] to being more generally accepting of childless women, powerful ideological views of motherhood do continue to exist.[13] Even the terminology used to describe a woman without a child has become loaded with meaning, with some feminists identifying with the phrase 'childfree' (which is intended to emphasise that childlessness can be an active and fulfilling choice),[14] some qualifying their reproductive status and choice with terms such as 'voluntary' or 'involuntary',[15] and yet others attempting to situate themselves outside of the value laden debate by using the phrase 'not-mother'.[16] Contiguous to this idealised view on womanhood, however, exists an equally idealised concept of what it is to be a 'normal' mother, which ultimately limits who might actually experience motherhood, with those women who do not conform being expected to forgo mothering in the interests of the child.[17]

Meyers suggests that there is an autonomy deficit in relation to many women's decision-making about motherhood and that this is reinforced by resilient matrigyno-idolatry: childbearing is women's destiny and 'heterosexuality is not only normative, it is imbued with a procreation imperative'.[18] She suggests that 'heedlessly imbibing cultural attitudes valorising procreation together with a romanticised image of motherhood removes motherhood from the realm of choice ... '.[19] Matrigyno-idolatry, however, has collaborators in feminist scholarship, and this is becoming increasingly evident within the first-person narrative of third-wave feminist writings in which motherhood has been embraced as 'the ultimate personal fulfilment'.[20]

To be assisted mother

Feminist debate about ARTs has replicated the wider debate about motherhood generally, i.e. whether ARTs constitute the empowerment or oppression of women. ARTs were heralded by Firestone as a means of avoiding the oppression of pregnancy and childbirth, with the potential (as yet unrealised) for parthenogenesis and ectogenesis.[21] The potential benefit of ectogenesis has been questioned, however, with Jackson suggesting that a viable artificial womb might ultimately lead to a reduction in choice about abortion and to some women's wombs being perceived as unsafe environments.[22] The reality of ART treatment today is limited to hugely invasive techniques which have very low success rates.[23] As such it has been argued that they 'reinforce the degradation and oppression of women to an unprecedentedly horrifying degree. They reduce women to living laboratories: to "test-tube women".'[24] Furthermore, the availability of reproductive technology is not driven merely by female demand:[25] it is largely dominated by the medical and scientific profession, business and the state. Some feminists believe that the price that has been paid for ARTs is medicalisation and over-regulation, resulting in 'medical violence against women'.[26]

However, ARTs, when they are successful, do allow women to have babies when they otherwise could not. It is arguable that the very availability of ARTs thus reinforces prevailing familial norms. Nonetheless, ARTs simultaneously have the potential to subvert the traditional family by opening up the possibility of reproduction to post-menopausal, single and lesbian women as well as non-gestational mothers through surrogacy. Jackson suggests that, paradoxically, to eschew assisted reproduction for its reinforcement of the traditional family unintentionally bolsters a view of natural motherhood whereby women can only experience motherhood from within a heterosexual partnership.[27] What is clear, however, is that the more the mother status is revered in society, the greater the demand for ARTs will be, inside or outside of the traditional family norm. However, it has been suggested that 'women's choice to participate in infertility treatment is so conditioned by the socially constructed stigma of infertility and a societally imposed norm of maternity as to be no real "choice" at all'.[28] This lack of choice is identified and explained by Orenstein in her personal narrative about her quest to have a baby

> That's the insidious thing about infertility treatments: the very fact of their existence, the potential, however slim, that the next round might get you pregnant creates an imperative that may not have otherwise existed. If you didn't try it, you'd always have to wonder whether it would've worked. That's how you lose sight of your real choices, because the ones you're offered make you feel as if you have none.[29]

Paradoxically, the very availability of ARTs in conjunction with second-wave feminism's message that women could 'have it all'[30] and say 'yes' to careers and 'no' to early motherhood,[31] has contributed to a social understanding or expectation that late mothering (via ART) is possible and women are thus lured into infertility.[32] As a result, ARTs might be constructed as a lifestyle choice. In Western society, the dominant cultural message sent out to women is that early pregnancy (before a career) is failure[33] and that teenage motherhood is a social ill.[34] Thus, the ideal medical age for pregnancy and childbirth (around eighteen to twenty years old) 'no longer comports with social and cultural values and expectation'.[35] Goodwin argues that 'soft' pregnancy and motherhood discrimination leads women to delay pregnancy and forces them into late mothering by a 'fertility penalty'[36] in terms of lost income and lost position on the career ladder. This creates a 'double bind' for women who believe that they have to choose between a career and early motherhood: 'If women truly possessed the right to choose motherhood without fear of discrimination, some might mother earlier when it is biologically safer to do so.'[37] For Goodwin, the invasive and risky procedures involved mean that ARTs therefore offer an *illusory* choice.

> ART accommodates the very social inequities which limit women's opportunities to simultaneously pursue careers and families equal to their male counterparts. Thus it indirectly reifies problematic norms by providing a secondary 'out' for the private sector by appearing to provide an unburdened utopian dream for women. This secondary option is not without its own murky socio-legal constructions and medical drawbacks.[38]

The choice to use ARTs does not, therefore, exist in the abstract but is conditioned by general societal norms of mothering, as well as the economic and social reality within which mothering can be realised. Furthermore, any specific treatment choice will be conditioned by the contextual presentation of that choice, based upon the information available, the ability to understand that information and the intimate social context of the choice.[39] For women in the UK, once the choice to use ARTs has been made, their reproductive autonomy is dependent upon the provision of ARTs under the HFE Act 2008 and access to them.

The provision of ARTs in the UK

Resource availability

Maternal age

Unless resources are available, there can be no choice to access them. In the UK some treatment is available under the NHS, at least theoretically. The National Institute for Clinical Excellence (NICE)[40] guideline recommends providing three full cycles of IVF for women aged between twenty-three and thirty-nine who have identified fertility problems or unexplained infertility persisting for at least three years.[41]

No age limit for treatment is expressed by the 2008 Act, and the issue is determined by clinics' discretion under the welfare principle (discussed below). While the recommended maximum age is thirty-nine for women (there is no age limit for men) to access publicly funded treatment, some primary care trusts (PCTs) impose an age limit as low as thirty-five years for women while some impose maximum age limits for male partners varying from forty-six to fifty-five years.[42] Some centres do treat women slightly older than thirty-nine. The imposition of a specific age limit is justified on the grounds of allocation of scarce resources: those that are more likely to succeed in a live birth are more likely to receive treatment and the chances of a live birth decline rapidly with age.[43] Yet there are other factors that affect fertility, such as obesity, but the NICE guideline does not state a specific BMI above which a woman should not be offered treatment in the way that it states a specific age. This method of resource allocation is not necessarily rational – a woman aged thirty-six who fails to conceive has potential access to NHS resources, but a woman aged thirty-nine does not, simply by virtue of her chronological age. The thirty-nine-year-old, however, may have had a potentially higher success rate due to other indicators of fertility: age alone does not therefore provide a rational determination of outcome. Furthermore, there is evidence that IVF using donor eggs is not any more efficient in younger women as opposed to older women as fertility problems are caused by ageing ovaries rather than the uterus. An older uterus also does not increase birth defects.[44] Medical research does cite evidence of increased health risks to older pregnant women, but the risks are relatively low if the woman is in good health.[45] To choose thirty-nine as the cut-off age also appears at odds with social reality. The upward trends in the fertility of UK women in their thirties and forties over the past three decades (the number of live births in the thirty to thirty-four and thirty-five to thirty-nine age range has risen steadily, and there is a small but consistent increase in live births in the forty and over category)[46] indicate that women are choosing to conceive later in life. The woman who tries (but fails) to conceive after her mid-thirties is effectively penalised as she must show three years of unexplained infertility to access NHS resources. The autonomy of the woman in her late thirties to make reproductive choices is thus constrained by potentially discriminatory resource allocation. Were recognition of reproductive autonomy to be at the forefront of rationing decision-making, there is a good argument for suggesting that it is actually older women who should be prioritised as they need treatment more than younger women.[47] This, combined with the fact that women's choices to mother early are constrained by social and economic realities and the promise of ARTs, means that the subsequent denial of NHS treatment is a form of double jeopardy and arguably constitutes secondary victimisation.

The age limit imposed in the public sector appears all the more problematic in light of the fact that private clinics have discretion to treat older and post-menopausal women. The maximum age for treatment varies according to the clinic but it would appear that fifty is the currently accepted upper age limit in the UK. Private choices, however, appear to become public property when the mother is post-menopausal. The issue of post-menopausal mothering has received worldwide attention with women of up to age seventy giving birth.[48] At the time of writing there is controversy over whether fertility treatment should be offered in the UK to Sue Tollefsen aged fifty-nine. After initially being refused IVF treatment at home, Tollefsen became a 'fertility tourist' and obtained treatment in Russia, using donor eggs to give birth to her daughter, now aged two. This has led to calls, notably from older female MPs, for legal intervention in order to establish an upper age limit for women.[49]

Broadsheet and tabloid coverage of Tollefsen's case mirrors the negative stereotyping typical of media coverage of similar cases[50] in criticising post-menopausal mothering on four main grounds, namely, maternal health, the welfare of the child, that it is 'unnatural' and that older mothers are 'selfish'.[51] Shaw and Giles's analysis of how age and motherhood are 'framed' in the news media, for example, shows a higher incidence of negative stories than positive ones, with even the positive stories containing negative undertones: 'a broadly positive first-person account of older motherhood was full of caveats (e.g. "my goodness, though, it was tough"), as if to ward off any thoughts readers may have of trying it out for themselves'.[52]

These objections to post-menopausal mothering will be examined briefly in turn. First, as regards maternal health, as noted above, the risk to the mother is low. Revealingly, recent research links paternal age and birth disorders yet there have been no public calls for an upper age limit to be set for fathers in fertility treatment (although as noted above some PCTs do set an upper age limit for fathers).[53] This not-altogether-rational disparity between men and women is equally evident in relation to the other objections and demonstrative of the double standards that abound in society concerning male and female sexuality and parenting: as Millns puts it, 'While virile older men are congratulated for still having it in them, a woman's "shrivelled old uterus" ... is seen as past it.'[54] The second argument, that the welfare of the child is adversely affected, does not stand up to scrutiny when the benefits of older motherhood, such as commitment, better interaction with the child, greater experience, knowledge and affluence, are taken into account.[55] Although there are concerns about life expectancy, Cutas argues that, while it is not in a child's best interest to be orphaned, those in dangerous occupations are not denied reproductive autonomy.[56] If these concerns were genuine then they should apply equally to fathers and paternal age limits should be set. Older fathers are not criticised on the same basis.[57] The third argument, that post-menopausal pregnancy is 'unnatural', is rarely aimed at younger women for whom treatment after early menopause would be equally 'unnatural'. Rather, it is suggested that the idea of unnaturalness is really a smoke screen for distaste at the subversive sexuality of a pregnant older woman.[58] Finally, older mothers are perceived as selfish for having chosen to postpone motherhood for education and a career: good mothers are self-sacrificing. But this may not be a choice at all. In summary, the arguments put forward against post-menopausal motherhood are not really based on age alone but on moral suitability.[59]

Other rationing criteria

In addition to age limitation, PCTs have been found to employ a range of arbitrary and unsubstantiated social criteria aimed at rationing treatment.[60] Amongst the non-clinical access criteria are smoking criteria, no existing children, one partner has no living children, no children under sixteen living with the couple, no children living in the household, no children in current relationship.[61] Access to treatment is therefore a complete postcode lottery. The use of such non-clinical social criteria to determine funding was not recommended by the NICE guideline and is not evidence-based.[62] Furthermore, the reference to infertility made by the NICE guideline means that single and lesbian women who are, in themselves, fertile but simply (male) partnerless may be excluded. This pushes 90 per cent of patients into the private sector,[63] where one round of IVF costs from £4,000.[64] Reproductive autonomy is thus compromised by cost: lower-income families will be excluded. Relegation to the private sphere for those who can afford it has knock-on effects: Lord Winston suggests that 'exploitation is a real issue. The combination of desperation and high costs is corrosive not only to the patient but to medical practice'[64] because in the private sector these patients are given IVF whether or not it is medically indicated. This also occurs in the USA where clinics offer deals such as 'live birth or your money back'.[65] Furthermore, financial restrictions lead to choices that otherwise would not be made, such as the implantation of more than one embryo to achieve a multiple birth, egg-sharing to receive free treatment and fertility tourism when IVF can be obtained cheaper abroad. Whether or not treatment should be provided free of charge (and academics and clinicians have argued strongly that it should)[66] is an ethical and policy issue that cannot be discussed here. Nonetheless, it is clear that financial cost operates to exclude poorer women from treatment and curbs their reproductive autonomy. The net result is that even when the law widens the goalposts to access, the actual provision of treatment by PCTs will restrict poorer women.

Embryo (de)selection

While the UK's regulatory regime remains permissive, the HFE Act nonetheless maintains tight regulatory control over treatment provisions and this has repercussions for reproductive choice. Perhaps some of the most closely regulated provisions are those that control the characteristics of the child which can be created and these tend to be steeped in ethical concern and debate. Although such controls are more concerned with concepts of ideal children rather than idealised mothering, they are worthy of brief mention because they do affect the reproductive autonomy of certain women. The UK permits (within strict legal limits) the use of pre-implantation genetic diagnosis[67] (including the creation of so-called 'saviour siblings')[68] and this gives women who are (potential) carriers of serious hereditary genetic disease the possibility to have a healthy genetically related child free from disease and thus to participate in mothering choices from which they would be otherwise excluded. Nonetheless, there are two legislative dictates that negatively impact upon reproductive autonomy to have the kind of child desired, namely, the prohibition of sex selection for social reasons such as family balancing[69] and the non-preferral of embryos and gamete donors which have an abnormality[70] which arguably sends a symbolic-expressive message as to the undesirability of disability[71] and may restrict the reproductive autonomy of those labelled as disabled.[72] Thus, legislation permits reproductive choice in terms of creating a specific type of child, at an abstract level, but the goalposts are set by law and maintained by clinicians.

Access and the welfare principle

Access to treatment in the UK is not specifically prescribed by law, in contrast to other regulatory regimes in Western Europe such as Italy, where the law clearly states that only heterosexual couples married or living together may have access to homologous treatment.[73] Rather, access is regulated by the 'welfare principle' under Section 13(5) of the HFE Act 1990. In its original form, the welfare principle read: it is a condition of licensing that clinics consider 'the welfare of any child who may be born as a result of the treatment (including the need of that child for a father) and of any other child who may be affected by the birth'. Following the 2008 Act, the words 'including the need of that child for a father' have been replaced by the words 'including the need for supportive parenting'. This will be discussed below. The issue of access is pragmatically devolved to the Human Fertilisation and Embryology Authority (HFEA), the licensing authority, to issue guidance through its Code of Practice, and, as a consequence, to clinics' discretion, thus exonerating the legislature from any enunciation of categorical access policy. The welfare principle has elicited criticism as it provides a forum for state invasion of decisional privacy: the infertile are in essence subject to a discriminatory 'tax' from which the fertile are exempt – no control is exercised over the reproductive autonomy of the fertile on grounds of their future fitness to parent. As a result, Jackson argues, 'the welfare of the child thus occupies a curious middle ground, in which it is always *less* important than fertile couples' bodily integrity and sexual privacy and *more* important than infertile couples' decisional privacy'.[74] Yet research demonstrates that children born through ARTs are, if anything, doing better than naturally conceived children.[75] Despite the Select Committee's recommendation that the welfare principle be abolished because of its unjustifiable discrimination against the infertile,[76] the welfare principle has been retained (albeit in a modified form) under the 2008 Act.

There is no doubt that in the past the welfare principle has been used to justify subjective assessments of potential parents on grounds of social factors, commitment to and suitability for parenting and adherence to certain family forms.[77] This was recognised by the HFEA's own research and subsequent adoption of a 'risk of serious harm test' in its Code of Practice.[78] The

HFEA's 8th Code of Practice, issued subsequent to the 2008 Act, provides the following guidance as to the meaning of 'supportive parenting':

> It is presumed that all prospective parents will be supportive parents, in the absence of any reasonable cause for concern that any child who may be born, or any other child, may be at risk of significant harm or neglect. Where centres have concerns as to whether this commitment exists, they may wish to take account of wider family and social networks within which the child will be raised.

Although the Code states that the assessment 'must be done in a non-discriminatory way ... patients should not be discriminated against on grounds of gender, race, disability, sexual orientation, religious belief or age', it is clear that clinics and not women have the final say as to access. It might be suggested that as ultimate power continues to lie with clinics, less visible strategies such as delaying access procedures which are difficult to challenge could obscure social judgements over fitness to parent.[79] Under the welfare principle, women's reproductive autonomy remains subject to patriarchal control, albeit in much diluted form: a clinician may scrutinise a private choice; thus, medical paternalism continues to trump decisional privacy.

Lesbian and solo women

The requirement of 'the need for a father' as part of the welfare principle justified the exclusion of lesbian and solo women from infertility treatment. The phrase had its origins in the 1984 Warnock Report which declared (without substantiation) that 'it is better for children to be born into a two parent family, with both father and mother'.[80] This part of the welfare principle was thus the heteronormative expression of ideal mothering: mothering within the two-parent family unit based on (hetero)sexual ties operating to marginalise lesbian and single women as deviant and 'other'. The effect of this clause was compounded by the fact that a child born to a single woman was legally father*less*, which further implied the desirability of being born to a heterosexual couple.[81] While access was not specifically denied by law, ample anecdotal evidence demonstrates that discrimination under the guise of the welfare of the child against lesbian and solo women did take place.[82] Some women who did not fit within this idealised notion of family adopted deceptive practices in order to gain access.[83] This legislative assumption that children born to lesbian and single women are emotionally and developmentally disadvantaged is not borne out by research; indeed, if anything, the opposite has been found,[84] and lesbian co-mothers have been found to be more involved parents than fathers.[85] The correlative devaluation of lesbian and single parenting[86] on this alleged basis is thus unacceptable, and this has now been recognised by the Government.[87] The 2008 Act has accordingly expunged the 'need for a father' from the welfare principle, but this was not without significant debate and controversy both within and outside Parliament. Opponents to the abolition of the 'need for a father' argued vociferously that removing the provision would be to state that fathers were not needed in the family and that the clause is symbolically important for fatherhood. Conservative MP Iain Duncan Smith, for example, claimed in the *Mail on Sunday* that 'another nail will have been hammered into the coffin of the traditional family. And another blow will have been struck against fatherhood.'[88] In essence, the 'need for a father' appeared synonymous with the wider debate about social breakdown and absentee fathers, yet only a very small percentage of (the already small number of) ART births are to single or lesbian mothers: ARTs are hardly responsible for the erosion of the 'traditional' family.[89] The 'importance of fatherhood' arguments are fallacious in this context: they fail to recognise that the retention of the clause would have no effect in returning absent fathers to the family, and, in terms of symbolic value, its retention symbolises unacceptable discrimination on grounds of marital status and sexuality.

In light of Labour government policy on sexual orientation, equality and parenting,[90] it would have been untenable to retain the 'need for a father'. In particular, the Civil Partnership Act 2004 recognises the validity of same-sex unions. In line with this, the parentage provisions of the 2008 Act (which passed with very little attention despite their radical nature),[91] bring the position of same-sex couples into line with that of heterosexual married and unmarried couples by providing a parallel regime allowing the civil partner or partner of the birth mother to become the second legal parent: thus, two women can be the child's legal parents.[92] While the result of the law is to equalise the legal position for same-sex couples, the alternative parenting model is set out as a mirror image, rather than the two regimes being combined into one. It is certainly arguable that this construction is symbolically suggestive that the same-sex regime is secondary or even 'other'.[93] In conjunction with the fact that there is a presumption of parental status for the husband and civil partner it might be suggested that the 2008 Act, by effect if not purpose, maintains a heteronormative statement based upon the primacy of the biogenetic two-parent model of the sexual family.[94] Significantly, while a child born to a single woman can remain legally fatherless under the 2008 Act, a single woman can name a male friend as the 'father' or a female friend as second female parent. This provides for a further type of legitimate alternative family form which may obviate concerns about the legally fatherless child but simultaneously maintains the importance of the two-parent model, suggesting that single mothering has not been accepted in quite the same way as same-sex parenting. The abolition of the 'need for a father' in conjunction with the new parentage rules is thus symbolically important in the recognition and legitimisation of women's reproductive choices to create alternative families. However, it must be recognised that the law is simultaneously also perpetuating motherhood as the norm for even more women.

Conclusion

It is suggested that the amendments to the HFE Act 1990 have made substantial progress in challenging societal concepts of ideal mothering and have permitted a wider use and acceptance of ARTs for women who were previously excluded. To the extent that what is not permitted remains more indicative of procreative liberty than what is permitted,[95] attention needs to be paid to the limitations upon autonomy under the Act evident in restricting motherhood for older women, the content and operation of the welfare principle and the controls over the prospective characteristics of children created. While these limitations may affect an extremely small number of ART users, they are nonetheless steeped in ethical implications, and it should not be forgotten that 'it is easy to grant people the freedom to do what is agreeable to us; freedom is important only when it is the freedom for people to do what is disagreeable'.[96] Furthermore, it has been suggested that the presumption concerning the legitimacy of state intervention in ART needs to be challenged as it 'allows the imposition of the values of one group on others'.[97] Overall, despite these limitations and caveats, the British legislation does provide more choice to women, and patriarchal control has, to that extent, consequently been diminished. This is important in acknowledging that ART does (sometimes) give babies to women who want them.[98] However, it should not be forgotten that, paradoxically, by opening up motherhood to previously excluded categories of women, patriarchy is also reinforced to the extent that mothering remains constructed as the idealised status for even those women historically categorised as 'other'.

Notes

1 E. Jackson, 'Degendering Reproduction?', *Medical Law Review*, 16 (3) (2008): 346–68.
2 D. T. Meyers, 'The Rush to Motherhood: Pronatalist Discourse and Women's Autonomy', *Signs*, 26 (3) (2001): 735–73; p. 736.
3 E. Jackson, *Regulating Reproduction: Law, Technology and Autonomy* (Oxford: Hart Publishing, 2001), p. 175.
4 C. MacKinnon, *Sex Equality* (New York: Foundation Press, 2001), p. 1192.
5 Given women's greater investment in fertility treatment, this chapter will only look at women's rights. This is not to suggest that men do not have interests at stake.
6 R. F. Storrow, 'Quests for Conception: Fertility Tourists, Globalization and Feminist Legal Theory', *Hastings Law Journal*, 57 (2) (2005): 295–330.
7 Jackson, *Regulating Reproduction*, p. 2.
8 Ibid.
9 C. MacKinnon, *Toward a Feminist Theory of the State* (Cambridge, Mass.: Harvard University Press, 1989).
10 C. MacKinnon, 'Feminism, Marxism, Method and The State: Toward Feminist Jurisprudence', *Signs*, 8 (4) (1983): 635–8; p. 638.
11 A. Rich, *Of Women Born: Motherhood as Experience and Institution* (New York: Norton, 1976); quoted in MacKinnon, *Sex Equality*, p. 1191.
12 M. Stanworth, 'The Deconstruction of Motherhood', in M. Stanworth (ed.), *Reproductive Technologies: Gender, Motherhood and Medicine* (Cambridge: Polity Press, 1987), pp. 10–35; p. 15.

13 See, for example, the public and media response to Nadya Suleman, so-called 'Octomom', in B. Crawford and L. Buckner Inniss, 'Social Factoring the Numbers with Assisted Reproduction', *Texas Journal of Women and the Law*, 19 (1) (2009): 2–26, at p. 25.

14 R. Gillespie, 'Childfree and Feminine: Understanding the Gender Identity of Voluntarily Childless Women', *Gender and Society*, 17 (1) (2003): 122–36, p. 123.

15 G. Letherby and C. Williams, 'Non-Motherhood: Ambivalent Autobiographies', *Feminist Studies*, 25 (3) (1999): 719–28.

16 A. Belcher, 'The Not-Mother Puzzle', *Socio-Legal Studies*, 9 (4) (2000): 539–56; p. 539.

17 Stanworth, 'The Deconstruction of Motherhood'.

18 Meyers, 'The Rush to Motherhood', p. 759.

19 Ibid., p. 747.

20 See Bridget J. Crawford, Chapter 17.

21 S. Firestone, *The Dialectic of Sex: The Case for Feminist Revolution* (London: The Women's Press, 1979).

22 Jackson, 'Degendering Reproduction?', p. 6.

23 S. Bewley, M. Davies and P. Braude, 'Which Career First?', *British Medical Journal*, 331 (2005): 588–9.

24 R. D. Klein, 'What's New About the "New" Reproductive Technologies?', in G. Corea et al. (eds.), *Man-Made Women: What Future for Motherhood?* (London: Pandora Press, 1985).

25 J. G. Raymond, *Women as Wombs: Reproductive Technologies and the Battle over Women's Freedom* (Melbourne: Spinifex Press, 1995).

26 Ibid.

27 Jackson, *Regulating Reproduction*, p. 178.

28 J. Gallagher, 'Eggs, Embryos and Foetuses: Anxiety and the Law', in M. Stanworth (ed.), *Reproductive Technologies: Gender, Motherhood and Medicine* (Cambridge: Polity Press, 1987), pp. 139–50; p. 146.

29 P. Orenstein, *Waiting for Daisy* (London: Bloomsbury Publishing, 2008), p. 220.

30 G. Greer, *The Female Eunuch* (London: Harper Perennial, 1971); Firestone, *The Dialectic of Sex*.

31 M. Goodwin, 'Assisted Reproductive Technology and the Double Bind: The Illusory Choice of Motherhood', *The Journal of Gender Race and Justice*, 9 (2) (2005): 1–54; p. 5.

32 Bewley et al., 'Which Career First?'.

33 Goodwin, 'Assisted Reproductive Technology', p. 45.

34 For example, in 1999, the UK Government pledged to halve teenage pregnancy rates by 2010 and allocated £260 million to achieve this. See http://news.bbc.co.uk/1/hi/education/8531227.stm and also http://www.dcsf.gov.uk/everychildmatters/healthandwellbeing/teenagepregnancy/about/strategy (both accessed 8 May 2010).

35 Goodwin, 'Assisted Reproductive Technology', pp. 45–6.

36 *The Independent*, 9 February 2010.

37 Goodwin, 'Assisted Reproductive Technology', p. 3.

38 Ibid., p. 52.

39 T. Glennon, 'Regulation of Reproductive Decision-Making', in S. Day-Sclater et al. (eds.), *Regulating Autonomy: Sex, Reproduction and Family* (Oxford: Hart Publishing, 2009), pp. 152–5.

40 NICE is an independent body providing guidance on promotion of good health and preventing and treating ill-health.

41 Available online at http://www.nice.org.uk/nice media/pdf/CG011niceguideline.pdf (accessed 11 March 2010).

42 Available online at http://www.dh.gov.uk/en/Publicationsandstatistics/Publications/PublicationsPolicyAndGuidance/DH_101073 (accessed 11 March 2010).

43 Available online at http://www.nice.org.uk/nicemedia/pdf/CG011niceguideline.pdf (accessed 11 March 2010).

44 J. Parks, 'On the Use of IVF by Post-menopausal Women', *Hypatia*, 14 (1) (1999): 77–96.
45 *The Times*, 29 May 2009; J. Berryman, K. Thorpe and K. Windridge, *Older Mothers: Conception, Pregnancy and Birth After 35* (London: Pandora, 1995), p. 93.
46 Available online at http://www.statistics.gov.uk/cci/nuggtet.asp?id=951 (accessed 11 March 2010).
47 Parks, 'On the Use of IVF', p. 92.
48 For example, Rajo Devi Lohan, *Guardian*, 6 March 2009.
49 Ann Widdecombe and Nadine Dorries in the *Mail on Sunday*, 17 January 2010.
50 D. Cutas, 'Postmenopausal Motherhood: Immoral, Illegal? A Case Study', *Bioethics*, 21 (8) (2007): 458–63.
51 *Mail on Sunday*, 17 January 2010.
52 R. L. Shaw and D. C. Giles, 'Motherhood on Ice? A Media Framing Analysis of Older Mothers in the UK News', *Psychology and Health*, 24 (2) (2009): 221–36, at p. 225.
53 See, for example, E. Frans et al., 'Advancing Age and Bipolar Disorder', *Archives of General Psychiatry*, 65 (9) (2008): 1034–40.
54 S. Millns, 'Making "Social Judgments That Go Beyond the Purely Medical": The Reproductive Revolution and Access to Fertility Treatment Services', in J. Bridgeman and S. Millns (eds.), *Law and Body Politics: Regulating the Female Body* (Aldershot: Dartmouth, 1995), pp. 79–104, at p. 93.
55 See J. C. Berryman, 'Perspectives on Later Motherhood', in A. Phoenix, A. Woollett and E. Lloyd (eds.), *Motherhood, Meanings, Practices and Ideologies* (London: Sage, 1991), pp. 66–85.
56 Cutas, 'Postmenopausal Motherhood'.
57 E. Watkins, 'Parsing the Postmenopausal Pregnancy: A Case Study in the New Eugenics', *New Formations*, 68 (spring 2007): 27–34. Available online at http://www.lwbooks.co.uk/journals/newformations/articles/60%20watkins.pdf (accessed 18 January 2010). Contrast the difference in reporting about sixty-seven-year-old Paul McCartney's parenting of a young daughter in the same edition of the *Mail on Sunday*, 17 January 2010, which carried Tollefsen's story.
58 Millns, 'Making "Social Judgments"'.
59 Parks, 'On the Use of IVF'.
60 R. Kennedy et al., 'Implementation of the NICE Guideline', *Human Fertility*, 9 (3) (2006): 181–9; p. 181.
61 Available online at http://www.dh.gov.uk/en/Publicationsandstatistics/Publications/PublicationsPolicyAndGuidance/DH_101073 (accessed 11 March 2010).
62 Kennedy et al., 'Implementation of the NICE Guideline'.
63 Lord Winston, Hansard, 4 December 2007, col. 1614.
64 Ibid.
65 Clinics make money on these offers because they give IVF treatment to those who do not really need it and thus who are likely to achieve a live birth; D. Schmittlein and D. Morrison, 'A Live Baby or Your Money Back: The Marketing of In Vitro Fertilization Procedures', *Management Science*, 49 (12) (2003): 1617–35; p. 1617.
66 For example, Lord Winston, Hansard; E. Jackson, 'Conception and the Irrelevance of the Welfare Principle', *Modern Law Review*, 65 (2) (2002): 176–203; p. 176.
67 Schedule 2 1ZA (1) a–d.
68 See S. Sheldon and S. Wilkinson, 'Hashmi and Whitaker: An Unjustifiable and Misguided Distinction?', *Medical Law Review*, 12 (2) (2004): 137–63.
69 See S. Wilkinson, 'Sexism, Sex Selection and Family Balancing', *Medical Law Review*, 16 (3) (2008): 369–89, at p. 369.
70 HFE Act 2008, Sections 14 and 13(9) respectively. Whilst no particular abnormality is referred to by the legislation or the explanatory notes, a high-profile US case in which a deaf lesbian couple used a deaf sperm donor to create a deaf child is specifically

referred to by the public consultation and the Select Committee 2005, and it is therefore possible that obviating this type of situation was the background to governmental policy.

71 Savalescu, 'Deaf Lesbians, "Designer Disability" and the Future of Medicine', *British Medical Journal*, 335 (2002): 771–3, at p. 772.

72 R. Fenton, 'Catholic Doctrine Versus Women's Rights: The New Italian Law on Assisted Reproduction', *Medical Law Review*, 14 (1) (2006): 73–107.

73 Jackson, 'Conception and the Irrelevance of the Welfare Principle', p. 184.

74 E. Jackson, *Medical Law: Text Cases and Materials* (Oxford: Oxford University Press, 2010), p. 774.

75 Science and Technology Committee, *Human Reproductive Technologies and the Law*, 24 March 2005, HC 7–I 2004–5, para. 107.

76 See, for example, R. Probert, 'Families, Assisted Reproduction and the Law', *Child and Family Law Quarterly*, 16 (3) (2004): 273–88; p. 273.

77 HFEA, *Tomorrow's Children: Report of the Policy Review of Welfare of the Child Assessments in Licensed Assisted Conception Clinics 2005*; HFEA, *Code of Practice*, 7th edn, 2009.

78 Jones suggested this in relation to single women under the previous regime – see book review of C. Jones, 'Why Donor Insemination Requires Developments in Family Law: "The Need for New Definitions of Parenthood", by S. Fovargue', *Medical Law Review*, 16 (8) (2008): 458–64.

79 *Report of the Committee of Inquiry into Human Fertilisation and Embryology*, Report Cm 9314, 1984.

80 HFE ACT 1990, Section 28.

81 See, for example, Probert, 'Families, Assisted Reproduction and the Law'; Jones, 'Why Donor Insemination Requires Developments'; E. Sutherland, '"Man Not Included": Single Women, Female Couples and Procreative Freedom in the UK', *Child and Family Law Quarterly*, 15 (2) (2003): 155–71; p. 155.

82 Jones, 'Why Donor Insemination Requires Developments'.

83 F. MacCallum and S. Golombok, 'Children Raised in Fatherless Families from Infancy: A Follow Up of Lesbian and Single Heterosexual Mothers at Early Adolescence', *Journal of Child Psychology and Psychiatry*, 45 (8) (2004): 1407–19; p. 1407.

84 Probert, 'Families, Assisted Reproduction and the Law'.

85 Stanworth, 'The Deconstruction of Motherhood'.

86 Department of Health, *Review of the Human Fertilisation and Embryology Act: A Public Consultation*, 2005, para. 3.27.

87 *The Mail on Sunday*, 17 November 2007.

88 Probert, 'Families, Assisted Reproduction and the Law'.

89 See Jeffrey Weeks, Chapter 20.

90 J. McCandless and S. Sheldon, 'The Human Fertilisation and Embryology Act 2008 and the Tenacity of the Sexual Family Form', *Modern Law Review*, 73 (2) (2010): 175–207; p. 175.

91 HFE ACT 2008, Sections 35–53.

92 The way in which the Department of Health worked out the regime is also indicative of this. See interview by McCandless and Sheldon, 'The Human Fertilisation and Embryology Act', p. 196.

93 See also Ibid.

94 Sutherland, 'Man Not Included'.

95 Savalescu, 'Deaf Lesbians'.

96 S. McClean, quoted in Jackson, *Medical Law*, at p. 826.

97 Jackson, 'Degendering Reproduction?'.

98 Ibid.

Chapter 19

Motherhood and autonomy in a shared parenting climate

Susan B. Boyd

Introduction

This chapter explores the limits that shared-parenting norms can place on women's autonomy over life decisions for themselves and for their children. In particular, it identifies the tensions between women's autonomy and modern expectations of mother-caregivers who do not live with the fathers of their children. While the focus on opposite-sex parents reflects the historic dominance of such relationships in parenting disputes that receive legal attention, the norms discussed are also relevant to the increasing number of disputes between lesbian mothers and sperm donors. Feminist approaches to autonomy and to relationships are discussed first. The discourse then turns to the implications of normative shared parenting for mothers who either never had, or no longer have, a relationship-based motivation for facilitating the child's relationship with the other parent. Finally, the concept of relational autonomy is used to suggest a way to shift the normative force of shared parenting.

Autonomy and relationships

Feminism has been centrally concerned with freeing women to shape their own lives rather than accepting a male-dominated definition of womanhood.[1] Objectives have included the freedom to choose one's own relationships, the ability to leave destructive relationships, the ability to choose when or whether to bear children and the ability to choose work that was not defined as appropriate for women. Both the liberal concept of 'choice' and the individualist version of autonomy at the core of liberalism and formal equality have been critically assessed by feminists, particularly when it was realised that, for women, achieving autonomy is complex.[2] Choices are shaped and often constrained by forces such as the ties of family commitments, familial and heterosexual ideology and economic dependency. Individuals are deeply influenced by social contexts and by power relations and ideologies connected to gender, race and class. Complete autonomy might, then, only be feasible in a socio-economic system that was free of, say, gendered power relations. In the meantime, the concept of autonomy must be considered within the context of power relations and ideologies that shape and constrain choices. The still male-dominated nature of these relationships and ideologies must be kept in mind.

Women's potential for autonomy is often constrained by relationships, although relationships can also enable autonomy. In fact, the very relationship between women as mother-caregivers and their children illustrates the ways in which relationships can facilitate as well as constrain autonomy. The caregiving that mothers provide children enables children to become autonomous persons, yet, at the same time, this caregiving relationship constrains maternal autonomy. Given the still-powerful societal expectations that mothers will provide primary care for children and the strong sense of responsibility that many/most mothers feel towards the well-being of their children, the constraints that parenting imposes on women's autonomy are more significant than those on men's.[3] Women's 'pregnant embodiment', their more continuous physical experience in relation to children as a result of pregnancy, breastfeeding, and caregiving responsibility, typically prevents them from being able to opt in and out of involvement with children in the way that men predominantly still can.[4] Despite long-standing calls for men to share parenting and for society to support work–life balance, the landscape of parenting remains surprisingly gendered due to a mix of biological and ideological factors.[5]

The ideology of motherhood affects women's autonomy, because women are often not viewed as persons in their own right, 'with choices to make about ways of being and living'.[6] This ideology is born of a still powerful public–private divide, which holds women responsible for children and family and constructs women as separate and distinct from men, who still dominate the public sphere.[7] Moreover, although the ideology of motherhood has changed, modern expectations of mothers arguably produce an equally constraining cultural norm.[8]

Motherhood must also be seen as contextualised within larger social and economic structures. Without a generous social or familial structure surrounding a woman's mothering (for example, a childcare system that might allow her time to pursue her own interests), her ability to make choices for herself is inevitably constrained. Enhancing a woman's autonomy means not an absence of state interference but 'the positive provision of resources to enable someone to have a meaningful set of options'.[9] The problem is that in most Western societies the family is also constructed as autonomous and as part of the non-public sphere.[10] Parenting is very often accomplished in isolation from extended families and/or without adequate childcare and other social supports so that maternal autonomy is correspondingly limited. Moreover, as Fineman has documented, the inevitable dependency of young children generates a derivative (economic and structural) dependency in their caregivers, usually women.[11] Social and economic structures that fail to fully recognise or accommodate this derivative dependency in turn negatively affect the ability of mother-caregivers to exercise autonomous choices or to achieve the economic stability necessary for them to do so.

A feminist and relational approach to autonomy acknowledges that most if not all individuals live their lives 'from within relationships with others' and that autonomy 'is not realizable without the ongoing support, care, and guidance provided by others'.[12] The question is how to support women's autonomy within the context of these relationships, some of which may be oppressive, and in a society that does not yet properly support mother-caregivers or women's reproductive labour, but, rather, relies on and exploits their relational labour.[13]

Trends in child-custody law over recent decades have arguably constrained, rather than enhanced, women's potential for autonomy. Much has already been written about modern trends in child-custody law, the rise of the fathers' rights movement, the normative push towards joint custody and shared parenting and the implications for maternal claims for custody.[14] However, little of this work has explored in any depth the question of women's autonomy in the face of these trends.[15] It has become taboo to emphasise women's issues when the interests of children are being addressed, especially in the face of expectations that mothers should be selfless.[16] That said, the ways in which normative encouragement of shared parenting, typically in the name of the best interests of the child, constrains women's ability to protect themselves *and* their children from abusive conduct by the other parent have been well documented. That literature best captures the tension between autonomy and safety versus shared parenting norms, but even beyond the context of domestic abuse consequences of normative shared parenting for women's autonomy can be identified. We have already begun to see the problematic consequences of a bifurcated approach whereby maximum contact between children and fathers is presumed to be in the best interests of most children, with exceptions carved out for the 'minority' who have been subjected to abuse.[17] It is also important to reinsert the question of women's autonomy into the picture, even in scenarios where abuse or violence is not at issue.[18]

Normative shared parenting and women's autonomy

The current normative framework encourages shared parenting for parents who live apart. There is a trend away from awards of sole custody to one parent. Family-law policy has encouraged men to take responsibility for childcare by emphasising maximum contact between children and 'both' parents after separation or divorce, as fathers' rights have increasingly been emphasised by fathers' rights advocates and policy-makers, not always in a manner that is friendly to feminism or women's autonomy.[19] Joint custody is awarded in almost half of Canadian divorce court-determined custody cases.[20] There is much anecdotal and academic testimony concerning the normative power of shared parenting in current decision-making.[21] Although more sharing of parenting responsibilities should in theory enhance women's autonomy, in some cases the ongoing ties that mothers must perforce have with the fathers of their children can diminish their potential for autonomy. Moreover, joint custody or shared parenting orders do not necessarily mean that fathers share responsibility for parenting equally with mothers. Rather, mothers tend to be responsible for managing and facilitating their children's lives, and children live with their mothers for the majority of the time in most cases.[22]

Nevertheless, as a result of a rethinking of paternal responsibility in child welfare and development and the emergence of new socio-legal norms around shared parenting, understandings about parenthood are being reshaped.[23] Fatherhood has become a new policy concern, with initiatives to promote 'good' fathering and social responsibility on the part of men, whether they are fathers within intact families or outside that structure. Fathers are now viewed as having 'a more direct, unmediated relationship to their children' than in the past.[24] In other words, paternal relationships with children are no longer seen as mediated by the relationship that a father has with the mother. Some of these trends are positive, particularly from the perspective of heterosexual women who seek greater and more direct sharing of parenting responsibilities by their male partners. Fathers are expected to engage directly with children in addition to assuming financial responsibility for them. Children can benefit from a less rigid sexual division of labour between their mothers and fathers and from the opportunity to receive engaged attention from more than one parent. Many may benefit from child-support enforcement as well. However, enhanced child-support obligations have also spurred the fathers'-rights movement in its push for shared parenting, with less than clearly positive results for mothers and children.[25]

While many women seek an engaged father with whom to co-parent, the trends towards shared parenting present serious challenges to women who prefer to parent without the biological father for reasons, for example, of abuse at the hands of such a man, concerns about his ability to be a constructive parent, plans to parent with a same-sex partner or a wish to parent autonomously or without a partner (an increasing phenomenon as 'single mothers by choice' increase in number).[26] Gender convergence has increasingly characterised modern accounts of fatherhood, with gender neutrality and formal equality dominating discussions about parenthood in a way that tends to obscure the ongoing gendered nature of reproductive labour and to enlarge formal rights for fathers.[27] These rights can translate into greater control over a pregnant woman or mother, in relation to decisions that will have more consequences for *her* life and body. The centrality of the female role in reproduction and parenting is being challenged, which, paradoxically, compromises women's autonomy. Not only are women still held more responsible for children and caregiving, but their autonomy over decisions in relation to children is now restricted in the name of father's equality.

In relation to parenting apart, a responsible mother-caregiver is now expected to nurture a child's relationship with the father, unless he is proven to be harmful. Otherwise, she may be labelled as an 'implacably hostile' or alienating mother.[28] Mothers who raise what may be legitimate concerns about the safety of contact arrangements can be vilified as 'no contact mothers'.[29] In some cases, they lose custody as a result, not because they are poor caregivers but because they have not facilitated paternal contact. The ability of women to assert autonomy from the fathers of their children in the face of this normative expectation is dubious. Moreover, the preference for joint parenting effectively binds only resident or primary caregiver parents, usually women, with no penalties being incurred by fathers who fail to live up to non-financial parenting responsibilities.[30]

Especially if a woman has at some stage cohabited with the father or the child has a schedule of contact with the father, it is increasingly difficult for her to choose at a later point to formulate a life that is marked by geographical distance from the father or to make decisions that may limit his involvement with the children. Restricting a mother-caregiver's choices in this regard may well have negative consequences for her relationships with her wider family and new partners and impact upon her career and her economic autonomy. In relocation applications, for example, a woman might be denied the opportunity to move with her child to be nearer family support networks, to take a better paying job or to join a new partner. In some cases, custody is changed to the non-moving parent, sometimes regardless of whether the move actually happens.[31] Some custodial parents (more often mothers) will choose not to even try to move, when the move may actually be in the best interests of their own or their child's security, or both, as well as their economic well-being. Even if the decision cannot be proved to be in the best interests of the child, or it may take time to tell, questions can be raised about the trend towards second-guessing a mother's judgement about her own and her child's interests in the face of disagreement by the other parent.

The dominance of the heterosexual and patriarchal family, historically a challenge for women's autonomy, is reproduced in this imposition of equal parenting by 'both parents' (a term that implies a biological mother and father regardless of actual familial circumstances, or the possibility of same-sex or multiple parents in a child's life) in the name of children's interests. As Fineman asserts, 'some recently enacted family laws make it much more likely that traditional patterns of paternal right and responsibility will continue even in a world in which the form of many families will otherwise not be traditional'.[32] Indeed, some fathers'-rights discourse is marked by a heterosexist concern with the consequences for children who are raised without a male (heterosexual) role model.[33] In the name of children's interests and rights, it has been forcefully asserted that children have the right to know the identity of their (biological) fathers.[34] In family law, the prioritisation of maximum contact has been legislatively promoted and embraced by judges, regardless of marital status or, sometimes, even of demonstration of a father's commitment to parenting.[35] Often, the family-law developments are inspired by a state interest in the father assuming financial responsibility for children so that the state does not have to, but these developments suggest parenting rights as well as financial responsibilities.[36]

Questioning the shared parenting climate: social-science research

Parenting almost inevitably imposes some limits on parental autonomy, but the question is to what extent limits should be imposed by legislation or judges in the name of children's best interests, especially when the scientific evidence remains unclear. Such constraints (for example on the ability to relocate) *may* be acceptable if they are negotiated respectfully between two adults, with flexibility regarding changes in plans and an ability to adjust arrangements according to adult and child needs.[37] However, in cases that go to adjudicated dispute resolution, such respectful negotiation has usually failed and flexibility is unlikely. In these cases, the question is what norms should guide resolution of disputes. This raises another question: do we develop aspirational norms that guide parents who can come to relatively easy resolutions of their issues, or do we more cautiously focus norm creation on those who are in higher conflict? In most cases that go to court, a high level of conflict is present, meaning that joint custody or shared parenting, which requires a reasonable degree of communication and cooperation between parents, is rarely appropriate.

Nevertheless, judges (and lawyers and mediators assisting in negotiations) increasingly feel that the normative starting point for decision-making is some form of shared parenting even if the governing legislation does not state a presumption in favour of joint custody. Where the governing statute does indicate a preference for some form of shared parental responsibility, subject to exceptions, as in Australia, the normative power is even greater.[38] Even in cases where problems with one parent's behaviour have been identified, such as substance abuse interfering with good judgement in care of a child or abusive behaviour towards a child or caregiver, judges are reluctant to limit contact. Supervised access is increasingly being ordered in the face of (usually paternal) behaviour that does not necessarily show any promise of changing over time.[39] An undifferentiated notion of parenthood seems to be applied, which views paternal involvement as crucial regardless of the quality of the relationship between the father and the child and/or the primary caregiver.

Yet research shows that any effort to impose a 'one size fits all' approach, for example, shared parenting, is both ill-conceived and ineffective, not only for mother-caregivers but also for children. The increased burden that is now placed on mothers to ensure that children have contact with the other parent, sometimes at significant costs to themselves or even their children, has been criticised.[40] Assuming formal equality between mothers and fathers in post-separation parenting is misguided because

> The research ... suggests that children do not necessarily benefit from greater contact with their non-custodial parent – rather it is the type of parenting the non-custodial parent engages in, *not the amount of time* that parent spends with the children, that is most significant. ... The research to

date indicates that children do not fare better post-divorce in joint custody arrangements than they do in sole custody, and some children – including those in high conflict families – may fare worse. Finally, the research confirms findings on the role of conflict that have been well known for some time – parental conflict significantly increases the risk of reduced well being on the part of children who have experienced their parents' divorce.[41]

The research reveals that false assumptions are often made about gender symmetry, showing that child well-being is consistently associated with the economic contribution of the father and the closeness of the mother–child relationship.[42] Children value the quality and flexibility of relationships with parents rather than quantity of time, and yet quantity may be being used as a proxy for quality.[43] Concerns have been raised about the impact on children of legislated shared-care regimes, which may be a key variable in generating poor emotional outcomes in children when their parents are in conflict.[44]

In addition, the attributes that increase the likelihood of shared arrangements working smoothly are not typically characteristic of parents who litigate or otherwise require significant support in order to determine and administer shared-parenting plans. This research raises serious questions about the durability of shared arrangements in high-conflict climates, as well as questions concerning the power of shared arrangements to improve parental cooperation and to diminish children's perceptions of parental conflict.[45] Studies that focus on adult relationships and the viability of shared parenting show that cooperative self-selection of shared parenting arrangements is the key to successful shared-care outcomes. Yet we see increased rates of shared parenting in populations of disputing parents.[46] Bastard and Cardia-Vonèche explain the variable patterns of contact and parenting after separation in the face of a growing socio-legal consensus concerning the need for both parents to have a strong ongoing relationship with children by reference to the correlation between how parents functioned during their partnership and how they function afterwards. They conclude that the norm of shared parenting after separation may be simply irrelevant for parents who did not share that role prior to separation.[47] Gender asymmetry in adult parenting relationships is, then, difficult to alter via child-custody law reform.

Social engineering through the introduction of legal norms in the complex field of parenting relations is thus quite questionable. On the other hand, some norms are necessary. The question is: what should they be and can they take account of complex social relations? If norms can take account of gendered factors such as women's primary care and some of the research results discussed above, then they may also enhance women's autonomy.

Seeking new norms

Feminist approaches to relational theory may assist in identifying appropriate norms in this field, ones capable of enhancing women's autonomy.[48] Relational theorists generally seek, in contrast to liberal individualist approaches, to understand individuals as socially embedded and as developing their identities and capacities within the context of a complex web of social relationships. One family-law scholar in Canada has argued that family law now assumes and produces 'contextual subjects', that is, 'subjects regarded as rooted in their relationships and social settings'.[49] These 'thick' interdependent relationships (ideally) enhance the autonomy of each individual involved.[50] Others suggest that 'to be autonomous, in a relational sense, is to be responsive and responsible to others, and interdependent within complex networks of relationships'.[51]

The problem with this thesis is that being responsive and responsible to others remains a highly gendered concept, especially within the heterosexual family, wherein women tend to take more responsibility – and to *feel* more responsibility – for the care of others than men tend to. In emphasising the importance of care, relationships and connection, there is a danger that a woman's interests and her autonomy may be overridden in the name of the family (and all the attendant social norms about women's roles within family). Therefore, in developing a relational approach that attends to women's autonomy interests, the larger social context discussed earlier is fundamental to understanding the choices women make when parenting, the difficulties that post-separation parenting disputes pose in the face of complex, gendered relationships and what sort of parenting arrangement is appropriate. As already discussed, the normative imperative for shared parenting further impedes a mother's capacity for self-determination. The highest truth of good parenting is taken to be facilitation of a child's relationship with the father, almost regardless of the circumstances.

What, then, might law and society do differently to enhance women's relational autonomy in the parenting context? Social and economic structures that enable human interactions to flourish would help. Parenting a child might ideally involve multiple adults and/or greater societal involvement in care for children, so that the onerous responsibilities do not fall on one individual (usually a woman), thereby unduly limiting her autonomy. But remedies such as these are unlikely to emerge in the context of privatised family-law disputes; certainly they cannot be ordered in a dispute between two parents (although sometimes a parenting plan might involve a third party such as a grandmother). Critically, though, an approach that says that 'both' parents must have contact with a child is not the same thing as providing greater social and economic supports for mothers. The responsibility cast upon mothers to ensure contact between children and fathers increases a woman's burdens without giving her any more social support or autonomy as a mother; it privatises and extends her responsibility.

The implications of this insight for legal norms are complex. As Maclean and Eekelaar have pointed out, it is 'hard for the law to allow complete autonomy to each of two people in dispute who are party to a joint enterprise – parenting – when not only are they in conflict, but the interests of the child and the state have also to be taken into account'.[52] At the same time, they suggest that the system can, and, I would add, *should*, seek a resolution that gives as much scope as possible to the autonomy of each parent. In difficult, conflicted cases over contact, they suggest that the work of the family barrister is crucial and that there continues to be a role for the courts in redressing the potential domination of weaker parties and protecting the interest of the children.[53] We need to ensure that legal norms permit lawyers and judges to perform this role, even in the face of the increased emphasis on (sometimes mandatory) mediation and collaborative methods that have accompanied the normative rise of shared parenting. Lawyers can play an important role in redressing the vulnerability of (female) clients in negotiating family law disputes.[54] Legal norms should also encourage lawyers to engender a sense of self-trust in their mother-clients, so that they do not bow too readily to normative pressure to share parenting in inappropriate circumstances.[55] Yet legal norms that prioritise shared parenting tend not to permit this flexibility. The preoccupation with elevating maximum contact through the language of shared parenting creates a pressure, generated by mediators, mental-health professionals, judges and lawyers, to agree to some form of joint custody. Neither will resorting to a general best-interests test address these concerns, despite the attraction of its flexibility to deal with varied fact scenarios; 'best interests' is now too often interpreted to mean shared parenting, barring exceptional circumstances.

The 'open-ended "best interests" rule is an obvious invitation to contextual assessment', but its uneven effects caution against 'uncritical calls for more contextualism'.[56] Leckey suggests that the difficult question often is not whether contextualism is appropriate or not but whether something is appropriately included within a relevant context or excluded from it. He indicates that 'a context will come into view shaped by the already existing relationships'.[57] I would add that the way in which relationships are defined and considered is crucial to this method. It is not adequate to consider only the relationship between those involved in parenting. The wider relational context must be brought into sight. Autonomy scholars working in other fields have emphasised this point. For instance, in the context of post-natal decision-making, developing meaningful autonomy requires attention to the coercive effects of oppressive social norms.[58] Overall, reproductive autonomy must include respect for women's human rights and an appreciation of the political and legal contexts that shape their options.[59]

Child-custody law therefore needs to look not only to children's best interests and parental rights and responsibilities but also to the normative principles that create the subordinate positions occupied by those who fail or refuse to live in accordance with prevailing norms. For women in custody disputes, resisting prevailing norms may mean not living according to dominant norms of motherhood or failing to live up to demanding norms of post-separation parenting that may overvalue contact between fathers and children. It may also mean escaping relationships that are exploitative or demeaning. An adequate normative framework must enable an understanding of, and account for, how post-separation norms and discourses gloss over the inequalities, economic and otherwise, that complicate parenting relationships. Women must not be prevented from distancing themselves from problematic relationships or from trusting their own judgement about what is best for themselves and their children. This sort of approach 'envisages autonomy from *within* structures of power and authority' and is 'sensitive to structural inequalities and material conditions in the position of women'.[60]

Child-custody norms should not, then, take the form of a decontextualised formal equality between fathers and mothers, with shared parenting as the normatively desired outcome, but should look at the context and lived relations of the family, including patterns of care and responsibility (which may well involve primary caregiving responsibility by mothers), any controlling or abusive conduct and the levels of meaningful engagement with children.[61] As McIntosh has suggested, based on research indicating that it is ill conceived to encourage all parents to 'give shared parenting a try', we need to bring finer distinctions to our inquiries than have typically been drawn concerning shared parenting.[62] Her relational approach would ask questions such as what are the influences of various shared-care climates and patterns on each parent's emotional availability to their children. For instance, the imposition of a rigid shared arrangement might impede parents from adapting arrangements to their children's developmental needs. I would add that the wider social setting should be considered, including the ideology of motherhood, the sexual division of labour and power relations within the family. This wider context would assist in highlighting any gender asymmetries that should be considered when making decisions about appropriate parenting arrangements. In turn, women's autonomy issues may come more sharply into focus even in an area of law that affirms the importance of relationships.

Conclusion

This chapter suggests that women's autonomy interests are problematically compromised in the current climate of normative shared parenting. In determining the rights and responsibilities that adults should have in relation to children, the legal system should rely less on a notion that rights should automatically accompany genetic definitions of parenthood and focus more on relational aspects of parenting. This approach would promote women's relational autonomy, taking account of the broader social context within which they engage in parenting. Judges in family-law contexts typically pride themselves on their ability to distinguish fact situations from one another and to apply flexible norms to these varying situations. They should, then, be well equipped to make the finer distinctions outlined above. Our normative frameworks, accompanied by education about social context, should guide judges in their application of the law by directing them towards significant factors. These would include factors connected to the relationship between the adults and the relationships between the adults and the children, as well as the larger relational social context (gendered division of labour, violence, etc.). To be more explicit, these factors should include past patterns of care and responsibility, including primary caregiving, the type of relationship each parent has with a child, any patterns of domination or any climate of coercion and fear, whether the parents have elected a shared arrangement, degree of geographical proximity between residences, ability of the parents to communicate, confidence in the other parent's parenting competence and the impact of proposed arrangements on a caregiver's ability to be emotionally available and attentive to a child and the child's views and needs.[63] A relational approach would require attention to the potential for healthy, cooperative relationships between the adults themselves and between the adults and children. For mothers who attempt to achieve a degree of autonomy from what they regard as unhealthy relationships, this approach may afford some greater degree of ability to determine the terms under which they parent. If legal norms can emphasise relational autonomy rather than formal equality rights, they may permit more fine-tuned decision-making, which in turn holds more promise for women's autonomy within modern legal approaches to regulating disputes between parents who live apart.

Acknowledgements

This chapter was supported by funding from the Social Sciences and Humanities Research Council of Canada and the UBC Law Class of '68 Award, and benefited from the assistance of Eiad el Fateh (J. D. UBC 2009). A more developed version of the ideas presented in this chapter was published as 'Autonomy for Mothers? Relational Theory and Parenting Apart' in *Feminist Legal Studies* 18(2) (2010): 127–158.

Notes

1 J. Nedelsky, 'Reconceiving Autonomy: Sources, Thoughts and Possibilities', *Yale Journal of Law and Feminism* 1 (1989): 7–36; p. 8.
2 C. McKenzie and N. Stoljar (eds.), *Relational Autonomy: Feminist Perspectives on Autonomy, Agency, and the Social Self* (New York: Oxford University Press, 2000), pp. 5–12.
3 See J. Nedelsky, 'Dilemmas of Passion, Privilege, and Isolation: Reflections on Mothering in a White, Middle-Class Nuclear Family', in J. E. Hanigsberg and S. Ruddick (eds.), *Mother Troubles: Rethinking Contemporary Maternal Dilemmas* (Boston, Mass.: Beacon Press, 1999), pp. 304–34.
4 R. Collier and S. Sheldon, *Fragmenting Fatherhood: A Socio-Legal Study* (Oxford: Hart Publishing, 2008), p. 60.
5 Although this landscape has begun to shift, women still account for 89 per cent of stay-at-home parents in Canada: K. Marshall, 'Converging Gender Roles', *Perspectives on Labour and Income*, 7 (7) (2006): 5–17; p. 11.
6 K. O'Donovan and J. Marshall, 'After Birth: Decisions about Becoming a Mother', in A. Diduck and K. O'Donovan (eds.), *Feminist Perspectives on Family Law* (London and New York: Routledge, 2006), pp. 101–22; p. 103.

266 Susan B. Boyd

7 See, generally, S. B. Boyd (ed.), *Challenging the Public/Private Divide: Feminism, Law, and Public Policy*, Toronto: University of Toronto Press, 1997.

8 O'Donovan and Marshall, 'After Birth', pp. 110–11.

9 E. Jackson and S. D. Sclater, 'Introduction: Autonomy and Private Life', in S. D. Sclater, F. Ebtehaj, E. Jackson and M. Richards (eds.), *Regulating Autonomy: Sex, Reproduction and Family* (Portland, Oreg.: Hart Publishing, 2009), pp. 1–16; p. 2.

10 M. Barrett and M. McIntosh, *The Anti-Social Family* (New York: Verso, 1991); M. Fineman, *The Autonomy Myth: A Theory of Dependency* (New York: New Press, 2004).

11 Fineman, *The Autonomy Myth*, pp. 35–7.

12 C. Ball, 'This Is Not Your Father's Autonomy: Lesbian and Gay Rights from a Feminist and Relational Perspective', *Harvard Journal of Law and Gender* 28 (2) (2005): 345–79; pp. 358–9, drawing on M. Friedman, *Autonomy, Gender, Politics* (Oxford: Oxford University Press, 2003); see also H. Reece, 'Review Article: The Autonomy Myth – A Theory of Dependency', *Child and Family Law Quarterly*, 20 (1) (2008): 109–24.

13 A. Donchin, 'Toward a Gender-Sensitive Assisted Reproduction Policy', *Bioethics*, 23 (1) (2009): 28–38.

14 For example, S. B. Boyd, *Child Custody, Law, and Women's Work* (Ontario: Oxford University Press, 2003); M. A. Fineman, 'Fatherhood, Feminism and Family Law', *McGeorge Law Review*, 32 (4) (2000): 1031–50.

15 But see H. Reece, 'UK Women's Groups' Child Contact Campaign: "So Long As It Is Safe"', *Child and Family Law Quarterly*, 18 (4) (2006): 538–61.

16 D. T. Meyers, 'Gendered Work and Individual Autonomy', in D. T. Meyers, *Being Yourself: Essays on Identity, Action, and Social Life* (Lanham, Md.: Rowman & Littlefield, 2004), p. 257.

17 See H. Rhoades, 'The Dangers of Shared Care Legislation: Why Australia Needs (Yet More) Family Law Reform', *Federal Law Review*, 36 (3) (2008): 279–99.

18 Reece, 'UK Women's Groups' Child Contact Campaign'.

19 See, for example, Collier and Sheldon, *Fragmenting Fatherhood*; Boyd, *Child Custody, Law, and Women's Work*; R. Collier and S. Sheldon (eds.), *Fathers' Rights Activism and Law Reform in Comparative Perspective* (Portland, Oreg.: Hart Publishing, 2006); J. E. Crowley, *Defiant Dads: Fathers' Rights Activists in America* (Ithaca, NY: Cornell University Press, 2008).

20 Statistics Canada, *Women in Canada: A Gender-based Statistical Report*, 5th edn, Catalogue no. 89–503–XIE (Ottawa: Ministry of Industry, 2006), p. 40.

21 H. Rhoades, 'The Rise and Rise of Shared Parenting Laws: A Critical Reflection', *Canadian Journal of Family Law*, 19 (1) (2002): 75–115.

22 B. Fehlberg, C. Millward and M. Campo, 'Shared Post-Separation Parenting in 2009: An Empirical Snapshot', *Australian Journal of Family Law* 23 (3) (2009): 247–75; at p. 263.

23 C. Smart, 'The "New" Parenthood: Fathers and Mothers After Divorce', in E. B. Silva and C. Smart (eds.), *The New Family?* (London: Sage Publications, 1999), pp. 102–14.

24 Collier and Sheldon, *Fragmenting Fatherhood*, p. 117.

25 Crowley, *Defiant Dads*; Boyd, *Child Custody, Law, and Women's Work*; Fehlberg et al., 'Shared Post-Separation Parenting'; Rhoades, 'The Dangers of Shared Care Legislation'.

26 C. Humphreys and C. Harrison, 'Squaring the Circle: Contact and Domestic Violence', *Family Law*, 33 (2003): 419–23; H. Rhoades, 'The "No Contact Mother": Reconstructions of Motherhood in the Era of the "New Father"', *International Journal of Law, Policy and the Family*, 16 (1) (2002): 71–94; F. Kelly, 'Nuclear Norms or Fluid Families? Incorporating Lesbian and Gay Parents and Their Children into Canadian Family Law', *Canadian Journal of Family Law* 21 (1) (2004): 133–78; R. Hertz, *Single by Chance, Mother by Choice: How Women are Choosing Parent Without Marriage and Creating the New American Family* (New York: Oxford University Press, 2006).

27 Collier and Sheldon, *Fathers' Rights Activism*; see also Donchin, 'Toward a Gender-Sensitive Assisted Reproduction Policy'.

28 C. Smart and B. Neale, 'Arguments Against Virtue: Must Contact Be Enforced?', *Family Law*, 27 (5) (1997): 332–3.

29 Rhoades, 'The "No Contact Mother"'.

30 It is very unusual for a father to be penalised for *not* exercising access or relocating, although he might later have trouble claiming custody or access later as a result.

31 D. A. R. Thompson, 'Ten Years After *Gordon*: No Law, Nowhere', *Reports of Family Law*, 35 (6) (2007): 307–31; at pp. 322–3.

32 Fineman, *The Autonomy Myth*, p. 185.

33 S. B. Boyd, 'Backlash Against Feminism: Canadian Custody and Access Reform Debates of the Late Twentieth Century', *Canadian Journal of Women and Law*, 16 (2) (2004): 255–90.

34 For example, in Great Britain, the Human Fertilisation and Embryology Authority (Disclosure of Donor Information) Regulations 2004, SI 2004/1511.

35 Divorce Act, RSC. 1985, (2nd Supp.), c. 3 s. 16 (10); J. Cohen and N. Gershbain, 'For the Sake of the Fathers? Child Custody Reform and the Perils of Maximum Contact', *Canadian Family Law Quarterly*, 19 (1) (2001): 121–83.

36 S. Boyd and C. Young, 'Feminism, Fathers' Rights, and Family Catastrophes: Parliamentary Discourses on Post-Separation Parenting', in D. Chunn, S. Boyd and H. Lessard (eds.), *Reaction and Resistance: Feminism, Law, and Social Change* (Vancouver: UBC Press, 2007), pp. 198–228.

37 Even negotiated or mediated agreements can be agreed to under coercive circumstances: W. Wiegers and M. Keet, 'Collaborative Family Law and Gender Inequalities: Balancing Risks and Opportunities', *Osgoode Hall Law Journal*, 46 (4) (2008): 733–72.

38 Rhoades, 'The Dangers of Shared Care Legislation'.

39 G. Sheehan, J. Dewar and R. Carson, 'Moving On: The Challenge for Children's Contact Services in Australia', in M. Maclean (ed.), *Parenting after Partnering: Containing Conflict After Separation* (Oxford: Hart Publishing, 2007), pp. 147–67.

40 For example, Rhoades, 'The "No Contact Mother"'; Cohen and Gershbain, 'For the Sake of the Fathers?'.

41 M. Shaffer, 'Joint Custody, Parental Conflict and Children's Adjustment to Divorce: What the Social Science Literature Does and Does Not Tell Us', *Canadian Family Law Quarterly*, 26 (3) (2007): 285–313; p. 287. (Emphasis added.)

42 P. R. Amato and J. G. Gilbreth, 'Nonresident Fathers and Children's Well-Being: A Meta Analysis', *Journal of Marriage and the Family*, 61 (3) (1999): 557–73.

43 C. Smart, B. Neale and A. Wade, *The Changing Experiences of Childhood: Families and Divorce* (Malden, Mass.: Polity Press and Blackwell Publishers, 2001).

44 J. E. McIntosh and R. Chisholm, 'Cautionary Notes on the Shared Care of Children in Conflicted Parental Separations', *Journal of Family Studies*, 14 (1) (2008): 37–52; Rhoades, 'The Dangers of Shared Care Legislation', p. 280.

45 J. E. McIntosh, 'Legislating for Shared Parenting: Exploring Some Underlying Assumptions', *Family Court Review*, 47 (3) (2009): 389–400; p. 397.

46 Ibid., pp. 391, 393.

47 L. Cardia-Vonèche and B. Bastard, 'Why Some Children See Their Father and Others Do Not; Questions Arising from a Pilot Study', in M. Maclean (ed.), *Parenting after Partnering: Containing Conflict After Separation* (Oxford: Hart Publishing, 2007), pp. 29–39. See also C. Smart and B. Neale, *Family Fragments* (Cambridge: Polity Press, 1999).

48 For example, Nedelsky, 'Dilemmas of Passion'. See also McKenzie and Stoljar, *Relational Autonomy*.

49 R. Leckey, *Contextual Subjects: Family, State, and Relational Theory* (Toronto: University of Toronto Press, 2008), p. 3.

50 Ibid., pp. 20–1.
51 Jackson and Sclater, 'Introduction: Autonomy and Private Life', p. 6.
52 M. Maclean and J. Eekelaar, 'Legal Representation and Parental Autonomy', in S. D. Sclater et al. (eds.), *Regulating Autonomy: Sex, Reproduction and Family* (Portland, Oreg.: Hart Publishing, 2009), pp. 93–107; p. 93.
53 Ibid., p. 96.
54 See, for example, B. Batagol, 'Fomenters of Strife, Gladiatorial Champions or Something Else Entirely? Lawyers and Family Dispute Resolution', *Queensland University of Technology Law and Justice Journal*, 8 (1) (2008): 24–45.
55 See S. Goering '*Postnatal* Reproductive Autonomy: Promoting Relational Autonomy and Self-Trust in New Parents', *Bioethics*, 23 (1) (2009): 9–19.
56 Leckey, *Contextual Subjects*, p. 81.
57 Ibid., p. 268.
58 Goering, '*Postnatal* Reproductive Autonomy'.
59 Donchin, 'Toward a Gender-Sensitive Assisted Reproduction Policy'. See Rachel Anne Fenton, D. Jane V. Rees and Sue Heenan, Chapter 18.
60 Donchin, 'Toward a Gender-Sensitive Assisted Reproduction Policy', p. 38.
61 Smart and Neale, *Family Fragments*, make similar recommendations, drawing on a feminist ethic of care, pp. 192–7.
62 McIntosh, 'Legislating for Shared Parenting', p. 397, quoting B. Smyth, 'A 5-Year Retrospective of Post-Separation Shared Care Research in Australia', *Journal of Family Studies*, 15 (1) (2009): 36–59.
63 This draws on Smart and Neale, *Family Fragments*, pp. 192–7 and McIntosh, 'Legislating for Shared Parenting'.

Part VI

Relationships, law and sex

Chapter 20

A very British compromise?
Civil partnerships, liberalism by stealth and the fallacies of neo-liberalism

Jeffrey Weeks

Introduction: the significance of civil partnerships

Since Denmark led the way in 1989, the idea of legalising same-sex unions or marriage has moved from the realm of the unthinkable to the terrain of the possible, if not yet the inevitable. It has become a touchstone issue concerning the state of our culture. Since the 1980s, controversy has raged in the USA about same-sex marriage and related issues over parenting, reflecting a deep national fissure and the continuation of the culture wars that have been burning since the 1970s.[1] Other jurisdictions from Canada to Argentina, South Africa and most of Western Europe have more or less willingly implemented domestic-partnership arrangements, registered civil unions and, in a number of cases, marriage, though not without fierce local oppositions.[2] Each country has taken its own path, reflecting its own cultural bias and political balance.[3]

The Pacs legislation in France (1999), for instance, followed classic republican traditions by refusing to recognise the separate cultural identities of lesbians and gays.[4] It allowed civil-partnership arrangements for heterosexuals and homosexuals alike and was clearly distinguished from marriage, the legal status of which was not affected: the partners remained individualised, no new legal entity was created, and no challenge was offered to the permanence of sexual difference or rights of inheritance. The legislation was opposed by conservatives of left and right but has bedded down as a normalised and widely accepted reform, favoured by heterosexuals as much as by non-heterosexuals.[5] In the Netherlands, radical changes came about through what Waaldijk called the 'law of small changes', an incrementalism that fitted in easily with the tradition of pillarisation that assumed the coexistence of different rights claims and was committed to recognising them.[6] The legalisation of same-sex civil partnerships and then of marriage in the early 2000s therefore seems a logical next step in the Netherlands' famous liberalism – though it characteristically did not lack critics who felt that same-sex marriage represented merely a sexual settlement that normalised conservative norms.[7] In Spain, same-sex marriage was enacted by a socialist government in 2005, in the face of fierce opposition from the Roman Catholic Church. In Portugal, on the other hand, same-sex marriage came in 2010 with little political opposition. In South Africa, same-sex marriage followed on the adoption of a radically egalitarian new constitution.[8]

Precisely because it touches on such a traditionally key subject as marriage, and behind that the complex patterns of family law, kin, the rearing of children and the transmission of property, the debate over same-sex relationships has a way of illuminating the social in a dazzling way. It casts light not only on the legacies of the past and the confusions of the present but also on the possibilities for the future. The experience of the UK is especially revealing. For a long time, it was classically hesitant in pursuing the legalisation of same-sex partnerships – or indeed any liberalisation of attitudes towards homosexuality.[9] Yet within a very short period at the beginning of the new millennium a series of legal reforms belatedly modernised British sexual law, culminating in the Civil Partnership Act 2004, which established a marriage-like framework for same-sex couples. When, a year later, civil partnerships were finally launched with a flurry of media coverage and little hostility, it seemed an inevitable, almost uncontroversial, move. From having, notoriously, the most authoritarian legal regulation and moral censure of sexual unorthodoxy in the Western world in the 1950s, by 2005 Britain had amongst the most liberal laws and attitudes in what has become one of the most secular and tolerant of countries.[10]

The introduction of civil partnerships is significant for what it tells us about the changing nature of our society and, in particular, the shift in patterns of intimate life. We can certainly see continuities with Britain's cultural traditions, not least in the absence of fervent ideological debate, and the pragmatic manner in which reform was enacted. But we can also see the shape of a post-traditional society bursting to be born. The changing relationship of non-heterosexual peoples to the wider culture and to themselves illustrates this acutely.

Drawing the lines

Logic would usually suggest that de-heterosexualising marriage by promoting same-sex unions/marriages is a potentially transgressive and subversive assault on its heteronormativity, an undermining of its cornerstone role and a destabilising of the hetero–homo binary that constitutes the gendered and sexual order. That is clearly what the conservative movements assume and why they are so violently hostile to same-sex marriage.[11] But the queer critiques of same-sex marriage, particularly strong in the USA, in effect argue that marriage can never be free of its heterosexual assumptions. Brandzel has argued that 'marriage is a mechanism by which the state ensures and reproduces heteronormativity, and absorbing certain types of gay and lesbian relationships will only further this process'.[12] Marriage, Warner writes, 'sanctifies some couples at the expense of others. It is selective legitimacy.'[13] This is why social conservatives and queer theorists can both oppose it: conservatives because it confers legitimacy on the illegitimate and normalises the abnormal; radicals because it elevates one type of same-sex relationships over others – it normalises a particular type of couple relationship and undermines the subversive and transgressive possibilities that sexual radicalism implies.[14]

For radical critics, marriage is at the apex of a hierarchy that marginalises single people, lesbians and gay men generally and also marginalises the complex forms of friendship and intimacy that have emerged in lesbian and gay communities.[15] The potentiality for different types of relationships offered by the 'friendship ethic' that underpins and sustains much of lesbian, gay, bisexual and transgender (LGBT) life is threatened by this apparent reversion to normalising couple relationships.[16] The formalisation of same-sex unions, it is argued, is based on an exclusive notion of love, which is still locked into ideas of possession and wrapped in violence. And it channels sexuality into forms of monogamy and lifetime commitment which the sexual transformations of the 1960s and 1970s sought to undermine, 'marriage comes with a baggage that is difficult to wrestle free from'.[17]

Such views are deeply rooted in the LGBT community and continue to have some resonance even several years after the successful implementation of the Civil Partnership Act.[18] But there were good historical reasons for strong latent support amongst lesbians and gays for stronger recognition of same-sex relationships. Two experiences, particularly since the 1970s, had dramatised the disadvantages of their legal standing. The first was the absence of parenting rights, especially amongst lesbians who had formerly been in heterosexual marriages, which led to a long-lasting and difficult campaign for the rights of lesbian mothers.[19] The second was the experience of the HIV/AIDS epidemic, especially amongst gay men, where there was a multitude of personal experiences of partners of people living with AIDS being denied anything remotely like partnership rights.[20] Both experiences underlined the denial of full citizenship to lesbian and gay people.[21] Yet, while there was a widespread belief amongst non-heterosexual people that they had as much right to marriage as heterosexuals, and most people wanted some form of legal recognition for lesbian and gay relationships on grounds of equal citizenship, that did not necessarily mean that they themselves intended to seize the opportunity.

The major reason for this was a strong sense that lesbian and gay relationships had genuine strengths and possibilities. Most of the self-defined LGBT people interviewed in *Same Sex Intimacies* believed that they had unique opportunities to lead more egalitarian lives than their heterosexual fellow citizens, precisely because they were excluded from the gendered and hierarchical relationships that traditional marriage represented.[22] They are, as Adam puts it in his study of relationship innovation in male gay couples, 'condemned to freedom' in the absence of strong traditional guidelines about how to live partnerships.[23] The evolving norms, rooted in the necessity of living lives against the grain, are based on the assumption of equality, disclosure and negotiation. Differences and divisions do of course survive: there are inequalities of income, power, opportunity, even of class, age and ethnicity, but the ethos is based on relationships of autonomy and choice, unconstrained by external rules.[24] For Giddens, lesbian and gay relationships, based on confluent love and freed of traditional bonds, were models for the development of the 'pure relationship'.[25] The pure relationship was a relationship based on honesty, trust and full disclosure to the other, which would survive only as long as both partners felt committed to it and was part of the logic of late modern patterns of intimacy. What was a matter of necessity in an era of oppressive legal codes and endemic prejudice has become normative within the gay community itself in more liberal times and a model for heterosexual society.

Given this background, it is not surprising that LGBT people on the whole were long sceptical about the merits of same-sex marriage or legalised partnerships in so far as they replicate traditional marriage. The sort of conservative justification for same-sex marriage put forward by Sullivan and similar gay conservatives, that it will mark the full integration of lesbians and gays into conventional society, does not seem to have been echoed in British research.[26] An online survey of mainly LGBT people drawn from twenty-seven countries, reporting in 2006, found strong support for equal rights, and for same-sex marriage on these grounds.[27] A smaller qualitative study at the same time found attitudes towards marriage 'more messy' than the debates tend to assume.[28] Instead, we find an interesting duality. On the one hand, there was a conscious desire for formal equality with the heterosexual majority in the whole range of citizenship rights, from benefit entitlements to care responsibilities, up to and including marriage. On the other hand, there was a widespread reluctance to simply 'mimic' straight society.[29]

Although there had been little popular pressure for change when, in December 2005, it finally became possible in Britain for same-sex couples to legally confirm their relationships under the Civil Partnership Act, same-sex couples appeared to welcome it with open arms, and there was an early rush to local registry offices.[30] Though carefully not officially deemed same-sex marriage, the legislation was deliberately framed by the Labour Government in parallel terms to heterosexual civil marriage. The only significant differences, ironically, given the obsessive cultural tradition of defining LGBT people solely by their sexuality, concerned the absence of sex: unlike heterosexual marriage, sexual consummation was not required to complete the partnership, and adultery could not provide evidence for the dissolution of the union. Many in the gay community ignored these subtle distinctions, decided to call it marriage right away and took up the offer with enthusiasm.[31] During the first nine months, over 30,000 lesbians and gays took advantage of the new legislation, with, initially, twice as many men entering civil partnerships as women, a pattern that was common in most jurisdictions.[32]

Towards equality

The Civil Partnership Act was part of a radical series of legislative changes that signified the formal move to homosexual equality: an equal age of consent, equality in the armed services and in relation to immigration, the repeal of repressive legislation directed specifically at lesbians and gays (such as Section 28 of the Local Government Act 1988 and the offence of 'gross indecency'), equality in relation to adoption and employment protection, in the delivery of goods and services, as well as the granting of new rights to transgendered people through the passing of the Gender Recognition Act 2004.[33] This was an unprecedented series of reforming changes, the most significant since the 1960s and probably the most decisive shift of sexual regulation in modern British history. The goal of equality between heterosexuals and gay people had been signalled by Tony Blair as long ago as 1994, before he became prime minister, but did not feature prominently in the early years of the post-1997 Labour Government.[34] This was liberalism by stealth rather than confrontation. Yet the changes were potentially very radical and constitute some of the most important achievements of the Blair Government.

The Civil Partnership Act went significantly further than had been signalled in the earlier consultation. Ministers had consistently reiterated that the Government was not endorsing same-sex marriage. In part, this was obviously a way of avoiding the divisive debates seen in the USA which had threatened at one stage to block parliamentary progress in the UK. From this point of view, the introduction of civil partnerships can be seen as a characteristically pragmatic way of adjusting to changing social realities without abandoning traditional forms and without arousing too much political hostility: a very British compromise. Although conservative religious organisations and pro-family groups voiced strong opposition, they were by now very much minority voices, and the legislation eventually had cross-party support as it went through Parliament. What especially diminished religious opposition was that what seemed to be on offer was a marriage-like arrangement separate from but parallel to civil marriage. As a further concession, unlike civil marriages, civil partnerships were specifically forbidden to be held in churches.

From another perspective, the introduction of civil partnerships can be seen as part of the Europeanisation of British social legislation and the anticipated outcome of the introduction of a European-style Human Rights Act.[35] The Government had already been pressured by the European courts to concede various forms of equality, regarding spousal rights in housing, pensions and the like, and there was a clear logic in going further.[36] In one area, however, Britain went beyond European norms. The area of consistent conservatism across Europe has been less concerned with sexual relationships than with parenting. At first, legislation in EU countries explicitly excluded equal adoption and fostering rights. Indeed, until 2005, even Belgium's granting of same-sex marriage excluded these. Children and childcare remained a last taboo. With the passage of the Adoption and Children Act 2002, Britain suddenly leapt ahead. This suggests that the pragmatism displayed in the implementation of the new policy was underpinned by a developing set of values about parenting and relationships, whether they were heterosexual or non-heterosexual.

The pragmatism behind the British legislation obscured an ideological colouring that fitted into the residual communitarian commitments that underpinned the Government's social philosophy.[37] From this perspective, the granting of strong guaranteed rights and agreed responsibilities to same-sex couples who entered legal partnerships fulfilled communitarian principles about building stable relationships (which up to this point in the wider debate initiated by Etzioni and his followers had signally ignored same-sex relationships) while not immediately undermining the legal status of marriage. Diversity in relationships was no longer seen as a problem, but instability in relationships was. This has led some commentators to emphasise civil partnership and same-sex marriage as involving a new form of regulation, which produces new types of subjects: the legalised and legitimised couple.[38] Butler has critically remarked on the dangers of the 'normalizing powers of the state' defining same-sex marriage as the only right and proper way for lesbians and gays to commit to relationships, and there is no doubt that the civil partnership and related legislation carries with it the danger of separating off the respectable gay from the unrespectable, the stable couple from the promiscuous, and of imprinting new normativities onto the gay community.[39] There is no doubt that the Blair Government was anxious to support some patterns of relationships over others. However, its ultimate preoccupations were not about stigmatising relationships that it disliked – its general tone in relationship to consensual activities, whether heterosexual or same-sex, was broadly permissive – but about supporting types of relationship that worked. Williams has argued that 'a new normative family is emergent, which … revolves around the adult couple whose relationship is based on their parenting responsibilities, and whose priorities are rooted in work, economic self-sufficiency, education and good behaviour'.[40] It is easy to see how this model could fit in closely with simultaneously supporting strong gay relationships, especially as they embrace parenting experiences. However, we must be careful not to try to fit everything together too neatly into a preordained explanatory framework. It is tempting for radical critics of initiatives such as civil partnerships to attempt to place them within the frameworks with which they are familiar: we live in a neo-liberal climate; the Labour Government supported neo-liberal economic reforms; therefore, civil partnerships must be a manifestation of neo-liberal sexual governance. Civil partnerships may indeed express values which are complementary to a form of neo-liberalism, but they are also rooted in a form of communitarianism and, beyond that, in an older social democratic tradition.[41] Values of reciprocity and strong communities underpin these developments as much as neo-liberal rationalism does.

It is even more difficult to agree with those critics who have argued that new citizenship claims, including same-sex marriage, are complicit with neo-liberal strategies when looked at from a wider international perspective.[42] The USA, the most neo-liberal of states, has been, on an official level, the most hostile of all Western nations to same-sex citizenship rights, while the European country most hostile to globalisation and to Americanisation, France, has pioneered partnership rights, via Pacs, but is similarly reluctant to go down the road of same-sex marriage, though for different reasons.[43] The legalisation of same-sex relationships as a process has many roots in different late-modern societies and cannot be reduced to an adjunct of wider socio-economic processes. Too much energy has been spent by activists in campaigning for sexual change to justify such a deterministic position. Richardson makes the point that though many contemporary campaigns for lesbian and gay citizenship rights may seem to mimic the cautious homophile movements of the 1950s and 1960s in seeking acceptance into existing value structures, their real purpose is elsewhere.[44] Their focus is no longer on demanding the right to exist in private, 'where the boundaries of private are marked by the limits of tolerance, but on the right to public recognition *and* the right to privacy'. Far from creating new types of relationships as an imposed norm, the new legislation confirmed existing relationships. As Shipman and Smart show, most people seeking legal recognition were already in stable partnerships with shared obligations and mutual responsibilities.[45]

Why marry?

Governments and legislators may seek to develop and shape new normative frameworks, but there can never be a one-to-one fit between intention and effect, and the unintended effects of state action are usually more potent than the intended in relation to sexual and intimate life. This is why governments are usually reluctant to do anything that looks too obviously like moral engineering. The future of civil partnerships and same sex-marriage will depend ultimately on how the subjects of these policies respond.

All the evidence suggests that thus far they have responded positively. Despite all the earlier hesitations when the opportunity arose, people rapidly lost their inhibitions. In practice, new meanings and realties are being created as LGBT people have formulated their own norms of acceptable behaviour and articulated their rationales and motivations for seeking legal recognition of partnerships. Three forms of legitimisation are common, which we can broadly label rights, commitment and recognition.

The rights agenda resonates with the larger claims to full equality that is the prime motivation of LGBT activism. We have already seen the range of arguments that lesbians and gays have put forward, amounting to a claim for equal justice and full sexual citizenship.[46] The recognition of rights and entitlements implies simultaneous parallel responsibilities. Civil partnerships have implications for social-security benefits, and pensions, such as the circumstances in which a civil-partnership union would be treated as a couple for assessment purposes. This now applies even to couples who have not contracted a civil partnership in the same way as it does to non-married heterosexual couples. There are also implications for joint parenting, and mutual care in health. So the responsibilities are real and ongoing. Civil partnerships did not invent new rights; by and large, they transferred existing individual entitlements to the couple. And, in a welfare society such as the UK, some of the passion behind the campaign for same-sex marriage experienced elsewhere was weaker precisely because of these pre-existing entitlements. For example, the claim that marriage was important for securing spousal health-care protection, which Butler felt to be important in the USA, diminished in a society which took for granted free health care for all.[47] Nevertheless, the new entitlements were considerable and provided a very material motivation to enter a civil partnership.

Important as the rights and accompanying responsibilities were, the underlying motivation is often more abstract, reflecting, above all, the desire to signify commitment.[48] Long before civil partnerships seemed likely, gay couples had been finding various ways of marking commitment: from the exchange of rings and gifts, celebrating significant events such as date of first meeting or first sex, birthdays or Christmas, to participating in full-scale commitment ceremonies.[49] 'We see the act of celebrating a same-sex union in the absence of legal recognition as an opportunity to create symbolic transformation', write Liddle and Liddle.[50] That symbolic transformation is a way of claiming legitimacy for the relationship and in changing individual attitudes, but clearly for many couples the symbolism has even deeper resonances. The lesbian and gay Christians who supported same-sex marriage in Yip's research saw their partnership in religious terms as a symbolic confirmation, or covenant before God, of commitment and love.[51] But even for those of an ardently secular disposition, the affirmation of commitment was a critical moment. For many, a civil partnership did involve a firm commitment to traditional monogamy, 'forsaking all others'. For others, however, the really important commitments were emotional, with sexual monogamy a matter of negotiation rather than prescription.[52]

Beck and Beck-Gernsheim argue that, in the new era of choice, love becomes an essential integrating glue: 'For individuals who have to invent or find their own social settings, love becomes the central pivot giving meaning to their lives.'[53] As my co-authors and I noted in *Same Sex Intimacies*, British lesbians and gays seem to be less open than, for example, their American sisters and brothers, in using the language of love as a legitimising or authenticising value.[54] But though ideas of eternal, romantic love tend to be absent from narratives of relationships, a quieter version is implicit. In its broadest sense, it embraces a range of emotions, including care, responsibility, respect and mutual knowledge – 'mutual recognition between equal subjects, and an awareness of the necessity, yet delicacy, of reciprocal relationships'.[55] We can compare this with Giddens' notion of confluent love, as an 'active, contingent love' that jars with eternal, once-and-for-all notions of love but is also without the highly gendered and power-ridden implications of high romance.

Conclusion

Affirming commitment and love in the civil partnership is usually an intensely private experience – often those who enter a civil partnership hold a very private ceremony, sometimes with the barest minimum of formal activity above signing the register.[56] But it has a necessary public resonance, which in the end is the real purpose of the event: public recognition of a private transaction but also public recognition of LGBT citizenship. The stories of same-sex unions suggest very clearly the importance of public affirmation. For some it is like 'a second coming out' – not simply a declaration of one's gayness, but an affirmation of one's most intimate commitments, and for some, this was as challenging as the first moves out of the closet.[57] Here, getting married is a 'fateful moment' that disorders previous life narratives and requires new scripts, a reshaped life story and new possibilities.[58]

Recognition by families and friends is one thing. But recognition has a wider resonance, as Taylor especially has discussed in the context of a multicultural society.[59] The denial of legal rights for same-sex unions can be seen, in Fraser's famous phrase, as one of the 'injustices of recognition' that mark contemporary society.[60] The bringing of LGBT people into full citizenship is therefore not a trivial act. In the end, if it is to mean anything, it must also entail confronting the forces that have inhibited full recognition. The goal of legitimising civil partnerships or same-sex marriages, I suggest, is better seen as a form of struggle for recognition than a ruse of power. Such unions are, of course, legally binding commitments, and, inevitably, that must have an implication on wider norms and values. Whether the impact of this is, in Yep et al.'s categorisation, assimilationist or radical will depend ultimately on the degree to which the practice of same-sex unions can transform both the normative meanings of marriage and the everyday practices of LGBT people themselves.[61] But within a very short time in the LGBT community within the UK, as elsewhere, legally recognised same-sex relationships are becoming rapidly routinised as one option amongst others – not the only or necessary choice, but a new possibility among many.

Notes

1 See A. Sullivan (ed.), *Same-Sex Marriage: Pro and Con. A Reader* (New York: Vintage Books, 1997); D. M. Estlund and M. C. Nussbaum (eds.), *Sex, Preference and Family: Essays on Law and Nature* (Oxford: Oxford University Press, 1997); E. Fassin, 'Same Sex, Different Politics: "Gay Marriage" Debates in France and the United States', *Public Culture*, 13 (2) (2001): 215–32; S. Cahill, '"Welfare Moms and the Two Grooms": The Concurrent Promotion and Destruction of Marriage in US Public Policy', *Sexualities*, 8 (2) (2006): 169–89; P. Kandaswamy, 'State Austerity and the Racial Politics of Same-Sex Marriage in the United States', *Sexualities*, 11 (6) (2008): 706–25; 'Gay Marriage: Courtroom Drama', *The Economist*, 16–22 January 2010, pp. 41–2.

2 R. Wintermute and M. Andenaes (eds.), *Legal Recognition of Same-Sex Partnerships: A Study of National, European and International Law* (Oxford and Portland, Oreg.: Hart Publishing, 2001); Y. Merin, *Equality for Same Sex Couples* (Chicago, Ill.: Chicago University Press, 2002); E. Bonthuys, 'Possibilities Foreclosed: The Civil Union Act and Lesbian and Gay Identity in Southern Africa', *Sexualities*, 11 (6) (2008): 726–39; M. Banens and R. Mendès-Leite, 'Nouvelles Visibilités, nouvelles discriminations? Report à l'adresse du ministère de L'Emploi, de la cohésion sociale et du logement

et du ministère de la santé et des solidarités', unpublished document, University of Lyon, 2008.

3 K. Waaldijk, 'Towards the Recognition of Same-Sex Partners in European Union Law: Expectations Based on Trends in National Law', in R. Wintermute and M. Andenaes (eds.), *Legal Recognition of Same-Sex Partnerships: A Study of National, European and International Law* (Oxford and Portland, Oreg.: Hart Publishing, 2001), pp. 635–52.

4 Fassin, 'Same Sex, Different Politics'; E. Fassin, *L'Inversion de la question homosexuelle* (Paris: Éditions Amsterdam, 2005).

5 Fassin, 'Same Sex, Different Politics'. See also C. Velu, 'Faut-il "pactiser" avec l'universalisme? A short history of the PACS', *Modern and Contemporary France*, 7 (4) (1999): 429–42; D. Borrillo, 'The *"Pacte Civil de Solidarité"* in France: Midway Between Marriage and Cohabitation', in R. Wintermute and M. Andenaes (eds.), *Legal Recognition of Same-Sex Partnerships: A Study of National, European and International Law* (Oxford and Portland, Oreg.: Hart Publishing, 2001), pp. 475–92; C. Johnston, 'The PACS and (Post)queer Citizenship in Contemporary Republican France', *Sexualities*, 11 (6) (2008): 688–705.

6 K. Waaldijk, 'Small Change: How the Road to Same-Sex Marriage Got Paved in the Netherlands', in R. Wintermute and M. Andenaes (eds.), *Legal Recognition of Same-Sex Partnerships: A Study of National, European and International Law* (Oxford and Portland, Oreg.: Hart Publishing, 2001), pp. 437–64, at p. 440.

7 G. Hekma, 'How Libertine is the Netherlands? Exploring Contemporary Dutch Sexual Cultures', in E. Bernstein and L. Schaffner (eds.), *Regulating Sex: The Politics of Intimacy and Identity* (London and New York: Routledge, 2005), pp. 209–24; p. 220.

8 Bonthuys, 'Possibilities Foreclosed', pp. 726–7. See Elsje Bonthuys and Natasha Erlank, Chapter 21.

9 R. Bailey-Harris, 'Same Sex Partnership in English Family Law', in R. Wintermute and M. Andenaes (eds.), *Legal Recognition of Same-Sex Partnerships: A Study of National, European and International Law* (Oxford and Portland, Oreg.: Hart Publishing, 2001), pp. 605–22.

10 J. Weeks, *The World We Have Won: The Remaking of Erotic and Intimate Life* (London and New York: Routledge, 2007), pp. 1–22, 167–98.

11 Fassin, 'Same Sex, Different Politics'.

12 A. L. Brandzel, 'Queering Citizenship? Same-Sex Marriage and the State', *GLQ: A Journal of Lesbian and Gay Studies*, 11 (2) (2005): 171–204, at p. 195.

13 M. Warner, *The Trouble with Normal: Sex, Politics and the Ethics of Queer Life* (New York: The Free Press, 1999), p. 82.

14 See discussion in P. A. Robinson, *Queer Wars: The New Gay Right and its Critics* (Chicago, Ill.: University of Chicago Press, 2005); E. D. Rothblum, 'Same-Sex Marriage and Legalized Relationships: I Do, or Do I?', *Journal of GLBT Family Studies*, 1 (1) (2005): 21–31.

15 C. Donovan, 'Why Reach for the Moon? Because the Stars Aren't Enough', *Feminism and Psychology*, 14 (1) (2004): 24–9, at p. 27.

16 K. Weston, *Families We Choose: Lesbians, Gays, Kinship* (New York: Columbia University Press, 1991); P. Nardi, *Gay Men's Friendships: Invincible Communities* (Chicago, Ill.: Chicago University Press, 1999); J. Weeks, B. Heaphy and C. Donovan, *Same Sex Intimacies: Families of Choice and other Life Experiments* (London and New York: Routledge, 2001), pp. 17–19.

17 Donovan, 'Why Reach for the Moon?', p. 27.

18 Weeks et al., *Same Sex Intimacies*, pp. 187–8; M. Mitchell, S. Dickens and W. O'Connor, *Same-Sex Couples and the Impact of Legislative Changes*, Report prepared for ESRC (London: National Centre for Social Research, 2009); E. Peel, 'Civil Partnership: Exploring the Meanings of Commitment, Ritual and Recognition for Same-Sex Couples', unpublished document, Aston University, UK, 2009.

19 G. Hanscombe and J. Forster, *Rocking the Cradle: Lesbian Mothers – A Challenge in Family Living* (London: Sheba Feminist Publishers, 1983); L. Harne and Rights of Women, *Valued Families: The Lesbian Mothers' Legal Handbook* (London: Women's Press, 1997); see also E. Lewin, *Lesbian Mothers: Accounts of Gender in American Culture* (Ithaca, NY: Cornell University Press, 1993); K. Griffin and L. Mulholland (eds.), *Lesbian Mothers in Europe* (London: Cassell, 1997); J. Stacey, 'Gay Parenthood and the Decline of Paternity as We Knew It', *Sexualities*, 9 (1) (2006): 27–53. See Rachel Anne Fenton, D. Jane V. Rees and Sue Heenan, Chapter 18.

20 B. Heaphy, C. Donovan and J. Weeks, 'A Different Affair? Openness and Non-monogamy in Same Sex Relationships', in J. Duncombe, K. Harrison, G. Allan and D. Marsden (eds.), *The State of Affairs: Explorations in Infidelity and Commitment* (Mahwah, NJ: Lawrence Erlbaum Associates, 2004), pp. 167–84; Weeks et al., *Same Sex Intimacies*, pp. 17–19; Weston, *Families We Choose*.

21 S. Watney, *Practices of Freedom: Selected Writings on HIV/AIDS* (London: Rivers Oram Press, 1994), pp. 159–68.

22 Weeks et al., *Same Sex Intimacies*, Chapter 5.

23 B. D. Adam, 'Relationship Innovation in Male Couples', *Sexualities*, 9 (1) (2006): 5–26, at p. 6.

24 Weeks et al., *Same Sex Intimacies*, pp. 109–13.

25 A. Giddens, *The Transformation of Intimacy: Sexuality, Love and Eroticism in Modern Societies* (Cambridge: Polity Press, 1992).

26 A. Sullivan, *Virtually Normal: An Argument about Homosexuality* (London: Picador, 1995). Discussed in Robinson, *Queer Wars*, 2005.

27 R. Harding, and L. Peel, '"We Do"? International Perspectives on Equality, Legality and Same-Sex Relationships', *Lesbian and Gay Psychology Review*, 7 (2) (2006): 123–40.

28 V. Clarke, C. Burgoyne and M. Burns, 'Just a Piece of Paper? A Qualitative Exploration of Same Sex Couples' Multiple Conceptions of Civil Partnership and Marriage', *Lesbian and Gay Psychology Review*, 7 (2) (2006): 141–61, at p. 155.

29 Weeks et al., *Same Sex Intimacies*, p. 193.

30 See B. Shipman and C. Smart, '"It's Made a Huge Difference": Recognition, Rights and the Personal Significance of Civil Partnership', *Sociological Research Online*, 12 (1) (2007). Available online at http://www.socresonline.org.uk/12/1shipman.html (accessed 2 March 2009).

31 Weeks, *The World We Have Won*, p. 188.

32 P. Curtis, 'Twice as Many Men as Women Start Civil Partnerships', *The Guardian*, 23 February 2006, p. 14.

33 Weeks, *The World We Have Won*, pp. 188–9.

34 J. Weeks, 'Labour's Loves Lost? The Legacies of Moral Conservatism and Sex Reform', in D. L. Steinberg, and R. Johnson (eds.), *Blairism and the War of Persuasion: Labour's Passive Revolution* (London: Lawrence & Wishart, 2004), pp. 66–80.

35 See Waaldijk, 'Towards the Recognition of Same-Sex Partners'.

36 M. Bell, 'Sexual Orientation and Anti-discrimination Policy: The European Community', in T. Carver and V. Mottier (eds.), *Politics of Sexuality: Identity, Gender, Citizenship* (London and New York: Routledge, 1998), pp. 58–67.

37 A. Etzioni, *The Spirit of Community: Rights, Responsibilities and the Communitarian Agenda* (London: Fontana, 1995).

38 J. Halley, 'Recognition, Rights, Regulation, Normalisation: Rhetorics of Justification in the Same-Sex Marriage Debate', in R. Wintermute and M. Andenaes (eds.), *Legal Recognition of Same-Sex Partnerships: A Study of National, European and International Law* (Oxford and Portland, Oreg.: Hart Publishing, 2001), pp. 97–112, 108–11. See discussion in Mitchell et al., *Same-Sex Couples*, pp. 75–97.

39 J. Butler, *Undoing Gender* (London and New York: Routledge, 2004), p. 104.

40 F. Williams, *Rethinking Families*, ESRC CAVA Research Group (London: Calouste Gulbenkian Foundation, 2004), p. 244.
41 Weeks, *The World We Have Won*, pp. 192–3.
42 See D. Richardson, 'Locating Sexualities: From Here to Normality', *Sexualities*, 7 (4) (2004): 391–411.
43 Fassin, 'Same Sex, Different Politics'; Fassin, *L'Inversion de la question*.
44 Richardson, 'Locating Sexualities', p. 405.
45 Shipman and Smart, 'It's Made a Huge Difference'.
46 K. Plummer, *Telling Sexual Stories: Power, Change and Social Worlds* (London and New York: Routledge, 1995); K. Plummer, *Intimate Citizenship: Private Decisions and Public Dialogues* (Seattle, Wash.: University of Washington Press, 2003).
47 Butler, *Undoing Gender*, p. 109.
48 Compare J. Lewis, *The End of Marriage? Individualism and Intimate Relations* (Cheltenham and Northampton, Mass.: Edward Elgar, 2001), pp. 124ff.
49 Weeks et al., *Same Sex Intimacies*, pp. 127–32, E. Lewin, *Recognizing Ourselves: Ceremonies of Lesbian and Gay Commitment* (New York: Columbia University Press, 1998).
50 K. Liddle and B. J. Liddle, 'In the Meantime: Same-Sex Ceremonies in the Absence of Legal Recognition', *Feminism and Psychology*, 14 (1) (2004): 52–6, at p. 53.
51 A. Yip, 'Same-Sex Marriage: Contrasting Perspectives among Lesbian, Gay and Bisexual Christians', *Feminism and Psychology*, 14 (1) (2004): 173–80, at p. 177.
52 Heaphy et al., 'A Different Affair?', pp. 173–7.
53 U. Beck and E. Beck-Gernsheim, *The Normal Chaos of Love* (Cambridge: Polity Press, 1995), pp. 1–2, 170.
54 Weeks et al., *Same Sex Intimacies*, pp. 70–1. Compare Lewin, *Recognizing Ourselves*, Chapter 6.
55 Weeks et al., *Same Sex Intimacies*, p. 124; see also J. Weeks, *Invented Moralities: Sexual Values in an Age of Uncertainty* (Cambridge: Polity Press, 1995).
56 Shipman and Smart, 'It's Made a Huge Difference'; Weeks, *The World We Have Won*, p. 197.
57 Weeks, *The World We Have Won*; Shipman and Smart, 'It's Made a Huge Difference'.
58 A. Giddens, *Modernity and Self-Identity* (Cambridge: Polity Press, 1991), p. 113.
59 C. Taylor, *Multiculturalism and the Politics of Recognition*, ed. Amy Gutmann (Princeton, NJ: Princeton University Press, 1992); C. Taylor, *The Ethics of Authenticity* (Cambridge, Mass.: Harvard University Press, 1992); see also Plummer, *Intimate Citizenship*, p. 111.
60 N. Fraser, *Justice Interruptus: Critical Reflections on the Postsocialist Condition* (London and New York: Routledge, 1997); see L. Adkins, *Revisions: Gender and Sexuality in Late Modernity* (Buckingham: Open University Press, 2002), p. 27.
61 G. A. Yep, K. E. Lovanas and J. P. Elia, 'A Critical Appraisal of Assimilationist and Radical Ideologies Underlying Same-sex Marriage in LGBT Communities in the United States', *Journal of Homosexuality*, 45 (1) (2003): 45–64.

Chapter 21

Attitudes to same-sex marriage in South African Muslim communities

An exploratory study

Elsje Bonthuys and Natasha Erlank

Introduction

Following a series of judgments and legislative amendments which gradually extended the legal rights of same-sex couples, South Africa became the first country outside Europe and North America to adopt legislation permitting same-sex couples to enter into marriage or a union akin to marriage (civil union). This legislation, known as the Civil Union Act 17 of 2006, mirrors the legal requirements and consequences of heterosexual marriage, as governed by the Marriage Act 25 of 1961, for same-sex marriage/union. Couples who marry under the Civil Union Act can choose to have their relationships registered as either marriages or civil unions and can thereby share in the social and symbolic value associated with marriage. Civil unions can be concluded by either same-sex couples or opposite-sex couples, while marriages can only be concluded by opposite-sex couples. In this chapter we will refer to the heterosexual *institution* as marriage and the same-sex *institution* as civil unions.[1]

The Civil Union Act aims to give effect to the equality provision (Section 9 of the Bill of Rights) in the South African Constitution and to protect the inherent dignity of same-sex couples by extending legal recognition to their relationships.[2] However, the progressive aims of the Civil Union Act can most easily be realised by couples who are aware of its existence and who have the social, cultural, religious and economic space to do so. For example, the gay white men studied by Phillips reported increased confidence to openly acknowledge their sexual orientation after the adoption of the Constitution, but most of these men experienced little difference in their personal lives.[3] Their greater integration into mainstream society could simply be due to the social and economic privilege associated with their status as middle-class white people and may not be shared by those lesbians, gays, bisexuals and transgenders who lack similar privilege.[4] Van Zyl adds that

> the sexual orientation section in the Bill of Rights has had a profound impact on the lives of people *who identify* as lesbian and gay ... A significant aspect of having sexual orientation in the Constitution is that it creates

legitimised discursive spaces, for example in the media, for every-day representations of same-sex relationships (though this also needs to be problematized) – opportunities for normalizing our identities and relationships.[5]

In other words, the extent to which same-sex couples will actually exercise their legal rights to enter into civil unions depends, first, on social and community attitudes towards their relationships and, second, on the degree to which civil unions resonate with the actual same-sex practices within a particular community. Bonthuys has argued elsewhere that the close modelling of civil unions on marriages means that same-sex practices within African communities are often excluded from legal recognition and that those couples who most closely resemble middle-class, heterosexual spouses are more likely to enter into civil unions.[6] This can also be classified as 'responsible relationships' seen through a Western/racist lens.[7]

The aim of this contribution is to study the attitudes to same-sex relationships within a sector of the South African community which is widely believed to be inherently conservative and intolerant of different (or deviant) sexual behaviour. Our research examined how same-sex practices are conducted within the Muslim community and whether community attitudes in a relatively small Muslim community in Johannesburg could create space for Muslim South Africans to utilise the provisions of the Civil Union Act. In particular, we aimed to find out whether our informants were aware of the existence of the Civil Union Act and if this statute, together with the Constitutional equality guarantees, would increase the tolerance for same-sex relationships.

In order to provide a context to our research findings, it is important to understand the legal status of Muslim marriages in South Africa. Marriage in South African Muslim communities takes two forms. On the one hand, there is the religious ceremony of Nikah, involving solemn promises by the spouses. Generally, a practising Muslim – an imam – officiates at the Nikah, which is held at a mosque or other place of worship. However, South African law does not give full legal effect to these marriages. In addition to the Nikah, therefore, couples who wish to have their marriages legally recognised must also enter into a civil marriage ceremony, usually conducted by a government official. Many Muslim couples only conclude religious marriages, with the result that their marriages lack full legal status. Although moves have been afoot since 2000 to legalise and regulate all Muslim marriages, the suggested reforms have not been adopted, partly because of disagreements between the diverse sectors of the Muslim community.[8] Ironically, civil unions under the Civil Union Act have full legal validity. They can be conducted either by Government marriage officers or by religious institutions. The first form of civil union would be of a purely secular nature, but the latter would involve some version of the Nikah. To our knowledge there are currently no Muslim organisations registered to conduct civil unions for Muslim couples. Attitudes to gay and lesbian people within the Muslim community may indicate the reason.

Attitudes and acceptance

Perceptions of Muslim communities as intolerant and vehemently opposed to same-sex relationships are fuelled by contemporary media accounts of condemnation and persecution of gay men and lesbians in Islamic countries such as Iran and Zanzibar and through condemnatory statements by Muslim clerics, both locally and abroad.[9] Nevertheless, academic literature describes a certain degree of acceptance and tolerance in historical and contemporary African Muslim communities. For instance, Murray and Roscoe, in an overview of same-sex practices in East Africa, cite a study of the Islamic Harari by Bieber, showing that 'sodomy is not foreign to the Harari'.[10] The authors also refer to nineteenth- and twentieth-century reports of widespread sexual activity between men and boys in the predominantly Muslim cities of Mombassa and Zanzibar, while Murray cites evidence of bride-price being paid for boys in certain Muslim groups in the Sudan.[11] Similarly, Muslim societies in West Africa tolerate same-sex sexual relationships, even as they disapprove of them on religious grounds, while gay men continue to play an important role in certain religious celebrations of the Islamic Hausa in northern Nigeria and approximate a self-defined 'gay community' within that group.[12] Of course, the existence of these same-sex relationships, even if they were very widespread, does not imply social or religious acceptance. For instance, Murray and Roscoe refer to Buxton's 1963 study of the Mandari, an Islamic society in southern Sudan, in which homosexuality clearly exists but is associated with witchcraft.[13]

Literature on lesbian, gay or transgender behaviour within South African Muslim communities is scant. The existing material, which indicates a limited level of community tolerance, mainly focuses on the coloured community in Cape Town, which includes both Muslims and Christians. Chetty describes the media portrayal of the Cape Town drag scene in the 1950s and 1960s, representing the drag queens as 'a kind of humanity and desire that is grotesque, unspeakable – and titillating'.[14] Certain drag queens became celebrities within their communities, and several gay men worked as well-known and sought-after hairdressers and beauticians.[15] It could, therefore, be suggested that there were some very visible persons in the community who were tolerated, at least to the extent that their services were popular. Chetty describes one of these hairdressers, 'Piper Laurie' or Ismail Hanif, who always dressed as a woman and was a famous dancer with a touring revue company: 'His family was devoutly Muslim, and Piper was very much a member of the faith. While his father was less accommodating of Piper's early expressions of gay identity, his mother and the rest of the family acknowledged his difference at an early age.'[16]

Similarly accepted was 'Bobby', another gay Muslim hairdresser. Chetty mentions that he was referred to as 'Aunt Bobby' by his nephews and nieces.[17] These manifestations of gay identity and community tolerance continued in places such as Steenberg, Salt River and Mannenberg after the Apartheid removals and dispersal of the coloured District Six community.[18] Nevertheless, the degree of tolerance should not be overstated. Although women frequented gay hairdressers and envied men dressed in stylish women's clothing, both Derese, an informant of Lewis and Loots, and Achmat, mention a gay man called Sis Gamat.[19] He was well known in the community as a caterer for weddings and parties. Of him it was said, 'Sis Gamat is a moffie. Sis Gamat sends all the women into hysterics; the men twitter nervously around him and ignore him. I hear the whispers: "Sis Gamat likes men."'[20]

Acceptance/tolerance was therefore not unqualified. Effeminate gay men were accepted while being regarded as freakish and strange. Children sometimes taunted them.[21] In addition, Achmat notes a perception that 'And it's the white man who likes moffies! You never see a brown man or a Native going round with moffies.'[22]

Derese, a lesbian Muslim, states that her strictly Muslim family does not accept her sexual orientation. This is, however, linked to their disapproval of extra-marital sex in general and a belief that lesbians are promiscuous.[23] This is echoed in a short interview with Zubeida, a bisexual Muslim woman from a conservative religious family in Fordsburg.[24]

With the exception of Zubeida, all of the information on Muslim attitudes towards same-sex relationships relate to the Cape community. Their attitudes and practices are not necessarily representative of Muslim communities elsewhere, especially not communities which are more religiously homogeneous or which have different cultural roots. In particular, Muslims who have recently immigrated to South Africa from West Africa, Somalia and the Sudan may have different attitudes and practices around same-sex relationships than those in 'coloured' or 'Indian' communities. Moreover, the information is not current. The latest information, contained in Gevisser and Cameron's book *Defiant Desire*, was gathered before its publication in 1994. Public attitudes would therefore not have been influenced by the non-discrimination provisions in the Constitution or by the adoption of the Civil Union Act twelve years later.

Background to the study

Before the adoption of the Civil Union Act, the Department of Home Affairs convened a series of public consultations in various communities throughout the country. Together with religious bodies of other faiths and African traditional leaders, the Muslim Judicial Council expressed dismay at the prospect of legalising same-sex relationships. Their official submission spoke of the 'traits our religion deems abominable, unnatural and a cause of the anger of Allah' and predicted that 'the spread of homosexuality and lesbianism will invite the anger of Allah, erode the family structure and expose young, innocent children to an unnatural lifestyle'.[25] Similarly, the Council of Muslim Theologians of South Africa related the cautionary tale of the inhabitants of Lŭt, whose homosexual acts caused their town and its inhabitants to be destroyed entirely.[26] Theologians regard same-sex conduct as 'a perversion and a serious deviation from the inherent nature of man ... even viler and uglier than adultery', which causes public shame and disgrace for parents and family members.[27] The Council advise people to shun temptation by avoiding 'looking at and staying in the company of beardless, young lads or even pictures of them' and by entering into heterosexual marriage.[28]

Nevertheless, this discourse is not unchallenged in the Muslim community. At the same Home Affairs consultative meeting, a group of Muslims called the Inner Circle argued that there were diverse opinions within the Muslim community and that certain interpretations of the Qur'an could justify recognition of consensual same-sex relationships.[29] The group describes itself as follows:

> The Inner Circle (TIC) was established by a concerned group of Muslims in 1996 as an underground social and support group. It started out at the house of Imam Muhsin Hendricks in the form of halqaat (study circles). These study circles ... have proven to be very successful in helping Muslims who are queer to reconcile Islam with their sexuality.[30]

Although the Inner Circle is not registered to perform legally valid civil unions under the Act, it has, since the passing of the Act, conducted a number of Nikahs for Muslim same-sex couples and is currently investigating the possibility of obtaining approval to conduct valid civil unions.[31]

In order to investigate tolerance we conducted a small-scale pilot study of community perceptions towards same-sex relationships. To this end we interviewed householders who were not, to our knowledge, involved in same-sex relationships. In addition, we also set out to interview Muslim South Africans who identified themselves as lesbian and gay to gauge their perceptions of community tolerance to their relationships.

Community members interviewed lived in Mayfair, a suburb just to the west of the centre of Johannesburg. Until the end of the 1980s, Mayfair was a predominantly white area, despite a long history of illegal mixed-race settlement. Although a multi-ethnic area, it is predominantly Indian and Muslim, its inhabitants including older, South-African born residents, as well as more recently arrived residents from areas including Bangladesh, Pakistan and the Arabian Peninsula. There are no current demographic figures for the suburb. Mayfair is home to several mosques and madrasas. It is a mixed-use area, incorporating shops with apartments above, as well as residential housing, most of which is free-standing.

We chose Mayfair because of its status as a relatively 'tight' Muslim community. The researcher began with known contacts and used these to find other informants. She worked according to a set of criteria, which included length of residence in the area. The informants ranged in age from early twenties into their seventies, with a median age in the forties. They included both men and women from the upper working class to the middle classes. Most had some degree of post-school education. Interviews were open-ended and semi-structured. The researcher collected basic data from all the informants, followed by a set of questions designed to elicit information first on attitudes towards sexuality and second on same-sex sexuality in particular. The interviews ranged from one to several hours. All interviewees were guaranteed anonymity: names are changed in following discussion. Fifteen of these interviews have been conducted to date.

In addition to gathering information on community perceptions of homosexuality, our researcher also conducted interviews with people who self-identified as being homosexual or transgendered. In order to increase the size of our sample and to ensure confidentiality, we did not require these informants to live in Mayfair, although some of our informants did. Participants were either pointed out to the researcher by other members of the community in Mayfair or by members of other Muslim communities in Johannesburg. Muslim lesbians proved extremely difficult to find, and all but one of our homosexual informants were men. A similar interview schedule was followed with the gay men as with the non-gay informants, although they were more directly questioned about their homosexuality. Names here have also been changed.

It must be stressed that the initial intention of this research was to see whether investigation could uncover attitudes of the members of the Muslim community we interviewed towards homosexuality. At the outset we anticipated some reluctance to speak to our researcher but we have generally been pleasantly surprised by the degree to which people have been willing to speak. Although we managed to engage two *maulanas*, who were not residents of Mayfair, in conversation, they had only limited willingness to participate in the study. We acknowledge that the study is not representative of the views of all South African Muslims. It is not a representative sample, just an exploratory study of some Muslims in one community (South African Muslims), nor is it representative of the experiences of all gay and lesbian Muslims. It should be followed up by more interviews with lesbian Muslims and a comparison with Muslims from different cultural backgrounds, including West and East African Muslims and Muslims from the Western Cape. Nevertheless, we believe our interviews have brought new and interesting material to light.

Our findings

Attitudes towards marriage

Attitudes toward civil unions are invariably linked to attitudes towards (heterosexual) marriage. Our informants were unanimous in stating that strong social and religious pressures to marry were brought to bear by friends, family and the wider community. Tariq summarised these pressures as follows

> marriage is encouraged in Islam to the T and to a greater extent you are told to marry, marry, marry and of course it's natural that not everybody will get married, so if a person is not married then there's no stigma against that person but marry, marry, marry all the time. Unlike if you go to the Christian religion, their St Paul says it is better to marry than to burn, but it

is better not to get married, he says, so they discourage it. The Hindu's highest form is that you will remain celibate. We are told to get married.

(Tariq, retired male)

One of our gay interviewees indicated that, even though he had been living with his male partner for twenty-five years and was fifty-two years old, certain family and community members continued to enquire when he would get married. Many of our informants shared this belief in the importance of marriage. Some young unmarried men expressed regret that they were not yet married but hoped that they would be well married soon. Despite the high value placed on marriage, many informants acknowledged that not all marriages are happy. Many people mentioned what they perceived as an alarmingly high incidence of adultery, while young unmarried informants told us that they were anxious to marry the right person and to avoid the bickering and unhappiness which they had observed in certain marriages.

Although many South African Muslims opt to conclude a (legally valid) civil marriage in addition to the religious Nikah, it appears that the social and religious significance attaches only to the Nikah. Informants who spoke of the need or the wish to marry never mentioned civil marriage but always referred to the Nikah. No one indicated that the lack of legal recognition of the Nikah would prevent people from concluding one. People may have been either unaware of the legal problems associated with the Nikah or this may not have been a morally significant issue for them.

A surprising number of household informants believed that gay and lesbian people should be encouraged to enter into heterosexual marriages in order to counteract the urge to have relationships with people of the same sex. A Johannesburg Moulana indicated that he would advise gay people to take this course of action but cautioned that they should tell their intended spouses about their same-sex relationships in the past. Two of our interviewees were associated with an NGO offering counselling for sexual, social and family problems to members of the Muslim community. Both agreed that the number of people who admitted to having same-sex relationships or desires had increased in the recent past. Both also indicated that they would attempt to persuade gay or lesbian callers that same-sex relationships were forbidden by Islam and would advise them to marry. However, one of the counsellors added that this would not be wise in situations where the callers had just emerged from a same-sex relationship, since they needed time to 'live a normal life' before entering heterosexual marriage. This approach accords with the advice offered on the website of the Council of Muslim Theologians of South Africa.[32]

One particularly striking interview was with an unmarried professional woman in her thirties. Although there had been indications throughout her serious relationship with a man that her boyfriend might be gay, and although her sister had warned her of this possibility, the informant refused to think about the issue until he terminated the relationship and told her that he was gay. Despite her distress, the respondent maintained contact with her former boyfriend and candidly admitted that she was prepared to marry him, even though he was gay. She said that she would accept his attraction to other men and would not require sexual fidelity, because in all other respects this man had treated her well and was a wonderful person.

Nevertheless, people who believed that gay and lesbian people should enter into heterosexual marriages also acknowledged that there was a risk that they would eventually end their marriages in order to pursue same-sex relationships, or that they would have same-sex sexual relationships while they were married. Our gay informants were aware of several married Muslim men who also had same-sex relationships, including even Muslim clerics. One informant also indicated that some married Muslim men had joined a support organisation for gay and lesbian Muslims. Understandably, our gay informants were opposed to pressurising gay and lesbian people to marry. While they sympathised with people who succumbed to pressures to marry, they believed that these marriages tend to disintegrate and would lead to unhappiness and frustration for both spouses and their children.

Attitudes towards same-sex relationships

Community attitudes to same-sex relationships are linked to the high value placed on Islamic religious marriage and to the belief that sex outside of marriage is wrong. Nevertheless, it seems that gay or lesbian sex is more vociferously condemned than heterosexual adultery or pre-marital sex. A few of our informants expressed morbid curiosity and disgust concerning same-sex sexual practices but others were far more tolerant. Some young males wished to witness sexual behaviour between women but indicated that they would be 'freaked out' by seeing two men kissing or embracing. A common theme was that same-sex *practices*, rather than mere desires or thoughts, were condemned because 'every person, when they're going through their teenage years and later teenage years, everyone has fantasies and thoughts … ' (Sophia, middle-aged woman).

Many informants had heard of gay or lesbian people being disowned by their families. Workers at helpline services told us that they had encountered families who, upon learning that their children were gay or lesbian, had ejected them from their homes. One informant indicated that he was aware of gay and lesbian young people who had committed suicide as a result of being rejected by their families. Other families do not resort to such drastic measures: 'sometimes they keep them in the house to contain the whole matter, but sometimes they just chuck them out. I think parents' initial reaction, many parents' initial reaction, is just get out of my house' (Zeynab, middle-aged woman, counsellor at Muslim helpline).

Despite citing these instances of community and family rejection of gay and lesbian people, virtually all our informants repeated that they themselves would not totally ostracise lesbians and gay men. Although they would disapprove of their sexual practices and seek to convince them to refrain from their wrong-doing, they would still greet them, and some would be prepared to invite individual lesbians and gay men, including same-sex couples, into their homes or to celebratory events. Furthermore, informants agreed that it was not their prerogative to judge these people, since judgement belonged to Allah. This was the case even for the respondent who expressed the most extreme homophobia. One reason for this tolerance and reluctance to judge can be located in the Islamic standards of proof and punishment as articulated by a Johannesburg Moulana and several other informants:

> where a person is found to be guilty of homosexual sins, they should be killed immediately ... But wait, don't just write down what I said about them being killed, because you must remember also according to Shariah, that if someone is accused of an act like adultery or homosexuality they must have four witnesses ... And all four witnesses must individually testify the same story and if one person's story does not correlate with another's, even in the minutest detail, that law cannot apply. Therefore it is almost impossible to accuse someone of such an act unless they themselves admit it.
>
> (Middle-aged religious married couple)

This might explain a number of contradictions in the interviews. First, it may be the reason why having desires or fantasies about same-sex sexual relations is not regarded as an indication of being gay or lesbian. For instance, one respondent said, 'If he's really involved in the relationship physically or whatever, *and there's existing proof of it*, probably I'll categorize him in that category. But just having thoughts about it and, I don't think anything strongly about that' (Mohammed, middle-aged man; emphasis added).

Second, our gay informants have indicated that they usually do not experience overt discrimination or rejection from family members or community members. Indeed, some of them are regarded as pillars of the community, accepted in mosques, and consulted on community matters. Many have social circles that extend beyond gay or lesbian people and are active in public projects. These informants themselves express a dislike of those who flaunt their sexuality:

> I have a problem with all these gay marches and things that they have. What is the need? Yes, we need to let people know that there are people with different sexual orientations within any community and people should be tolerant, but I don't believe in people dressing up weirdly and whatever the case is to advertise who they are. It doesn't work for me, it doesn't work for me. You know what, you want to dress up weirdly, well, then do it in the privacy of your home and you don't have to advertise it to the rest of the world.
>
> (Faizel, middle-aged gay man)

The essence of a great deal of community tolerance seems to lie in the fact that whatever cannot be proven by way of four identical eyewitness accounts must be ignored. Gay informants confirm this. They tell of several gay and lesbian cohabitation relationships which are regarded by the community as simply 'friendships' or as instances of economic and social convenience. One informant tells how, despite openly sharing a bedroom with his male partner for twenty-five years to the knowledge of his family members, many still do not acknowledge that he is gay, even though they invite both him, his partner and their foster child to family celebrations. This form of tolerance is, however, dependant on lesbian and gay relationships not being openly flaunted as such:

> 'if you don't advertise it and you don't go out there and make it public and show affection in public to each other and hold hands and do what normally straight people would have done' (Faizel, middle-aged gay man).

'He is not going to leave what he is doing, but you can tell him that he can't do it in public, because it is wrong and he can't just go around messing in the streets and so on. If he wants to do it he can do it privately if he wants' (Tasneem, middle-aged woman).

Although there is a level of tolerance of individual lesbian and gay people and of same-sex relationships which are not publicly flaunted, this tolerance does not extend to civil unions. With very few exceptions, and including some of the most tolerant of our informants, participants vehemently rejected the idea of civil unions, and several interviewees reported that they were 'shocked and disgusted' by the legislation. Several informants predicted that the adoption of the Civil Union Act would have dire consequences for the community and even the country. These consequences included an increased visibility of same-sex relationships, an increase in the confidence of gay and lesbian people and in acceptance of these relationships by other people in the Muslim community. People therefore feared that same-sex relationships would be exhibited in public and that, by implication, the community would no longer be able to ignore their existence. Other predictions included an increase in HIV, increased interpersonal violence, increased crime and child molestation.

Even more vehemently rejected was the notion that civil unions could include a Nikah. Although rumours circulated that one or more same-sex Nikahs had been performed in Mayfair, most people were adamant that the community would never recognise such marriages. We were unable to locate people who were party to same-sex Nikah's in Mayfair or elsewhere.

Some of our gay interviewees also rejected the idea of a same-sex Nikah. Although they perceived certain advantages from the legislation, including increased financial security for same-sex couples, they also thought that publicly entering into a civil union, especially one involving a Nikah, would be hurtful to family members. One interviewee argued that people who openly entered into civil unions were very brave or perhaps even somewhat foolish, especially if they had business interests in the Muslim community. For various reasons, they themselves did not plan to enter into civil unions. One informant said that it was not necessary, since there was a strong commitment between himself and his partner, and, in any case, a civil union would embarrass and hurt family members. Another respondent felt that it would curtail his independence and create intrusive sexual demands which he would be obliged to satisfy.

> Like I said, when we cross the street, he wants to hold my hand. I can't be possessive over someone and I don't want someone to be possessive over me ... Another thing is this – if I am busy making roti and this guy wants sex, I am not prepared to leave my roti. This is what these people are doing.
>
> (Fatima, elderly male-to-female transsexual)

Conclusion

Murray argues that deliberately ignoring instances of moral and especially sexual transgression forms part of a common Islamic ethos. As long as sexual transgressions are discreet, Muslim communities seem willing to overlook them and to assume that all people act in accordance with religious prescripts. This not only protects individual adulterers and those who engage in sex with people of the same sex but it also serves to uphold religious sexual norms by creating the impression that they are universally observed.[33]

If tolerance to same-sex relationships in Muslim communities is based on deliberately looking the other way and a widely held assumption that relationships are not sexual until proven to be so, then the widespread opposition to civil unions becomes understandable. When two people enter into a civil union, there is no longer any space for the community to ignore the nature of their relationship. People who celebrate their civil unions by way of Nikah are regarded with horror because they directly and publicly challenge the community's understanding of Islamic sexual norms. Same-sex couples' reluctance to enter into civil unions make sense when we understand that, paradoxically, their relationships are, to some extent, tolerated when they are not officially partnered but that they would be strongly condemned if they were to enter into an official civil union. There is an additional irony in the fact that, currently, a same-sex civil union has higher legal status than a Muslim marriage and civil-union partners receive more legal protection from the state than do spouses in an Islamic marriage.

Returning to the quote by Van Zyl that 'the sexual orientation section in the Bill of Rights has had a profound impact on the lives of people *who identify* as lesbian and gay', we could argue that, for gay and lesbian Muslims, identifying as gay within their communities is not the best strategy.[34] For this reason, the impact of the Constitution on their personal lives remains limited, while, paradoxically, the adoption of the Civil Union Act can be regarded as exposing them to the danger of being ostracised from their communities.

We may even agree with Wafer that 'In countries where Islam is the dominant religion, equal rights for gays and lesbians are unlikely to be achieved by means of secular arguments that do not pay due respect to the sacred sources of Islamic culture. Such an approach is more likely ... to result in a backlash.'[35]

The same may apply on a smaller scale, to Muslim communities. Wafer cites Duran, who argues that a more fruitful way to increase tolerance for lesbians and gay men would be to engage with the religious interpretations that underlie the community belief that same-sex relationships are wrong.[36] In the South African context, this may be achieved by Muslim groups such as the Inner Circle, who seek to challenge orthodox textual interpretations. On the other hand, if they were publicly to conduct same-sex Nikah ceremonies, this may be regarded as a deliberate challenge to community religious views and thus undermine their aim of increased tolerance.

Acknowledgements

Thanks to our excellent researcher, Taahirah Chothia for her enthusiastic and inspired work on this project. Thanks also to the members of our writing group for their useful comments and suggestions for further research.

Notes

1 Just for clarity, references to marriage mean opposite-sex marriages under the Marriage Act. Civil unions are same- or opposite-sex marriages or civil unions conducted under the Civil Union Act. Muslim marriage is the religious ceremony which has limited legal effect.
2 Preamble, Civil Union Act.
3 O. Phillips, 'Ten White Men Thirteen Years Later: The Changing Constitution of Masculinities in South Africa, 1987–2000', in M. Van Zyl and M. Steyn (eds.), *Performing Queer: Shaping Sexualities, 1994–2004* (Cape Town: Kwela Books, 2005), pp. 150–1.
4 Ibid., pp. 156, at p. 159.
5 M. Van Zyl, 'Shaping Sexualities: Per (Trans)forming Queer', in M. Van Zyl and M. Steyn (eds.), *Performing Queer: Shaping Sexualities 1994–2004* (Cape Town: Kwela Books, 2005), p. 19.
6 E. Bonthuys, 'Possibilities Foreclosed: the Civil Union Act and Lesbian and Gay Identity in Southern Africa', *Sexualities: Studies in Culture and Society*, 11 (6) (2008): 726–39.
7 Jackie Jones, Chapter 22, and J. Jones, 'The Responsibility of the EU: Familial Ties for All', in C. Lind, H. Keating and J. Bridgeman (eds.), *Taking Responsibility: Law and the Changing Family* (Aldershot: Ashgate, forthcoming).
8 South African Law Reform Commission, *Report on Islamic Marriages and Related Matters*, July 2003. The investigation started in 2000.
9 A. Cline, 'Iran: Gay Teens Executed by Hanging' (2005). Available online at http://atheism.about.com/b/2005/07/25/iran-gay-teens-executed-by-hanging (accessed 2 May 2008); Independent Online, 'Homosexuality on the Rise, Say Muslim Clerics' (2005). Available online at http://www.mask.org.za/article.php?cat=islam&id=739 (accessed 2 May 2008); P. Tentena, 'Muslims Back Orombi' (2006). Available online at http://www.mask.org.za/article.php?cat=islam&id=996 (accessed 2 May 2008).

10 S. O. Murray and W. Roscoe, 'Horn of Africa, Sudan and East Africa: Overview', in S. O. Murray and W. Roscoe (eds.), *Boy-Wives and Female Husbands: Studies of African Homosexualities* (New York: St Martin's, 1998), pp. 21–40; p. 22.

11 Ibid., pp. 30–4. See also D. P. Amory, '*Mashoga, Mabasha, and Magai:* "Homosexuality" on the East African Coast', in S. O. Murray and W. Roscoe (eds.), *Boy-Wives and Female Husbands: Studies of African Homosexualities* (New York: St Martin's, 1998), pp. 67–87, for a detailed discussion of cross-dressing and contemporary gay identities in Swahili-speaking, Islamic East African societies; S. O. Murray, 'The Will Not to Know: Islamic Accommodations of Male Homosexuality', in S. O. Murray and W. Roscoe (eds.), *Islamic Homosexualities: Culture, History and Literature* (New York: New York University Press, 1997), pp. 14–54; p. 40.

12 S. O. Murray and W. Roscoe (eds.), 'West Africa: Overview', in S. O. Murray and W. Roscoe (eds.), *Boy-Wives and Female Husbands: Studies of African Homosexualities* (New York: St Martin's, 1998), pp. 91–110; p. 107, citing nineteenth- and twentieth-century studies in Senegal; R. P. Gaudio, 'Male Lesbians and Other Queer Notions in Hausa', in S. O. Murray and W. Roscoe (eds.), *Boy-Wives and Female Husbands Studies of African Homosexualities* (New York: St Martin's, 1998), pp. 115–28.

13 Murray and Roscoe, 'Horn of Africa, Sudan and East Africa: Overview', p. 35.

14 D. R. Chetty, '"A Drag at Madame Costello's": Cape Moffie Life and the Popular Press in the 1950s and 1960s', in M. Gevisser and E. Cameron (eds.), *Defiant Desire* (Johannesburg: Ravan Press, 1994), pp. 115–27; p. 115.

15 Ibid., pp. 123–6.

16 Ibid., p. 124.

17 Ibid., p. 125.

18 J. Lewis and F. Loots, '"Moffies en manvroue": Gay and Lesbian Life Histories in Contemporary Cape Town', in M. Gevisser and E. Cameron (eds.), *Defiant Desire* (Johannesburg: Ravan Press, 1994), pp. 140–57; pp. 142–3.

19 Z. Achmat, 'My Childhood as an Adult Molester: A Salt River Moffie', in M. Gevisser and E. Cameron (eds.), *Defiant Desire* (Johannesburg: Ravan Press, 1994), pp. 325–47; at p. 335; Lewis and Loots, 'Moffies en manvroue', p. 144; Achmat, 'My Childhood as an Adult Molester', p. 328.

20 Achmat, 'My Childhood as an Adult Molester'. 'Moffie' is a derogatory term for an effeminate gay man.

21 Ibid., p. 330.

22 Ibid. My translation.

23 Lewis and Loots, 'Moffies en manvroue', pp. 144, 145, 151.

24 T. C. Sam, 'Five Women: Black Lesbian Life on the Reef', in M. Gevisser and E. Cameron (eds.), *Defiant Desire* (Johannesburg: Ravan Press, 1994), pp. 186–92; p. 190.

25 Department of Home Affairs, 'Minutes of the Home Affairs Portfolio Committee Public Hearings on the Civil Union Act, 16 October 2006'. Available online at http://www.pmg.org.za/viewminute.php?id=8331 (accessed 5 October 2007).

26 Jamiat Ulama of South Africa, 'Homosexuality and Lesbianism'. Available online at http://www.jamiat.co.za/library/homosexuality_and_lesbianism.htm (accessed 9 June 2008).

27 Ibid.

28 Ibid.

29 Department of Home Affairs, 'Minutes'.

30 Available online at http://theinnercircle.org.za/index.php?page_id=2 (accessed 2 September 2009).

31 Personal communication with Imam Muhsin Hendricks who is the executive director and founding member of the Inner Circle.

32 Jamiat Ulama of South Africa, 'Homosexuality and Lesbianism'.
33 Murray, 'The Will Not to Know', p. 14.
34 Van Zyl, 'Shaping Sexualities', p. 19.
35 J. Wafer, 'Muhammad and Male Homosexuality', in S. O. Murray and W. Roscoe (eds.), *Islamic Homosexualities: Culture, History and Literature* (New York: New York University Press, 1997), pp. 87–96; p. 87.
36 Ibid.

Chapter 22

Taking 'sex' out of marriage in the European Union[1]

Jackie Jones

Introduction

In February 2010 Viviane Reding, the new Commissioner for Justice, Fundamental Rights and Citizenship, stated that the European Union (EU) Charter 'will be the compass for all European Union policies', providing the background against which all EU policies will be impact-assessed, with a no-tolerance zone for any member state that does not adhere to the Charter.[2] She proclaimed that 'our EU Charter represents the most modern codification of fundamental rights in the world. We, Europeans can be proud of it.'[3] I hope so. In June 2010 she reiterated these sentiments and stated that

> the Commission will present later this year a communication on the EU fundamental rights policy which will set out its strategy for an effective enforcement of the Charter. My key objective is to render as effective as possible the rights enshrined in the Charter for the benefit of all people living in the EU.[4]

The speeches were given at a time of anticipation in the EU as negotiations for EU accession to the ECHR (Convention for the Protection of Human Rights and Fundamental Freedoms) are under way. That human-rights convention was written in the late 1940s – a time of open wounds, turmoil and rebuilding. On the whole, the ECHR has served its constituent members well in times of peace as it was a forward-looking international convention at the time of its drafting, enumerating rights that are accessible by individuals not just states. The traditionalist/original intent interpretation of some articles has given way to positive duties on the states to ensure not just compliance with the Convention but also that the rights are not stripped of their essence. That kind of progressive, purposive interpretation has yielded some positive results in the area of family rights (Article 8) but less so for marriage (Article 12). Whether or not accession to the ECHR and the content of the differently worded Article 9 EU Charter (marriage) is able to fulfil the hope of 'us Europeans' to be able to 'be proud' of the EU Charter is the subject of this chapter. In particular, it will be questioned whether or not a newly rebranded Article 9 is able to fulfil the hopes of status recognition of those same-sex couples who wish to have their relationship recognised as a marriage anywhere in the EU. Will either the ECJ (European Court of Justice) or the ECHR (European Court of Human Rights) be able to adjudicate for a citizen-orientated, inclusive Europe or will it be left to member states alone to decide whose relationship is worthy of legal recognition?

The EU and same-sex relationships

Recently there has been an expansion in the number of legal jurisdictions recognising different types of stable same-sex relationships in law and in society. Most progress has been made in the recognition of same-sex civil unions, registered partnerships or the like, but not of same-sex marriage. Although a full survey is beyond the scope of this chapter, the importance for present purposes concerns the large number of different types of relationships recognised by states that are marriage-like, possessing all, most or many of the rights of marriage. More than 50 per cent of EU member states now have civil-partnership legislation, including Austria (2009), Belgium (2003), Czech Republic (2006), Denmark (1989), Finland (2001), France (1999), Germany (2001), Hungary (2007), Italy (in different cities), Luxembourg (2004), the Netherlands (2000), Portugal (2001), Romania (2006), Slovenia (2005), Spain (2005), Sweden (2009) and the UK (2004). The Irish Government has included it in its 2010 programme of Bills. The speed of acceleration post-2000 or post-recent accession is startling. It recognises the increased importance of choice, dignity and equality for same-sex intimate relationships in the legal systems at issue here. That acceleration and acceptance, I would argue, has been helped by EU equality laws outlawing sexual-orientation discrimination. Article 19 of the Treaty on the Functioning of the EU, alongside secondary legislation banning discrimination on the basis of sexual orientation in the workplace have helped in the process of ending discrimination against lesbians and gay men, both in terms of their status as legal subjects of law as well as rights bearers. Underpinning the recognition of same-sex intimacies is the symbiotic relationship between the member states and the EU's values/principles as enshrined in the case law of the ECJ, the *acquis communautaire*, EU Treaties, the fundamental values of international obligations, and many national laws and constitutions as they originate from 'common constitutional traditions' of the member states.[5] These values are also part of the general principles of EU law and fundamental rights of the EU.[6] Those common EU and member-state values are now codified in the EU Charter. The same articles can be used in cases both domestically and before the European courts. For example, Article 20 EU Charter ensures that everyone is equal before the law, and Article 21 provides that the EU prohibits 'any discrimination based on any ground such as sex, race, colour, ethnic or social origin, genetic features, language, religion or belief, political or any other opinion, membership of a national minority, property, birth, disability, age or sexual orientation'. The articles in the Charter are important when read in light of the other articles, laws and policies because they assist in winning cases on the basis of substantive equality arguments before both national courts and the ECJ. Indeed, the EU Charter can aid in the process of purposive interpretation for which the ECJ is famous.

The EU charter and a mandate for marriage

The EU Charter became legally binding in December 2009 and now has the same legal value as the Treaties. There are, however, limitations to its scope. It is addressed to the EU and the member states only when they are implementing EU law. Article 6(1) EU Treaty states that the EU gains no new competencies nor does the Charter extend the application of EU law. Under Article 6(2) EU Treaty, the EU will accede to the ECHR. Article 6(3) makes clear that where the EU Charter rights correspond to those guaranteed by the ECHR, the Charter rights shall have the same meaning as under the Convention, although EU law may provide 'more extensive protection'. Any extended protection may prove difficult to accomplish, however, as the jurisprudence under the ECHR forms part of the general principles of the EU.[7] Accordingly, it is in the area where the texts of the Convention and the EU Charter diverge that the ECJ may retain some supremacy of interpretation, including over Article 9 EU Charter.

The explanatory guidance of the original Charter states that Article 9 is based on Article 12 ECHR. However, the wording of Article 9 has been modernised, providing that 'the right to marry and the right to found a family shall be guaranteed in accordance with the national laws governing the exercise of these rights'.[8] Article 12 ECHR, on the other hand, states that 'men and women of marriageable age have the right to marry and to found a family, according to the national laws governing the exercise of this right'. The deletion of the reference to 'men and women' from Article 9 is significant as it means that the case law of the ECHR need not necessarily be followed. This may be a crucial differentiating point because the case law in relation to Article 12 on marriage has always retained its (conservative) heteronormative format, with some exceptions, most notably concerning transsexuals being able to exercise the right to marry the person of their choice, even if that person is of the same sex as the transsexual's own birth sex.[9] There has thus been some erosion in the heteronormative character of the right. Cases using Articles 8 and 14 ECHR have led to a more progressive reading of 'family life' or 'private life' for same-sex couples. In March 2010, the ECHR in the case of *Kozak* v. *Poland* held that the Polish authorities' blanket exclusion of same-sex couples from succession could not be justified as necessary for the legitimate purpose of protection of the family founded on a 'union of a man and a woman' as stipulated in Article 18 of the Polish Constitution; it violated Articles 8 and 14 ECHR.[10] The Court stated that there is a need for governments to recognise 'developments in society and changes in the perception of social, civil-status and relational issues, including the fact that there is not just one way or one choice in the sphere of leading and living one's family or private life'. It also held that laws adversely affecting the 'intimate and vulnerable sphere of an individual's private life' need strong justifications. Thus, the margin of appreciation, even in the EU member state of Poland with its very 'conservative', recently amended Constitution, is getting narrower, a further indication that more progressive changes may not be altogether foreclosed in this area. Indeed, if one were to follow the pattern of national laws (see below), these provide a good indicator that full equality of treatment will eventually follow. *Kozak* dealt with 'private life'. It is in this sphere that the ECHR has been more generous to same-sex couples. On the other hand, there was no recognition of 'family life' for same-sex couples until June 2010. In *Schalk*, the ECHR for the first time dealt *directly* with the issue of legal capacity of same-sex partners to marry.[11] Although the first chamber rejected the arguments of two gay Austrian men that the denial of their right to be able to marry under Austrian law was a violation of Article 12 ECHR, I would argue that there were several positive points worthy of note in the judgment. First, the Court based its ruling on a traditionalist interpretation of the 1950 ECHR (para. 55) and a lack of consensus among its constituent members (para. 58).[12] Yet, at the same time, it acknowledged that in nineteen Council of Europe member states there was the possibility of same-sex couples either entering a marriage or a registered partnership and that social change was progressing at great speed. Second, the Court held that because of a lack of European consensus the margin of appreciation was still wide. Third, and interestingly, from the point of view of this chapter, the Court undertook a comparison between Article 9 EU Charter and Article 12 ECHR, demonstrating an unease with the significance of the difference in wording. The Court reiterated its previous statement in *Goodwin*, but then went one step further by explicitly stating that:

> the Court would no longer consider that the right to marry enshrined in Article 12 must in all circumstances be limited to marriage between two persons of the opposite sex … However, as matters stand, the question whether or not to allow same-sex marriage is left to regulation by the national law of the Contracting State.[13]

The reference to persons of the opposite sex is significant because the Court was not referring to a *Goodwin* situation (transsexuals) but rather to a biological non-binary coupling. In terms of an Article 12 right, therefore, there is a slight shift towards no longer foreclosing the possibility of legal recognition of same-sex intimate relationships. In effect, the Court was saying, it is just a matter of time. That point of view is reinforced by the Court's statements in relation to 'family life'. For the first time, the ECHR accepted that a same-sex couple *could* enjoy 'family life'. What is even more startling is that the Court considered this as a natural, evolutive step, with 'artificial' distinctions no longer tenable between opposite and same-sex couples.[14] The significance of that step cannot be overstated because a survey of national progression of the rights and status recognition of same-sex couples reveals that this type of progress leads to the opening of same-sex relationship recognition and, eventually, same-sex marriage. But what the Court gave with one hand, it took away with the other. In the instant case, it was held by a majority 4:3 split, that there was no 'family life' as, again, there was no European consensus yet, only 'evolving rights'.[15]

In the setting of the Council of Europe, where many of the states are more 'traditionalist' than in the EU, it is unsurprising that the Court is still reluctant to grant full equality of recognition under Article 12. Even here, however, there has been some recognition of social changes that need to be reflected in national laws, albeit under Articles 8 and 14. In a union of twenty-seven states, with more than 50 per cent of member states enacting legislation recognising same-sex unions and seven allowing same-sex marriage, there is what the ECHR would call a 'European consensus' and thus the chances for a progressive jurisprudence under a twenty-first century, modern charter are much greater. Indeed, the explanatory notes accompanying the EU Charter make such a position tenable, asserting that modernisation of Article 9 is:

> to cover cases in which national legislation recognises arrangements other than marriage for founding a family. This Article neither prohibits nor imposes the granting of the status of marriage to unions between people of the same sex. The right is thus similar to that afforded by the ECHR, but its scope may be wider when national legislation so provides.[16]

In fact, the ECHR already accepted this position in its 2002 *Goodwin* decision: 'the Court would also note that Article 9 of the recently adopted Charter of Fundamental Rights of the European Union departs, *no doubt deliberately*, from the wording of Article 12 of the Convention in removing the reference to men and women' (emphasis added).

The exercise of the right to marry gives rise to social, personal and legal consequences. It is subject to the national laws of the contracting states but the limitations thereby introduced must not restrict or reduce the right in such a way or to such an extent that the very essence of the right is impaired.[17]

What is meant by 'no doubt deliberately' is fundamental to this chapter. National laws can diverge on this point. The explanation above may simply represent the EU's version of the margin of appreciation. However, analysing the case law under Articles 8, 12 and 14 ECHR in this area, it becomes apparent that the margin has shrunk significantly in recent times. It is no longer tenable for a state to hold that transsexuals have an Article 12 right to marry (that they can marry someone of the opposite gender of their birth sex), yet that they may not choose to marry a person of the opposite sex *after* they have 'acquired a new gender'. In other words, there is now an acknowledgement of the right to marry the person of your own choice rather than being limited to someone of the opposite gender, and, most importantly, an acknowledgement that the right itself cannot be stripped of its essence.[18] Not providing choice of marriage partner, it is argued, *does* strip the right of its essence. The narrowing of the margin of appreciation and the recognition of 'family life' is significant in EU terms, as the explanatory guidance of the EU Charter states that 'where the right is similar (not the same) to that afforded to the ECHR, … its scope may be wider when national legislation so provides'. The provision does not simply give permission to individual member states to grant equality to same-sex marriage within their borders; rather, it expresses an aspiration (at the very least) indicating where all EU states must head. Equally, it encapsulates the wider definition of marriage that is coming soon to more and more EU member states. Indeed, Article 9 EU Charter provides an EU framework for a purposive interpretation, in line with the general principle of EU law which holds that when acting in their field of competence member states must, nonetheless, adhere to equality as a fundamental right of EU law. In other words, equality must trump a traditionalist/ originalist interpretation. This means that member states' room for manoeuvre is limited, as further evidenced by the EU case of *Maruko*.[19]

In any event, states are moving towards this position at their own speed. The EU Charter, the development of human-rights jurisprudence, general principles of EU law as well as the advent of sexual-orientation-discrimination legislation at EU level all ensure that there is a congruent relationship between national and EU-level enactments in the field of familial ties. At the same time, we witness a contemporary series of tensions: the bedding-in of laws prohibiting sexual orientation in the workplace, the contracting of EU citizenship (due to asylum and immigration fears), in turn sitting in uneasy relation to the call for full equality (status recognition). The tensions between all of these aspects of present developments are real but manifest differently across the various member states. In terms of same-sex relationships, the normal process in countries with a short history of the decriminalisation of homosexual sexual relationships will not be at the vanguard of permitting relationship recognition for lesbians and gays. However, in countries not only with a longer history of laws prohibiting sexual-orientation discrimination but also receptive to rights claims, calls for relationship recognition may well succeed. In this light, it is interesting to reflect on examples of current trends in laws and policies and to observe the myriad of ways in which equality for lesbian and gay long-term relationships is being recognised in different member states.

National laws

The continued influence of the ideological conflation of family and marriage is demonstrated by the fact that many of the EU member states' constitutions guarantee, and often protect, marriage and the family. Most see marriage as the precursor to the family. The relative position of marriage-guarantee clauses within the member states' constitutions or in their national legislation inevitably reflects the values of that society. So, for instance, where marriage is seen as a fundamental right, it will normally be interpreted by constitutional courts using an original intent or historical interpretative method. Thus, typically, the default position is that marriage remains juridically constructed as heterosexual despite equality guarantees. One can describe this as the default position. 'Traditionalist countries', in this framework, are ones in which the institution of marriage is interpreted in a historical or religious fashion: it has been, is and remains irreducibly heterosexual (e.g., Poland, Lativia, Malta, Greece). There is, in these contexts, very little, if any, movement towards recognising (same-sex) marriage (or marriage to the partner of your choosing) as a constitutional right. At the vanguard of this traditionalism are Poland and Latvia, changing their constitutions post-accession to make marriage gender-specific and banning Pride marches. But there are signs of change for such traditionalist countries on two fronts. First, grass-roots activism. For example, in 2008, a mayor of a Greek island performed two same-sex marriage ceremonies, and in Bulgaria the first religious same-sex marriage took place in June 2006.[20] This mirrors informal marriage registers and the 'weddings' celebrated in some cities across Germany and the UK before enactment of civil-partnership legislation. Grass-roots activism and strong lobbying are precursors to more fundamental changes which are then taken up by political parties trying to garner votes. If elected, parties then put forward legislative proposals which are often subject to constitutional challenge before being enacted into law. The arguments for effecting change will often employ the language of obligation under EU law in order to ban sexual-orientation discrimination and to progress equality. Indeed, this has happened for marriage and civil-partnership regimes in several member states (for example, Germany, Portugal and Spain). Second, there are a decreasing number of 'hard-line' EU countries that refuse to enact any civil-union or life-partnership laws, including Bulgaria, Cyprus, Estonia, Greece and Latvia.[21] Poland would be part of this list, except that in 2003 it introduced same-sex civil-partnership legislation into Parliament that ran out of legislative time. It was never reintroduced. Some form of same-sex partnership recognition now exists in more than 50 per cent of states, with many granting same-sex partnerships all the rights of a married couple. There is therefore a critical mass of acceptance. More states will soon join this list, especially after the European Parliament Resolution of January 2009 calling for mutual recognition of same-sex relationships across the EU.[22] Ireland is perceived as one of the countries with the most conservative reputation. Its constitution is fiercely defended, debated and followed, especially in relation to family matters. Unsurprisingly then, Ireland's constitution does not recognise same-sex marriage.[23] Despite opposition to civil same-sex partnerships by the Roman Catholic Church, it looks more than likely that the Civil Partnership Bill 2009 will be enacted into law before the end of 2010.[24] Importantly for the free movement of persons (no doubt influenced by EU substantive law), Clause 5 will recognise civil partnerships legally sanctioned in other countries. What is happening in Ireland, then, appears to be the normal pattern of progression towards status recognition evident in hard-line countries in the EU. Other countries have started with registration of partnerships and then moved on to opening up marriage, even giving the parties a choice of conversion. For example, in the Netherlands, over 6,000 same-sex partnership registrations have taken place in three years, and the conversion rate from partnerships to marriage stands at over 60 per cent since 2005.[25]

In most countries, court cases are not enough, especially where the influence of the Church is still strongly felt. Cases have to be followed up with activism and political will. Grass-roots action, such as Pride marches, all help to galvanise actions to change the attitudes of politicians and the public. Politicians often hold the key to effective change as, for example, in Spain and Portugal. Marriage is enshrined in Article 32 of the Spanish Constitution but has always been upheld as a heteronormative societal institution primarily for the purpose of procreation. Despite this traditional view, the Government brought forward a law on gender-neutral civil marriage in 2005, including same-sex adoption (a highly contested area in most countries around the world).[26] The Government advocated that a twenty-first-century reading of the Spanish Constitution is essential for a modern Spain. That meant substantive equality, dignity, the right to the development of the person and the right to privacy as enshrined in the Constitution trumped discrimination against same-sex couples and a religious or traditionalist interpretation.[27] The significance of this position resides in the fact that a staunchly Roman Catholic country which had for years been oppressed by Franco decided on a progressive interpretation when it seemed an unlikely step. At the time, only three countries in the world permitted same-sex marriage. By the end of 2008, 12,648 same-sex marriages had taken place, and Spain has thus become one of the 'progressive countries', permitting not just same-sex registered partnerships, but also taking 'sex' out of marriage.[28] In some member states, the courts changed their mind over a short span of time. In February 2010, the Portuguese Parliament, despite a three-to-two Constitutional Court decision in July 2009 that held not permitting same-sex couples to marry was not against the Constitution, voted in favour of making the definition of marriage gender-neutral. This was despite strong opposition from the Roman Catholic Church. When the draft law was challenged in April 2010, the Constitutional Court ruled that 'the extension of marriage to those of the same sex' did not conflict with the recognition and protection of the family as a 'fundamental element of society', emphasising that marriage is a 'concept' that 'admits of several political views'.[29] The law came into effect in May 2010.

By 2010, five EU member states had opened marriage to same-sex couples: Belgium, the Netherlands, Spain, Sweden and Portugal.[30] Five may appear to be a small number, but the goal of taking sex out of marriage is getting closer in several other member states. Two others are very close: Slovenia and Luxembourg. Slovenia is a country whose timeline from the invisibility of same-sex relationships to one of embracing progressive familial ties was very short. The Slovenian Registration of a Same-Sex Civil Partnership Act (ZRIPS) was adopted in June 2005.[31] Registrations started in July 2006. In response to a constitutional challenge in July 2009, the Constitutional Court held that Article 22 of the new law violated Article 14 of the Slovenian Constitution on the basis of violations of a human right to property and sexual-orientation discrimination.[32] The Court gave the Government six months in which to remedy the situation. As a result, the Slovenian Government brought forward a progressive family-code-reform Bill in September 2009 calling for equalisation of same-sex unions with other family unions, including same-sex marriage and adoption.[33] The proposal passed the first reading in Parliament in March 2010. Once enacted, Slovenia will become the first former Eastern European country to accept gender-neutral language for marriage. Finally, Luxembourg is set to permit same-sex marriage before the summer recess without any fanfare.[34] There will then be seven EU member states which have changed their national laws in order to better accommodate calls for substantive equality and dignity for all of their citizens concerning one of the most traditionalist institutions to ever exist on the planet.

From this survey, it can be seen that all of these countries have utilised the language of compliance to EU (formal and substantive equality) law and dignity alongside domestic (constitutional equality) values in order to open up the space for relationship recognition for same-sex couples. We can arguably conclude that the impetus for change at national level has been influenced by EU-level enactments that prohibit sexual-orientation discrimination. At the very least one can argue that the *aquis* on sexual-orientation discrimination has been and continues to be used by national actors either before national courts or by references to the ECJ (and the ECHR) to legally recognise an expanding set of relational ties as normatively acceptable. That much is evident in the most recent reference to the ECJ concerning rights tied to legal couple relationships. In the *Maruko* case, the ECJ ruled that the unequal and separate regime of pension entitlements for same-sex couples and married ones in Germany was discriminatory.[35] As the Court makes clear, it is the fact that the rights for married couples and registered partners are moving ever closer that triggers the assessment of the disparity as discrimination. The Federal Constitutional Court stated that:

> the referring court considers that, in view of the harmonization between marriage and life partnership, which it regards as a gradual movement towards recognizing equivalence, as a consequence of the rules introduced by the LPartG (German life partnership law) and, in particular, of the amendments made by the Law of 15 December 2004, a life partnership, while not identical to marriage, places persons of the same sex in a situation comparable to that of spouses so far as concerns the survivor's benefit at issue in the main proceedings.[36]

In other words, the fact that the two regimes are similarly situated but separate offends the very essence of equality of treatment. The ECJ further stated that:

admittedly, civil status and the benefits flowing therefrom are matters which fall within the competence of the Member States and Community law does not detract from that competence. However, it must be recalled that in the exercise of that competence the Member States must comply with Community law and, in particular, with the provisions relating to the principle of non-discrimination.[37]

One can also argue that the general principle of non-discrimination trumps national laws that discriminate on the basis of sexual orientation in the sphere of community competence. Indeed, when the case returned to the Federal Constitutional Court, it was on the basis of Article 3 Basic Law (equality) as understood in the light of EU case law that the Court ordered equalisation in pension rights for registered partners and married couples. The Article 6 'special protection of marriage' duty of the national constitutional order was no longer tenable in this respect.[38] It is this supremacy in areas traditionally left to constitutional courts that, I would argue, will become the battleground under Article 9 EU Charter (and the Charter in general). EU competency in relation to civil status has been expanded by the inclusion of Article 9 EU Charter, contracting into the ECHR and having equality and non-discrimination as core values of the EU constitutional order, despite any limitation in interpretation.[39] That has necessarily to be the position, otherwise the supremacy of community law itself is challenged.[40] In the EU, member states have different practices, especially in the area of private relationships. The proliferation of the number of same-sex partnership and marriage laws nonetheless make the exercise of EU rights – as an EU citizen – much more difficult. For example, in the UK, a married Belgian same-sex couple will not have their marriage recognised. Instead it will be converted into a civil partnership. Arguably, in the UK this does not cause too many legal or practical problems because the Civil Partnership Act 2004 and other laws bestow nearly all the rights of marriage to civil partners (apart from status recognition!). However, in Poland, for example, where same-sex relationships are not recognised at all, the EU right of free movement of citizens, persons and workers will not be fully realised. According to long-established case law of the ECJ, *any* obstacle to the free-movement right is prohibited, including mere administrative obstacles.[41] And that has not only been recognised by the European Parliament but is precisely why the European Parliament has called for relationship recognition across the EU. With the enactment of Article 21 EU Charter banning sexual-orientation discrimination, such obstacles become even less tenable. In addition, there is little doubt that the ECJ *will* rule on civil status under Article 9 as references are brought by NGOs in the member states. This is still the case regardless of any opt-out member states may have negotiated.[42] Indeed, Commissioner Reding announced in December 2009 a plan to consider enacting a European Civil Code.[43] Civil codes cover, among other things, both contracts and torts. Many also regulate family laws, including the civil status of marriage and the family. It seems likely therefore that the 'covert' regulation (competence in the field) of family status will become 'overt' in the near future. In addition, if civil status is not part of the competence of the EU then why was Article 9, with different wording from Article 12 ECHR, incorporated into the EU Charter?

Conclusion

This chapter has outlined several arguments as to why it is possible to imagine an EU that no longer penalises those who want to marry the person of their choice. The horizontal and vertical relationship between EU and national laws and policies make the EU a hugely successful *sui generis* supranational organism. Apart from the legal arguments presented here, there are other, societal ones as well. If the EU is to become a union for its people, traditionalist arguments about procreation tied to heteronormativity and religious dogma cannot be sustained. In 2006, a Eurobarometer survey found that 44 per cent of EU citizens were in favour of same-sex marriage.[44] That figure is most probably higher now, especially as the number of EU member states which have legalised same-sex marriage has increased. Forty-four per cent is a very high rate considering the types of countries included in the survey: from very traditional, religious ones to modernist, secular states. The institution at issue in this chapter is civil marriage, as sanctioned and recognised by the state or by the EU. Opening civil marriage to people of the same gender would not encroach upon religious marriage. It would encourage stable relationships, and that may be something that a state or the EU would invest with considerable importance, especially in the context of our increased longevity and the states' predilection to privatise care.[45] We tend increasingly to enter, remain and exit multiple (liquid) relationships of varying lengths. The question of the nature of varying relationships and their interaction with stability and commitment is a complex matter. We enter relationships for different reasons at different points in our lives. Some relationships may be 'temporary', and some provide the context in which our first same-sex sexual experience is gained. Moreover, sexual preference identification is not a fixed matter either. Some individuals try very hard to 'fit in' or do not acknowledge their sexual feelings until much later in life. Relating this to considerations affecting marriage and the family, this 'coming out' can occur after a heterosexual marriage has broken down and the children have left the home. It is precisely then that individuals may want to settle down with someone of their own sex, and it is important to acknowledge that any status, obligations and rights attached to that relationship choice are just as important as those attached to a heterosexual marriage. Full legal, societal and cultural recognition of the need for diversity and freedom of choice in the construction of familial ties is arguably key to full equality, dignity and personhood in this complex context. Marriage, accordingly, should be seen as one of the valid range of choices that should be fully available to same-sex couples. It should be mandated and adjudicated by the EU, not simply left to a postcode lottery of individual states.[46]

The EU Charter presents an opportunity to progress this equality agenda. A challenge such as *Schalk* will eventually come before the ECJ. When it does, I believe it will be much more difficult for the ECJ than it was for the ECHR to deny same-sex couples the right to marry because of the emphasis on equality as a fundamental principle of EU and the 'common constitutional traditions' of national law. Indeed, there is an EU consensus building that recognises registered partnerships and same-sex marriage (with more than half of its states recognising same-sex relational ties and at least seven states permitting gender-neutral marriages as of 2010). If the ECJ decides in favour of the same-sex couple, then we can start to speak about gender-neutral marriage and what it will bring to the gender relations inside familial ties (of all kinds).

Notes

1 This chapter does not address the feminist arguments against marriage as a legal institution here although the author accepts many of those arguments. This chapter talks to equality as a substantive right.
2 V. Reding, speech entitled, 'Towards a European Area of Fundamental Rights: The EU's Charter of Fundamental Rights and Accession to the European Convention of Human Rights', Interlaken, 18 February 2010.
3 Ibid.
4 V. Reding, Speech/10/324, 'How to make the Charter of Fundamental Rights the Compass for All EU Policies?', Brussels, 22 June 2010.
5 Article 13, Treaty of Amsterdam; Council Directive 2000/78/EC of 27 November 2000 establishing a general framework for equal treatment in employment and occupation, OJ L 303, 2.12.2000; Directive 2004/38/EC of the European Parliament and of the Council of 29 April 2004 on the Right of Citizens of the Union and Their Family Members to Move and Reside Freely Within the Territory of the Member States Amending Regulation (EEC) No. 1612/68 and Repealing Directives 64/221/EEC, 68/360/EEC, 72/194/EEC, 73/148/EEC, 75/34/EEC, 75/35/EEC, 90/364/EEC, 90/365/EEC and 93/96/EEC, OJ L 158, 30 April 2004, 77; Commission Proposal for a Council Directive Implementing the Principle of Equality Regardless of Religion or Belief, Disability, Age or Sexual Orientation, Extending the Scope of Directive 2000/43/EC to all other forms of discrimination (COM 2008 0426).
6 T. Tridimas, *The General Principles of EU Law*, 2nd edn (Oxford: Oxford University Press, 2007).
7 Article 6(3) EU Treaty.
8 S. Peers, 'Taking Rights Away? Limitations and Derogations', in S. Peers and A. Ward (eds.), *The EU Charter of Fundamental Rights* (Oxford: Hart Publishing, 2004), Chapter 6; OJ C 364, 18 December 2000, p. 1.
9 *Rees* v. *UK*, Series A, No. 106 (1986) 9 EHRR; *Cossey* v. *UK*, Series A, No. 184 (1990) 13 EHRR; *Sheffield and Horsham* v. *UK* (1997) 27 EHRR 163; *Goodwin* v. *UK* and *I* v. *UK* (2002) 35 EHRR 18; *Karner* v. *Austria* (2004) 38 EHRR 24.
10 Application No. 13102/02.
11 *Schalk and Kopf* v. *Austria*, Application No. 30141/04.
12 *Schalk*, Paras 55 and 58 respectively.
13 *Schalk*, Para. 61.
14 *Schalk*, Para. 105.
15 *Schalk*, Para. 105.
16 OJ C 303, 1; explanatory notes.

17 *Goodwin*, paras 100–1.
18 *B. and L. v. the United Kingdom*, No. 36536/02, §34, 13 September 2005, and *F. v. Switzerland*, 18 December 1987, §32, Series A, No. 128.
19 Case C-267/06 *Tadao Maduko* v. *Versorgungsanstalt der deutschen Bühnen*, Common Market *Law Review*, 46 (2) (2009): 723–46.
20 *Kathimerini* online, 4 June 2008. Available online at http://www.ekathimerini.com/4dcgi/_w_articles_politics_100003_04/06/2008_97375 (accessed 12 October 2009). M. Dohi, '"Seful" homosexualilor s-a insurat religios ieri'. Available online at http://www.libertatea.ro/stire/seful-homosexualilor-s-a-insurat-religios-ieri-154747.html (accessed 12 October 2009).
21 See, generally, R. Wintemute and M. Andenæs (eds.), *Legal Recognition of Same-Sex Relationships: A Study of National, European and International Law* (Oxford: Hart Publishing, 2001).
22 European Parliament Resolution of 14 January 2009 on the Situation of Fundamental Rights in the European Union 2004–8, 2007/2145 (INI), P6_TA (2009)0019.
23 Article 41.3.1. 'The State pledges itself to guard with special care the institution of Marriage, on which the Family is founded, and to protect it against attack.'
24 Available online at http://www.oireachtas.ie/documents/bills28/bills/2009/4409/b4409d.pdf (accessed 23 October 2009).
25 K. Waaldijk, *More or Less Together: Levels of Legal Consequences of Marriage, Cohabitation and Registered Partnership for Different-Sex and Same-Sex Partners. A Comparative Study of Nine European Countries* (Paris: Institut National d'Études Démographiques, 2005); K. Waaldijk, 'Partnerships in the Netherlands', *Euroletter*, 87 (2001). Available online at http://www.france.qrd.org/assocs/ilga/euroletter/87.html (accessed 18 June 2002).
26 *Ley* 13/2005.
27 J. Jones and E. Merino-Blanco, 'The Influence of Constitutional Law on Family Forms in Germany and Spain', *Child and Family Law Quarterly*, 20 (1) (2008): 23–44; N. Pérez Cánovas, 'Spain: The Heterosexual State Refuses to Disappear', in R. Wintemute and M. Andenæs (eds.), *Legal Recognition of Same-Sex Relationships: A Study of National, European and International Law* (Oxford: Hart Publishing, 2001), pp. 493–504.
28 Spanish National Statistics Institute. Available online at http://www.inc.es/en/welcome_en.htm (accessed 21 October 2009).
29 Available online at http://www.publico.pt/Pol%25EDtica/acordao-que-da-luz-verde-ao-casamento-gay-publicado-hoje-em-diario-da-republica_1434406&prev=_t (accessed 11 May 2010).
30 Norway opened marriage to same-sex couples in 2009 which in turn influenced Sweden to do the same only months later. Iceland followed in June 2010.
31 *Zakon o registraciji istospolne partnerske skupnosti*, Official Journal of RS, No. 65/2005.
32 *Blažič and Kern* v. *Slovenia* U-I-425/06-10. Available online at http://odlocitve.us-rs.si/usrs/us-odl.nsf/0/2d889887e4205f81c1257604003479fc/$FILE/U-I-425–06.pdf (accessed 25 October 2009).
33 Available online at http://www.sta.si/en/vest.php?id=1428986&s=a (accessed 22 October 2009).
34 Available online at http://luclebelge.skynetblogs.be/post/7606466/grandduche-du-luxembourg-le-mariage-gay-avant (accessed 20 March 2010).
35 Case C-267/06 *Tadao Maruko* v. *Versorgungsanstalt der deutschen Bühnen* (2008) ECR I-621.
36 *Maruko*, para. 69.
37 *Maruko*, para. 59.
38 1 BvR 1164/07 of 7 July 2009. Available online at http://www.bverfg.de/entscheidungen/rs20090707_1bvr116407.html (in German). See J. Jones, 'The Prospects of Legal Recognition of Same-Sex Marriage in Germany', *Equal Opportunities International*, 28 (3) (2009): 221–32.

39 J. Bengoetxea, N. McCormick and L. Moral Soriano, 'Integration and Integrity in the Legal Reasoning of the European Court of Justice', in G. de Búrca and J. H. H. Weiler (eds.), *The European Court of Justice* (Oxford: Oxford University Press, 2001), pp. 43–87; p. 46.

40 That is why the ECJ first 'discovered' fundamental rights as general principles of community law as early as 1969 in the case of 29/69 *Stauder* (1969) ECR 419. In addition, national courts are under a community mandate to protect EU fundamental rights as general principles of EU law. Case C-260/89 *ERT* (1991) ECR I-2925.

41 EU Directive Free Movement of Persons and their Families; see R. Cholewinski, 'Family Reunification and Conditions Placed on Family Members: Dismantling a Fundamental Human Right', *European Journal of Migration and Law*, 4 (3) (2002): 271–90; H. Stalford, 'EU Family Law: Human Rights Perspective', in J. Meussen, M. Pertegás, G. Straetmans and F. Swennen (eds.), *International Family Law for the European Union* (Antwerp: Intersentia, 2004); E. Guild, 'Free Movement and Same-Sex Relationships: Existing EC Law and Article 13 EC', in R. Wintemute and M. Andenæs (eds.), *Legal Recognition of Same-Sex Relationships: A Study of National, European and International Law* (Oxford: Hart Publishing, 2001), pp. 677–93.

42 R. Lane, 'The EU Charter of Fundamental Rights and the Subsisting Commitments of EU Member States under the ECHR: More Variable Geometry', *Croatian Yearbook of European Law and Policy*, 3 (2007): 355–89; A. Torres Pérez, *Conflicts in Rights in the EU: A Theory of Supranational Adjudication* (Oxford: Oxford University Press, 2009).

43 18 December 2009. Available online at http://www.euractiv.com/en/opinion/eu-justice-chief-plans-civil-code-privacy-laws/article-188417 (accessed 23 December 2009).

44 Eurobarometer, *Final Results* (Brussels: EU Commission, 2006), 66, p. 42. Available online at http://ec.europa.eu/public_opinion/archives/eb/eb66/eb66_highlights_en.pdf (accessed 14 September 2010).

45 M. A. Fineman, *The Autonomy Myth* (New York: New Press, 2004).

46 Torres Pérez, *Conflicts in Rights in the EU*, p. 45.

Chapter 23

From Russia (and elsewhere) with love
Mail-order brides

Jennifer Marchbank

Introduction

Some time ago I made a presentation to a public audience on the topic of 'mail-order brides'. The press in Canada picked up on this, and I was asked for interview after interview for both press and broadcast media. It seemed that, as Langevin and Belleau found, the

> exotic and mysterious phenomenon of 'mail-order' brides arouses curiosity. Moreover, many people are sceptical of its existence in Canada. The idea of men looking for wives in far-off lands is intriguing. Who are these men in search of brides? What exactly are they looking for? How do they go about it? … Who are the women who immigrate to Canada in this way?[1]

I had my fifteen minutes of fame but I also had something more. I realised that the public and the media had a very limited knowledge about mail-order brides and that mostly they – the brides – are seen as passive victims not as active agents of change in their own lives. This is important, for public perceptions influence public policies. In this chapter I shall situate mail-order brides in the context of international marriages, primarily in North America, and examine some of the policy responses from both receiving and sending societies.

Background and numbers

The term 'mail-order bride' is one applied to women who advertise (through an agency or a pen-pal website) their aim to marry a man from a more developed society, or one with more opportunities. The term carries with it images of women as a commodity to be purchased rather than of women seeking romance and potential marriage. Yet, as Constable's research shows, the issue is more complex than mail-order brides being either the hapless victims of Western men or calculating scammers only out for a 'green card' or equivalent.[2] Nor are the men all abusers. Many of these marriages, are, in fact, successful, loving unions.

Whilst the development of technology such as the Internet has permitted the exponential growth of agencies that organise introductions (among other services), the migration of women to North America as future wives is far from a modern phenomenon.[3] As early as the seventeenth century, over 750 young French women, *filles du roi*, were sponsored by Louis XIV to become the brides of men in New France; while the Gentlemen's Agreements of 1907 and 1908 made it possible for Japanese women to marry by proxy before joining their husbands in the USA.[4] Canada also received Japanese picture brides, over 6,000 between 1908 and 1924, with the practice of proxy marriages enduring until the 1980s in Italian Canadian communities.[5] In addition, mail-order brides and agencies have been around for decades, developing from print-based advertisements to interconnected websites containing photographs of a plethora of women on each. Technological advances have also led to an increase in the number of agencies, often referred to as International Marriage Brokers (IMBs), simply due to the ease with which websites can be established, images displayed and information provided. Technology also allows agencies to host thousands of women. A Foreign Affair, which operates out of Phoenix, Arizona, boasts 30,000 plus women, and AnastasiaDate, based in Maine, claim 14,500 Russian women, all to entice visitors to their sites.[6]

Determining the numbers of women and men involved is fraught with difficulties. Time and again, I have followed references to numbers, only to find that the original source of the figures is from the 1990s and must be taken as an underestimation given the vast increase in the number of agencies.[7] On the whole, governments do not collect data on the numbers of mail-order brides, as separating out this form of marriage from all spousal migrations is virtually impossible. Similarly, most IMBs fail to collate robust statistics, and, thus, making estimates becomes necessary. Scholes's well-known first estimates for the USA are that in 1996 around 4,000 US marriages resulted from introductions through IMBs.[8] By 1998, he adjusted his estimate to be 4,000–6,000 annually, due to rapid technological developments increasing the numbers of women listed and the entry of women from the nations of the former Soviet Union.[9] Nonetheless, these figures indicate that mail-order marriages account for only '2.7 per cent to 4.1 per cent of all immigration involving female spouses' into the USA.[10] This is supported by a further study conducted by the Immigration and Naturalization Service (USA) in which all applications for fiancée (K1) visas for one month were examined, revealing that 5.5 per cent appeared to be likely mail-order introductions.[11] An examination of the number of former fiancé(e) visas transferred into permanent-resident status in the USA in 2002 shows that 18,621 former fiancé(e)s were transferred, of whom: 4,739 were from Europe (including 1,476 from Russia and 861 from the Ukraine); 9,358 from Asia (including 1,361 China; 2,392 Philippines; 2,418 Vietnam) and 966 from South America (including 346 Brazil; 301 Colombia).[12] However, there is no way to determine how many of these were relationships formed through IMBs. Acquiring figures for Canada is even more difficult, as recognised by government report writers:

The absence of empirical studies and statistics on the subject prevents us from finding out how many women, or how many consumer-husbands, are involved in this international trade ... we cannot determine the number or identity of the MOB [mail-order bride] agencies ... Yet, despite the lack of statistics, all the documentation shows that this phenomenon has skyrocketed in the last decade.[13]

The explanation for this dramatic increase may lie not just in the exponential growth of the Internet but also in the agency of women, as Petrova, the owner of an internet introduction site, states:

Russian women ... seek contacts with foreign men with the intention of future marriage. Those women are educated, intelligent and smart. They are not going to become intimate submissives or maids. They seek equal relationships and will not tolerate infidelity or abuse. There is nothing wrong with them; they are not doing anything different from the women who place ads in ... local personals. There is a lack of men in their country, why can't they look elsewhere?[14]

Characteristics of mail-order brides and consumer husbands

Mail-order brides are far from being a homogenous group, a fact utilised by the IMBs when marketing women, precisely in order to exploit the positive characteristics of women's ethnicities.[15] Previous research has shown that brides range in age from fifteen to fifty-two though, worryingly, Donna Hughes found several sites based in Russia that, in 2001, had listed underage girls as potential correspondents, with some sites containing contact information for children as young as ten years.[16] Recent searches found no agency listing anyone under eighteen, and some listing women up to seventy-one years old.[17] In the past, it was found that 'these girls tend to be younger (by an average of 15 years) than the man', with the average age of Asian women being considerably lower than that of women from the former Soviet Union (31 per cent of former Soviet women are listed as under twenty-five compared to 61 per cent of Asian women).[18] However, an analysis of several sites shows greater complexity now than in 1998: AnastasiaDate, which specialises in Russian women, has 49 per cent of its listings as being between eighteen and twenty-five years; A Foreign Affair's extensive listings of women from former Soviet countries shows that only 24 per cent are aged between eighteen and twenty-five, yet its Asian listings show that 49 per cent are in the same age range.[19] For some sites, youth is not the only marketable factor, as indicated by Orient Brides, which has ten women featured on their front page: four of whom are over forty; three over thirty and the remaining two over twenty-five.[20]

Very little is known about consumer husbands beyond Jedlicka's 1994 research, which shows that, in contrast with popular stereotypes, consumer husbands are not social 'losers' but, rather, quite successful, educated white (94 per cent) men with an average age of thirty-seven.[21] Just over half had been previously married, a third already had a child, and 75 per cent planned to have further children. Constable's ethnographic study of mail-order marriages confirms this profile of American men, while analysis of the members of one site revealed that men, again predominantly white, from eighteen to fifty-six, are seeking women through this single IMB.[22] One observation regarding European men (seeking Polish wives) is that 'French men tend to be 25 to 40 years old, wealthy and good looking. German men tend to the 50 plus years old and financially stable (sic)'.[23]

The stereotype of men who seek marriage through IMBs is not complimentary, usually portraying such men as being in search of a submissive, domestically focused woman untarnished by Western feminism. However, there are some elements of truth to this, for example, as one site maintains, 'French farmers ... are rejecting ... French women as too haughty, finicky, picky and demanding. They want Polish women.'[24] These stereotypes are also mediated alongside other messages, such as those urging respect for the women (while, nonetheless, deriding local women) as shown in the following quotes from testimonials:

> First, DO NOT look at foreigners as backwards and stupid. ... my wife IS NOT stupid. Indeed sometimes she scares me with how much she does know. Treat your correspondent with respect. If you tell them you are planning to do something, do it or be willing to explain why you cannot if you have to. Are Asian women, (and I speak of this cause my wife is Asian and I only know from experience with her) submissive and docile? In a way, yes. But, more importantly, they can be very strong willed if they need be. They ARE NOT Americanised, and that is important. And is that not why you are seeking a foreign spouse? To get away from the American woman? The Hillary Clinton who say (sic) they are truly independent of their husbands but will stick around them because they are interested in nothing but power?

> [Y]ou want something that is truly submissive and docile? If so, resign Cherry Blossoms and buy a puppy. At least they do not hit back or run away when you beat them.[25]

It appears that although these two men seek respect both for themselves and for their wives, they continue to insult other women. For example, in the former quote, successful women are implied to only have achieved any greatness by riding on their husband's coat-tails. In addition, both these quotes are deeply misogynistic, and the latter not only implies that women are interchangeable with dogs but also acknowledges, perhaps even condones, the use of violence. It may be the case that such men are not seeking respect for mail-order brides in their own right but to bolster their own masculinity through being a man with a respected wife.

The men and women on these sites present themselves in ways not dissimilar to other internet dating sites, and it appears that both play to the romantic, fairy-tale, traditional ideal of marriage:

> I look forward to meeting a kindhearted, friendly and honest girl. She should be friendly and capable of love and being loved. I want a girl that knows how to and enjoys making her man happy and can appreciate a man that wants to make her happy also. Wanting to share our bodies, minds and souls. I will hold you in my strong arms forever and wish to love you night and day.[26]

And from women:

> I am a soft person, good-hearted and have good traditional values. People know they can count on me to be around in times of need. I am wonderful, natural person, patient, friendly, charming and I am open to many points of view.[27]

> im simple,sincere,faithfull,loyal and I am a romantic, affectionate, caring. I am looking for a romantic, honest, affectionate, passionate man who wants to be in love with me for the rest of his life.[28]

Women also display their strengths as well as their dreams:

> I have always been dreaming about having a strong family with children and a great husband, who will support me and love me. I have a rather strong character, but at the same time soft and tender. I value respect and equality in the relationship.[29]

However, looking at thousands of images across hundreds of sites, certain common elements are clear in how women are presented. As Luehrmann observes, the advertising of Russian women is similar to the stereotyping of Asian women as feminine and submissive, 'beautiful, caring, family-orientated ladies, unspoilt by luxury ... eager to please even the older Western visitor'.[30] Yet other very sexualised presentations exist, and my research indicates that it is more frequent for Russian and Ukrainian women to be presented as 'sexy', with Asian women more often described as 'feminine' and 'pure', and Poles, Slovaks and Czechs as 'beautiful'. In addition, Luehrmann reports that promotional materials also indicate that Russian women are of middle- and upper-class backgrounds, and she concludes that 'women in Russia seem to offer all the traditional values men used to look to Asia for, but fit more neatly into the racial hierarchies of the US'.[31] So for some the attraction may be the exotic 'other', and for others the attraction may be a traditionally focused woman who can 'pass' as a non-mail-order bride. The intersections of gender relations, 'race' relations and economic disparities are all very evidently aspects of the IMB industry.

For some men, sexual purity is something they seek. Many of Constable's respondents 'answered that they were attracted to Filipinas partly for their sexual purity, morality, Christianity, and their "traditional" values, and that they therefore had greater respect for women who protected their virginity and refused to have sex before marriage'.[32] However, other aspects of national attributes are also obvious, such as comparisons amongst nationalities, with sites promoting women from one area over others, often reflecting fears that male clients hold:

> Don't fall prey to the countless Ukrainian and Russian mail-order bride … agencies … [they] are known for scams, an issue that you will not have to worry about with Czech and Slovak mail-order brides, as they live in modern, economically stable and safe EU countries, no different from any other Western country … It is not a secret that Czech and Slovak women are extremely beautiful, surpassing … Russian women.[33]

This UK-based site goes on to remind potential clients that these women enjoy good health care and education, that they speak good English, come from modern countries with good internet access and, very importantly, need no visa to travel to the UK, Canada or the USA unlike, for example, Thai or Ukrainian women.[34]

Motivations of brides

One of the motivations of consumer husbands appears to be a desire for a wife more traditional than Western women, but what of the brides? What motivates them? Some, such as some middle-class, professional Mexican women, are 'influenced by fantasies of "the American way of life" … more equitable and communicative marriage partners, a stable middle-class lifestyle, more mobility, and access to education and sometimes careers'.[35] Luehrmann has 'characterized international arranged marriage as a female migration strategy' conducted for the purposes of living in the West.[36] However, the Russian women she interviewed also spoke about being lonely, wishing to have a family and the difficulty of finding a suitable man in Russia (where male life expectancy is fifty-nine years, with over 40 per cent dying from alcohol-related conditions).[37] The Slavic women in Canada interviewed by Rossiter also mentioned seeing Canadian men as superior to Ukrainians, who were reported to drink, smoke and cheat.[38] However, also motivating these women were desires for an increased standard of living and a safer and healthier environment for their children. So, romantic images of Western men are certainly one influence, but so too are these women's experiences of poverty, sometimes economic, sometimes environmental, and frequently a lack of gender equality within their own societies.

Some women join agencies without initially seeking a spouse, but for those who are in search of a partner, it seems that what they seek is the same as other women.[39] In studies of women, both with agencies and without, from Colombia, Russia and the Philippines, Baez Minervini and McAndrew conclude:

> Across the board, we found a pre-occupation with the very same characteristics (e.g. ambition, commitment to a relationship and children, sexual fidelity, a mate that is somewhat older) that have been documented by other researchers. In short, women willing to become MOBs do not appear to have a different agenda than other mate-seeking women.[40]

It appears that although aspects of the stereotypes remain, and strong elements of marketing, including comparative marketing, are most definitely present, the majority of women seeking international marriages are acting as agents of their own lives, albeit within circumstances more restricted than those many women in the West enjoy.

Vulnerability and protection

One of the main debates regarding mail-order brides revolves around concerns that these women are particularly vulnerable both to trafficking organisations and to the men they marry.[41] Women's organisations, such as the Center for Women's Policy Studies, include regulation of IMBs in their campaigns against trafficking.[42] They are seen by some, such as Hughes, as possible conduits to organised trafficking gangs, though Luehrmann concludes 'that the literature on "trafficking" contains more generalizations than case studies to support them', while describing Nordic marriage farms (where Russian women visit in the hopes of finding a husband) in the same article.[43]

It is true that some of these marriages are abusive and not what the woman anticipated:

> At the start of our relationship, we were okay, but as time passed, we began having arguments. My husband didn't want me to send money to my family in the Philippines. We have so many arguments when it comes to this issue. He can't understand why I want to help out my parents. Luckily, I got a job because he is not giving me any money at all.[44]

Existing studies show that a number of problems are present, from the social isolation experienced by Slavic women in rural Alberta, Canada; unmet expectations within couples, such as Russian women not being as submissive as some American men had thought; to differences in opinions about obligations to extended family, concerning childcare and other household matters; and poor language skills, restricting employment and social opportunities.[45] In addition, although admitting that most of the data is anecdotal, the Immigration and Naturalization Services in the USA reported to Congress that 'the argument that immigrant women in mail-order marriages are more at risk [of] abuse seems plausible, given the discrepancy in power' in the couple.[46] Further, where abuse does exist, these women frequently have fewer resources, such as family members, friends or knowledge of their rights and local services than women originally from the host society.

Sometimes the experience of such marriages is extremely abusive, and some have ended in tragedy. Although it is impossible to calculate what percentage of mail-order brides suffer abuse (as we do not know how many such brides there are), there are several well-reported cases. One such case was Anastasia Solovieva, whose husband, Indle G. King Jnr., killed her after she tried to divorce him because of the domestic abuse she suffered at his hands.[47] Another, Susanna Remerata Blackwell, was killed while pregnant (with another man's child) when her husband shot her as their divorce case was coming to a close in the courthouse.[48] These high-profile cases from the USA support the contention held in the public imagination that such marriages are abusive and that the men involved merely seek someone to dominate and control. In addition, many women's organisations hear directly from women experiencing abuse within these marriages.[49] Yet, as Scholes' report to the Immigration and Naturalization Services in the USA shows, there is little evidence to suspect that there is a greater degree of abuse in mail-order marriages than in other immigrant marriages.[50] Nonetheless, any instance of abuse is unacceptable, and cases such as the two above have stimulated new legal provisions in the USA.

The legal context

Regulation of the mail-order bride situation does exist in some countries. The Philippines led the way in 1990 with the passing, by the Aquino Government, of an Act to make IMBs illegal in that country.[51] This was supported, in 2003, with other provisions to protect against trafficking and, from 1999, a series of provisions to protect women in the Philippines from more general acts of violence and gender discrimination have been passed.[52] These Acts may have made life in the Philippines more acceptable for women but have limits in that Filipinas can still join overseas IMBs, and many women also leave the country through established labour-migration routes. As these laws have 'little effect on international marriage brokers who do a lot of their advertising and matching online', enforcement is difficult.[53] However, these provisions do indicate that the Philippine Government has recognised that regulating IMBs alone is not sufficient to prevent women seeking foreign husbands and that amelioration of gender discrimination at home is also required.

By contrast, another main 'sending' country, Russia, has no legislation at all to regulate IMBs, though Luehrmann reports that, due to fears held by Western men that Russian women are 'scammers', some agencies offer security to overseas clients by providing background checks on the women they list.[54] This lack of legislation may reflect the local culture, which has few laws and services devoted to issues such as domestic violence.[55]

In some 'receiving' countries, such as Canada and Australia, standard immigration regulations offer a degree of protection to foreign spouses of all kinds. For example, Australia requires that, for citizens wishing to sponsor an overseas partner, the prospective partner 'must be personally known to [the] fiancé(e) and [they must] have met as adults'.[56] Australia also limits the number of sponsorships to two, a minimum of five years apart.[57] However, Australia does not regulate IMBs. Likewise, Canada offers protection, not through regulation but via general immigration legislation, and no political party has plans to introduce any legislation.[58] One such protection is that whereas both the USA and Australia permit immigration as a fiancé(e), Canada requires that a couple already be married.[59] Many receiving countries also have provisions that permit foreign spouses experiencing abuse to leave their marriages prior to the end of their sponsorship period.[60]

In Europe, from whence many brides originate, considerations have been given to regulating mail-order marriages under the auspices of human rights, with the Council of Europe issuing a *Report on Domestic Slavery: Servitude, Au Pairs and Mail-Order Brides* in April 2004. This report was considered in the deliberations of the draft Convention of Action against Trafficking in Human Beings, and, although this Convention has subsequently been ratified, there is no explicit mention of mail-order brides amongst the specific and general regulations and actions on victims of trafficking.[61]

Perhaps one of the most controversial pieces of legislation passed to protect foreign spouses, and to regulate the IMB business, is the USA's International Marriage Broker Regulation Act 2005 (IMBRA).[62] This Act resulted from an attachment to the Violence Against Women Act 2005, encouraged by feminist lobbying, and from the examples of several states which had already imposed restrictions upon IMBs.[63] Influencing politicians to act on an area often viewed as 'outside' of politics – the family – is a major achievement. However, although the result is legislation to protect women from abuse, it situated the issue of IMBs outside of family or even immigration policy and labelled all as violence. That is one reason why so many men are so angry about it.[64]

The IMBRA requires that the Department of Homeland Security maintains a database to track multiple visa applications filed for fiancé(e)s and spouses; that government agencies devise a pamphlet on the 'legal rights and resources for immigrant victims of domestic violence' to be distributed to prospective spouses in their own language; and that IMBs provide foreign clients with background information about their US clients, disclosing any history of any violence or sex related offences.[65] IMBs which do not comply are liable for substantial fines.

The arguments for the IMBRA are that the economic, social and informational inequities that can exist in mail-order marriages, and which sometimes lead to extreme abuse, can be reduced by offering prospective brides information on their rights and the ability to uncover whether or not a man has a history of violent behaviour and/or serial marriage. While many recognise the inherent value in such aims, opponents argue that the constitutional rights of US men are being infringed; that such strict regulation may send IMBs either underground or overseas; and that previous legislation was already adequate.[66] Across the World Wide Web, examples of sites opposing this law abound, most blaming feminists and ranting against feminist organising (an obvious target, as many of the informal sites on this topic are clearly anti-feminist).[67] However, despite feminists being blamed, some are also critical, as Wendy McElroy wrote in an often-reproduced blog: 'What view of the American man does the IMBRA broadcast to the world? American men are so predatory and violent that the U.S. government must protect foreign women by providing police checks before allowing the men to say "hello".' The 'Ugly American' has become an article of federal law, supported by Congress.[68]

However, despite all the efforts on both sides, these may be moot points, as a report by the US Government Accountability Office uncovered that the government departments charged with implementing IMBRA are failing to do so in some respects, such as notifying overseas clients about multiple petitions, tracking multiple petitions and, by 2008, having still not completed a final draft of the information pamphlet.[69]

Conclusion

It would appear then that the issue of mail-order brides is vastly more complex than the common assumptions of both the public and policy-makers would allow. In those countries that have taken steps to regulate these relationships, it seems that policies have been shaped by concerns regarding the motives of participants – in particular, but not exclusively, men. These concerns include the possibilities of exploitation of women, including physical and other abuse, and of abuse of immigration laws. In acting to protect national boundaries and potential brides, such women are viewed simultaneously as victims and as conniving migrants. Neither view permits space for true agency. In the end, it may very well be the case that mail-order brides are victims not just potentially of (some) individual men (as is the case for all women) but of the international political economy, which creates conditions of material inequalities and fosters a desire for migration.

Notes

1 L. Langevin and M.-C. Belleau, *Trafficking in Women in Canada: A Critical Analysis of the Legal Framework Governing Immigrant Live-in Caregivers and Mail-Order Brides*, Status of Women, Canada, October 2000, Introduction, Section 1.

2 N. Constable, *Romance on a Global Stage: Pen Pals, Virtual Ethnography, and 'Mail-Order' Marriages* (Berkeley, Calif.: University of California Press, 2003).

3 A Google (www.google.com) search for mail-order brides generated 5,730,000 hits on 9 October 2009, compared to K. M. Morgan's 2006 search which generated

1,750,000 hits: K. M. Morgan, 'Here Comes the Mail-Order Bride: Three Methods of Regulation in the United States, the Philippines, and Russia', *George Washington International Law Review*, 39 (423) (2007). Compare this to the 1994 estimate by Glodava and Onizuka that put the number of introduction agencies at 100, mostly relying on print catalogues: M. Glodava and R. Onizuka, *Mail-Order Brides: Women for Sale* (Fort Collins, Col.: Alaken, 1994).

4 See *The Canadian Encyclopedia*. Available online at http://www.thecanadianencyclopedia. com/index.cfm?PgNm=TCE&Params=A1ARTA0002799 (accessed 9 October 2009); C. Lee, *Prostitutes and Picture Brides: Chinese and Japanese Immigration, Settlement, and American Nation-Building, 1870–1920* (San Diego, Calif.: The Center for Comparative Immigration Studies, University of California, 2003).

5 R. Sumida, 'The Japanese in British Columbia', MA thesis, University of British Columbia, 1935; cited in D. Kaduhr, 'Picture Brides in Early Japanese Immigration to Canada', *Osaka Shoin Women's University Faculty of Liberal Arts Collected Essays*, Vol 39, 9–21. Available online at http://ci.nii.ac.jp/naid/110000040522/en (accessed 28 September 2009). S. Iuliano 'Donne e buoi dai paesi tuoi: Italian Proxy Marriages in Post-War Australia', *Australian Journal of Social Issues*, 1999, 34, 4: 319–35. Available online at http:// findarticles. com/p/articles/mi_hb3359/is_4_34/ai_n28748403 (accessed 9 October 2009).

6 A Foreign Affair. Available online at http://www.loveme.com (accessed 15 October 2009); AnastasiaDate. Available online at http://www.anastasiadate.com/?gclid= CI7xzOWxwp0CFRQpawodLCD9tA (accessed 15 October 2009).

7 Frequently Glodava and Onizuka, *Mail-Order Brides*; or R. J. Scholes, 'The "Mail-Order Bride" Industry and its Impact on U.S. Immigration', in Commissioner of the Immigration and Naturalization Service and the Director of Violence Against Women Office at the Department of Justice, *International Matchmaking Organizations, A Report to Congress* (Washington, DC, 1999).

8 R. J. Scholes, 'AF ISO WM: How Many Mail-Order Brides?', *Immigration Review*, 28 (spring 1997).

9 Scholes, 'The "Mail-Order Bride" Industry'.

10 AILA InfoNet Doc. No. 99030999, posted 9 March 1999, p. 11. Available online at http://www.aila.org/content/default.aspx?bc=1016%7C6715%7C16871%7C17119% 7C13775 (accessed 21 July 2009).

11 AILA InfoNet Doc. No. 99030999, p. 11.

12 United States Citizenship and Immigration Services, *2002 Yearbook of Immigration Statistics*. Available online at http://uscis.gov/graphics/shared/aboutus/statistics/ IMM02yrbk/IMM2002.pdf; cited by M. A. Clark, presentation to US Senate Committee on Foreign Relations, 13 July 2004. Available online at http://www.protection project.org/commentary/brides.htm (accessed 18 October 2009).

13 Langevin and Belleau, *Trafficking in Women in Canada*, Section 1.4.1.

14 E. Petrova, 'Mail Order Brides? Not!!!' Available online at http://www.russian womenmagazine.com/dating/brides.htm (accessed 2 December 2009).

15 For example, ThaiLoveLinks. Available online at http://www.thailovelinks.com/ ?ovchn=GGL&ovcpn=English+Canada+Content+Image+Ads+Thai+Brides&ovcrn= image+ad&ovtac=PPC&gclid=CNDxxZmqwp0CFSUsawodxFFjrg (accessed 18 October); ChnLove: The Leading Matrimonial Site in Asia. Available online at http://www.chnlove.com (accessed 18 October); HotRussianBrides. Available online at http://www.russianbrides.com (accessed 18 October 2009).

16 Figures quoted by Langevin and Belleau, *Trafficking in Women in Canada*; see also D. Hughes, 'The Role of "Marriage Agencies" in the Sexual Exploitation and Trafficking of Women from the Former Soviet Union', *International Review of Victimology*, 11 (2004): 49–71.

17 Searches conducted by the author, 16 October 2009.

18 R. J. Scholes, 'How Many Mail-Order Brides?', Center for Immigration Studies, March 1997. Available online at http://www/www.cis.org/MailOrderBrides (accessed 16 September 2009); Scholes, 'The "Mail-Order Bride" Industry', Appendix A.

19 Sites were selected by taking the first Google hit for Russian and Asian brides: Anastasia-Date and A Foreign Affair.

20 Orient Brides. Available online at http://www.OrientBride.com (accessed 16 October 2009).

21 D. Jedlicka, cited in Scholes, 'The "Mail-Order Bride" Industry'.

22 Constable, *Romance on a Global Stage*. Analysis for author of the demographics of men posting on http://www.cherryblossoms.com (accessed 2 May 2006).

23 Anon., 'French Farmers Dump Demanding French Women for Pretty Hard-Working Poles'. Available online at http://www.masterpage.com.pl/outlook/200608/french farmers.html (accessed 6 November 2009).

24 Ibid.

25 Testimonials, Cherry Blossoms. Available online at http://www.cherryblossoms.com/cgi-bin/htmlos.cgi/5880.1.1098583183121469027 (accessed 24 May 2006).

26 From the profile of a fifty-three-year-old US man. Available online at http://www.filipinokisses.com/view.php?l=&id=128180randm=2&randw=3 (accessed 2 November 2009).

27 One prospective bride on Foreign Ladies. Available online at http://www.foreign ladies.com/search-results.html?_SEARCH_RS_=16917837224af2524d9988d121083194 (accessed 2 November 2009).

28 Posted by a twenty-eight-year-old Filipina woman. Available online at http://www.filipinokisses.com/view.php?l=&id=181674randm=2&randw=3 (accessed 2 November 2009). (Errors in the original.)

29 Twenty-eight-year-old Ukrainian woman. Available online at http://www.hotrussianbrides.com/mail-order-brides/profile-208751.aspx (accessed 2 November 2009).

30 S. Luehrmann, 'Mediated Marriage: Internet Matchmaking in Provincial Russia', *Europe-Asia Studies*, 56 (6) (2004): 857–75, p. 863.

31 Ibid.

32 Constable, *Romance on a Global Stage*, p. 153.

33 Destiny Woman. Available online at http://beautiful-czech-women.com/russian-women-vs-czech-women (accessed 9 October 2009).

34 The process of achieving visas is often problematic, and applicants face legal barriers if the purpose of the application for a non-immigrant visa is believed to be for migration. See Embassy of the United States in Ukraine, 'Information Concerning the Use of Marriage Brokers, Dating Services and Catalogues'. Available online at http://kiev.usembassy.gov/amcit_marriage_brokers_eng.html (accessed 21 July 2009).

35 F. Schaeffer-Grabiel, 'Cyberbrides and Global Imaginaries, Mexican Women's Turn from the National to the Foreign', *Space and Culture*, 7 (1) (2004): 33–48; p. 38.

36 Luehrmann, 'Mediated Marriage', p. 864.

37 Available online at http://news.bbc.co.uk/2/hi/health/6752515.stm (accessed 6 November 2009).

38 M. J. Rossiter, 'Slavic Brides in Rural Alberta', *Journal of International Migration and Integration*, 6 (3) (2005): 493–512.

39 See Constable, *Romance on a Global Stage*, who had respondents seeking pen pals, and Luehrmann, 'Mediated Marriage', who cites some as exploring travel opportunities.

40 B. Paez Minervini and F. T. McAndrew, 'The Mating Strategies and Mate Preferences of Mail Order Brides', *Cross Cultural Research*, 40 (11) (2006): 111–29.

41 See Hughes, 'The Role of "Marriage Agencies"'.

42 See Center for Women's Policy Studies, *Report Card on State Action to Combat International Trafficking* (Washington, DC: CWPS, 2007). Available online at http://www.

centerwomenpolicy.org/documents/ReportCardonStateActiontoCombatInternational Trafficking.pdf (accessed 30 October 2009).

43 Hughes, 'The Role of "Marriage Agencies"'; Luehrmann, 'Mediated Marriage'. These farms are destinations, usually rural, in, for example, Norway, where Russian women visit for a period of time. Norwegian, and other, men then visit to find a woman. A relationship, sometimes brief, may happen, and some women make return trips.

44 Philippine Women's Centre of British Columbia, *Canada: The New Frontier for Filipino Mail-Order Brides*, 2000, available online at http://www.scs-cfc.gc.ca/pube.html (accessed 15 December 2006).

45 Rossiter, 'Slavic Brides in Rural Alberta'; L. Visson, *Wedded Strangers: The Challenges of Russian-American Marriages* (New York, Hippocrene Books, 2001); B. Beer, *Deutsch-philippinische Ehen: Interethnische Heiraten und Migration von Frauen* (Berlin, Reimer, 1996).

46 AILA InfoNet Doc, AILA InfoNet Doc. No. 99030999, Section 4.

47 L. Mobydeen, 'Something Old, Something New, Something Borrowed, Something Mail-Ordered?', *Wayne Law Review*, 49 (939) (2004).

48 International Marriage Broker Regulation Act: Hearing Before the Senate Foreign Relations Committee, 149 Cong. Rec. S9, 960-01 (25 July 2003), statement of Senator Maria Cantwell.

49 Philippine Women's Centre of BC, *Canada*.

50 Scholes, 'The "Mail-Order Bride" Industry', Appendix A.

51 An Act to Declare Unlawful the Practice of Matching Filipino Women for Marriage to Foreign Nationals on a Mail Order Basis and Other Similar Practices Including the Advertisement, Publication, Printing or Distribution of Brochures, Fliers and Other Propaganda Materials in Furtherance Thereof and Providing a Penalty Therefore, Republic Act No. 6955 §2(a)(1) (1990) Philippines.

52 An Act to Institute Policies to Eliminate Trafficking in Persons Especially Women and Children, Establishing the Necessary Institutional Mechanisms for the Protection and Support of Trafficked Persons, Providing Penalties for its Violations, and for Other Purposes, Republic Act No. 9208 §3(a), §4 (2003), Philippines. See Morgan, 'Here Comes the Mail-Order Bride', p. 423.

53 S. Maldonado, 'Criminalizing Matchmaking: Mail Order Marriage Laws', *Concurring Opinions*. Available online at http://www.concurringopinions.com/archives/2009/06/whats-wrong-with-mail-order-marriages.html (accessed 14 December 2009).

54 Ibid., p. 7; Luehrmann, 'Mediated Marriage'. Scammers are women who pose as potential brides merely to extract money or travel opportunities from men. See http://www.dangersofinternetdating.com/articles/mail orderbrides.htm (accessed 20 July 2009).

55 Morgan, 'Here Comes the Mail-Order Bride'.

56 Australian Government, Department of Immigration and Citizenship, *Sponsorship for a Partner to Migrate to Australia*, Form 40SP. Available online at http://www.immi.gov. au/allforms/pdf/40sp.pdf (accessed 30 October 2009).

57 Australian Government, Department of Immigration and Citizenship, Form 40SP.

58 M.-C. Belleau, 'Mail-Order Brides and Canadian Immigration Policy', *Canadian Women's Studies*, 22 (3/4) (2003): 94–103. Personal correspondence between author and the main political parties, 2007.

59 Immigration and Refugee Protection Act, 2001.

60 See, for example, Australian Government, Department of Immigration and Citizenship, *Statutory Declaration Relating to Family Violence*, Form 1040. Available online at http://www.immi.gov.au/allforms/pdf/1040.pdf (accessed 30 October 2009).

61 Recommendation 1663 (2004), Council of Europe Convention on Action against Trafficking in Human Beings, Warsaw, 16 May 2005. Available online at http://conventions.coe.int/Treaty/EN/Treaties/Html/197.htm (accessed 2 November 2009).

In 2008, the Convention was ratified by Albania, Armenia, Austria, Bosnia and Herzegovina, Bulgaria, Croatia, Cyprus, Denmark, France, Georgia, Latvia, Malta, Moldova, Montenegro, Norway, Poland, Portugal, Romania, Slovakia and the UK and has been signed by twenty other Council of Europe member states: Andorra, Belgium, Finland, Germany, Greece, Hungary, Iceland, Ireland, Italy, Lithuania, Luxembourg, Netherlands, San Marino, Serbia, Slovenia, Spain, Sweden, Switzerland, 'the former Yugoslav Republic of Macedonia' and Ukraine.

62 As evidenced by the huge number of posts, blogs and websites on this matter.
63 See CWPS, *Report Card on State Action*.
64 I have lost track of the number of blogs I have read and emails I received from people angry about the IMBRA.
65 Violence Against Women and Department of Justice Reauthorization Act of 2005, Subtitle D International Marriage Broker Regulation.
66 G. Bala, *Press Release on International Marriage Broker Law*. Available online at http://usaimmigrationattorney.com/PressReleaseIMBRA.html (accessed 19 February 2008).
67 See, for example, Online Dating Rights. Available online at http://www.online-dating-rights.com; Roissy in DC, available online at http://roissy.wordpress.com/2009/10/19/repeal-the-imbra-now/IMBRA – Deems American Men Abusers. Available online at http://www.melindapenpals.com/blog2 amongst others (all accessed 2 November 2009).
68 W. McElroy, 'Mail Order Bride Law Brands US Men Abusers'. Available online at http://www.ifeminists.net/introduction/editorials/2006/0111.html (accessed 20 July 2009).
69 US Government Accountability Office, 'International Marriage Brokers Regulation Act 2005: Agencies Have Implemented Some, But Not All of the Act's Requirements', report to Congressional Committees, USA, August 2008. Available online at http://www.centerwomenpolicy.org/programs/trafficking/federallaws/documents/IMBRAGAOReport.pdf (accessed 2 November 2009).

Index